GENDER, CHOICE AND COMMITMENT

To Jess Sommerlad
and his grandmothers
Madeleine Sommerlad and Ronda Gehling

Gender, Choice and Commitment

Women solicitors in England and Wales and the struggle for equal status

HILARY SOMMERLAD
PETER SANDERSON

Routledge
Taylor & Francis Group
LONDON AND NEW YORK

First published 1998 by Dartmouth Publishing Company Limited and
Ashgate Publishing

Reissued 2018 by Routledge
2 Park Square, Milton Park, Abingdon, Oxon, OX14 4RN
52 Vanderbilt Avenue, New York, NY 10017

Routledge is an imprint of the Taylor & Francis Group, an informa business

A Library of Congress record exists under LC control number:

ISBN 13: 978-1-138-38506-1 (hbk)
ISBN 13: 978-1-138-38503-0 (pbk)
ISBN 13: 978-0-429-42735-0 (ebk)

Contents

List of Figures

List of Tables

Acknowledgements

A great many people have contributed to this book in one way or another. Clearly the greatest debt is to the women and men who responded to questionnaires and requests for interviews so positively, and gave their time even though they had so many other calls on it.

Dave Campbell, with the support of various members of the Law Department at Leeds Metropolitan University (then Leeds Polytechnic), including Pauline Joyce, set up the initial research project. Janet Allaker was a partner in the first stage of the data-gathering exercise, and the legacy of her organisational and data-processing skills continued to be important right through the life of the research. She was also instrumental in launching the second stage of the project during her time at the Institute for the Study of the Legal Profession, Sheffield University.

We are grateful to the Law Society for funding the initial stages of the project; in addition, the staff of the Research and Policy Planning Unit at the Law Society were most helpful throughout: in particular, Carole Willis supported the research and helped to obtain financial support, and Eleni Skordaki, Judith Sidaway, Verity Lewis, John Jenkins and Bill Cole responded to requests for information with great generosity. Mike Shiner at the Policy Studies Institute was similarly helpful. Over the years many members of the Association of Women Solicitors, at both local and national levels, have been extremely supportive; Eva Crawley, Alison Parkinson, Judith Willis, Katy Paxton, Jenny Staples, Judith McDermott and Cathy Baxendall were extremely helpful in variously providing contacts, information, and access to some of the rich material in the AWS archives. At Leeds Metropolitan University, the second stage of the research was supported by the Policy Research Unit (later Institute), and Viv Smith, Simon Baldwin, Sarah Holden and Geraint Hughes provided technical expertise. Other colleagues from the Law Department were also very helpful.

We would also like to thank those who agreed to read all or part of the manuscript. Clare McGlynn, who helped in many other ways as well, identified anomalies and provided additional material. Janet Lodder, Isobel Manley, Richard McSwean commented on issues of substance and style. Paul Bagguley made helpful and supportive comments on the sociological material. The errors of style and substance which remain are of course entirely our own responsibility. Susan Smith prepared the format of the text with great skill, care and patience.

Finally, as we argue in the pages which follow, a task like this is impossible for anyone with childcare responsibilities without access to considerable social capital; in our case we had the invaluable support of Teresa Bolger, Sue Attwood and Rosemary Daley, and the cheerful tolerance of Jess Sommerlad, who has lived with this project from the beginning and who didn't complain about the loss of either parental or computer time.

List of Abbreviations

ACLEC	The Lord Chancellor's Advisory Committee on Legal Education and Conduct
AWS	Association of Women Solicitors
CPS	Crown Prosecution Service
PD	Practice Development
PI	Personal Injury
PR	Public Relations
UK	United Kingdom

Cases Cited

Balfour v. Balfour (1919) 2 KB 571
Bamber v. Fuji International Finance (1996) unreported IT decision, case no. 28081/94
Beaumont (1992) CR App R (S) 270
Bebb v. Law Society (1913) 109 LT Rep 36
Bebb v. Law Society (1914) 1 Ch 286
Beresford Hope v. Lady Sandhurst (1889) 23 QBD 79
Bradwell v. Illinois (1873) 83 US (16 Wall) 130
British Telecommunications plc v. Roberts EOR No. 70 (1996)
Brooks v. Canada Safeway Ltd. (1989) 1 SCR 1219
Chorlton v. Longs (1868) LR 4 CP 374
De Souza v. Cobden (1891) 1 QB 687
Edwards v. Attorney-General of Canada (1930) AC 124
EEOC v. Sears Roebuck 839 2d 302 (1988)
Ezold v. Wolf, Block, Schorr & Solis-Cohen, 983 F 2d 509 (3d Cir. 1992)
re. French (1905) 37 NBR 359
Gillespie Case C - 342/93 (1996) 1 RLR 214 (ECJ)
re. Goodell (1875) 39 Wisc 232
Jex-Blake v. Senatus of Edinburgh University (1873) 11 M 784
Ministry of Defence v. Cannock (1994) 1 RLR 509 (EAT)
Nairn v. St Andrew's University (1906) AC 147
Robinson v. Oddbins (1996) unreported IT decision, case no. 4224/95
Rur (1991) 4 All ER 481
Graham Sherman (1990), Guardian, 27 February
Viscountess Rhondda's Class (1922) 22 AC 339

Statutes

Interpretation Act 1889
Solicitors Act 1843
Lord Brougham's Act 1850
Medical (Registration) Act 1858
Interpretation Act 1889
Sex Disqualification (Removal) Act 1919
Sex Discrimination Act 1975

1 Introduction

> My own wife is a personal injury solicitor in a large firm and she has worked in other firms. She has never experienced discrimination. In her last firm she was offered a full equity partnership but turned it down for domestic reasons. You may not like it, but I think it is a fact that many women solicitors do, in fact, put their families before their careers.
> (Letter Martin Mears, President of the Law Society to Clare McGlynn and Caroline Craham, cited in Smerin, Law Society Gazette, 25 October 1995, p.2)

> We must stop presenting women as 'victims' or as an undifferentiated mass of mindless zombies whose every move is determined by other factors and social forces... Women are responsible adults, who make real choices and are the authors and agents of their own lives. Some women choose to be home-centred, with work a secondary activity. Some women choose to be career centred, with domestic activities as a secondary consideration. Female heterogeneity is a result of the choices women make, reflecting not just different but conflicting preferences between two qualitatively different life courses. (Hakim, 1996a; 186-7)

This book is concerned with understanding the experiences of women solicitors in private practice in the UK. The last fifteen years have seen a very rapid growth in the numbers of women qualifying as solicitors, and obtaining employment at junior levels of private practice. However, as in other professions such as medicine and accountancy, the upper reaches of private practice remain dominated by men (Sommerlad, 1994; Skordaki, 1996; Helena Kennedy, 1992; Allen, 1991; Jackson, 1997): the structural changes which facilitated, and also stemmed from, the increased participation of women, do not seem to have led to this participation being on equal terms. Why this should be the case is a matter of controversy.

As Anne Witz has argued, there is a lengthy history of commentators attributing women's failure to reach the top echelons of the professions to problems of reconciling typically male career patterns with family life (1992, p.2; Fogarty, Allen and Walters, 1981; Davies and Rosser, 1987).

Even explicitly feminist work struggles to escape from the ideology that it is perverse for women to expect to be able to combine a career with parenthood, and that therefore the 'penalties' that they experience are the consequences of their own choices rather than the construction of motherhood and the prevailing social arrangements for child care and employment (an ideology which we will describe in shorthand as 'voluntarist'). Moreover, there has recently been a renewed emphasis on this notion that women's own choices and preferences, rather than structural inhibitions or the direct discriminatory behaviour of individuals, are the principal influence on their career destiny. The quotations which head this chapter represent the strength of the voluntarist perspective, both in the legal profession itself, and in academic comment on the labour market. Consequently, any work examining the relationship between gender and the labour market must confront this issue of choice, and the many questions it raises. How free are women in reality to make choices in the labour market as it is currently structured? When they make their choices, to what extent are they influenced by the general social sense of what is and is not possible? To what degree are their career decisions shaped by their experiences of employers' attitudes and practices? To what extent are choices available to exceptional individuals, but not to women collectively? Finally, perhaps the most fundamental question we should ask is why the issue continues to be constructed as a 'women's problem', where the central issue is women's right to participate in the workplace, rather than the difficulty of equalising care responsibilities in the home (see Liff, 1997, p.558; Lewis and Lewis, 1996).

This book is concerned to set the taken for granted conception of how women make choices within the context of the complex network of social relationships that make up the labour market, and, in particular, to examine the extent to which the structure of gender relations provide a delimited set of parameters within which choices can be made. This issue is particularly significant in a profession like law. Firstly this is because it might appear that, as a result of extensive training and the high status of the profession, women lawyers possess an exceptional degree of authority and power in terms of their decision-making. Secondly, because law, and hence legal practitioners, play a major part in constructing social reality, and, in particular, gender identities and roles. As Bourdieu argues: 'Law is the quintessential form of the symbolic power of naming that creates the things named, and creates social groups in particular' (1987, p.838).

We are equally concerned with the idea of commitment. Where it is clear that women are equal to men in terms of ability, questions are often posed about whether they are equal in terms of their 'commitment to work' (Hakim, 1995; 1996). We shall argue that the concept of commitment is itself gendered. It is predicated on a naturalised view of the independence of the public and private spheres, and the role of men and women in each. Thus studies of commitment which look at the hours which men and women are prepared to work, and the extent to which their desire to work is dependent on financial reward, rarely if ever use the data to illuminate the question of men's commitment to their home lives, and the distinct work which is undertaken in the private sphere. It is similarly rare for such studies to question to what it is that women and men are expected to be committed at work, and the precise way in which such commitment may be measured. It is our contention that commitment is an ill-defined, and ideological concept. Women lawyers are not in fact facing the same kind of job that men lawyers are, and employer perspectives on the respective potential and career trajectories of women and men are starkly different. Furthermore, we will be arguing that in common with other occupations, expectations of performance in law work are not only profoundly gendered, but also sexualised. Women's perceived sexuality can be a management resource, and is consequently a significant element in the degree to which they are regarded as suitable for some specific types of work and unsuitable for others. However, the gendered aspects of law work tend to be implicit, and it may be that most women only become aware of the baggage that goes along with the job after some time in post.

The fact that there is a variety of types of work that solicitors may engage in is particularly significant in deciphering women's positions in the profession. The legal labour market is highly differentiated. Although all lawyers are members of the same profession to the extent that they are products of the same system of legal education and belong to the same self-regulating association, they practise in very different arenas, where the character of their business, their associations with clients and other fellow professionals determine the prevalence of specific cultures (Collier, 1998; Cain and Harrington, 1994). So, for example, an insolvency lawyer and a criminal legal aid practitioner may each have more in common in terms of culture with their respective clients than they have with each other. This extreme differentiation has created strains within the nominally unitary profession, but has also provided the framework for a complex patterning of women's experience, so that success is more possible for them in some areas than others. Indeed it is the case that it may be easier for a certain type of woman to succeed in some areas, at certain stages of their career, than a man.

Is it therefore valid to attempt any generalisation about the experience of women solicitors, especially given the criticism that studies which take gender as their primary focus are thereby inevitably characterising women as a homogeneous category (for instance, see Morgan, 1984; Menkel-Meadow, 1989; Barrett, 1987; Spelman, 1988; Bacchi, 1996)?[1] Specifically, Bottero has argued that 'The problem with the literature on women's entry to male-dominated professions is that by stressing continuity, and focusing on aggregate gender differences, the complexity and specificity of women's employment situation tends to be lost' (1992, p.332). This charge may appear especially pertinent to this study since we not only seek to generalise about the position of women, but are also concerned with the historical legacy of professional culture. This does not mean that we do not recognise the dangers of working within a framework which appears to treat as unproblematic the categories of 'women' - and indeed 'men' (Collier, 1998). Our data clearly revealed the need to distinguish between for instance, the experiences of our black and working class respondents and those of, say, middle class white women, as well as the differences generated by the various working environments (Dixon and Seron, 1995). Nevertheless, we contend that the results of both our research and those of other surveys (for instance, The Hansard Society, 1990, pp.43-51; Reynell, 1997; Sidaway, 1997; McGlynn and Graham, 1995; Ross, 1990) demonstrate that gender remains a principal determinant in the career trajectories of women solicitors, and, as we observed above, of the shape of legal practice. As Jackson has written, 'gender has historically been constitutive of a certain group identity, and, since we cannot exist in a chronological vacuum, we need to acknowledge the significance of that history' (1993, p.407). It is not only academic commentators who tend to reify gender. It is the profession (and of course mainstream society) which reifies it, and a focus on women solicitors as a category is therefore justified, if only on strategic grounds (Braidotti, 1993).

However, our claim to be able to generalise may be regarded as even more tenuous since this study draws particularly on data on women's position in the larger, more commercially oriented firms, and refers less to the experience of women in, for example, the sector that has specialised in legal-aided work. This has been in part because the big commercial firms are the largest employers of women, and yet are also viewed as particularly 'macho' and hostile to women returners (that is women who return to work following a career break, generally a maternity leave). It is also because such firms may be viewed as paradigmatic of private practice culture. Whilst we are therefore aware that some of the discussion may be less relevant to some legal workplaces than to others, a particular focus on such firms is warranted because of the influence they have as the professional elite[2] and because they are in the vanguard of professional restructuring. Moreover, both our data and that of the other surveys cited above indicates the existence of many commonalities between women lawyers across the spectrum of practices. In particular, they face discrimination in terms of pay, and this begins at the very start of their careers (Moorhead, 1997), and they also tend to share with each other the common destiny that their career trajectory will be flatter than a man's: even if they manage to climb on to the same incline at the beginning of a career, they will be likely to fall off (or be pushed) before that career has progressed to a pinnacle.

This complex relationship between women and the law jobs they seek to obtain and maintain is further overlaid by the long waves of economic prosperity and decline which radically affect the shape of the profession, both in terms of its overall size, and in terms of its internal composition. For example, whilst the last recession brought an end to the period of rapid general expansion, and a sharp decline in areas like commercial conveyancing, it saw an increase in insolvency practice and in criminal legal aid work (Goriely, 1996). Our research indicates that the position of women in the profession is intimately linked to these 'long waves' in a fashion that tends to support theories of the existence of a 'segmented' labour market. Their entry into the profession in large numbers in the UK, as in practice in North America and Australia, coincided with a period of unparalleled expansion in law work, and, in many cases, they appear to have been the first victims of decline.

As we have already noted, women's careers are also systematically influenced by life course factors in a way not experienced by men. Some commentators, notably 'human capital' and 'preference' theorists, tend to attribute women's position in the labour market in general almost entirely to these factors. They endorse the 'natural' inflexibility of the labour market which refuses to accommodate carers on equal terms, and the 'natural' fact that few men in full-time employment wish to, or are able to, demonstrate a substantial commitment to the private realm. This approach has been criticised, and the point has been frequently made that 'men's work' in the public sphere is heavily dependent on, indeed advances as a result of, women's work in the 'private' sphere: this domestic work, which facilitates an enhanced involvement in 'public' work, has been described as 'social capital' (Seron and Ferris, 1995), and access to this servicing is asymmetrically distributed between genders. However the relationship between the two spheres is more complex, and related to the construction of masculinity and femininity. For instance, we would argue, along with many recent writers on organisational culture (Hearn and Parkin, 1995; Sheppard, 1989) that sexuality, as well as gender, heightens the significance of motherhood as a factor in women's labour market destiny.

In attempting to develop an understanding of the relationship between women and their labour market, we have had to confront the resilience of the human capital approach to gender differences in career trajectories, exemplified by Caplow (1954), and, latterly, Becker (1991). In particular we contest the idea that individuals are judged according to a neutral evaluation of the properties and attributes they possess, or indeed that these attributes or skills can be and are objectively evaluated (see Markus, 1987), and that a change in their currency value is a function of technical obsolescence. In fact, desirable attributes are socially constructed, and mirror a hierarchical ordering prevalent in society outside the closed world of the law: their construction is drawn from and in turn validates judgements about the type of person fitted for certain work. In this process people are privileged on the basis of their class, gender and ethnic history. In discussing these issues, we have used the term cultural capital to refer to these socially validated attributes (Bourdieu, 1987, 1991; Hagan and Kay, 1995), and to understand the way in which women are articulated into the legal labour market so that skills and attributes which they believe to be significant are devalued.

A further aspect of private practice which we explore is the cultural milieu which shapes the experiences of women lawyers. This professional culture is the product of a lengthy historical process: a project of 'professionalisation' well documented in specialist literature, the goal of which was monopoly control over the provision of certain services. In the case of the exclusion of women from the provision of these services, the ideological justification was drawn from the character of the Common Law itself,[3] so there is an intimate link between the character and practice of law in the UK, the legal professional project and 'social closure' against women. The topic deserves a dedicated book in itself, but we have sketched an outline which provides a context for the contemporary data.

Finally, it is worth stressing in this brief introduction to the issues thrown up by our research, the extent to which many of our women respondents have frequently been baffled, angered and shocked by their experiences.[4] We believe this to be in part a function of the power and prevalence of the belief that modern society and its institutions are characterised by formal, rational procedures, and objective decision-making, and the resulting confusion when experience proves otherwise. This is reinforced by the dominance of human capital theory in vernacular understanding of the labour market, and the emphasis in public policy on formal qualifications and accreditation. This image of modernity and rationality is however being increasingly challenged, and the significance of the personalist relationships which underpin power hierarchies and key decision-making processes is being recognised. These personalist networks reinforce male dominance and subordinate women, since many of them are maintained through nominally private activities and institutions which either formally exclude women, or make it difficult for them to feel at home. The significance of these institutions and processes often only becomes apparent to women over time. For similar reasons, this is a difficult area to research: as Catherine Hakim remarks, 'some of the most important processes that contribute to greater career success among men than women are invisible, not just unmeasured but unmeasurable' (1996, p.183). We have explored this area through interviews, but again it begs for further systematic research.

The underlying issue which we are seeking to address through this book is the extent to which women and men are able to exercise real choice over the way in which they work and construct their careers. For there is no doubt that the template of the lawyer into which both genders have to fit constricts men as well as women. Male respondents as well as female perceived the working conditions as a yoke, and resented the damage to their relationships with their family, though there was a greater tendency amongst men to accept some of the burdensome terms as simply given.

The research project

A full description of the methods used in this research, including details of sampling procedures, sample sizes, response rates and analytical techniques, is included in the Appendix. At this point, we would simply like to introduce the origins and rationale of the project, and trace the development from an initially quite limited focus, to the broader enquiry which we report here.

In 1990, the Law Society and a local Training and Enterprise Council commissioned some research from the then Leeds Polytechnic into the kind of training necessary to support the re-entry of women solicitors into the profession. This work was undertaken by one of the authors in conjunction with a research assistant, and the project subsequently reported to the Law Society (Sommerlad and Allaker, 1991). The project took the opportunity offered by a limited regional study to survey the women on the records of two local Law Societies, investigate their intentions in relation to taking a career break, the deterrents that they might confront, or that had confronted them on return, their preferences in relation to training for return, and the conditions under which they would like to return.

The project had attracted the interest of the Law Society because of the threatened shortage of solicitors in the late 1980's consequent on the commercial property boom. It was therefore premised on the assumption that women solicitors were, and were regarded as, a valuable human resource which employers would want to attract back to the profession, and that the main problem was how to ease their re-entry. It was clear to the principal researcher that before the efficacy of returner training could be evaluated, there were general issues relating to the profession's attitudes and practices in respect of women employees which needed to be addressed, and the focus was shifted slightly, with the approval of the Law Society, to gather data on these issues from women themselves and from all Senior or managing Partners in the research region. The data gathering exercise took the form of a postal questionnaire consisting of both closed and open items, a limited programme of in-depth interviews, and observation of returner training programmes.

By the time the project reported, the concern with preventing the loss of women to the profession had waned, as the recession had led to a position where the supply of lawyers exceeded demand. Moreover, the findings of the research did not point to an easy route to successful retention strategies, as the principal deterrents to women returning to the profession were not the problems of skills' deficit which human capital theorists argued were the distinctive property of women employees, but rather the ethos, working practices and career structure of the profession itself (Sommerlad and Allaker, 1991; Sommerlad, 1994a; Sommerlad and Sanderson, 1997). Due to the adapted form of the survey instrument a substantial amount of baseline data was available for the sample, and this offered the prospect of being able to undertake a longitudinal panel study. This prospect was partially realised when the Law Society offered a contract for up-dating the research in 1994, and a limited follow-up study was undertaken (Sommerlad, 1994a), using the same methodology but a smaller random sample of the original cohort. This allowed for the tracking of the experiences of the cohort through the difficult period of the recession. The follow-up study supported and strengthened the findings of the earlier research: of particular interest were the experiences of the committed career women lawyers who in the earlier survey had not perceived the structure and ethos of the profession as a problem, but who four years later viewed the situation more negatively and had adapted their career plans accordingly.

In the planning of a treatment of the research materials for this book, it appeared important to develop the quality of data in relation to some of the issues which had been mentioned frequently, but not in depth, in the responses to open questions on the survey instrument, and in previous interviews. In particular, some of our women respondents, especially those from the large commercial practices, had made references to the 'world' of practice development, and the prevalence of personalist male networks, which had made clear the focal role of this kind of activity in solicitors' career progression. Many of their references were to the way in which networking revolved around activities which were either exclusively male, or which made women who participated uncomfortable. We decided it would be appropriate both to conduct interviews with women which concentrated on this professional domain, and to try to elicit from a sample of men what was involved in the more 'closed' activities, and how the men themselves felt about their exclusiveness. It had also become clear that the social processes which were involved in the accommodation between the profession and women practitioners were complex and multi-layered. This is confirmed by research which has been undertaken in other jurisdictions, in particular Mona Harrington's account of women lawyers in the USA (1992), and Margaret Thornton's similarly qualitative treatment of Australian women lawyers (1996). The complexity of these processes is only accessible through a more in-depth interview procedure. Consequently, between November 1996 and June 1997 a further series of interviews was conducted with a range of respondents, in part drawn from the original sample. This stage of sampling was not random, but purposive, as we were seeking further data on the emergent issues, and the women who had already volunteered responses in these areas were the most likely fruitful sources of data. However, we also interviewed women who worked or had worked either in types of firm in which we were interested, or whose accounts would 'triangulate' others, or who had moved into areas connected with the law, which had not been the subject of the previous research, like teaching law or in-house lawyering. A 'snowball' sampling technique was used both for this group and for the new sample of men solicitors. The interviewing was conducted by telephone, which we feel enabled respondents to provide more detailed information on some quite difficult areas: one of the surprising and moving aspects of the research has been women's readiness to volunteer quite intimate and harrowing details of their experiences. For this we are very grateful, and we hope our treatment of the material does their honesty justice.

Another aspect of the research which appeared more significant as we worked on it was the historical dimension to the 'culture of lawyerdom': it became obvious that whilst some practices were relatively recent, and although the mode of masculinity in the law was changing substantially in the 1980's and 1990's, the 'cultural inertia' of the profession was a powerful force working against the equal inclusion of women. We consequently sought accounts of the profession before the 1980's from both men and women who had worked in a range of legal settings, and we have supplemented these accounts with substantial documentary and secondary library research.

Hilary Sommerlad was the principal researcher at all stages of the work, and conducted the overwhelming majority of the interviews personally. During the initial research programme (1990-1991), she was assisted by Janet Allaker, and Peter Sanderson advised on questionnaire design and data analysis. During the next stage (1994), she was supported by staff from the Policy Research Institute of Leeds Metropolitan University. The design of the third stage of interviewing was conceived jointly, but carried out by Hilary Sommerlad. The theoretical framework and the final data collation and analysis has been a joint project, as has the writing, although we have taken primary responsibility for the drafting of particular chapters.

The structure of the book

This book attempts to make sense of our data concerning women's experience in law careers by using a wide range of theoretical perspectives. We have tried to achieve a balance between the evidence and the discussion which does justice to both, without either trivialising the data, or overburdening the text with references. We would like the book both to be accessible to women who work in the law, and yet also to stand up as a work which attempts to locate the experiences we recount within a tradition of feminist and critical sociological and sociolegal theory. This brief guide is intended to help readers identify which sections to search out or avoid.

In Chapter Two, we critically examine theories of gender and the labour market, concentrating on women's experience in the professions. This is the chapter where we also explicitly lay out the source for our theoretical framework. For those readers who don't wish to see the way in which we ground this in the literature, we have provided a summary at the beginning. Specifically, we identify the following concepts as significant for our work: Carole Pateman's theorisation of the 'sexual contract', as the device with which public and private worlds are simultaneously separated and bound together, is linked to the concept of 'social capital' as the form in which this fraternal contract enables men to gain systematic labour market advantages; Bourdieu's discussion of legal culture (1987) and his concept of 'cultural capital' is developed and expanded to provide a link between women's variable characteristics, and employers' variable demands, and this is situated within a model of occupational and organisational labour markets; and finally, the Weberian notion of 'social closure' is used as an overarching description of the way in which social processes work to exclude or marginalise women in the profession.

In Chapter Three, we examine the history of the entry of women into the solicitors' profession in England and Wales. We have tried to provide a factual account of key events. This is set in the context of an analysis of the patriarchal character of the law as an ideology and a profession, and we have attempted to demonstrate how the closure of the profession up to 1919, and its ratification by Common Law judgments, was underpinned by a tight network of personal relationships and shared opinions. This symmetry between the ideology and the practice of law, we argue, forms the basis of the subsequent informal, cultural exclusion of women.

In Chapter Four, we trace the persistence of this culture in both the profession and the academy during the fifty year period following the end of formal exclusion, when women's participation rates in England and Wales remained below 10 per cent (and for the bulk of that period the rate was below 5 per cent; Abel, 1988, p.415). In support of the historical record, we use the accounts of men and women respondents who were practising during this period. Our exploration of the professional culture during this period includes a brief discussion of the nature of law and legal training. Finally, we provide a summary of the era of expansion of women's participation, and explore the statistical picture of their distribution in the profession, before examining the characteristics of our sample in relation to this wider national picture.

In Chapters Five and Six, we attempt to broadly delineate the culture and structures of the profession which provide the context within which choices must be made. Chapter Five, drawing largely on qualitative data, focuses on the patriarchal and personalist culture of the legal workplace and identifies the key mechanisms in 'doing business' and developing a career, which ensure that it is specifically masculine cultural capital which is valued most highly. Chapter Six deals with the same material as the previous chapter, but from the perspective of women; in particular it considers the way in which women have been accommodated within the patriarchal structures and culture described in Chapters Four and Five. We attempt an examination of the ways in which gender and sexuality are key elements in the management of women's careers in the solicitors' profession. We identify how women's 'difference' can represent a form of cultural capital, but one which is continually subject to valuation or devaluation by men. In particular, the data in this chapter indicates the tension between the way in which women are judged simultaneously according to contradictory individualist ('each person is appointed strictly on merit') and collectivist ('well of course it's a fact of life that women go off and have babies') criteria.

Chapter Seven examines career breaks for reason of maternity. It is pivotal to the book as a whole, both because it is the break for childcare in a law career, as in so many others, that marks the point at which male and female career trajectories begin to diverge, and also because the response of the profession to motherhood and the private world it represents serves to illuminate some particularly murky corners of the law as a patriarchal profession. In this chapter, we subject human capital and preference explanations of the career break to a thorough critique. In particular, we criticise the role of the concepts of commitment and choice and the way they are mobilised to both effect and justify women's marginalisation in the professional labour market. The ambiguity of both terms is construed as an essential component of the profession's capacity to respond to women's increased presence in the profession with practices that ensure continued closure.

Chapter Eight is a prospective conclusion: whilst summarising the rather bleak picture drawn by the book of women's position in the profession, it also looks at various ways in which a more equitable occupational culture could be achieved. This is not intended as a policy-oriented report, and one of the messages of the book is that the obstacles in the way of women's full and equal participation in the law, as in many other occupational spheres, are remarkably durable both because of the tenacity of the culture of brotherhood, and also because of the conventional social script. Nevertheless, it is instructive to look at ways in which change might take place and the kind of policies and culture that support change.

Notes

1 Clearly, both legal workplaces and the homes of many professionals are characterised by intra-gender hierarchies. Women solicitors benefit from the 'difference' between

themselves and women in more 'traditionally female' jobs, for instance, legal secretaries, cleaners and nannies. However, the concern of this book is with the fact that, even given this support, women inside the 'ringfence' of the profession have been unable to achieve equal status.

2 This is also the standpoint of various commentators on the American legal profession, as Kaye has written: 'The big firms cast a giant shadow, in terms of public perceptions of the profession, parallels in other fields, and standards within the legal community ... the actual influence of the big firms and their alumni ... extends far beyond their numbers' (1988, p.113); see also Epstein's comment on their influence on legislation (1981, p.176), and Nelson's observations on their contribution to the development of the professional paradigm (1988).

3 For instance, see Phillimore, L.J. in Bebb v. Law Society (1914) 1 Ch. 286, p.298, discussed below in Chapter 3.

4 McGlynn has written: 'To many young women lawyers, discrimination is an unfamiliar concept and many consider this will always be the case. The grim reality is that discrimination will affect many women lawyers ...' (1997, p.19).

2 Gender and the Legal Labour Market

Introduction and theoretical summary

This chapter reviews some of the literature concerned with women's position in employment in general, and in the professions in particular, with the aim of crafting a theory of women solicitors' articulation into the professional labour market. In this introductory section we provide a precis of our ideas for the non-academic reader. We then move to a fuller discussion of the work which has influenced our own perspective. We have tried to avoid the kind of summary which has been described as 'a tedious British-style review of all the literature on gender and the professions' (Cohn, 1994). However, given that this particular area of study is both complex and controversial (Crompton, 1997), there is some substantial exposition of the theories and the way we will be applying them.

A framework for understanding women's experiences in the legal profession needs to be flexible enough to accommodate the fact of individual differences between women, whilst having the explanatory power to elicit the commonality which tends to distinguish their experiences from those of men. A key element in this framework must be the interdependence of the public and the private spheres,[1] and Carole Pateman's conception of the sexual contract (1988) challenges the common assumption of many labour market theories that practices in the public world of work (such as recruitment, determination of remuneration, the development and peopling of organisational hierarchies within workplaces) are entirely independent of the private world of work in the home and family. On the contrary, the continual processes of reproduction of male power occurs through the circular relationship between the labour market and the private sphere. This is illustrated in the legal profession by the fact that the kind of participation which is demanded of most women and men who wish to 'build careers' is predicated on domestic servicing, which some commentators have designated 'social capital'. Nor is this just an incidental characteristic, but rather an underlying principle: the 'natural fact' of the domestic division of labour underpins the way in which business is done in the profession.

This conception of gendered difference, operating reciprocally in the public and private spheres is central to women's professional marginalisation, and therefore to women lawyers' 'contingent authority' (Thornton, 1996). Women have ascribed to them 'essential', natural qualities, such as 'caring', and these qualities, seen as appropriate to their role in the private sphere, tend to be viewed as similarly inappropriate for the public sphere, which is held to require attributes commonly characterised as masculine (Young, 1987). This Aristotelian dichotomy then facilitates what sociologists of the professions describe as 'social closure', namely, restricted access to privileged occupational roles. The creation and maintenance of social closure is a historical process, and in the following chapter we identify the legacy of the construction of the profession as a 'fraternity'.

We trace the development of an ideology, a culture, and exclusionary practices which limit the scope for women's participation. Although such ideologies, cultures and practices are commonplace in other occupations, we would argue that they have had a particular force in the Law, because of the ideological construction of the Common Law itself as a sanctified mode of tradition and 'common sense', and because of its central role in constituting the meaning of womanhood. It took major social change outside the profession, and major structural change inside it, for women's participation on a large scale to become a possibility. Nevertheless, when women did finally enter in large numbers, they did not step into neutral jobs, the 'empty places' spoken of by Hartmann (1979). They were assigned work roles which were gendered, which the law itself designated as 'natural' for someone with particular gender characteristics to occupy. Those which are gendered as male tend to be the higher status roles within the profession, and women's representation in these is both sparse and tenuous.

A wealth of evidence suggests that those roles which are gendered as female correspondingly tend to have lower status and attract lesser rewards. However, the issue is complicated by the diversity of occupational roles covered by the term 'solicitor'. Statistics which are based on averaged figures of earnings and status indicate a tendency towards segregation in the legal labour market which is both vertical (women are much less likely to be equity partners or to earn a large salary) and horizontal (women are more prominent in some branches of the profession than others). However, the patterning of this distribution is quite complex, and at the moment statistics are not collected and analysed on a basis which would allow for a comprehensive picture to be drawn of women and men solicitors' respective positions in all the different sectors of the solicitors' labour market. Our own research indicates that 'successful' women appear to be the exception, and that the characterisation of the legal labour market as gendered is justifiable. In addition to being gendered, we would argue that some work roles are sexualised, in demanding that the women who occupy them behave in ways that conform to heterosexual male expectations.

The gendering of work roles erodes the foundations of the human capital view of the labour market as a neutral site of exchange. Women do not come to the market place bearing just skills which they can cash in for economic reward. They bring a range of other attributes which we describe using the concepts of cultural capital and symbolic capital (Bourdieu, 1991). This capital consists not only of attributes which are achieved, but also some which are ascribed to them by the prejudices of those who exert most power in the market: the 'difference' of women therefore becomes a way in which the value and status of their achieved human capital can be undermined. A woman can work hard, perform exceptionally in examinations, become expert in her field, only to discover that she is regarded as 'a good technician' and a 'back room girl', since what may be required for 'partnership material' is someone who is 'clubbable', or 'ladsy' or attractive.

This is because, underpinning the rhetorical view of the law and the legal profession as a neutral arena where one is judged by professional expertise,[2] much of the business is founded on patron-client relationships (Kaufman, 1974), which we describe as 'personalist', and which are the stuff of 'relational capital' (Granovetter, 1985; Dezalay and Garth, 1997; Hanlon, forthcoming), and where values altogether distinct from professional expertise come into play. These personalist, or clientelist, relations are constructed by, and dominated by men, and the changes necessary to make this network of relationships routinely accessible to women are inconceivable to most of the participants. Hence women also find it difficult to accumulate the relational capital of client networks which is a key aspect of the promotion process (see Hagan and Kay, 1995). The consequence is that women tend to have flatter career trajectories in the law than men, and are more likely to leave the profession in mid-career. From the human capital perspective, one might expect this to be regarded as a wasteful disaster by firms (indeed it was this view within the Law Society which prompted support for the original project which initiated this research: Sommerlad and Allaker, 1991; Sommerlad, 1994a).

However, in spite of a stream of reports delineating the problem, and the sponsorship of high profile 'exceptional women' (Mills, 1997), there are few if any indicators of positive change, either in the UK or comparable jurisdictions (Harrington, 1992; Hagan and Kay, 1995; Thornton, 1996). In part, this is due to structural factors: processes of rationalisation and concentration, combined with practices such as basing remuneration and corporate strategy on billable hours, have all combined to create an environment in which there is a need for a stratum of workers who will never achieve the professional dream of partnership. In this context, women tend to be regarded as a category of worker ideally suited for this stratum, as we have found that employers typically place a five year horizon on women's career prospects. Our research has demonstrated that a cycle of consequences flows from this fact: this shortened horizon, reinforced by prejudices about women's 'difference', leads to a reduction of opportunities, and perpetuates an environment in which many women simply do not feel at home. In particular, if they take career breaks, or have domestic caring commitments, they are likely to find their prospects drastically reduced, and their working environment even less friendly. As a consequence, many women 'choose' either to downgrade their career ambitions, move to friendlier environments where they can practise law (for instance, in bureaucratic alternatives such as the Crown Prosecution Service, local authorities or to positions as In-house Lawyers), or leave the profession altogether. Thus the processes we have described can be seen as clearly leading to a segmented labour market, with the possibility that, if the profession undergoes a radical restructuring, which has been debated as a possibility (Derber, 1982; Abel, 1988, pp.24-5; Halpern, 1994, pp.100-1; Sommerlad, 1995; Paterson, 1996), women may be predominantly represented in a subsidiary or secondary labour market of salaried employees, or in non-private practice environments where career routes are limited. In as much as women may be more liable to redundancy in times of recession and over-supply of labour, they might be said to represent a 'reserve army' of professional labour (Braverman, 1974; Breugel, 1979).

The traditional tactic adopted by women entering single sex professions has been that of assimilation. The ideology of liberal legalism in which all solicitors have been inculcated predisposes many women towards this human capitalist course, based on a belief in the legal labour market as a neutral sphere in which workers are autonomous individuals who make it through their own merit (Bourdieu, 1987, p.820). Traditionally therefore women lawyers have requested formal equality, not special treatment, and in this way, the culturally male patterns of work, and the social relations of domination which characterise private practice have if anything been legitimated by female participation. However the liberal viewpoint appears to be losing some ground, as the current construction of legal work, which is characterised by increasingly lengthy working patterns, is beginning to be challenged by more and more women, and even by some men. Nevertheless, most women, like men, are obliged to conform to the dominant ethos, and some women choose to adopt an extreme version of assimilation in an effort to reach the top. We examine this tactic and argue that its pursuit does not necessarily exempt its exponents from the consequences of the patriarchal culture of the profession. It can, in any event, only work for a few women as individuals, and not for women as a category, and is especially problematic for women who wish to become mothers, since men remain the norm, the 'measure of all things' (MacKinnon, 1987, p.34).

There is a final issue to be considered in this summary of our theoretical framework: to what extent is women's experience in the law the consequence of the individual, purposeful intention of men to discriminate against them, and to what extent is it the consequence of systemic factors over which neither gender has control? Our data does clearly implicate individual men, and groups of men, in acts of discrimination, disparagement and, occasionally, even harassment, though the cultural roots of this behaviour in the legal profession are complex, and the motives at times seem more subtle than fear of economic competition. However, the strength of this culture (or as Crompton and Sanderson describe it, 'cultural inertia', 1990, p.33) is such that it is difficult for men socialised inside it to deviate from the norm (Collier, 1998), even where they find aspects of it uncongenial in the extreme. As Fredman has argued, discrimination should rather be seen as a result of 'social structures and institutions ...' (1997, p.2). Ultimately, therefore, change is to be sought in a cultural transformation (Itzin, 1995) which loosens up the notion of what it means to be a lawyer for both men and women, and, relatedly, transforms the nature of gendered responsibilities in the private sphere.

The rest of this chapter is concerned with putting flesh on the bones of this argument by looking at theories of the labour market and the professions which develop an understanding of women's position. We begin by reviewing the principal general approaches to the differential position of women in the labour market, and in particular contrast the rational choice school of theories, such as human capital and preference theories, with gender stratification theories. We then translate these theoretical perspectives to the specific position of women in professions, identifying these as special categories of labour market, and examine the extent to which the situation of the women in our research conforms to the models we have discussed. We conclude the chapter by identifying the key concepts which underline the analysis of our data. As we acknowledged both above and in the Introduction, gender is simply one element in the ordering of opportunities in the profession, but although British African Caribbean and 'Asian' women were represented in our sample, the empirical base of the study necessitates the limitation of our principal focus to the experiences of women solicitors as women.

Gender and the labour market

Sociological work on the relation between gender and the labour market is concerned with both the product and its process: the product being the mapping of women's distinct position in the market, and the process being the ways in which this position is brought about. Theoretical and empirical studies of the gendering of the labour market tend to cluster in colonies which are often circumscribed by the boundaries of academic disciplines or their subsets. For example, the study of the professions could reasonably be regarded as a subset of labour market studies, but many of the insights of labour market sociologists are omitted from work on the professions. In the remainder of this chapter, we aim to integrate the insights to be derived from a range of theorists from different sites in this theoretical archipelago.

The fact of the gendered distribution of workers between different sectors of the world of occupations is well established. This differential distribution embraces a number of dimensions of occupations. Women are asymmetrically distributed between the public world of employment and the 'private domestic sphere' (Bradley, 1989); between different specialised occupations - 'horizontal segregation' (Hakim, 1979; 1992); between different strata of the labour market in terms of rewards - 'vertical segregation' (Corti, Laurie and Dex, 1995; Arber and Ginn, 1995); and between full-time and part-time work (Beechey and Perkins, 1987; Hakim, 1995). Although the issue of the extent of women's participation in the labour market in the UK, and its historical variation, has recently become a matter of controversy (Hakim, 1995, 1996a; Crompton, 1997), and patterns of segmentation and segregation are clearly subject to historical change, the fact of occupational segregation by gender remains well established in a range of studies (Hakim, 1979, 1992; Crompton and Sanderson, 1990).

In examining the processes through which this asymmetrical distribution occurs, analyses tend to operate at two levels. At the level of social structure, we are concerned with why this asymmetry occurs: is it the result of biological imperatives, powerful forces of socialisation, or the exercise of power in the cause of economic self-interest? If the latter, is it the result of capitalism or patriarchy; of men acting in the interests of their class or their gender, or some combination of the two? At the level of social process, we consider how the distribution occurs: by what mechanisms are women excluded from, or constrained not to choose, particular occupations? Here we are concerned both with phenomena which may be explicit and easily observable, such as formal legal exclusion and direct discriminatory behaviour unsheltered by formal exclusion, as well as indirect discriminatory processes, or the development of unfriendly environments which inhibit women from participating.

This chapter will therefore discuss theoretical perspectives on reasons for particular patterns of distribution, and here it is important that we recognise that the causes of asymmetrical distribution can not be simply read off from the surface 'facts'. There is a tendency on both sides of the argument in some of the debates to assume that the fact of segregation and segmentation self-evidently demonstrates the validity of either discrimination or choice as a determining factor. So, for example, Hakim has argued that the case study methods used by feminist researchers tend to overplay the impact of structural discrimination, because of a failure to distinguish between the differing career orientations of a heterogeneous population of women workers (1995, 1996a). Breugel, on the other hand, has criticised Hakim for inferring women's preferences from labour market outcomes (1996). The debate which has developed from this controversy clarifies the need for analysis which is representative and sophisticated enough to account for a heterogeneous female population, together with methods which allow us to understand the processes by which women make choices about their careers.

An account of the distribution of men and women into different sectors of the labour market is not enough on its own. Such an account should be combined with an analysis of the process of the articulation of women with the labour market which embraces the complexity of the relationship between the 'demand' and the 'supply' side, and the heterogeneous nature of each side. The employers in the legal labour market are composed of large corporate firms, small general practices, firms heavily dependent on legal aid work, firms which undertake no legal aid work at all; firms whose perspective is international and firms whose perspective is local (Collier, 1998; Cain and Harrington, 1994; Flood, 1996; Lewis, 1996). The way in which this kaleidoscope of employers views equal opportunities issues also varies widely (McGlynn and Graham, 1995). The supply side is similarly varied. For instance, the preferences and motivations of women pursuing a career as a solicitor are clearly differentiated: some women fit Catherine Hakim's definition of the career-centred woman who invests in training and has no intention of having a family (1995, 1996a). Others may have regarded their career as having a fixed horizon; however the majority of our respondents appear to have entered the profession with the objective of combining child-bearing and child-rearing with the achievement of a position in the profession commensurate with their abilities. Our evidence suggests that the difficulties of realising this last objective largely stem from the current structure and culture of legal workplaces in a variety of forms. Therefore, whilst recognising the heterogeneity of the characteristics of each side of the labour market, we agree with those commentators who argue that this does not preclude accepting the fact that, overall, the labour market may operate in a way in which it is systematically gendered; a proposition which is supported by evidence that women throughout the profession, and at all stages in their careers, earn less and enjoy lower status than their male counterparts (Sidaway and Lewis, 1996).

Segregation and segmentation in the labour market

Segregation and segmentation are concepts which can help us to construe the complex patterning of women and men in different occupations, or sectors of occupations, and at different levels of remuneration and labour market mobility. The two terms are sometimes mistakenly used interchangeably, and in relation to the solicitors' profession it is important to be clear about the distinctions. Hakim defines occupational segregation as 'when men and women do different kinds of work, so that one can speak of two separate labour forces, one male and one female, which are not in competition with each other for the same jobs' (1996, p.145). She further defines segregation as taking two forms: 'horizontal occupational segregation exists when men and women are most commonly working in different types of occupation. Vertical occupational segregation exists when men are most commonly working in higher grade occupations and women are most commonly working in lower-grade occupations or vice versa' (1979, p.19).

For the concept of segregation to have any meaning, it is necessary to rely on statistics which are generated using clear occupational boundaries. However conceptual difficulties arise from the fact that these boundaries are social constructions. For example, several members of staff, in a solicitor's office, each belonging to a different occupational category, may draft wills, take statements from clients and clerk for counsel in the crown court. Perhaps more significantly, several members of the 'legal profession' in any one town may be differentiated not just by an occupational specialism, but also by a corresponding career trajectory, remuneration and working conditions. Therefore, an index of segregation which uses the category of 'lawyer' or 'solicitor' is likely to be a blunt instrument. This is a problem which is accentuated by historical change and development in occupations, as the following illustration demonstrates.

From the 1880's onwards, it could be argued that the solicitors' profession has exhibited both vertical and horizontal segregation even though Hakim argues that these phenomena are 'logically separate' (1979). On the one hand, women were formally excluded from taking professional qualifications and from admission to the Roll until 1919, and subsequently did not constitute more than 5 per cent of those with practising certificates until 1975 (Abel, 1988, p.415). On the other hand, women, after their first entry into law offices in the 1880's (Abel-Smith and Stevens, 1967) rapidly came to dominate the base of clerical work on which the profession rests and which in many cases involves law work such as drafting documents and attending counsel in court (see for example data on the use of clerks at police stations, Sanders, 1996, pp.270-71): by 1978 women clerical staff constituted 50,000 of the 98,000 people working in solicitors' offices (Sachs and Wilson, 1978, p.178), and by 1976, 49 per cent of the new fellows admitted to the Institute of Legal Executives were women.

However, the solicitors' profession exemplifies the problems with segregation indices. Their dependence on the clarity of occupational boundaries renders them ineffective when dealing with the extreme diversity and differentiation of types of solicitors' work described above, and the impact of restructuring. The extremely rapid increase in the number of women entering the profession in the 1980's and 1990's could be seen as exemplifying a complete collapse in segregation. Nevertheless, the resulting notion of 'feminisation' needs to be considered both in the context of the simultaneous structural changes taking place which have reshaped career opportunities and trajectories (Sommerlad, 1994, 1995, 1996; Crompton and Sanderson, 1990, p.38), an issue which we examine further below, and also in the context of the resilience of patriarchal culture and the refurbishment of certain exclusionary mechanisms.

Theories of segmentation which concentrate on the broader characteristics of the market and its occupants allow for a rather more subtle analysis. Crompton and Sanderson, in analysing women's experience in a range of occupations, have produced a model of the occupational structure which aims to bring 'together within a single framework both the nature of the labour market and the characteristics of individuals within it' (1990, p.38). The model is composed of a matrix organised around two principle axes. One axis describes the continuum of skills and qualities on offer by employees (in essence a human capital axis). This axis makes a fundamental division between 'primary' and 'secondary' markets. The primary market is for individuals or groups with high levels of credentials and qualifications. By contrast, the secondary market is for employees who lack skills and qualifications, and is characterised by inferior conditions and unstable employment; as a result, here occupational mobility is controlled by firms.

The second axis makes a distinction between external and internal labour markets. External markets are those where there is a requirement for specific skills, probably accredited or certificated, and which therefore allow employees to move relatively freely between firms. In internal markets, the demand is for general skills which are specifically related to the needs or working practices of the firm, with the consequence that employees leaving jobs are likely to suffer a penalty (such as unemployment resulting from being unable to sell their firm-specific skills to another employer). In terms of the general labour market, the market for solicitors is clearly a primary one. There are however, within that primary labour market, also different markets on the external/internal axis. Firstly, 'occupational labour markets', which are external markets that 'include individuals whose skills and qualifications provide a market shelter which enables them to move between jobs without incurring any employer penalty' (Crompton and Sanderson, 1990, p.40). Secondly, there are 'firm internal labour markets', which are 'characterised by limited entry ports combined with movement up job ladders' and forms of firm-specific training and socialisation which restrict the mobility of staff outside the firm (id.). A median point on this latter axis is occupied by 'occupational internal labour markets', of which, in the legal profession, the market for in-house lawyers would provide the paradigmatic case.

The variety of employment sites which make up the legal profession straddle this model. On the one hand, it might appear that law firms would be located in an occupational labour market, since, like the medical profession, they are bounded by the formal criteria of qualification underpinned by statute and self-regulation. However, in both professions, the particular character of areas of the labour market limits the ability of qualified professionals to move freely. In medicine, general practitioners are bonded together in partnerships which restrict mobility. This is also the case for many solicitors, but the structure of partnership also affects solicitors who are not partners. This derives in part from the significance for lawyers and law firms of what Hagan and Kay describe as 'reputational capital' (1995), a crucial component of cultural capital.

More important than a lawyer's 'technical skills' is her or his capacity to attract and maintain a sound client base.[3] Therefore, in order to limit the mobility of their employees, some law firms tend to adopt the strategies of 'inclusion' and 'encirclement', such as writing restrictive covenants into contracts of employment (see The Lawyer, 28 October 1997, p.1), more typical of organisational labour markets. Conversely, certain types of solicitors may be unattractive to firms, because they lack reputational capital, or are deemed incapable of accumulating it. We explore the implications of this feature of the legal labour market, which is to be found in both the traditional 'family firm' and the modern 'corporate' sector, for women's employment below. It is worth noting here, however, that this characteristic relates to the social construction of the paradigmatic solicitor as male. Furthermore, because relational capital reflects the current values of whichever 'market' it operates in, its importance similarly increases the tendency to stereotyping employees, and gender-typing work.

A key aspect of the segmentation model is that it accounts for the dynamic processes of change, 'opening', closure, and 'encircling', in the labour markets we are discussing, and is therefore closely related to neo-Weberian theories of professionalisation, which we discuss further below. Crompton and Sanderson point out that it is labour markets with clear occupational boundaries which are most likely to be gendered, but that the association of such occupational boundaries with specific qualifications allows for the atypical group to use the 'qualifications lever' to gain entry (1990, p.44), which has clearly been the historical case with the legal profession. Informal exclusionary practices which operate at the level of the firm, however, are more difficult to surmount.

By contrast, human capital theories which seek to explain occupational segregation and segmentation by gender are concerned with problems of matching the demands of specific sectors of the labour market with employees, and would focus attention on issues of quality and reliability in the female supply of labour (see Becker, 1985; Hakim, 1996). However, a crucial difficulty with such analyses is that they have tended to accept employers' accounts both of the quality of female labour, and of essential demand characteristics. Crompton and Sanderson argue that in fact segregation and segmentation are the products of historic processes of conflict and adaptation between employers and employees, generating a cultural inertia through which a gender typing of occupations is accepted and propagated by interested social actors: 'occupational segregation is being reproduced by cyclical practices which are the outcome of past conventions regarding the "proper" relations between the sexes, the particular characteristics of national economies and so on, as well as being transformed by divergent practices such as the "qualifications lever"' (1990, p.43).

These historic processes can be viewed at two degrees of magnification. From a distance, we can observe the changing relation between women and the public world of wage labour, as well as continuities in the processes that maintain gender distinctions both in the public and private spheres. It is the examination of these processes of continuity and change which is the subject of the next section. Close up, we can observe the processes which support or impede the attempts of women to gain access to particular occupations. This involves a deconstruction of the voluntarist theories which attribute the 'glass ceiling' to women's choices or work orientations. Instead, attention is focused on what is involved in the gendered social construction of occupational roles and the qualities and 'skills' deemed necessary to fulfil them.

The origins of segregated labour markets

In examining the causal origins of segregated and segmented labour markets, we are not simply engaging in a theoretical debate, but looking at the direction in which opportunities and avenues for change lie. If we follow the arguments of human capital and rational preference theorists, then there would appear to be little need to examine the behaviour of employers, or to search for underlying social processes which work to women's disadvantage, as women will continue to make choices to work in less well rewarded areas, and to restrict their commitment both to waged work in general and to continuity with particular employers (Hakim, 1996a). This is attributed to the economic efficiency of a division of labour between heterosexual couples (though presumably it should apply to any couple where it is logical for one partner to specialise in domestic labour) (Becker, 1985, 1991).

However, what of employers' behaviour? In her initial, more extreme endorsement of rational choice theory, Hakim implied that in distinguishing between apparently less committed, less stable (women) employees, and more committed men employees, employers were, again, simply making rational choices as to the form of human capital in which it was profitable to invest (Hakim, 1996a). However, in her fuller, more layered account, she points out that even Becker's original theory acknowledged discrimination as a significant factor in accounting for gender-based earnings differentials (1996, p.14). This clearly undermines the claims which are made regarding the neutrality of the labour market, which is in turn fundamental to the validity of the rational choice model, since when and if women do decide not to invest in their career to the same extent as men, they can be seen to be influenced by the well understood unevenness of the labour market's treatment of the two genders. This fact, that the choices made on each side of the labour market were reciprocally determined, was indeed the experience of many of our respondents. Some women explained that, despite the substantial investment in their training, their career plans had been developed on the basis of an understanding about the limitations on their scope for advancement. We examine this evidence in detail below in Chapter Seven. Human Capital theory offers no explanation for this initial prejudicial treatment of women which we argue persists even when women demonstrate clear commitment to a long term career plan.

Hakim cites Goldberg's version of a theory of 'natural gender difference' as one possible explanation for differentiated experience in the labour market. This account, which combines hormonal difference with socialisation, has, as Hakim notes, parallels with some feminist arguments about gendered behaviour patterns (for instance, Gilligan, 1982). We shall not dwell on this attempt to reduce explanations of human behaviour to the biological: Cynthia Cockburn has pointed to the difficulties involved in locating oneself in a strong position in the sameness/difference dichotomy (1991, pp.10-11). What is more significant is that the 'qualities' or attributes which are used to identify difference, the 'binary opposites' of gender, are negotiated social constructions, subject to variation according to culture, class, power and the specific contexts in which these all interact. More crucial than any 'difference' is the capacity for individuals or groups to ascribe that difference and use it as a means of subordinating others. As a result, whether women are, as a category, different, or whether such difference is a consequence of their social construction by men for purposes of sexual objectification and domination (MacKinnon, 1987), or whether there are identifiable female characteristics which should be valued (West, 1991), is not central to our current concern here. What is important is the power of the profession to construct them as different, and then to both exploit and devalue that difference.

As labour market expressions of liberalism, a central tenet of which is blindness to the structures of domination which underlie formal equality, human capital and psycho-biological theories lack both a general perspective on the materiality of power, and a historic perspective on its role in processes of gender differentiation. They are therefore deficient as causal explanations, and ultimately mimic the common sense rationalities of economic actors who wish to justify the fact of segmentation and segregation. More convincing are accounts of gender stratification which look at the process as a developing one, where structures and ideologies of power are renegotiated historically to meet changing economic and cultural circumstances. We will therefore move on to examine theories of women's experience in the labour market which do not seek to attribute their position solely to the behaviour and choices of women themselves, but who see occupational segregation and segmentation as the result of systematic behaviour by the demand side of the market.

The historical origin of public occupations segregated by gender has been seen as coeval with the development of a capitalist division of labour (Pateman, 1988; Hartmann, 1981; Walby, 1990; Crompton, 1997), and, in part, a response to the possibility of women's economic independence created by the availability of wage labour. The gendered structuring of the labour market gave scope for ensuring lower levels of remuneration for women's work, and their consequent continued dependence on institutionalised heterosexual relations. There are of course critics of this model of the origins of occupational segregation, but, as we have argued above, the causal models offered as substitutes are weak, depending on essentialist characterisations of gender difference, and parallel conceptions of 'voluntary' or 'natural' segregation (Hakim, 1996, p.146). Nevertheless, the argument highlights the difficult point about the reason for asymmetrical distribution referred to above, and recurrent throughout our discussion. Whilst the preference theory interpretation of women's career paths as the result of their own choices is rightly criticised for being excessively voluntarist, and for distorting concepts like choice, it is equally problematic to attribute direct agency to men in perpetuating occupational segregation without looking at the evidence of process and motive which supports this similarly voluntarist conception. Bourdieu's conceptualisations of the legal world provides one explanation: 'the effects that are created within social fields are neither the purely arithmetical sum of random actions, nor the integrated result of a concerted plan. They are produced by competition occurring within a social space' (1987, p.852).

The discussion of our data in the chapters which follow tends to illustrate this observation. Men's behaviour in legal organisations is structured though the historical legacy of a closed masculine culture, and its reaction to infiltration by the 'other'. At the same time this culture is shaped by the ideology and discourse of 'impartial reason', and the equation of this normative ideal with maleness in contradistinction to designated femaleness: the binary opposition which is rooted in the public/private dichotomy.

The interdependence of the public and the private

The classical liberal theory of the labour market presupposes the independence of the public and private spheres. That is, it assumes that paid employment in the public sphere exists independently of the domestic sphere which reproduces the means for the existence of the public.[4] Rational choice theory also assumes that the choices employers and employees make are grounded in a neutral interpretation of the immediate exchange: in other words, that employers' decisions as to whether to employ women are not bounded by presuppositions or prejudices about women's characteristics or behaviour as a category, and that women's decisions about selecting occupational avenues are not determined by foreknowledge of the actual or assumed gendering of labour markets. This formulation of the operation of the labour market has been alluded to in the earlier discussion of Crompton and Sanderson's model of the labour market. It privileges employers' reasoning: clearly they would not wish to assume an economic responsibility for the domestic sphere, nor would they want to admit to 'irrational' behaviour in the labour market. Rational choice theory, as we will argue throughout the book, therefore constitutes a rationale for the discriminatory behaviour which produces occupational segregation. In contrast, a range of alternative theoretical perspectives point to the interdependence of public and private spheres, and the historically specific character of current arrangements.

Carole Pateman locates the loss of women's potential for economic independence in the removal of production from the household into 'civil society' at the birth of capitalist production (1988, p.116). In delineating the impact of this economic transformation, she points to the indispensable (though sometimes conceptually invisible) links between the public and private worlds: 'the construction of the worker presupposes that he is a man who has a woman, a (house) wife, to take care of his daily needs. The private and public spheres of civil society are separate, reflecting the natural order of sexual difference, incapable of being understood in isolation from each other' (op.cit., p.131). Most other feminist writers are similarly united on the intimate links between the significance of unpaid domestic labour and occupational segregation. Hartmann argues that low wages keep women dependent on men through what Hakim terms the 'marriage market', and the domestic division of labour in which they are then enmeshed weakens their position in the labour market (1981, p.448). Similarly, for Walby the causal link between the labour market and family goes 'in the reverse direction from that conventionally assumed; it goes from the labour market to family, not vice versa, when we ask questions about causation at the structural level' (1990, p.57).

Whilst human capital explanations of women's predominance in the domestic sphere have relied on essentialist theories of a social ordering based on biology, psychology or economically rational choice, feminist structural explanations have focused on the deliberate acts of male participants in the labour market, and have identified manifold examples of ideologically driven acts of exclusion. Our own evidence indicates the prevalence of the ideology of 'separate spheres' as a rationality underpinning both the exclusion of women, where it occurs, and their incorporation into the legal profession on different terms. This is specifically linked to the construction of 'law work', particularly in the sectors which interact most closely with the commercial world, as a job which it is virtually impossible to undertake whilst having any domestic responsibility. The need for 'social capital' (domestic servicing; Seron and Ferris, 1995), and the fact that, even in more 'modern' economies such social capital tends almost invariably to accrue to men (Hochschild, 1989), reinforces the framework of gendered difference which surrounds the legal labour market along with others (for instance see Wajcman, 1996).

How does this ideology operate at the level of recruitment and selection, where women are articulated into the labour market? The history of the legal profession, as we shall see, contains examples and episodes of direct discrimination and exclusion, but increasingly it is being recognised (in work on organisations in both the public and private sector; Collinson et al, 1990; Itzin and Newman, 1995; Halford and Savage, 1995) that a theoretical framework which can encompass more subtle forms of closure in the labour market is required. In the following section we examine the social construction of gendered roles in greater detail.

Cultural capital, 'difference' and the labour market

We have argued above that the weakness of human capital and rational choice theories is embedded in their synchronic character, and their failure to take account of the fact that labour markets are shaped through historical processes where the two sides interact reciprocally to shape each others' attitudes and views. A model which uses a similar metaphor, but which can encompass the sense of process is Bourdieu's formulation of the idea of cultural capital, a term which describes the resources which can be brought into play by an individual (or group) to achieve a desired position within a 'social field' (and see Markus, 1987, pp.104-5).

Cultural capital is deployed within a field (like the legal labour market - or, as he describes it, the 'juridical field' (1987)) where it 'represents power over a field (at a given moment) ... The kinds of capital, like trumps in a game of cards, are powers which define the chances of profit in a given field (in fact to every field or sub-field there corresponds a particular kind of capital, which is current, as a power or stake, in that field)' (1991, p.230). So, for example, to be employed as a lawyer, rather than a clerk or legal executive, it is necessary to possess the formal cultural capital represented by the institutionally guaranteed qualifications and vocational training. However, even to complete the training, by obtaining a training contract (or, historically, articles), it may be necessary to possess the cultural capital which will be recognised by the desired firm: this cultural capital may take the form of a particular combination of educational experience, or significant family or social connections with key agents (relational capital) which may either be taken as given or may be achieved through participation in the right networks (sporting connections, clubs and societies). Alternatively, significant 'qualities' may be recognised ('drive'; 'forensic skills'; being 'clubbable' and so forth), and these can be viewed as a part of what Bourdieu defines as a person's 'habitus': sets of dispositions (attitudes, 'taste', linguistic and bodily traits) which people absorb in their primary and secondary socialisation and which contribute to their practical knowledge, the ability to function in an appropriate milieu. So, for example, as we shall observe in the next chapter, socialisation practices were a key aspect of ensuring the unity of each branch of the legal profession, and the function of pupillage and articles can be seen as partly ensuring that an individual was 'fit' and also that they would subsequently fit in. Of all such rituals in the legal world, the barristers' practice of dining in the Inns is both the most notorious, and best demonstrates the force of Bourdieu's analysis: Helena Kennedy vividly describes the feeling that 'Gray's Inn was another planet' (1992, p.39) and the way in which the rituals of dining were used to enforce a categorisation of 'insiders' and 'outsiders' (op.cit., pp.40-1). The 'practical knowledge' embodied in these rituals has to a considerable degree become entangled with the dominant view of what constitutes the law itself (an example may be the resistance to abandoning wigs and gowns in court because they represent the dignity and authority of the Law), and in the following chapters we explore the way in which this has embodied a particular form of masculinity at the heart of legal practice and discourse.

Bourdieu argues that individual agents or groups are defined in social fields by their relation to each other according to the properties (cultural capital) used in constructing this field or 'space', and that the field acts to determine the position of individuals within it 'as a set of objective power relations imposed on all those who enter this field, relations which are not reducible to the intentions of individual agents or even to direct *interactions* (his emphasis) between agents' (1992, p.230). This is a difficult but important point, in the context of looking at the relative position of men and women within the legal profession. To what extent do individuals determine, or have the capacity to challenge, the oppressive relationships within which they find themselves? To use one example, it has been argued that an increasingly dominant factor in the culture of the legal profession is the globalisation of legal practice (Flood, 1996), and the growing demands for the twenty-four hour availability of legal staff, and this was indeed mentioned both by senior partners and women practitioners themselves as limiting the participation of women with caring responsibilities 'because clients wouldn't like part-timers'. Whether or not this dictum was 'true', it nevertheless constituted an 'active property' constructing the field of international commercial legal practice, one which it would be difficult for an individual or even an individual firm, to reconstruct.[5] Therefore, for an individual disadvantaged in such a field there would be little alternative but to accept their position or to seek an alternative field within which to operate (and this might be a way in which to understand structural developments within the profession, such as increases in the numbers of sole practitioners in the solicitors' branch, or the creation of new chambers in the barristers' branch). Thus, as Bourdieu argues, the increasing differentiation of the juridical field in response to external pressures creates competitive forces which structure the realm of possibilities for individual practitioners (1987, p.850).

This theoretical perspective therefore has the flexibility to accommodate the existence of heterogeneous fields of practice in the law, distinguished by the types of cultural capital which create the conditions for success, as well as the characteristics specified in Crompton and Sanderson's model (1990). There are, it follows, fields in which the chances for women to succeed are considerably greater than in commercial law or insolvency practice; for example matrimonial law and conveyancing. We emphasise again therefore that our findings are particularly pertinent to specific fields and types of practice.

At the same time, the wider legal world represents an overarching field characterised by 'difference' and Bourdieu's principal concern has been to create a framework for the understanding of the reproduction of hierarchies, and whilst his principal focus is on class and gender receives only a fleeting, (and occasionally patronising, see 1991, p.50) mention, his conceptualisation nevertheless offers a great deal towards an understanding of how gender hierarchies work. Firstly, it recognises the way in which markets are socially constructed around ideas of difference which are neither neutral nor objective, but which reflect a hierarchical ordering more generally prevalent in civil society. Secondly, the recognition of a range of informal characteristics as constituting cultural capital (what Bourdieu describes as 'bodily hexis' or 'a permanent disposition, a durable way of standing, speaking, walking and thereby of feeling and thinking', 1990, pp.69-70) helps us to understand some of the problems which are embedded in discourses of formal equality. In particular, the notion of 'symbolic violence' offers a way of understanding how individuals can be kept in their place through interactions whose meaning is not objectively visible:

> The modalities of practices, the ways of looking, sitting, standing, keeping silent, or even of speaking ('reproachful looks' or 'tones', 'disapproving glances' and so on) are full of injunctions that are powerful and hard to resist precisely because they are silent and insidious, insistent and insinuating (1991, p.51).

It offers a way of understanding those virtually invisible social practices which generate segregation in the labour market whilst remaining difficult to detect and combat, such as the management and recruitment processes identified in a range of public and private sector organisations (Collinson et al, 1990). Thirdly, the model, and the idea of the price formation of cultural capital allows us to discern the way in which the qualities which women bring to the market may not realise the value which they expect, since the machinery of price formation is in the hands of the predominantly male elite who manage the profession.

Finally, this conceptualisation of the social skills and their valorisation which underpin a lawyer's placement in the labour market, brings us back to the ideology of separate spheres, and the sexual contract. The interrelationships between the creation of hierarchies and the construction of difference is dependent on the masculine/feminine dichotomy (Thornton, 1996). This, however, does not only mean that women are ascribed qualities which generally inhibit their successful participation in the public sphere; it also results in the ascription of a cultural capital to which they themselves might not attribute great value. In particular, this may apply to their sexuality. A number of commentators have pointed to the use of sexual harassment and 'compulsory heterosexuality' in the workplace as a means of sublimating the oppression suffered by male employees (Hearn and Parkin, 1995), 'bonding' male employees (Stanko, 1988; Cockburn, 1983), excluding women from non-traditional occupations

(Cockburn, 1985), and exerting male authority and control over women in the labour market (Cockburn, 1991). In a development of this perspective on sexuality and work, Adkins has argued that, in the service industries she studied, women's work roles were sexualised, and women were obliged to engage in forms of heterosexual interactions (1995). These ranged from being subjected to sexualised selection criteria and overtly sexualised dress codes to accepting work conditions that meant they were expected to deal with 'forms of sexual objectification from men customers and men co-workers' as 'an integral part of their work' (op.cit., p.145). Adkins argues that women's status as sexualised workers renders them a less powerful group in relation to male workers, and that men and women were constituted as different kinds of workers, 'even when they were located in the same jobs' (op.cit., p.147; see also Collinson and Collinson, 1996; Filby, 1992). This argument has important implications for rational choice theory which assumes a state of *ceteris paribus* in the decision-making and commitment of female employees. If we agree that men and women are ascribed differing subjectivities and have qualitatively different experiences, and are subject to different employer expectations even when occupying the 'same' jobs, then indices of choice and commitment become similarly incommensurate.

Adkins' argument also allows us to develop the conception of cultural capital to include sexuality. One way of accommodating women within the rapidly changing world of law work is to incorporate them as sexualised workers in specific roles, or to incorporate their sexuality in certain aspects of their work. We discuss this issue in relation to 'practice development' below. Therefore it can be argued that one form of cultural capital which women bring to the profession (even when they are not aware of it) is sexual, and we will use the term 'sexual capital' in our analysis. However, whereas Adkins' analysis tends to view the sexualisation of labour as one category of experience, in fact sexual capital is variable in type, and different types attract different values in different fields: the problem, even for women who might consciously deploy their sexual capital for occupational advantage, is that men control the processes of defining the field, and therefore women face the constant threat that they might behave 'inappropriately'. Our research also reinforced the perhaps obvious point that women's 'sexual capital' is subject to life cycle factors. Motherhood is a watershed in the careers of women, not simply because of its effect on their availability, or their (perceived) motivation and career plans, but also because after motherhood (or even marriage) their ascribed status can undergo a radical transformation (Brannen and Moss, 1991; Hochschild, 1989; Thornton, 1996).

An important issue which springs from this conjunction of the ideas of cultural capital and sexual difference is the fact that whilst theories which examine the embodiment of women as women have now a fairly lengthy history, the 'norm' from which women are distinguished is apparently assumed to be a monolithic entity, where the processes of embodiment are unproblematic (and also voluntary). Collier has argued the need to 'reconceptualise the social practices of law as … "masculinising agencies"' (1998, p.22), following the example of Collinson and Hearn in 'naming men as men' in organisations (1994). Whilst in Chapters Three and Four we are concerned with aspects of the construction of the legal profession as a brotherhood, in Chapter Five, we explore the character and construction of some of the legal masculinities which are represented in different sites in the profession, and argue that one of the processes taking place is the reconstitution of masculinity in response to the perceived threat posed by the increasing numbers of women in the lower branches of the profession.

In summary, we can understand the idea of cultural capital as a pivot of the relations between the two sides of the labour market, which enables decisions to be made on a level which may not involve explicit discrimination but which nevertheless reproduces the existing gender hierarchy of the profession. The concept avoids the weaknesses of explanatory frameworks which rely on 'essential' versions of gender characteristics, or which over-rely on simple primary socialisation arguments. 'Difference' is a product of the construction and reconstruction of attributes and dispositions which are then the subject of hierarchical discrimination by those with the power to discriminate. As a result, characteristics and qualities are not something an individual 'has' as the human capital model argues; rather, they are the product of ascription by others. In the case of gender this is particularly significant because the malleability of models of difference can allow qualities brought to the labour market to be disqualified (or rendered ineligible). To embrace this phenomenon, we have used the term 'variable' to qualify 'cultural capital'.

As we noted above, several writers have identified the difficulties inherent in regarding the 'attributes' of men and women as given, natural, and naturally distinct, particularly in relation to the workplace. Rowe and Snizek argue, 'gender is largely irrelevant to individual preferences for work values. Faulty assumptions that restrict the researcher to foregone conclusions and unnecessary differentiation are best discarded. Such differentiation has historically been the source of, as well as the justification for, general social inequality, which has resulted in blatant discrimination in the workplace' (1995, p.228). Despite the significant variations between female practitioners arising from characteristics such as class and ethnic identity, the position of all women in the legal labour market is based on the profession's construction of them as different and the simultaneous devaluation of that difference and consequent demand that it be eradicated and that they perform as men. Further, this is not, as we noted in our discussion of cultural capital, a consistent demand, in that at other times, or in other ways, they will be required to behave 'like women'. Epstein's study of women lawyers in the USA demonstrated that 'women who were tough-minded faced the disapproval of both men and women colleagues, and even of feminist attorneys who faulted them for assuming a "male model" of behaviour' (1991, p.329). Cockburn specifically links the patriarchal control of difference, the ability of men to define when it is important, to the reduction of the value of female labour power: 'women's skills, imputed and actual were set to work and under-valued. For the company, therefore, women's domestically-defined, sexually defined, differently perceived labour power was an important source of capital accumulation' (1991, p.163).

The value of the concept of cultural capital therefore is that it allows us to see difference as a currency which is used in the process of claiming labour market advantage, but the value of which is also subject to depreciation by external forces. However it should also be noted that the flexible nature of cultural capital is in part a reflection of the shifting nature of the professional labour market. As Anderson and Tomaskovic-Devey have argued in their study of the organisational context of gendered earnings inequalities, patriarchy should be regarded in the workplace as a 'dynamic set of organisational practices' where 'men's advantage is not assumed but rather is subject to defence, challenge, erosion and consequent reassertion' (1995, p.35). This is particularly the case in a historically contested field like the 'professions'.

Gender, professions and social closure

The growth and development of the 'professions' has attracted specialist attention from sociologists since the late nineteenth century, and an extended debate has been conducted over whether 'professions' exist as distinct modes of occupational organisation, or whether it is more appropriate to discuss processes or 'projects' of 'professionalisation' (Johnson, 1972; Larson, 1977; Parkin, 1979; Abbott, 1988). We are concerned, not so much with the terms of this well-rehearsed debate, but with the issue of whether the legal profession has distinctive characteristics as a labour market, in terms of gender effects.

The 'professions' can be seen as a species of the 'occupational labour markets' discussed by Crompton and Sanderson, and referred to above, in terms of the clarity of their boundaries, which are reinforced by specialist qualifications. As has been argued by many critics, the attempt by the traditional 'sociology of the professions' to invest them with additional distinguishing characteristics (a paradigm is Millerson, 1964) serves merely to support the justification offered by professionals themselves for their monopoly over the provision of specific services. These 'distinctive characteristics' need to be conceptually reformulated as socially constructed claims, and evaluated in the context of their role in the contest over monopoly. In terms of the solicitors' profession, a key issue is the attempt to construct a distinctive 'knowledge mandate', a body of technical expertise, structured enough to allow for the formal standardisation of the 'production of the producers', yet sufficiently indeterminate to resist appropriation by other groups. Legal education, from its inception, had a tenuous link with the world of practice, but it has been argued that one of its functions was to provide the key element of 'social closure', the term used by Neo-Weberian sociologists to identify the processes excluding non-conforming social groups from the practice of the occupational monopoly. The weakness of this strategy of closure is its accessibility through the 'qualifications lever': as was eventually demonstrated, it was comparatively simple, given the right conditions, for women to outperform men at the stage of formal educational credentials. However, Thornton argues that a corollary of the 'knowledge mandate' is the constitution of the lawyer as a 'legal knower', an embodiment of avowedly neutral (but actually male) technical-rational practice. The concomitant historical depiction of women as incapable of moral reason detracts from their ability to fulfil this role[6] hence the contradiction between women's capacity to achieve formal knowledge and their failure to achieve commensurate recognition. As she points out in relation to her account of legal education, 'the sexed body of the woman law student continued to get in the way of the idea of her becoming a rational legal knower' (1996, p.83).

In addition to the claim to expert knowledge, another key 'claim', which Burrage demonstrates was a focus of the collective endeavours of solicitors' association, was to 'gentlemanly' status and 'honour' (1996). The principal mechanism for reinforcing this status was the apprenticeship mode of training represented by 'articles', and we shall argue that this process has been profoundly gendered. Therefore, the formal qualifications may be seen as a proxy guarantee of social acceptability, whilst the 'real' induction into the profession was through the 'vocational' stage, during which an individual's cultural capital was consolidated and developed. We shall argue that when the formal training ceased to perform its screening function, by admitting large numbers of women, it became necessary to find another proxy for acceptability. That has become 'commitment' (see also Sommerlad, 1998), measured through specified patterns of work which can only be managed with domestic servicing: we would also argue that the development of the importance of commitment has been paralleled by processes of change in the profession which have transformed its 'gentlemanly status'.

This transformation has been the product of a historical contest, which can be seen as having both class and gender dimensions. During the course of this contest, a complicated one which involves competition between groups for occupational monopoly, as well as struggles to exclude some groups altogether, the character of the specific claims made by professions to justify their status leads to a corresponding set of strategies for the maintenance and erosion of monopoly. Witz distinguishes between the strategies employed by dominant social or occupational groups (1992, pp.46-7), and those employed by subordinate groups in the struggle over professional monopoly. Exclusionary strategies are concerned with the maintenance of control over the occupation through regulation of labour supply, and patrolling the boundaries of practice. Gendered exclusionary strategies involve the application of individualist criteria of eligibility for men, and collectivist criteria of ineligibility for women (so we would argue from our last paragraph that commitment is a gendered collectivist criterion of ineligibility). Demarcationary strategies involve the negotiation between occupational groups over control of spheres of competence, of the kind which characterised the struggles between solicitors, conveyancers, scriveners, barristers and others during the eighteenth and nineteenth centuries. It can also be used to describe instances where one occupational group is able to achieve control over the spheres of competence of another (described by Larkin as 'occupational imperialism', 1983). In the case of solicitors, this would characterise the relationship between the solicitors and legal executives (Abel, 1988, pp.207-8).

In looking at the strategies used by subordinated groups, Witz draws on the work of Parkin (1979) and Murphy (1984) to provide an account of 'usurpationary and dual closure strategies'. Usurpationary strategies involve a subordinate group mobilising power to transform collectivist criteria of exclusion into individualist criteria (generally involving a claim for formal equality), in order to effect entry. 'Dual closure strategies', which Witz describes as characteristic of female professional projects, are employed in an effort to maintain control over a sphere of competence against a threat from above, and to consolidate this control through the development of exclusionary devices of their own (1992, p.50). In the case of the solicitors' profession, we shall primarily be concerned to trace the development of a female usurpationary strategy, since the process of professional fission which might lead to a 'dual closure' strategy has yet to occur.

Witz correctly argues that the concept of 'profession' is itself gendered and that 'the first step towards purging analyses of their androcentric bias is to abandon any generic concept of profession and redefine the sociology of professions as the sociological history of occupations as individual, empirical and above all historical cases rather than as specimens of a more general, fixed concept' (1992, p.64). The sense of this approach is amply demonstrated by contrasting her account of the developing medical division of labour in the nineteenth and twentieth century with the contemporaneous developments in the legal profession which we discussed above. Whilst the medical profession was involved in a series of gendered demarcationary struggles which resulted in the development of a formalised gendered division of medical labour (in part, as Menkel-Meadow notes, the product of essentialist views of gender capabilities:

1989, pp.300-1), there was no equivalent process in the legal profession, where specialised spheres of competence did not have a gendered dimension (since women were equally unrepresented in both barristers' and solicitors' branches), and where the subordinated occupational group of legal executives had equal representation of both men and women (Abel, 1988, p.208).

A further dimension to Witz's analysis is her discussion of the distinction between autonomous (typified by control over qualifying examinations and membership of professional registers) and heteronomous (typified by statutory reinforcement of exclusionary shelter) forms of closure. She points to the fact that autonomous closure, functioning in civil society, has proved to be more effective than legalistic heteronomous strategies (1992, pp.65-8 for example). It is significant that women's initial usurpationary project in relation to the law challenged collectivist criteria of exclusion through just such a formal equality strategy which consequently implied the right to inclusion on an individualist basis of 'merit'. Hence, whilst the 1919 Sex Disqualification (Removal) Act removed the formal enshrining of the 'separate spheres' principle from the Common Law, it did not challenge the similar embodiment of that principle in the profession, as we shall observe in the next chapter. The institutionalisation of male power in key areas of the State and civil society, which provided the bulwark against women's entry to the legal and medical professions in the first place, remained fundamentally unchallenged.

Another important distinction between the legal and medical professions is that whilst in hospital medicine, there has been a substantial degree of formal specialisation, in both branches of the legal profession specialisation in legal education is still resisted (Saunders, 1996), and a key aim appears to have been to maintain the status of both barristers and solicitors as unitary professions. Clearly this apparent unity masks extensive differentiation in terms of the work undertaken, the mode of organisation of labour, and the concomitant rewards. So the apparent formal unity of the profession may also mask an implicit asymmetry in the areas to which women are being admitted; it has been argued that the legal labour market is in fact characterised by horizontal segregation (see Podmore and Spencer, 1986, and the patterns discussed in Chapter Four). Consequently, women solicitors' apparently successful usurpationary strategy needs to be interpreted in the context of the structural change which the private practice of solicitors, in common with other professional practices, is currently undergoing.

Gender and structural change in the legal profession

In an article which drew heavily on Braverman's labour process perspective, Carter and Carter argued in the early 1980's that the increasing participation of women in a range of professions coincided with 'a rapidly developing split in professional work between prestige jobs with good pay, autonomy and opportunities for growth and development and a new class of more routinised, poorly paid jobs with little autonomy' (1981, p.478), and that women would overwhelmingly be concentrated in this latter 'sector'.

This approach to understanding the character of women's participation in the professions is linked with the theories of gendered work, analysed above, in that it argues against the 'empty places' models of women's move into employment as a whole, and into previously male occupations in particular. Inside the legal profession there was a long period (outlined in greater detail in the next chapter) after the establishment of formal equality in 1919 when women's participation was minimal, and there were comparatively few structural changes in the profession: when, in effect, processes of social exclusion operating outside the profession, and informal social closure within, meant that the status quo obtained.

A number of commentators have argued that the processes, both inside and outside the profession, which allowed for women's participation ensured that the change in participation rates, when it came, was accompanied by major internal structural changes (for instance, Abel, 1988). For Hagan and Kay, the 'growth dynamic' which characterised particularly large law firms in the 1980's and 1990's was the consequence of an expansion and concentration of reputational capital generated by partners in such firms, which then required compliant qualified labour to service the clients represented by this cultural and reputational capital (Hagan and Kay, 1995, pp.33-5). The concentration of equity partnerships and the corresponding increase in the ratio of assistant solicitors to partners is necessary in order to increase the rate of profit. Combined with technological change, it could be argued that this dynamic is leading to a parallel process in the routinisation of legal work and the translation of much of this work to a paralegal stratum (a particular example is the development of law clinics in the USA). In the publicly funded sector, the pressures for cost reduction have, it is argued, made similar processes of specialisation and routinisation attractive (Sommerlad, 1995, 1996).

As Hagan and Kay point out, the consequent bottleneck on the route to partnership undermines one of the prime dynamic forces in legal labour market, namely the quest for advancement through partnership, the traditional process whereby the apprentice eventually becomes the 'master' (1995, p.33). They therefore argue that women are 'used' as a submissive form of skilled and well-educated labour, 'to play a vital demographic role in the centralisation and concentration of cultural capital that is transforming the legal profession' (id.). In the UK this structural change may be reflected in the creation in some of the larger corporate firms of the layer of salaried partners, which is a means of maintaining the rhetorical commitment to the ladder of advancement. Hagan and Kay also point out that, whilst the departure of a male lawyer from a firm is seen as damaging that firm's reputational capital, in that it is generally accompanied by a loss of clients, women are more likely to leave jobs but not take clients with them, 'and these departures may even be advantageous in limiting demands for promotion to partnership and increased earnings' (id.).

It could be argued that the restructuring of the profession is leading, therefore, to the creation of a secondary labour market for lawyers, in which women predominate, though this is disguised by the complex pattern of specialist and generalist firms of varying sizes, and with differing client groups and management philosophies. The existence of this secondary labour market both preserves the ladder of advancement for men, and provides 'a hedge on spiralling demands for rewards in periods of growth' (op.cit., p.340) since its occupants are regarded as more easily disposable during times of recession. As we have discussed above, the rationale for allocating women to this secondary market is sustained by an ideology which stresses women's biological destiny, their lesser need for work (the 'component wage' argument), their 'different' motivations and attributes, and their 'unreliability' as employees. It follows from this argument that, if women are successfully to fulfil this role of a secondary labour force, their greater participation in the profession, so far from liberalising attitudes towards them, will lead to an increased prevalence of an ideology which 'encircles' (Witz, 1992, p.47) or places distinct parameters around their participation.

We do not present this as a determinist theorisation of women's entry into the profession which implies that they are the passive victims of male power.[7] A number of accounts are coming forward which indicate that the relationship between gendered work roles and the people who occupy them changes in subtle ways as the gender composition of an occupation changes (Halford and Savage, 1995; Morgan and Knights, 1991; Bottero, 1992). However, we would endorse Epstein's fear (1981), that women's increasing participation in the professions has not been viewed neutrally by male lawyers, and that the concept of 'difference' can be used in such a way as to maintain control over specific areas and strata of practice. The conceptual apparatus discussed in this chapter will be used in the rest of the book to discuss the extent to which this can be seen to be happening in the solicitors' profession in the UK.

Conclusion

We have argued in this chapter for a combination of theoretical perspectives and analytical tools to elicit the processes which help to determine women's position in the solicitors' branch of the legal labour market. The application of theories which operate at the structural level, such as those of labour market segmentation and professional closure, is important in identifying the phenomenon of women's differential positioning, and the processes of historical change in occupations which have influenced this. With the assistance of some of the key concepts generated from these theories we can also analyse aspects of the behaviour of gendered groups; for example the prolonged struggle by the male legal hierarchy between 1880 and 1920 to establish and maintain the formal exclusion of women from the legal profession. Again, structural theories of gender segregation and differentiation can provide a framework for the analysis of the interdependence of the public and private realms and the fashioning of occupational roles to fit (and, it might be argued, to maintain) a gendered division of domestic labour.

However, we have also argued for the application of theories in the middle range, which can avoid the twin dangers of determinism and voluntarism in accounting for women's positioning. In particular, the intricate relationship between the social construction of 'women's qualities' and the 'capital' (human, cultural, symbolic, relational) required to qualify for occupational roles, requires a careful delineation. In addition, we need to account for the fact that the decision-making of actors in the real world is adaptive: conditioned by their 'knowledge' of the other parties. Employers decide whether or not to employ women on the basis of their 'knowledge' of the unreliability of women employees (reinforced by the ideological support of 'rational choice theory'). Women base decisions about career and life course on their knowledge of employers' views of women's prospects in general.

The research has been based on an appreciation of the complexity of the issue. Consequently, the study which follows explores the historical data which provides the evidence for the major transformations of women's position in relation to the legal profession, and uses contemporary data which embraces both sides of the labour market, the experiences of men as well as women, the private realm as well as the public. In spite of our best efforts, we risk being aligned with a strain of theory which regards the situation as a 'woman's problem', and all women as sharing the same problem. Our position is rather that, however problematic 'gender' is as a category (just as 'profession' is similarly problematic), it is an active property in the construction of opportunities in law work, and that both macrosocial and microsocial research tends to confirm this.

Notes

1 The terms private and public are ambiguous in that they can signify the freedom of individuals and the market from public (state) regulation, but are also commonly employed to signify the distinction between the private family and social relations outside of the family (Fredman, 1997, p.16). We are using the terms in this latter sense, but also argue that inequities in the legal workplace are able to persist because private practice resists the potential of state interventions to mitigate the effects of gender stereotypes.

2 Bourdieu identifies a commitment to this rhetoric, in particular the claim to the universal applicability of legal judgment as 'the entry ticket to the juridical field' (1987, p.820).

3 'Client development' skills have been identified as increasingly important since the recession in the early 1990's (Leigh-Kile, 1998, p.60).

4 This perspective is illustrated by the traditional exclusion of unpaid household labour from national accounts, and is challenged in a recent report from the Office of National Statistics which argues for the inclusion of accounts of household production because 'there can be no doubt that much value added takes place outside the formal economy' (Murgatroyd and Neuberger, 1997, p.69).

5 It must be emphasised, however, that whilst we acknowledge here that such a re-negotiation of working practices in this field would be difficult, it is not impossible; the ways in which the field could be re-shaped are the subject of our discussion of policy in the concluding chapter.

6 Similarly Young argues that the ideal of 'impartial normative reason' and its construction as the universal law of the public realm entails the expulsion of 'desire, affectivity and the body' and '... to the degree that women exemplify or are identified with such styles of moral decision making ...' excludes women from 'moral rationality' (1987, pp.62-63). Clearly the increasing focus on women lawyers' sexuality further undermines their claims to 'moral rationality'.

7 As Granfield has remarked, the 'reproduction of power is never complete nor uncontested' (1996, p.221).

3 'The Common Sense of Mankind': the Common Law and the Historical Exclusion of Women from the Legal Profession

> I believe that the common sense of mankind has taken a particular view of occupations that are fitted for women, and although you may have among women particular instances of great learning and great genius even, and in some respects the qualities that are appropriate to such a transaction as bringing an action, I do not think that the common sense of mankind will recognise the sort of thing that solicitors have to do as work which is appropriate to women.
> (The Earl of Halsbury, former Lord Chancellor, speaking in the debate in the Lords on the Solicitors (Qualification of Women) Bill, Lords Debates, HANSARD, XXIV, Col.269 (27 February, 1917))

This chapter combines an historical account of women's exclusion and subsequent admission to the profession with a brief consideration of the patriarchal foundation of the Common Law. There are three key themes to this combined discussion.

The first theme is the way in which women's formal exclusion from the profession in the United Kingdom, as in Australia (Thornton, 1996, pp.56-63), Canada (Hagan and Kay, 1995, p.6), and South Africa (Sachs and Wilson, 1978, p.36), exemplifies the judicial role, and its potential to articulate male prejudice as the Common Law (Rifkin, 1980); to 'make things true simply by saying them', by virtue of juridical social authority (Bourdieu, 1987). Whilst the legitimacy of the legal system rests on the principle that judges merely interpret the law, in fact they are continually involved in the process of making and remaking it (Fredman, 1997, p.2). What became known as the 'persons cases' illustrate this mix of judicial activism and proclaimed neutrality. Rationalised as based in the character of the Common Law's endorsement of custom and tradition, the judgments in these cases were delivered with a sense of their self-evident and obvious character by an apparently monolithic judicial establishment. As Sachs and Wilson remark, 'one of the characteristics of judicial pronouncement in England, particularly noticeable in these cases, was its lack of self-consciousness or strain' (1978, p.50).

In fact the contradiction between claimed neutrality and opinionated intervention is evident across a wide range of social issues (for instance see Griffith, 1977), but is particularly noteworthy in the use of the Common Law to establish the nature of women and hence to justify their subordination.[1] The second theme therefore concerns the common law tradition which, drawing in part on Roman law, held that it was 'immemorial custom' which 'revealed' that women were not persons as defined in, for instance, The Solicitors Act 1843, and which therefore excluded them from public office. The actual components of immemorial custom consist of views which reflect the Aristotelian depiction of women as the inferior, binary opposites of men. Finding concrete expressions in the ideology of the sexual contract,[2] such views are still to be found in legal discourse today (for instance, see Graycar and Morgan, 1990; Smith, 1993). Explored in greater detail in the following chapter, they include reference to women's essential domesticity, and resulting incapacity and need for protection. Consequently, as we noted in the previous chapter, the ending of formal collectivist criteria of exclusion did little to change such stereotyping of women, which instead formed the foundation for informal mechanisms of exclusion. Particularly noteworthy is the issue of the status of the married woman, the 'femme covert' (see Fredman, 1997, pp.40-58). Even in key cases such as Bebb v. Law Society (1913 and 1914),[3] and in legislative projects which contested formal exclusion, advocates did not, until after World War I, dispute the fact that married women and mothers could not hold public office.

A third theme is the way in which these 'obvious' impediments to female entry were deeply rooted in the solicitors' professional culture. The significance of the professional culture is especially clear given the limited role, until recently, of the academy in the training of lawyers. The centrality of modes of training which were concerned with socialisation rather than with credentials, and which revolved around an apprenticeship or articles with 'a strong fictive kin character' (Burrage, 1996, p.53), were a particular characteristic of the solicitors' branch of the profession.[4] The modality of this patron-client relationship, as described by Burrage (1996, p.54), could only be conceived of as male to male, and was of a nature that a woman could not possibly replicate; characterised by a ritualised hardship, a semi-servile form of male bonding, it was crucial to preparing the clerk to 'become' the master.

From the 1880's onwards, when women's admission to the legal professions became an issue for the courts and for Parliament, the elite of this male culture used all the informal avenues available to it to ensure that judgments and parliamentary decisions went its way, but although this legalistic response to women's usurpationary struggle was initially successful, it ultimately proved, as Witz argues (1992), to be the weakest element of the strategy of closure. However, the formidable barrier of professional culture proved able to compensate for the removal of the legal obstacle to women's entry. Shaped by the social script on which the arguments against female admission had been based, this culture generated less tangible processes of exclusion leading to the emergence of occupational segmentation and segregation.

The significance of the legal struggle over the exclusion of women therefore lies not so much in its effect, which was to delay the entry of a comparatively small number of women into the profession for a couple of decades, as in the norms and behaviour of legal culture which it revealed. In common with other instances of the 'malestream' culture (O'Brien, 1981) of civil society, legal ideology and ethos both perpetuated attitudes and facilitated acts which were deeply discriminatory, whilst masking this characteristic by endowing them with a 'natural', 'matter of fact' character (see Smith, 1993, p.20). In our discussion of the profession we will therefore argue that the character of the law, whilst drawing its strength from its claim to impartiality and universality (Bourdieu, 1987), in fact contains a patriarchal core (see also Kennedy, D., 1992). Correspondingly, assumptions about 'proper' and 'natural' gender roles have also been embedded within the processes of legal training (Graycar and Morgan, 1990; Frug, 1992; Thornton, 1996), and these will be discussed in the following chapter.

We would argue that such a historical view of the cultural practices of the profession is a necessary precursor to interpreting the experience of women in the law today.

Gender and the character of the Common Law

The 'natural' congruence between masculinity and the practice of law and the reciprocal harmony between femininity and domesticity has its basis in the law itself - in legal ideology, discourse, and practice (see Graycar and Morgan, 1990). As Olsen has argued in her discussion of the dualist structuration of classical liberal thought: 'Law is supposed to be rational, objective, abstract and principled, like men; it is not supposed to be irrational, subjective, contextualised or personalised, like women' (1990, p.201). However, not only is the law therefore 'sexed' as male, the law also plays a primary role in constructing both sex and gender;[5] that is in determining what 'natural' attributes can be held to constitute masculinity and femininity (see Smart, 1992; Naffine and Owens, 1997). Following on from this, the law both gave, and continues to give, expression and legitimacy to the social relations which result from this process, and is also a fundamental factor in shaping lawyers' attitudes (Bourdieu, 1987).

Consequently, one analytical approach to understanding the nature of the social order represented by law firms is through a focus on their working material. Law concerns the basic terms of social life: 'it is a plastic medium of discourse that subtly conditions how we experience social life … help(s) us to make sense of the world, … fabricate(s) what we interpret as its reality and construct(s) roles for us … and tell(s) us how to behave in the roles …' (Gordon, 1988, p.15). In other words, as a belief system which is concerned with the naturalisation of (gendered) hierarchies and categories, with the legitimation of power and the endorsement of proper codes of behaviour (Rifkin, 1980), it is as formative - if not more so - of the world view of the legal professional as of any other citizen (see Lahey for a discussion of the effect of this on women practitioners, 1991, p.4).

However, this contention appears to accept the claim by the law to comprise a unified body of rules, whereas in fact, as many commentators have pointed out, the law is in reality a complex of, frequently competing, norms (Hunt, 1993). Nevertheless, until the emergence of feminist jurisprudence, legal determinations of the distinct properties of the male and female legal subject were relatively uncontested. Furthermore, the professional orthodoxy is predicated on the univocal and coherent nature of the law, and, until recently, the profession was correspondingly, relatively homogeneous and conservative. Whilst the role of law as an arena of struggle and mediation between social groups is revealed in legal history through the competition between the traditional cultural order, generally represented by the Common Law, and modernising projects, generally represented by statute, an examination of the masculinist practices and ethos of both the legal workplace and of the judiciary, appears to indicate a continuing adherence by the professional mainstream to that traditional cultural order - certainly in respect of essentialist views of gender relations and roles.

A further caveat needs to be made to our opening assertion about the correspondence between the ideology and discourse of the law and the legal professional: when considering legal culture, is formal law of any more than marginal significance? It is now a commonplace that the private sphere has largely escaped its gaze (O'Donovan, 1981, 1985), and we will discuss in Chapter Five the ways in which the private sphere does not only comprise the family, but also other systems of personalist relations, including the 'old boy's club' and the law firm. As Fredman (1997) has observed, even today notions of freedom to contract remain paramount in the employment sphere, and there is an antipathy by both the liberal state and participants in the market, to intervention. At the same time, there is clearly an ideological interchange between such private and public spheres, resulting in part from the personalist ties which bind them. The results of this interchange subsequently find formal expression in case law, which, together with the ideology of liberal legalism, legitimates a hierarchical cultural order which may then be acted out, free from the constraints of the Rule of Law, in the private sphere.

The Common Law and the Judiciary: brotherhood in theory and action

Smart has observed that as a result of the intensification of legal oppression of women during the 18th and 19th centuries, the focus of the feminist campaigns in the 19th century was on equal rights through reform of the law: '(Law) ... formalised (women's) social and economic disabilities and, in many ways, extended and legitimised them' (1991, p.135). These campaigns, which ranged from the suffrage movement to individual attempts to gain admission to the professions, centred on the claim to be included in the universal language of the law, and to be acknowledged as juridical 'persons' and thereby to achieve entitlement to the same legal rights as men. Unsurprisingly, such attempts to win legal citizenship, waged mainly from the 1870's through till 1919, were consistently rebutted by the judges (see Gordon, 1984). Judicial reaction was justified by an evocation of the immemorial traditions of the common law, which the judges used, where necessary, to override the wide and nominally inclusive terms of statutes such as the Solicitors Act 1843, Lord Brougham's Act 1850 and the Interpretation Act 1889.

As Goodrich has argued, 'all vernacular law claims antique or immemorial status ...' (1993, p.281), and by discovering that women's disability was rooted in ancient custom, the judiciary could portray their decisions as entirely unrelated to political prejudice or male self-interest. The presentation of their judgments as purely declaratory meant that even where statutes used the apparently neutral and universal terminology of 'persons', the judiciary found that this did not indicate that they were exceeding their constitutional role. Rather, it was argued that a finding that women had been 'persons' would have been anti-constitutional, and this was the core of the Law Society defence in the case of Bebb: 'The admission of women is repugnant to the subject of the Act, as through all the centuries they have not acted as solicitors ... If such a departure is to be made from custom it must be made by statute' (Bebb v. Law Society (1913) 109 L.T. Rep.36).

The persons cases discussed below therefore exemplify the use of the Common Law to prevent social change and maintain an exclusively male public sphere through the mystification and sanctification of that Law. Such sanctification was, of course, integral to its legitimacy: 'And though this law be the peculiar invention of this Nation, and delivered over from age to age by Tradition, yet may we truly say, that no human law, written or unwritten, hath more certainty in the rules and maxims, more coherence in the parts thereof, or more harmony of reason in it; nay we may confidently aver, that it doth excell all other laws and is the most excellent form of government; it is so framed and fitted to the nature of this people, as we may properly say that it is connaturall to the Nation' (Davies, 1615, pp.2b-3a; cited in Goodrich and Hachamovitch, 1991).

Furthermore, this tactic is not just of historical interest; on the contrary, the above testimony to the moral and cultural basis for legal authority (represented in the tradition of Dicey) remains the professional orthodoxy on the common law. Despite attacks on its legitimacy and coherence from a variety of perspectives, for instance from the Critical Legal Studies movement (see, for example, Adelman and Foster, 1992; Horwitz, 1977; Fitzpatrick, 1991), the Common Law is still a 'master' discourse - represented as a coherent, univocal system which is intrinsically impartial because it is 'removed from the sphere of mundane and sectional interests, from the ebb and flow of historical change and contingency' (Harris, 1996, p.6), and whose claim to deliver justice firmly rests on its transcendence of power relations.[6] This claimed objectivity stems, in turn, from the fact that it presents as an organic expression of the particular character of the nation; hence, the preeminent source of its legitimacy is the claim, illustrated above by Sir John Davies' observations, to articulate the 'national Voksgeist' (Carty, 1991, p.182; and see Cotterell, 1989). Taken together these characteristics endow the common law and its interpreters with a unique authority, apparently uncontaminated by every-day prejudices. In Blackstone's words, judges are 'the depositories of the laws, the living oracles, who must decide in all cases of doubt' (Blackstone, 1809 1: 69; cited in Cotterell, 1989, p.25).

However the law must also evolve, and consequently the judge cannot be constructed as a purely passive spokesman of the law: 'An individual judge or court must subordinate individual reasoning and values to those enshrined in the law ... The judge is the privileged representative of the community, entrusted with its collective legal wisdom, which he is authorised to draw upon constructively in order to produce solutions to novel issues raised before the court' (Cotterell, 1989, p.26). The Common Law, is, after all, also known as 'judge made law'. This active role however imperils the vital claim of impartiality, since it indicates the policy-making aspect of judging. For of course, in reality, the law, in both substance and practice, is intimately related to matters of state - for example, as an expression and affirmation of existing social relations (Bourdieu, 1987, p.817), and, for its personnel, as a route to social and political power (both covert and overt). This was particularly true of the period under discussion, when it was common for the judiciary to be actively engaged in politics, frequently as MP's (see Heuston, 1964). Furthermore, and despite such overt political activism, an additional vehicle for judicial politics was the common law itself, which, as Sugarman has argued, following the Glorious Revolution became 'one of the important languages of English political thought ... the English state became increasingly dependent upon an autonomous legal profession and legal system in order to legitimate itself ... the legal community helped to constitute the state' (1996: 86).

Law, then, far from being devoid of social context, is, in a variety of ways, engaged in the legitimation of a political and social order, whilst judge made law is, inevitably, at times little more than a formalisation of contemporary popular prejudice as truth - an expression of fraternity. It may be argued, therefore, that in the judicial articulation of the common law relating to women in the 19th, and even for much of the 20th, century we see patriarchal personalist relations being dressed up and given legal sanctity. The unwelcome pretensions of women to inclusion in civil society, and, correspondingly, to independent legal status, required the legal ideologues to draw upon patriarchal custom to keep women firmly located in the private sphere, which, in accordance with the terms of the sexual contract (Pateman, 1988) removed them from the gaze of formal law.

However, one of the ways the state achieves legitimacy in liberal democratic society is through the provision of legal procedures and a discourse which does genuinely constrain arbitrary power; as Merry has argued 'as an ideology (law) contributes to the social construction of the world as fair and just, and at the same time provides a language and forums for resisting that order' (1992, p.360). Although judge made law may be, in relation to women, characterised as the public expression of private patriarchy, at the same time, the ideology of the law necessarily holds out the promise of equality: the Rule of Law is a belief system for both the rulers and the ruled. We shall observe the force of this as we track the way in which, in their challenge to their formal exclusion from the legal profession, women became tied to a usurpationary strategy of claiming formal equality before the law and thereby simultaneously maintaining its legitimacy (Elshtain, 1982), as well as, on occasions (as in the case of the distinctions drawn between married and single women), endorsing particular ideological constructions of women's 'state'.

The law and the public and private politics of formal exclusion

It is common to view women as being formally excluded from the profession until the passage of the Sex Disqualification (Removal) Act 1919. However, this formulation accepts both the authenticity of the ideological project which was involved in professionalisation, and the pronouncements of the judges who appealed to the common law tradition in formalising that exclusion in the persons cases at the end of the nineteenth century. Instead the formal legal bar of women from the solicitors' profession should be seen as the result of their usurpationary project (see Gordon, 1984, p.144).

Consequently it could be argued that formal exclusion only existed between the first of the persons cases which established the common law precedent on which the refusal of the Bar and the Law Society to admit women was based, and the subsequent admission of the first four women in December 1922[7] (Abel-Smith and Stevens, 1967, p.194). So whilst the synchronic framework of much sociology may see exclusion as a fact, it is more appropriate to see it as a process, grounded in specific historical circumstances, even though comparative analysis tends to demonstrate strong international parallels which indicate that the gendering of the professions is a *structured* process.

Women's formal exclusion depended on a number of related propositions: the status of the solicitor's occupation as a public office, which was closely linked to the success of solicitors in obtaining the State's support for statutory shelter in the 1843 Act; the declaration by judges that in employing common law principles, they should regard the lack of evidence of women's participation in advocacy as a legal incapacity which could only be overturned by statute; and the debate over whether women historically *had* held any public office.

The solicitor's profession emerged from an evolutionary process of demarcationary competition between various groups, whose boundaries were at times indistinct, over rights to practise in the range of courts in the UK legal system, and rights to practise different aspects of the legal process (Birks, 1960; Abel-Smith and Stevens, 1967; Abel, 1988, pp.139-42). The distinction between two branches of a largely unitary profession, as opposed to a market in which barristers, Doctors of Law, scriveners, attorneys and solicitors competed, gained and lost ascendancy, was not consolidated until the early nineteenth century (Baker, 1990, pp.177-97; Abel-Smith and Stevens, 1967, pp.19-24: Sugarman, 1996, pp.87-9). Until 1729, control over the 'profession' was exercised by the judiciary, with varying degrees of effectiveness (Sugarman, 1996, p.87), and the 'profession' could hardly be regarded as unitary, given the absence of any formal legal education (Sugarman, op.cit.; Abel-Smith and Stevens, 1967, p.26), and the diversity of sites in which the socialisation process took place. A common feature of all branches does appear to have been the absence of even any attempts by women to practise before the late 1870's: indeed the gendered character of the 'profession' seems to be so taken for granted, that it is not even commented on in many historical analyses.[8]

As we noted in the previous chapter, the solicitors' professionalisation project does not, therefore, seem to have explicitly involved competition between the genders for spheres of competence of the kind summarised by Witz in connection with the medical profession (1992, pp.104-16). Nevertheless there are strong parallels in the way that disparate branches of each profession were brought together as monopolies through legislation, which, although worded neutrally,[9] was subsequently used to justify male exclusivity. As Witz argues, 'gendered exclusionary mechanisms did not operate at the institutional level of the State but in the institutions of civil society' (1992, p.73): in the case of law, the Law Society, the Inns of Court, the Courts and the universities. The 'natural' and 'immemorial' constitution of the Law and legal practice as a sphere free from female influence or authority was a cornerstone of exclusion at this level. It enabled the judiciary to resist attempts by women to gain admission by tracing a genealogy from the Mirrour of Justices where along with 'serfs ... those under the age of twenty-one, open lepers, idiot attorneys, lunatics, deaf mutes, those excommunicated by a bishop, criminal persons', women were ineligible for appointment to the bench (cited in H. Kennedy, 1992, pp.56-7), to the judgment of Lord Fry in[10] De Souza v. Cobden where he compared the election of a woman to the election of a 'dead man or an inanimate thing' ((1891) 1 Q.B. 687).

In taking this position, the judiciary relied heavily on a statement by Coke which maintained that women could not be attorneys (Birks, 1960, p.277), and rejected historical evidence put forward for the plaintiffs in these various cases[11] that women had been able to exercise authority in feudal England. Recent scholarship has looked again at this question, and in the light of its findings the claim for a 'timeless tradition' of excluding women from public office may be deconstructed. Firstly, evidence does exist of women exercising authority: for example, in feudal England women had the right to receive vassal homage, to hold ordinary fiefs and to enjoy jurisdiction over their serfs and tenants in manorial courts (Murray 1995, p.81), as well as to sit as jurors, though there is little evidence that they sat or acted in the King's Courts (Murray, op.cit., p.82), and as the processes of justice became more bureaucratised, women appear to have lost this role. Women also seem to have enjoyed parliamentary rights under feudal and Tudor monarchy (Murray, op.cit., p.90). Contemporary supporters of women's struggle to gain admission also challenged the claim that women had never participated in the public sphere, and even the Law Times, in an uncharacteristically sympathetic Comment on women solicitors,[12] noted that both individuals had held high office and that women in general had 'been sextons, overseers and governors of workhouses' (10 March 1917, p.331). Secondly, the distinction between 'public' and 'private' spheres was not meaningful in pre-capitalist societies. The creation of the separate, private sphere was an aspect of the process whereby women lost the authority they had once enjoyed. It also formed a part of the reconstruction of the patriarchal order in the seventeenth century (Murray, 1995, p.90), one expression of which was the contemporary recreation of the common law by Coke, on whom subsequent opponents of women's admission to public life were to rely.

The first recorded refusal by the Law Society of a woman's request to take the professional examinations was in 1879 (Abel, 1988, p.173), and in the 1880's women began to be employed as clerks in solicitors' offices (Abel-Smith and Stevens, 1967, p.193). A formal legal challenge to the male monopoly in medicine had occurred in 1873, in the case of Jex-Blake[13] v. The Senatus Academicus of the University of Edinburgh (1873)

11 M 784 (Witz, 1992, p.91; Gordon, 1984; Bridgeman and Millns, 1998, pp.12-7), and the judgment in this case established a template on which subsequent cases were to be modelled. The rejection of women's claims to enter university was based, in Lord Neaves' view, on the 'fact' that members of public corporations such as universities were historically male, without exception, and therefore there could be no right to entry established in common law (Sachs and Wilson, 1978, pp.20-2). In support of the refusal to deviate from the long standing custom that only males could be admitted, Roman law was cited: 'for custom is the best interpreter of laws' (D. 1,3,37; in Gordon, 1984, p.144). However, as Gordon has observed, this text was not in fact as favourable to this line of reasoning as it might seem, but rather illustrates the point that it was through such cases that formal exclusion was established, since in full it says: 'if a question of interpretation of a law arises, the first point to investigate is what rule the community applied in cases like that in the past' (D. 1,3,37; cited in Gordon, id.). As Gordon goes on to point out: 'as this was the first recorded case in which women had applied for entry to a Scottish University it could well be said that there was no custom' (id.; and see the Sankey judgment, post).[14]

Subsequent to the Jex-Blake judgment, university education in England was partially opened up,[15] and from the 1880's onwards a number of women were able to obtain law degrees (Abel-Smith and Stevens, 1967, p.193). As a result, unsuccessful attempts to obtain admission to the Bar were made in 1903 by Bertha Cave and Ivy Williams, and, shortly after, Christabel Pankhurst, who applied to the Benchers of Lincoln's Inn and subsequently obtained a First in her LL.B (Pankhurst, 1931, p.179; Sachs and Wilson, 1978, p.172).[16] Following the rejection of their applications (for which no reason was given), Christabel Pankhurst was instrumental in setting up the Committee to secure the Admission of Women to the Legal Profession (Faulkner, 1997, p.3).

In 1912 John Waller Hills, a solicitor, and Lord Wolmer, with the support of Lord Robert Cecil, introduced a Bill to enable women to be admitted as barristers and solicitors. The proposal was strongly opposed by both the Bar and the Law Society, and the Bill made little progress (Birks, 1960, p.276). Following this, on 25 January 1913 The Times reported that the application by Gwyneth Bebb, Karen Costello, Maud Ingram (later becoming Crofts), and Lucy Nettlefold, all of whom had had brilliant academic careers at either Oxford or Cambridge (id.), to the Law Society to take the preliminary examination was refused on the ground of their sex. In the subsequent test case of Bebb v. The Law Society (1913) L.T., 109, 36, Lord Buckmaster for the plaintiffs contended that the definition of 'persons' in the Solicitors Act of 1843 included women, citing the support of the interpretation clause (Section 48) which stated that 'every word importing the masculine gender only shall extend and be applied to a female as well as a male ... unless in any of the cases aforesaid it be otherwise specially provided, or there be something in the subject or context repugnant to the construction' (pp.36-7). In the initial hearing Buckmaster argued that there was no incapacity which would prevent women from meeting the requirements to be admitted, other than the precedent that women were disqualified from exercising a public function (Chorlton v. Lings (1868) L.R. 4 C.P. 374; Beresford Hope v. Lady Sandhurst (1889) 23 Q.B.D. 79). As discussed above, he then sought to challenge the claimed tradition of female exclusion from the public sphere on which these precedents were founded, citing instances of women acting as attorneys from Select Civil Pleas, Bracton's Note Book. Significantly, he also attempted to turn Coke's reference to the Mirrour of Justices on its head by arguing that the 'femmes' who supposedly could not be attorneys were, clearly, 'femmes covert', and that therefore *single* women could practise. Here, as on other occasions in women's struggles in the late nineteenth century, the distinction between single and married women was conceded.[17] Judge Joyce, presiding at the initial hearing, had no difficulty in dismissing this 'novel and somewhat startling application', along with the 'reference made to Bracton, the Mirrour of Justices, and other authorities or supposed authorities of some remote antiquity' (p.38), and his judgment was confirmed by the Master of the Rolls with two other judges on appeal. Despite Joyce's disparagement of Buckmaster's use of antique authorities, the grounds given by all three were the fact that 'inveterate usage' showed that women had never, amongst any of the public offices cited by the plaintiff, been shown to have held office as attorney, and that therefore for the Appeal Court to agree to the plaintiff's case would be to engage in legislation, and, in the words of Cozens-Hardy, M.R.: 'I disclaim any right to legislate in a matter of this kind' (Bebb v. The Law Society (1914), 1 Ch.286, p.294).

In fact, underlying the reasoning which claimed to be grounded in a strict adherence to common law principles was a world view grounded in the ideology of separate spheres, in which the private, women's sphere was clearly seen as subordinate. Mossman has pointed out the way in which Mr Justice Barker, in Re. French,[18] a Canadian case which paralleled that of Bebb, felt able to couple the claim to judicial neutrality with a forceful expression of views about women's role: 'the expressed idea of detachment and neutrality both masks and legitimates judicial views about women's "proper sphere"' (1991, p.291), and such personal views are characteristic of the debate over women's admission to the professions which continued throughout the first two decades of the twentieth century.

Nevertheless, it is clear that the common law tradition did indeed provide support for such views. Goodrich argues that this 'common law view' of women's estate rested in fact an older body of thinking about divine and natural law; for instance the compilation of Roman law, the Corpus Iuris: 'The Digest provides an extensive ... medley of prohibitions, incapacities, and denigrations of women as persons alieni iuris, subject to another's control ... "women are debarred from all civil and public functions and therefore cannot be judges or hold a magistracy or bring a lawsuit or intervene on behalf of anyone else or act as procurators". By D. 16.1.1 it is reiterated that women, like children, cannot perform any civil functions, they cannot undertake obligations ...' (1993, pp.277-8). Goodrich also describes the way in which this source was built upon by reference to the law of Nature which 'subjects the female sex ... to the male in both social and domestic circumstance ... (detailing) female characteristics of simplicity, subservience, physical inferiority, lesser virtue, deformity, irrationality, slenderness of understanding, lack of heat, deficiency of construction, heedlessness, timidity, fear of death, and the proclivity to domesticity' (id., discussing Fortescue, 1466).

These views of women find clearest expression in the common law on couverture, which reduced married women to little more than slaves (see Mill, 1869, p.58). However, for Blackstone the resulting disabilities which the Common Law placed on women were 'for the most part intended for her protection and benefit, so great a favourite is the female sex of the laws of England' (Commentaries on the Laws of England, 1765, i, 433, cited in Mills, 1997, p.2). Consequently, women, as a result either of their natural inferiority or, at times, their moral superiority, had no independent legal identity,[19] and, married women were effectively their husband's property. Hence the 17th century dictum by Sir Matthew Hale that a husband could not be guilty of raping his wife, for, according to Blackstone: 'By marriage, the very being or legal existence of women is suspended, or at least it is incorporated and consolidated into that of the husband, under whose protection and cover she performs everything, and she is therefore called in our law a femme-covert' (cited in Holdsworth, 1988, p.18).

This position had then been elaborated upon in the 19th century in various ways; for example one refinement, congruent with the idealisation of Victorian womanhood, held that women were too delicate[20] - the frail vessels theme of Victorian literature (Mews, 1969; Smart, 1992). This meant that it could be adjudged that they were either incapable of engaging in the combative legal world, or that their virtue and innocence required protection from it.[21] An expanded version of this approach portrayed women in their idealised state as the guardians of man's humanity and happiness. As a result, prefiguring the human capitalist advocacy of a gendered division of labour (Becker, 1985; 1991), the 'natural' separation of spheres, and therefore gender inequality, was portrayed as essential for the entire social order. This was the rationale put forward by the Law Society Council for its opposition in 1870 to the Married Women's Property Bill, which it argued would constitute a 'serious ... disturbance of the existing social relations and the legal system' (cited in Sugarman, 1996, p.116). Forty-four years on their opposition to one of the private member's bill to remove women's disqualification from the legal profession was couched in similar terms: 'we do not believe any benefit will accrue to the ladies themselves, the Profession or to the public' (Law Times, 4 April 1914, p.578).

As Roberts has written: 'It was the sweet, passive, obedient wife, busy within her domestic setting, showing her concern and appreciation for her masculine protector, apprehensive for his comfort and safety, ever watchful of his situation, that brought emotion to the manly breast of Millais and his Victorian contemporaries ...' (1973, p.50). Clearly this view, endorsed by a line of male thinkers from Aristotle through to Rousseau, envisaged a role for women of safeguarding society's virtue; consequently man's happiness would be destroyed if women were contaminated by exposure to the public world (Young, 1987, p.66). As a result, the existence of separate spheres was portrayed not as anti-women, but, on the contrary, as a 'privilege of the sex ... admitting that fickleness of judgment and liability to influence have sometimes been suggested as the ground of exclusion, I must protest against it being supposed to arise in this country from any under-rating of the sex either in point of intellect or worth. That would be quite inconsistent with one of the glories of our civilisation - the respect and honour in which women are held ...' (Sir James Easte Willes in the 'Manchester Voters' case, cited in Sachs and Wilson, 1978, p.34).

A judgment delivered by the Supreme Court of Wisconsin, in 1875, encapsulates the contemporary legal justification of the subordinate position of women and their essential unsuitability of the legal profession:[22]

> The law of nature destines and qualifies the female sex for the bearing and nurture of the children of our race and for the custody of the homes of the world and their maintenance in love and honour. There are many employments in life not unfit for female character. The profession of the law is surely not one of these. The peculiar qualities of womanhood, its gentle graces, its quick sensibility, its subordination of hard reason to sympathetic feeling, are surely not qualifications for forensic strife. Nature has tempered woman as little for the judicial conflicts of the court room, as for the physical conflicts of the battle field. And it is not the saints of the world who chiefly give employment to our profession. It has essentially and habitually to do with all that is selfish and malicious, knavish and criminal, coarse and brutal, repulsive and obscene, in human life. It would be revolting to all female sense of the innocence and sanctity of their sex, shocking to man's reference for womanhood and faith in woman, on which hinge all the better affections and humanities of life, that woman should be permitted to mix professionally in all the nastiness of the world which finds its way into courts of justice (Re. Goodell (1875) 39 Wisc. 232).

Another, less courteous, perspective, which has also survived with remarkable tenacity, was that women were intrinsically incapable of participating in the neutral reasoning processes held to characterise the law; that, because of their domesticity, emotionality and irrationality they could not aspire to being 'technocratic' professionals (Thornton, 1996). In Thompson's words, women were 'debarred from access to ... (the) logic of the law' (1977, pp.262-3); or, as Lord Halsbury remarked in a House of Lords debate on the 1917 Solicitors (Qualification of Women) Bill: '... calm judgment and absence of partisanship are qualities which a solicitor ought to possess ... and those are qualities which are not commonly found in a woman' (Hansard, Lords Debates, 24, 1917, p.270). This approach is particularly evident in the reaction of solicitors to the possibility of female competition. In place of the judicial emphasis on womanly virtues such as modesty and delicacy, we tend to find questions being raised as to women's soundness of judgment, and even as to their honesty and integrity (Birks, 1960, p.276). According to a letter from 'A Country solicitor' to the Law Times in April 1914: 'There is only one bright spot in the proposal to admit women as solicitors, and that is, that the public well know that there was yet a woman who could keep her mouth shut on other people's affairs' (4 April 1914, p.580). Correspondingly the judges in the persons cases '... attributed to men a superior spirituality ... as reflected in loftiness of mind, a capacity for reverence, and the ability to indulge in abstract thought' (Sachs and Wilson, 1978, p.10), and Harrington's discussion of legal education at Harvard Law School reveals similar attitudes which were in part expressed comparatively, in the form of a deep misogyny (1994; see also Thornton, 1996). This equation of rationality and objectivity with masculinity and, concomitantly, of irrationality with femininity, and disregard of the evident fact that the 'neutral' perspective is in actuality white middle class male subjectivity, has for some time formed the basis of the feminist critique of orthodox jurisprudence (for instance see Scales, 1993; Smart, 1992).

What the persons cases also demonstrate however is the plasticity and inherently political nature of the Common Law and, correspondingly, the historically contingent nature of Judges' findings. After the massive social upheaval of the First World War women aged thirty years and over were enfranchised in 1918, and in the following year the Sex Disqualification (Removal) Act, which we discuss below, formally removed all disabilities preventing women from holding public office. However, neither statute contained an express, statutory declaration that women were now legally persons, and consequently this remained a matter for the judiciary, not all of whom were prepared to concede the issue. In 1922, Viscountess Rhondda, a former suffragette, sought to rely on the statutory removal of legal disabilities to claim a seat in the House of Lords.[23] Her application was considered by a special Committee of the House of Lords, composed of seven men, three of whom were judges. Despite the support of both the Attorney General and the majority of the Committee, which would normally have been conclusive, the decision was resisted by the Lord Chancellor, Lord Birkenhead, an active anti-suffragist. His opposition resulted in the referral of the matter to a larger committee, which decided against her. The argument again deployed all the tactics familiar from the persons cases. 'Inveterate tradition', which made it possible for the sense of the 1919 Act to be ignored was cited. According to Heuston, 'In a judgment covering thirty-two pages ... Birkenhead held that a peerage held by a peeress in her own right is one to which in law the incident of exercising the right to receive a writ is not and never was attached' (1964, p.402). Secondly, the device of parliamentary sovereignty was utilised. Parliament was not deemed to have expressly conferred on women the right to sit in the House of Lords: 'The Legislature ... cannot be taken to have ... employed such loose and ambiguous words to carry out so momentous a revolution in the constitution of the House' (Lord Birkenhead, p.375). It therefore had to be assumed that there was *no* intention to bestow such a right, and the judiciary could not exceed its constitutional role by legislating in this matter.

Following this, the first persons case to come before the English courts after the 1919 Act, and the last to be heard, was an appeal to the Privy Council, Edwards v. Attorney General of Canada, (1930) AC, 124. It represents an interesting coda to the struggle for formal equality. The decision, delivered by the presiding Judge, Lord Sankey, was in favour of the women applicants and, taken together with the previous judgments, represents a perfect illustration of the contingent and arbitrary nature of common law judging. Once again, the venerable precedents of the Common Law were referred to, but on this occasion distinguished. Thus the courts now found that the Common Law did *not* preclude them from giving expression to a re-ordered relationship between the genders, firstly because the term persons was ambiguous and secondly because women's previous absence from public life was not important since custom would have prevented any previous contestation of their exclusion.

As Mossman points out, although Sankey's judgment finally represented a victory both for women and common sense, because he obscured the reasoning behind his choice of precedent, he 'preserved the power and mystery of legal method even as he endowed women with the right to be summoned' to the Canadian Senate (1991, p.297). Since then, a host of subsequent judicial pronouncements has preserved the fundamentally patriarchal character of the Common Law. Despite the claim to neutrality and universality, the cultural, communal identity which the law articulated remained overtly male.[24] Furthermore, solicitors were able to exercise a conservative influence over legislative projects, both as advisers, but also, as Sugarman has argued, through influencing the 'available normative language and therefore the presuppositions of legislative and decision-making process. By helping to define the perimeters of what was proper and legitimate for authorities to undertake ... it played an important but neglected role in setting limits to political innovation' (op.cit., p.121). This power of the legal establishment was clearly revealed in the 'legislative' stage of women's usurpationary project.

The pursuit of formal equality through legislation

The Bebb judgment left legislation as the only avenue for the ending of formal closure. The Solicitors (Qualification of Women) Bill, a private member's bill introduced in 1914, again by John Waller Hills, had the support of feminists and suffragettes like Millicent Fawcett. It was scheduled for a Second Reading which it never, however, received. The Law Society had once more made their opposition clear, as they did to a further Bill introduced in the Lords by Lord Buckmaster in 1917, which again failed to receive government support or time, and which was opposed on grounds suggested by the Law Society in a postal campaign; namely, that with so many solicitors away at the front it was the wrong time to make the decision (see Law Times, Vol.142, p.234, 3 February 1917). The Lord Chancellor, Lord Finlay, made the point on their behalf: 'it is not so much a case of the danger of their places being filled up by women, as a question of this kind, which certainly is an important one for the whole profession, being decided in their absence and at a time when they have not had the opportunity of making their wishes on the subject known' (Hansard (Lords) XXIV, 267). However, in a later passage, after distinguishing the case of law from that of medicine, the same speaker enunciated the underlying ideology of the profession's opposition to the legislation in far more telling terms, which are worth citing in full:

> The question is, what is the proper sphere of women? I may be old-fashioned in these matters, but I do not believe that the active practice of a profession is compatible with the proper work of a woman which, after all, is that of a wife and a mother attending to her family. I recognise, of course, that there are a great many women who, as matters stand in this country, have not the opportunity of marrying. I wish things could be redressed in that matter. Possibly in the course of time means may be evolved of enabling them to find a sphere in other parts of the British Empire where they may become the mothers of mighty nations. But to introduce them as competitors with men in the professions is surely to aggravate the situation in this country. Wherever a woman is in a profession she presumably displaces a man who, if he succeeded in making a livelihood would take a wife. The sexes were not meant to be competitors in the professions; they were meant to be helps to one another. That is my view of the ideal of woman's work. The man should be the breadwinner. (Hansard (Lords) XXIV, 267-8)

This elegant exposition of the 'separate spheres' perspective which underlies human capital theories of women's estate, illustrates Carol Pateman's description of the way in which public and private spheres are implicated in each other in the sexual contract. The Lord Chancellor protested that the question was 'not one of trade unionism', and in a sense was justified in so claiming. Again, the threat was envisaged as being to the whole order of society, not just to the narrow interests of one occupation, and the sense of a visceral opposition to change is evident in the general professional response to change as well. The leader columns of the Law Times consistently railed against both the plaintiffs in the Bebb case, and the successive sponsors of legislation to allow women's entry:

> So far as this country is concerned we can only repeat what we have stated before and to which we adhere - namely, that the admission of women either as barristers or solicitors would not be for the good of the community, and would introduce into the active practice of the law difficulties which cannot be over-estimated.
>
> (Leader on the initial Bebb judgment; Vol.135, p.232, 5 July 1913)

> It is satisfactory to note that the council of the Law Society intend to oppose on the second reading the Bill dealing with this subject. Any other attitude would be impossible, for we have not the slightest doubt that the vast majority of the Profession are opposed to any further extension of their membership, certainly

> in this direction. As we stated last week, we may in the future have lady barristers and lady solicitors, but the advantage of such a change to any of the parties concerned, the ladies themselves, the Profession, or the public, is difficult to see.
> (Commenting on the Solicitors (Qualification of Women) Bill of 1914; Vol. 136, p.578, 4 April 1914)

Of interest in these leaders (only a sample of a consistent stream) is the absence of any coherent argument against women's admission; as Grata Flos. Greig, the first woman lawyer to practise in the Commonwealth (admitted in Australia in 1905) wrote: '... to many, the main question is, are women capable of performing legal work? Well, why not? Personally I have never heard one rational reason against it, though I have listened to heaps of twaddle' (Greig, 1909, p.149). It does not appear too harsh to describe many of the speeches against the reforming legislation as intellectually threadbare; take for instance Lord Halsbury's comment in the debate on the 1917 Bill that 'the things which solicitors have to do are inappropriate to women. I do not propose to go through any sort of description of what those things are' (Hansard, XXIV, Col.269, 27 February 1917). Perhaps this weak defence of the status quo is partly explicable by the fact that most of the participants in these debates believed that the unofficial exercise of power, and mobilising of male networks, rather than logic, would in fact determine the outcome. It is the bonds and relationships between key members of the judiciary, the legal and political establishment, and the anti-suffrage movement that we will examine next.

Judges, networks and anti-suffragism: political barriers to women's admission

We have discussed above how the common law was used as a vehicle by the profession not only to replicate and reinforce its misogynist views, but also to endow these with a natural and therefore doubly legitimate identity. As Sachs and Wilson have observed: 'It is understandable that Sylvia Pankhurst, as all other feminists, should have considered the decisions in the male monopoly cases to be bad law upheld by prejudice, just as their opponents considered it to be a good law maintained by neutrality' (1978, p.49).

The history of women's efforts to gain legal identity and citizenship status therefore reveals the interconnections between the common law as a crystallisation of existing power relations, and the legal profession as both enforcers of those relations and a social nexus. The Common Law, as has been argued above, is essentially judge made law. So, what was the character of this judiciary and the wider legal profession? For Thornton 'the concept of fraternity is central to the constitution of masculine identity that underpins the jurisprudential community' (1996, p.166), and examination of the links between anti-suffragism and some of the key members of that community renders this point particularly explicit. For the claim to disembodied neutrality and objectivity, linked in turn to the idea of the judiciary as mere legal archaeologists, is rebutted not just by the prejudiced nature of contemporary legal pronouncements, but also by the political activism of prominent legal figures at the time.

Law was perceived as a key arena by women in their struggle both for the vote and for wider equality,[25] and, by the beginning of the 20th century, several leading members of the suffrage movement held law degrees (Faulkner, 1997, p.3). Correspondingly, prominent lawyers were to be found amongst the principal anti-suffragists (many of whom were Conservative MP's). They included members of the judiciary who had presided over women's applications; for instance Lord Loreburn (who, as Lord Chancellor, heard Nairn v. St. Andrews University (1909) A.C. 147, concerning an application by five women graduates of Edinburgh University to vote), Lord Birkenhead (Lord Chancellor in 1922 and, as we noted above, prime mover in the continuing opposition to women peers), and Judge Fitzjames Stephen who has been described as having a 'pronounced zest for enforcing … (established authority)' (Harrison, 1978, p.33). Lord Finlay (Lord Chancellor in 1918), Henry James, the jurist H.S. Maine (who was fiercely opposed to all state intervention),[26] Sir Edward Clarke - prominent lawyer and Conservative MP, and influential academics such as Dicey, Bryce, and Warden Anson[27] were all also enthusiastic members of this powerful network. Harrison has written: 'As with the medical profession, so with the law - professional self-interest, politics, the classics and male clubbery bubbled up into a rich anti-suffragist brew', and, describing a dinner held in honour of Asquith:

'Proposing the toast of the guest, Sir Edward Clarke as senior bencher of Lincoln's Inn said, "I speak to both of you; to the Oxford of public honour and the Asquith of private friendship", thus concisely bringing together the three sections of the anti-suffragist world, and knitting together established institutions as such occasions customarily do' (1978, p.103).

Harrison's history of the anti-suffrage movement exposes the close relationships between these political and legal worlds and ideologies, which were continually cemented through a maze of gentlemen's clubs (see also Heuston, 1964),[28] which in turn built upon the networks developed at public school (Harrison, 1978, pp.97-100): 'Without the men of the smoking room, the three sections into which the diagram naturally falls - Oxford academic, legal-political and imperialist-political - would almost fall apart' (op.cit., p.97); and, 'The Oxford college was itself a small club ... (and) the transition from Oxford to the law was eased not only by the bridging personalities of Dicey, Bryce and Anson, but also by the fact that the two worlds were very similar' (op.cit., p.102). It is evident therefore that just as underlying the proclaimed rationality, objectivity and indeed legalism of the Common Law may be found the prejudices of existing power elites, so too beneath the surface of regulation and the neutral meritocratic order of the profession, there existed a complex web of personalist relations (see also Birks, 1960, p.275; and Sugarman, 1996). Through such ties men conspired to debar women in order that patronage might continue to be enjoyed by the fraternity alone: 'the clubbable established figures (of the legal profession) ... held in their hands a clutch of opportunities and eased the paths of the young men they patronised' (Harrison, 1978, p.103).

The persistence of these networks into the 1990's is evidenced by both our research sample, and by successful women lawyers like Barbara Mills (1997, p.8) and Helena Kennedy (1992) who identify them as inimical to the progression of women. They also demonstrate the importance of the historical legacy of the period when the profession was exclusively male, and built its relationships with the powerful institutions of civil society.

The removal of the formal bar; women become 'persons'

The Committee for the Admission of Women to the Solicitors' Profession, formed following the failure of the Bebb case, included prominent figures such as Humphrey Ward, Elizabeth Garret Anderson and Millicent Garret Fawcett. Effective lobbying by this group[29] with the backing of John Waller Hills, MP, eventually resulted in open Government support for legislation which would remove the sex disqualification imposed by the persons cases. Nevertheless, Hill's subsequent private member's bill failed at the second reading and the matter was postponed on the outbreak of war. As discussed above, the war and the resulting absence of so many solicitors was also put forward as the principal reason for opposition to Lord Buckmaster's attempt in 1917 to end the sex bar (Hansard, Lords Debates XXIV, 1917, p.267).

However, whilst the war delayed progress towards female emancipation, and provided its opponents with a further argument against it, it also furnished women with an opportunity to refute the stereotype of female incapacity. In 1909, Grata Flos. Greig had written that 'most men, when it comes to an argument as to what women could or could not do, generally argue "You have not ergo, you cannot"' (1909, p.150). In illustration of the reserve army of labour theory (Braverman, 1974; Breugel, 1979), the haemorrhage of male workers to the war front levered open all sorts of hitherto exclusively male sectors of the labour market to women. By 1916, the labour shortage was such that the government became engaged in a series of negotiations with Trade Unions and professional associations in order to facilitate women's employment (Holdsworth, 1988, pp.66-7); conferences were held to encourage the registration of women war workers (Pankhurst, 1932), and in March a Government Committee was set up to consider the best ways of substituting female for male workers (Faulkner, 1997, p.4). By January 1918, the numbers of female employees had risen from 3.23 million in 1914 to 4.8 million, with the result that many women were engaged in traditionally 'male' occupations (Rosen, 19744, pp.248-51). The specific impact of this massive social change on the legal profession is described by Milford: 'A figure given in 1917 of 4,000 solicitors and articled clerks away at the War demonstrates the scale of the problem faced by firms struggling to cope during those years. Many a man with a son at the Front, or who might never return, was grateful to have a clever daughter to bring into the Firm for the duration ... and by 1918 she was too valuable to lose' (cited in Skordaki, 1996, p.10).

That this irrefutable demonstration of female capacity across a range of occupations was a major factor in women's admittance to the public sphere (Pankhurst, 1932, p.607), is illustrated by the arguments in support of Buckmaster's Solicitors (Qualification of Women) Bill (1917). Buckmaster based his entire case for presenting the Bill during wartime on the role that women were now playing in society: 'I am not sure that it is generally recognised how much we owe women in this great struggle ... There are women, as we all know, engaged in almost every occupation that was hitherto considered to be the exclusive area of man's work ... I myself know a woman whose brother is fighting in France ... whose place she has taken, and she has discharged the work to the complete satisfaction of the firm with whom she is working ... and there are other women ... who are engaged actively in the legal profession at the present time ... There are women employed today in every kind of capacity in solicitors' offices ...' (Hansard, Lords Debates XXIV, 1917, pp.259-261). In this view he was supported by the Earl of Selbourne because: 'Women have shown in this war that they can do things that very few men believed they could do ... They have shown their adaptability; they have shown that when they are given the chance there are very few professions in which men shine in which women cannot shine too' (id., p.273).

Although Buckmaster's measure was defeated, it was clear that the intellectual argument had been won and that removal of the legal bar was now only a matter of time (Birks, 1960, p.277). In 1918, following victory in the Khaki Election won partly on the basis of promises of social reform, Lloyd George gave the vote to women over thirty, and made explicit government backing for the opening up of the civil professions. In 1919 Buckmaster introduced another Bill which this time covered the barristers' branch of the profession as well as the solicitors'. The solicitors' profession was resigned: 'A great change in the economic position of women has been wrought during the war, and their claim to equality of opportunity in professions for which they are neither physically nor intellectually disqualified can no longer be resisted with any reasonable chance of success' (The Law Journal, 1919; cited in Birks, 1960, p.277). Reflecting this, a special general meeting of the Law Society in March 1919 resolved by 50 votes to 33 that it was 'expedient that existing obstacles to (women's) entry into the legal profession should be removed' (Law Society, 1919, p.37).

In 1919 Buckmaster's Bill passed the House of Lords, but the government then decided to sponsor its own Bill, which would be of wider application, and in the same year the Sex Disqualification (Removal) Act was passed. By S.2 women were 'entitled to be admitted and enrolled as a solicitor after serving under articles for three years only if either she has taken such a university degree as would have so entitled her had she been a man, or if she has been admitted to and passed the final examination and kept, under the conditions required of women by the university, the period of residence necessary for a man to obtain a degree at any university which did not at the time the examination was passed admit women to degrees'. In 1930, as we discussed above, it was also conceded at Common Law[30] that there was no longer anything (to paraphrase the debate in Bebb) in the subject repugnant to the construction of women as legal persons.

On 18 December 1922 Carrie Morrison became the first woman to be admitted to the Law Society. Her excellent credentials were characteristic, of necessity, of many of the early women entrants; for instance, in addition to taking first class honours in French and German, she spoke Spanish and Catalan. However, despite the many interesting aspects of this particular entrant, the reaction of the legal establishment was to largely ignore her admission, and the legal press, previously so engaged with the question of women solicitors, did not mention it at all (Law Society Gazette, 22 February 1995). By contrast, there was quite extensive coverage of the early admissions by the national press, which, prefiguring subsequent reactions to female public figures, also engaged a trivial discussion as to the appropriate costume for women lawyers[31] (Skordaki, 1996, p.11). By the end of 1923 eight women had been admitted; however, the numbers of women solicitors remained tiny, and in 1923, these isolated early entrants set up the 1919 Club,[32] the purposes of which, according to one early member, was to offer each other 'mutual help and comfort' (Faulkner, 1997, p.5).

Conclusion

In one of the many debates over the question of women solicitors, one of the most ardent supporters of the cause argued: 'The whole history of the women's movement has been to show that there is no gate that guards the avenues of employment that has ever been freely opened from within; they have always been ruptured from without. And the reason is not far to seek ... each one of us is at heart a trade unionist ... anxious to secure that small part of the world's field of work which it is his lot to cultivate from the keen and bitter winds of untempered competition' (Buckmaster, Hansard, Lords Debates XXIV, 1917, p.266). Indeed, despite the pious and formal language in which the establishment case was presented, it is evident that naked self-interest was a primary motivation in the tenacious resistance put up by the legal profession to the admission of women: thus one correspondent to the Solicitor's Journal complained: 'a crowd of women are to be let loose further to cut up the profession' (cited in Birks, 1960, p.276).

Nevertheless, the intellectual case against women's entry was primarily expressed in the form of detached legal argument. When the courts finally found that women were legal persons after all, it was simply rationalising a social change which had already occurred and which the legitimacy of the law required it to register. What the persons cases expose therefore is the ambiguity of the universalist claim by the common law, which may act, in fact as a form of discursive and ideological exclusion, and a camouflage for the political and economic exclusion, which parallels the professional exclusion. Sustained through the personalist ties which had also been a prominent feature of the struggle against women's entry, these more intangible forms of gatekeeping were carried on long after formal inclusion had been conceded and were bolstered by the persistent identification of legal authority with maleness and the law's continuing reliance on the 'reasonable man' as the centre-piece of its logic, accompanied by the regular regurgitation and legitimation of misogynist stereotypes of women. However, the general acceptance by pioneering women lawyers of the ideology and culture of the law and of the profession[33] meant they were entrapped in these 'mystifications which supported the status quo' (Rifkin, 1980, p.85). Indeed, such 'miscognition' may be viewed as a necessary pre-condition of engaging in law work (see Bourdieu, 1987). Whilst, therefore, in practice female participation in the profession continued to be shaped by the ideology of the separate spheres, and circumscribed by continuing presumptions as to the maleness of law and legal practice, women's subscription to the legal ideology of neutrality and universality precluded them from mounting an effective, separatist challenge (Skordaki, 1996, p.14).

Notes

1 The 'production' of the legal subject by the law, and the obfuscation, through a discourse of nature and tradition, of the fact that male and female legal subjectivities are in fact legal artefacts, has recently been explored in a collection of essays edited by Naffine and Owens (1997); in particular, see Davies, pp.25-46. The reaction of the judiciary to women's claim to legal personhood exemplifies this process. See also Smart (1992).

2 For an absolutely explicit statement of this, see the American case of Bradwell v. Illinois 1873, 83 US (16 Wall) 130: 'civil law, as well as nature herself, has always recognised a wide difference in the respective spheres and destinies of man and woman'.

3 (1913) 110 L.T. Rep., 353; and (1914) 1 Ch. 286.

4 This remains a feature of the production of solicitors; for example the recent ACLEC report on legal education refers to its purpose as the socialisation of students into legal culture (1996, p.24).

5 This is not to discount the contribution of other disciplines to establishing and maintaining sex based hierarchies and gender identities (see Okin, 1979). For instance, scientific and medical authority also preached women's inferiority and the dangers of straying from their biological destiny.

6 Bourdieu comments on characteristic legal linguistic procedures such as the predominance of passive and impersonal constructions, which are designed to express the neutrality of the law (1987, p.820; see too Maley, 1994, p.45).

7 Carrie Morrison was the first woman solicitor, followed by Elizabeth Pickup, Maud Crofts and Elaine Sykes.

8 See for example, Sugarman (1996) and Burrage (1996). In Larson's pioneering work (1977) on professionalisation the words 'women', 'gender' do not even feature in the index. Heuston's study of Lord Chancellors (1964), entirely ignores the issue of women, even in his discussion of Lord Buckmaster, one of their champions.

9 The Medical (Registration) Act's parliamentary sponsor later claimed never to have intended such a monopoly to be created (Witz, 1992, p.73).

10 One of the persons cases relating to women's elections to local councils.

11 Evidence of women's previous capacity to hold public office formed the core of the case against the Law Society in the Bebb case (1914) 1 Ch. 256 post.

12 However, the date of this 'Comment' should be noted. The change in tone is no doubt a result of the passage of time and the general change in attitudes towards women as a result of the war.

13 The importance of male networking in resisting women's claims to enter the public sphere is specifically alluded to by Sophia Jex-Blake in her account of her efforts to gain admission to the royal infirmary of Edinburgh. She talks of a 'hostile clique' and of 'all powerful members of the Colleges of Physicians and Surgeons (who) had resolved to ostracise any medical men who agreed to give us instructions' and goes on to describe how they orchestrated opposition amongst the students (in English Woman's Review, April 1871, cited in Murray, 1984, p.315).

14 Edwards v. Attorney-General of Canada (1930) A.C. 124.

15 Although this was not universal; for instance Maud Crofts, one of the four women who acted in the 'Bebb case', took Honours in history and law at Girton College, 1980-12, but was unable to take her degree as at that time Cambridge University did not admit women.

16 An earlier attempt was made by Margaret Hall in Scotland to submit herself for the Solicitors' Preliminary Examination via the Society of Law Agents. Though not opposed by the Society, when the application was laid before the courts, it was, as in subsequent cases in England and Wales found that as she was not a 'person' she could not take the exam (Faulkner, 1997, p.3).

17 A distinction which, in illustration of the sexual contract, points up the centrality for patriarchy of women as male property; see Levi-Strauss (1969) and his assertion of the universality of the exchange of women as fundamental to the cultural order.

18 Re. French (1905) 37 N.B.R. 359.

19 The dichotomous approach to women, in which they are constructed as representing such dualities as disorder/docility; whore/madonna is discussed in Thornton, 1996. Smart similarly notes the inherent dualism in the legal category of women, 1992, p.29.

20 Clearly this approach to the position of women was near universal in the industrialised world; for instance; 'The law of Holland ... went out of its way to protect women, but ... as being the weaker vessels, and subject to natural legal disabilities' (Incorporated Law Society v. Wookey (1912) (cited in Sachs and Wilson, 1978, p.37)).

21 Sophia Jex-Blake records that the 'phalanx of opponents' to our application to enter Edinburgh University 'raised the cry of indelicacy' (in English Woman's Review, April 1871, cited in Murray, 1984, p.316).

22 This judgment is a clear articulation of the need to maintain the separation of the private and public spheres, with their dichotomous characteristics of 'affectivity' and 'rationality', neither of which should contaminate the other (Young, 1987).

23 Viscountess Rhondda's Claim (1922) 22 AC 339.

24 This cultural identity as a social practice is clearly related to what Smart describes as the law's role as a 'gendering strategy (1992, pp.34-7) whilst remaining theoretically distinct'.

25 This is not, of course, to underestimate the other fields in which women were struggling; education, in particular, was a focus of activity (see, for instance, Armytage (1964) pp.159-61).

26 See his attack on collectivism: Popular Government (1885).

27 It is interesting to note that whilst these prominent jurists were involved in the selective use of legal principles, and invented tradition in order to exclude women from the public sphere, the last three named figures were also involved in the movement to construct an objective 'science of law' (Sugarman, 1991). Dicey, in particular, of course, is noted for his formulation of equality before the law as a fundamental principle of the Rule of Law. His effective exclusion of women from this principle typifies the liberal tradition; see his 'Letters to a Friend on Votes for Women' 1909 (cited in Fredman, 1997, p.39).

28 So Lord Cozens-Hardy, MR, wrote to Lord Buckmaster in 1915: 'All the judges, without exception, are members of the Athenaeum, and I presume you will wish to be a member' (Heuston (1964), p.269).

29 On 28 March 1914 The Law Times reported that the Lord Chancellor, Lord Haldane, had received a deputation from the Committee, and had announced that 'he was in favour of the principle, as was the Prime Minister and the Law Officers of the Crown, whom he had consulted about the Bill to authorise the proposal' (p.578).

30 Edwards v. Attorney-General of Canada (1930) A.C. 124.

31 The appropriate dress for women lawyers remains an issue, indeed it has recently been causally linked with the glass ceiling: 'organisers of a solicitors' exhibition claim women are held back from promotion within firms because of the way they look ... In response to these concerns, the solicitors' exhibition engaged image consultants House of Colour to advise women solicitors on dressing respectably. They came up with The Rules, which include a ban on bare legs and see-through fabrics ...' (Longrigg, 1998, p.3).

32 By the 1960's there was so little support for the club that the possibility of winding it up was mooted. In 1969, following discussions which stressed the useful contribution to women's interests that the club could make, its name was changed to the Association of Women Solicitors (AWS), and it was decided that it should be less concerned with social events (Faulkner, 1997, p.7).

33 Whilst this faith in the intrinsic fairness of both the legal system and practice is less characteristic of the current generation of female lawyers, one of our women respondents clearly articulated her belief in formal equality, neutrality and individualism as key components of legal ideology and discourse: 'A woman solicitor should not expect positive discrimination. An employer should not expect to be concerned about domestic arrangements. A solicitor is a solicitor albeit male or female and should not expect any special favours. If we expect to be treated as equals then we should behave as equals' (1990).

4 'Bonds of Trust': From Informal Exclusion to Full Participation?

Introduction

The ending of formal exclusion through the Sex Disqualification (Removal) Act of 1919 did not mean that the worst nightmares of Lords Halsbury and Finlay were realised. Male solicitors who returned from the War were not ousted by female competitors, and their families continued to be supported. At first sight this might not appear that remarkable: the mass participation of women in higher education was still half a century away, so there was little prospect of large numbers of women following Carrie Morrison, Maud Crofts and Mary Sykes in using the credential route, or, as Crompton and Sanderson describe it, the 'qualifications lever', to challenge the male monopoly of private practice. However, as we have pointed out, the solicitors' profession was at this stage still far from being a graduate one, and although in the nineteenth century women had been also absent from the rank of clerks, by 1901 they represented 39 per cent of the 32,168 non-managing clerks in the profession (Abel, 1988, p.176). So why did this involvement at the base of the legal pyramid not lead to a greater level of qualification through the articled clerk route? Because there are no studies of women who worked at this level we do not know whether many of them even attempted this route; however the pattern of participation by the first women solicitors gives us some insight into the difficulties which would have been encountered by any women clerks who had tried to qualify in this way.

This chapter will sketch out aspects of professional culture between 1919 and the 1980's in an attempt to identify the informal barriers this presented to women, both in terms of participation rates and career progression. We will argue that multiple deterrents existed. These were principally to be found in the character of legal training (and, indirectly, in the nature of the law itself), in the fact that 'female usurpationary strategies' were a middle class phenomenon, and in the prevalence of male networking as a mode of appointing solicitors, the culture of which meant that for many firms women were viewed as entirely ineligible. As a result, we can identify certain features which characterise female participation from its inception: the need for patronage, the incidence of overt discrimination, the development of female specialisms, the problems for women with children, and an apparent internalisation of the legal ideology of neutrality and equality, inhibiting the development of a specifically women's voice. In the first part of the chapter we have used accounts of their experiences provided by women qualifying and joining the profession over the period from 1922 to the early 1980's to support our depiction of the culture within which they worked. In the second part we consider aspects of the role of legal education in the acculturation of solicitors and have summarised briefly some of the very considerable literature of feminist jurisprudence which names the ideology and practice of the law as male in order to clarify the influences on male attitudes towards women and contradictions for women attempting to make their careers as solicitors. Finally, as a prelude to our study in subsequent chapters of the experiences of contemporary women solicitors, we discuss various facets of the legacy of this period for the era of expansion in the 1980's, when the qualifications lever did allow for the large-scale entry of women. This last part of the discussion includes a summary of the statistical picture of women's skewed distribution across the profession, and a brief sketch of the character and experiences of our own sample.

Between formal inclusion and large-scale participation 1922-1979

As we noted above, the removal of the formal bar to women solicitors, and the issue of the first practising certificate to Carrie Morrison in 1922, did not presage large-scale female participation. This was the common experience of other jurisdictions where women had finally obtained entry (Rhode, 1991, pp.1743-4; Hagan and Kay, 1995; Thornton, 1996), and was arguably partly the consequence of the fact that the project to admit women had an extremely limited class base. Quite a substantial degree of prosperity was needed in order to become a solicitor; in the main higher education was open only to those who could support themselves, and in addition, up until the 1970's, articled clerks had to pay their principal for the privilege of their training (Maud Crofts had paid approximately £100 a year for her articles; AWS Archive).

However, the paucity of female candidates for admission to the profession should not be ascribed solely to this factor. As Sachs and Wilson argue, 'it was hardly to be expected ... that when the formal disabilities were removed, women would find a comfortable place for themselves in legal practice', and they go on to point out that the very list of female 'firsts' are reminders of 'continuing male domination rather than female advance' (Sachs and Wilson, 1978, p.178). Informal gatekeeping strategies repaired the breach made by legislation. The principal exclusionary mechanism was the refusal of articles or full employment; thus one woman who qualified in 1925, and practised into the 1980's, commented that 'most firms would not take a woman articled clerk' (1990, AWS Archive). Deterrence could also take the form of poor pay and promotion prospects (Faulkner, 1997, p.6), all of which could lead women to voluntarily exclude themselves in a way that could appear to be the result of free choice. As a result of such barriers, it was not uncommon for women who had studied law at university to fail to qualify as solicitors. Consequently, in the UK as in the United States, the first generations of women who did go on to be admitted and to practice as solicitors, usually had to have the kind of strong familial links with the profession which mirrored male patronage networks in their general form (Faulkner, op.cit., p.5). Maud Crofts, the only one of the four original plaintiffs in the Bebb case to qualify, was the daughter of a barrister, and became a partner with her brother and husband, and was therefore able to develop her own client base (Faulkner, op.cit., p.10). As her daughter observed of both her mother and the other women pioneers: '... they all had legal connections - I don't think anybody would have thought of doing it without' (1990, AWS Archive).[1]

Male domination of the profession was also maintained through an unchallenged culture: unchallenged partly because the first women to qualify and be admitted, as might be expected given their class background and familial links with the law, were strongly committed to the 'formal equality' route. In common with other representatives of the first wave of feminism, they generally wished to demonstrate that they could fill the existing places as well as men, without requiring any concessions or modifications (Skordaki, 1996, p.14). The daughter of Maud Crofts described this approach in the following way: '... the climate in Girton, which was founded by Emily Davies ... (was that) the only way you could get equality for women was through education and (she) insisted that the women take all the same exams as the men - so ... no quarter asked or given ... (it) was very much an equal idea' (1990, AWS Archive). Consequently, the founding of the 1919 club for women solicitors (renamed the Association of Women Solicitors (AWS) in 1969) was not perceived as part of the development of a separatist, distinctive women's voice, but was rather concerned with social events and the provision of mutual support. As one of the first woman solicitors, Sybil Warren, commented: 'it was never intended in any way to be a "women's movement"', and another of the first wave wrote: 'I have repeatedly said that I see little point in having an association of *women* solicitors. I see no difference between women and men solicitors. We all do the same job' (1990, respondent's emphasis, AWS Archive). That this approach was representative of the first generation of women was confirmed by a solicitor admitted in the 1950's, who recounted how the 'pioneers had wanted to be thought of as just solicitors', rather than as women. She also explained how her generation had similarly:

> adapted by trying to be like the men; that's what we wanted. We wore dark, plain clothes. We didn't push our femininity forward at all - not the way you sometimes see now. We wanted to do things the same way as the men - we thought that that's what the clients wanted.
>
> (Retired general practitioner, 1997)

So in practice the admission of women did not, until recently, represent any real threat, either numerical or cultural, to male domination of the 'juridical field'. This was explicitly articulated in 1954 when it was emphasised to the Law Society Council that the 1919 Club did not want to be 'militant but merely to take our place with our men contemporaries in the profession' (Club Minute Book, 21 October 1954; Faulkner, 1997, p.6).

Apart from modelling their dress and values on those of men, it is clear that the early women solicitors were also often single and therefore able to replicate males in other ways (and see Drachman, 1989). As Maud Crofts' daughter observed, marriage was likely to necessitate leaving the profession: '… a lot of the women who were available for higher education … wouldn't have married and if they did marry I don't think they would have bothered about having children … some of my mother's friends from Cambridge married and of course that was the end … you didn't do anything else' (1990, AWS Archive). On the other hand, the fact that most of the early women worked in family firms meant that some of them, including Maud Crofts herself, were in fact able to continue working after children. However the presence of mothers did nothing to disrupt the cultural milieu of the professional workplace. Quite apart from their negligible numbers, then as now, the ability of such women to delegate childcare to other women meant that they could effectively continue to function as men: '(my mother) … always practised … you had nannies and maids …' (id.).

Women were generally restricted to particular areas of practice - usually wills and probate and conveyancing, and sometimes family work (Skordaki, 1996, p.14), and often to female clients. Thus it appears that whilst the pioneers were generally committed to succeeding by endorsing male norms, nevertheless many of them found a place by developing a distinctively female market. For instance, Maud Crofts' daughter explained that her mother 'really provided the clients for my father and my uncle until they got the firm going' because 'there were all these very feminist women who in no way wanted to go to a man solicitor, and it so happened that a lot of them had quite a bit of money because you couldn't have taken up a cause unless you'd had private means …' (1990, AWS Archive). Correspondingly, the suspicions of non-feminist or male clients were cited as problems by some pioneers, and respondents who qualified in the 1950's, '60's and '70's all mentioned the predominance of male networking in much of the core business in a range of different kinds of practice; evidently both these factors would help to explain why these early women practitioners worked in 'female' specialisms. On the other hand, it may be that, at times, potential client hostility was put forward by the profession as a rationale for excluding and restricting women's participation (a device which some of our contemporary respondents also mentioned); thus a woman who qualified in the early 1950's, recounted how she only discovered that she was being ejected by one firm when a client told her, and how in fact she had 'such a good client base that there was quite a "stink" about it' (AWS Archive, 1990).

The fact that the early women solicitors generally offered no challenge to professional culture did not guarantee that, as a fraction of the labour force, they were regarded as co-equal with their male counterparts. Despite the fact that there had been women solicitors for over thirty years, the women who were admitted in the 1950's found that they were refused admission to the coffee room at the Law Society. Instead, until the success of their challenge to this policy, it was expected that they would confine themselves to the 'Ladies Annexe', a small room near the Ladies toilet.[2] Other, petty forms of discrimination also remained, similarly undermining women's status as professionals. A woman who qualified in 1940 explained that because she had run her own business she had met with very few obstacles, but that she had encountered problems at the Law Society: 'It had not occurred to me until I tried to take a woman friend there as a guest, that although women members were permitted, any friends they might wish to entertain must be male! Very embarrassing!' (1990, AWS Archive).

Unsurprisingly, therefore, finding articles and work also continued to be problematic well beyond the first generation of female solicitors. A woman who qualified at the end of the 1940's recounted how she had hoped to obtain articles outside the family firm, but was at first unsuccessful despite her personal contacts: 'My uncle had a friend who was a partner with one of the big city firms ... and they said (they were very nice but) "we wouldn't even consider having a girl" - just like that which actually really annoyed me ... I mean they hadn't even seen me, it wasn't personal, I wouldn't have minded if they'd seen me and said "no they couldn't stick me and they didn't want me" ...' (1990, AWS Archive). Her father then obtained articles for her with another firm through his acquaintance with one of its partners. When women did obtain work it was generally clear that their career was regarded as short-term; this was the experience of another woman in the early 1950's: 'after I'd qualified I found an ad. in the Gazette saying they wanted a woman; it was a small City firm. At the interview I asked "Why a woman?" and they said it was because there were no prospects and I was to be paid less too' (1997). The woman concerned accepted the arrangement because it did in fact fit in with her plans.

In the public arena the ubiquity of male values was taken for granted and therefore the presence of women could incite overt prejudice from colleagues necessitating the swift adoption of the 'habitus' of the field (Bourdieu, 1992). A 1950's qualifier told the following story:

> I do remember some open hostility. For instance, in the early 60's I went to a Law Society Conference which used to be held once a year in Oxford. It used to be a really big thing, very well attended; any member in theory could go. There were three women and about two hundred men there. When I got there I was told this wasn't on, this is a men's club - women can't come here. But when they found you didn't mind them telling dirty jokes and could drink with them, then you were accepted. (Retired probate lawyer, 1997)

Other women described similar experiences which indicated that their presence was frequently greeted with surprise, amusement or contempt; thus one woman stated that the firm to which she was articled in the 1940's 'were all very nice and ... treated me as a bit of a joke' (AWS Archive, 1990). On the other hand, the excessively hostile reaction that might have been anticipated from the language used in debate and in professional journals during the struggle to end formal exclusion appears to have been rarely encountered; perhaps partly because they were usually protected by the shelter of their family firms and partly because of the slender basis of women's participation. A male solicitor who had qualified in 1937 stated that, by the time the war broke out, he had still never come across a woman solicitor: 'later on in practice I had a client who claimed to have been the first woman solicitor. There was just a trickle of women coming in at this time and they made no impression - I don't remember anything about them' (former senior partner of a medium sized general practice, 1997).

The same respondent provided an evocative account of the way in which the male networking, on which much business was based, continued completely undisturbed by women's participation:

> Our firm was in Clement's Inn which was very near to the Law Society, and we used to go into the Law Society, a bunch of us - ex-officers - there was a snack bar at the Law Society which charged reasonable prices and that's where we'd meet; it had a club-like atmosphere, you got to know other people there,

from other firms. There were old stagers who'd held the fort while we were away at the war, and us. It was like a market, you formed friendships, bonds of trust, and you'd do business there with each other .... the City firm people tended to keep themselves to themselves - they formed another clique; there were dining clubs all around this area, where different sorts of circles would meet. It was very, well completely, male dominated I suppose. I don't remember any women going into that snack bar - it was very much a male environment.

An ability to mingle in these surroundings was clearly a fundamental feature of an individual's cultural and relational capital. Birks, writing about this era, commented on the crucial significance of building up networks both within the profession and with the public, especially given the restrictions on advertising, so that many firms had one partner whose main function was to bring in clients. 'He is to be found in many London clubs and attending every sort of social function' (1960, p.275), and the combination of this capacity with the 'kin character' of the partnership, which we will discuss further in the next chapter, formed a key aspect of recruitment practices. As we noted above, this could work to women's benefit where they could use family links either to obtain work, or to set up in the shelter of a family firm. Usually however, in the world of general legal practice, women's anticipated inability to bring 'business' with her into the firm might be regarded as a crucial handicap, and this would clearly be complicated by the issue of 'difference'. The process of 'representing the firm' and being 'socially acceptable was mediated by gender, and is evidently one reason why a 'girl' would not even be considered:

We had a relative, she's now a woman of sixty, a nice bright person, and I think I was asked if some approach could be made on her behalf, to see if she could be articled to the firm. This was in the early 1950's. At the time, women were just beginning to come in. We had a serious Partners' Meeting, and I said, "What about it?" and they said it would be all right but that the trouble was that some of the clients wouldn't like it.[3] Some of the clients were tough nuts and so it wasn't prejudice within the firms, it just wouldn't have been possible. (Retired senior partner, medium sized general practice, 1997)

Given these continuing barriers to women's participation, patronage generally remained the key to personal success. For instance, one woman recounted her experiences in the early 1960's in the following way: 'I had a very good boss and he encouraged me ... I was promoted quite well - over and above of some of the men ... partly because of the champion I had in my boss' (Academic, 1997). Another woman, a former equity partner of a medium sized general practice in a small town, explained that she had been taken on, and then been able to specialise in commercial work at a time when women were largely restricted to female specialisms like conveyancing, both because 'I was very good and because there was no one else and also because they had never had a female fee earner before ... when I went for Articles, the senior partner was intrigued - he said he had never had a woman before, but was prepared to take the risk ... he trained me up ... then I was made a partner ... they liked the novelty ...' (1994).

Correspondingly, failure to obtain the shelter of a patron usually meant that even by the 1960's admission (let alone success) was impossible. A female respondent who took a Law degree in the 1960's, found a place as a legal clerk at the Electricity Board, because 'you couldn't get anything better unless you had legal connections, and at that time you had to pay to get articles ... it was like a secret society which was not for the likes of you' (barrister and academic, 1997). The subtle forms of humiliation which women entering all male arenas are likely to endure run like a thread through her work history. No woman at the Board was allowed to send letters out under her own name, though recently appointed teenage male clerks could. She left to have children, and then decided to retrain for the Bar in 1975: when she applied for some exemptions from Bar finals she was patronised and humiliated, and when she went to see the sponsor allocated her from the local bar, he said "oh, we'll have to go up to London one weekend" - sort of sexual jokes - so of course I never used him for any help'. Of the six women who studied Law at university with her, the only two to make a career in practice did indeed have male relatives practising law. Similar experiences of prejudice and humiliation surface in the accounts of other women practising around this time. For instance a woman who had qualified in the 1950's described how 'the judges and registrars were always very prejudiced, in the main. One registrar in particular took barristers first, then male solicitors from out of town, then male solicitors locally and finally a woman' (1990, AWS Archive).

The environment in the 1970's was apparently often no more welcoming. Indeed, the accounts of women who qualified around this time contained more instances of prejudice and hostility than those of women admitted in previous decades. This is perhaps in part because the increase in numbers was beginning to represent the sort of threat to male hegemony which had been so feared around the turn of the century, and presumably in part because these newer entrants were no longer always accommodated by family firms. Many women recounted being openly told that their place was at home, and whilst for some this had ensured that they left on becoming pregnant, others explained that, in the absence of professional links to assist in overcoming this prejudice, it had meant that they had not progressed beyond the preliminary stages; for instance: 'I went to see the man who was head of the local Law Society in * (this was in 1972). He told me 'young ladies like you would be better off being secretaries or legal executives'. I also tried to get a job as a trainee, but the message was clear that women should be at home having babies. I was also struck by the snobbery of the profession, and was advised that if you don't have connections in the law, then forget it' (mature law student, 1997). Another woman, approximately twenty years qualified, recounted how, in the early 1970's she had placed two advertisements for employment in the Law Society Gazette, which were identical except that in one she disclosed that she was a woman; whereas this one produced only two responses, she had received 17 replies to the one which had made no mention of her gender (1990, AWS Archive).

Several respondents spoke of the problems women tended to encounter once they were in, for instance: 'I was never encouraged career wise by the partner I was articled to in the early 1990's … the other two articled clerks - both males - were encouraged and kept on, but I was never offered a chance even though I was as good as them - it was a boys' own network and women didn't get a look in' (matrimonial specialist, 1997). Another, also talking about the early 1970's said: I felt I was treated more like a tea girl than a trainee. I was articled to the litigation partner and basically he couldn't see why women were working, and made this quite clear' (solicitor and academic, 1997). Anticipating these views, she had removed her engagement ring for her interview, but had still faced the expected questions about her plans for children. Furthermore, despite being prepared for male resistance, she found the daily experience of work difficult: 'I used to go home from ... in tears, because I was very aware that he didn't think much of me. One of the things he used to do if he was interviewing certain clients, he would deliberately say things to embarrass me - I mean elicit details about their case - sexual, salacious details, to upset me'. In another instance, a woman who eventually achieved judicial appointment was known, when she practised as a defending barrister, as 'the rape queen' because it was considered by chambers and the managing clerk to be both amusing and effective to use her as defending counsel for rapists as often as possible.

The cultural continuity which these accounts reveal characterise the general experience of women in the all-male or predominantly male environment of private practice.[4] The tendency for women in relatively isolated positions to be subjected to greater degrees of hostile behaviour ranging from disparagement to harassment has been identified by international research (see for example Rosenberg et al, 1993; McGlynn and Graham, 1995). A labour market sociologist has recently attributed the tendency for employees of either gender to leave mixed occupations in favour of single-sexed occupations as most probably the result of the fact that 'working life is more psychologically or socially comfortable, or unproblematic, for many people when work colleagues are of the same sex' (Hakim, 1996, p.162). However, what our evidence describes is not just cultural solidarity of the neutral kind described by Hakim, but a cultural climate consolidated at its most extreme around forms of misogyny varying in degree but not in kind. It is therefore hardly surprising that our women respondents in many cases sought alternative career paths such as teaching, or public service, in organisations whose bureaucratic practices offered a greater degree of shelter, though clearly these male values (as explored below) are also present in the academy and other settings.

The statistical evidence confirms this picture of cultural continuity. In the 1920's women represented 1.7 per cent of those admitted to the profession, and admissions proceeded to grow slowly but steadily over the next half century (2.9 per cent in the 1940's, 6.7 per cent in 1959, 9.9 per cent in 1971) until the period of rapid growth in the 1970's and 1980's (Abel, 1988, p.415). Naturally, women represented a smaller proportion of those with practising certificates; 0.7 per cent in 1931 growing to only 3.2 per cent in 1971 (id.). However, during the contraction of private practice in the 1950's, women appear to have been affected disproportionately, their percentile representation in the profession shrinking along with their absolute numbers (from 2.7 per cent in 1951 to 1.8 per cent in 1957: id.). This appears to support Breugel's theorisation of the female workforce as representing a reserve army of labour (1979; and see Braverman, 1974), since it raises the possibility that the engagement of women might have been seen from the beginning as a luxury, and that they would have been obvious targets for dismissal or redundancy in difficult times. This issue recurs in our discussion of the 'slump' in the late 1980's and early 1990's,[5] and emphasises that women's participation in the legal labour market needs to be seen in the context of 'long wave' phenomena such as cyclical shifts in the economy, and major transformations in the character and class basis of occupations.

The profession was of course also influenced by the persistence of highly stereotyped gender roles and characteristics in society at large; roles and characteristics which the law itself helped construct. Obtaining the vote and the status of juridical personhood had not led to major gains in other areas. As Patricia Smith has written: 'until the 1970's the courts maintained the idea that separate spheres of endeavour for men and women were natural and good ... This assumption made women dependent on men and subject to their authority' (1993, p.20). This view (which, in fact, we would contend persists today) underpinned the profession's dealings with both the public and female employees. A Law Society guide entitled 'The Services of a Solicitor', published in the 1960's, gives a flavour of the contemporary discourse, and exemplifies the continuing relegation of 'the wife' to the private sphere and the attribution to her of 'womanly' qualities. Intended to advertise to the public the sort of help that could be obtained from a lawyer, various scenarios are presented in which a husband and wife have approached a solicitor. In each one the wife is characterised as emotional, excitable and irrational; the first scenario is entitled 'The dismissal of the Daily Help', a function which clearly falls to the wife who is nevertheless represented as incapable of exercising it responsibly:

> **The Wife**. She has stolen that £1 note out of my purse. I know she has ... When she comes tomorrow, I would like to send her off packing at once. Will that be all right, do you think?

By contrast, the husband, whilst a lay person, is nevertheless restrained in his reaction, and a calming influence:

> Steady, dear. We don't want trouble, you know. What's more, we must keep within the law ...
>
> **The Solicitor**. First, let's be practical about this. Have you got a replacement? ... The strict law is clear enough. Notice can be given to a servant on any day of the week ... but instant dismissal without notice ... can only be justified if the employer proves serious misconduct ...

Another scenario is entitled 'The Gossip' - a part played, of course, by the wife.

> **The Wife**. The way he is behaving is absolutely disgraceful! Don't you think that I ought to tell his wife all about it? What are friends for, if not to let you know about these things?
>
> **The Husband**. I am not so sure about passing these stories on. After all, we can't be certain that they are true and even if they are, remember that 'the greater the truth, the greater the libel'. Then suppose it came back to him and he even started a slander action? We might both be in real trouble. After all, a husband is responsible for his wife ...
>
> **The Solicitor**. You are perfectly correct that a slander action can be a most serious matter ... Does the husband have to pay for his wife's libels or slanders? Not any longer. That unreasonable rule was abolished some twenty-five years ago.

The subsequent scenarios similarly illustrate the apparently dangerous combination of responsibility for the domestic sphere and female impulsiveness and excitability; where the carpet in the lodger's room has been burned, the wife begins by exclaiming: 'Of course it must be his fault ... it must be his responsibility. I would never have taken him on as a lodger at all if I had known he would start burning holes in the carpet'. She then turns to her husband however, as the head of the household, to resolve the matter: 'It's up to you now. You must tackle him about it ...' (Cockshutt, 1961, pp.118-24).

These scenarios convey vividly the 'normal' representation by the profession of women's roles and capacities, expressed in language barely distinguishable from the views of the anti-suffrage movement half a century before, and the use of the noun 'men' and the masculine pronoun to personify solicitors seems more emphatic, and expressive of absence than the linguistic conventions of the time would demand. The construction of the scenarios delineates a fellowship between the male solicitor and client as expert and lay 'knowers' (Thornton, 1996), whilst the portrait of the woman implicitly contradicts the possibility of women being 'knowers' of any kind. The fictions of this guide to the profession also mirror the constructions of the scenarios which have long been the stuff of legal education, and demonstrate the continuity of the discourse between the private realm, 'public education', and the reproduction of lawyers through the academy (see Collier, 1991; 1998a).

In the following sections, we therefore move on to consider the contribution of both legal education and the law to the process of professional acculturations.

The production of lawyers: legal education and training

The role of legal education and training is a dual one: firstly it is a repository of 'knowledge' about what the law 'is', and so it projects from the past the gendered character of the Common Law and 'legal method' which we referred to in the last chapter, and which will be discussed further below. However legal education is also a repository of 'practical knowledge' about what it is to be a lawyer, projecting the past culture of the profession into the future:

> This training is a major factor in the hierarchical life of the legal profession. It encodes the message of the legitimacy of the whole system into the smallest details of personal style, daily routine, gesture, tone of voice, facial expression - a plethora of little p's and q's for everyone to mind. (D. Kennedy, 1992)

The culture of hierarchy and patronage which relegates women to the lower echelons, was seen by many respondents as particularly prevalent at the vocational stage of training: 'it's all put me off; articles is all about fagging anyway - the whole profession, it seems to me, is still based on that public school way of carrying on - lots of hierarchies and bullying - maleness and snobbery are still rife' (mature student, postgraduate diploma, 1997).

Such descriptions are born out by analyses of articles (Burrage, 1996), but seem even more applicable to the hierarchical culture of the Bar. As Helena Kennedy has argued, the dining which is a compulsory part of qualifying as a barrister is designed 'to create a camaraderie amongst the profession in which familiarity will help in the maintenance of high ethical standards ... also ... these events will provide the opportunity for new entrants to a profession to make contacts ... Patronage is an insidious feature of life at the Bar' (1992, pp.37-8). One of our male respondents gave an account of dining, which graphically characterises the issues of hierarchy and patronage.

> The ritual was an archaic vestige, originally probably more elaborate because originally you were attached to a senior barrister in your mess and that's where you would have learned your law. I think it was also designed to instil into people a sense of hierarchy and place which is what the law is about because the law is essentially a self serving machinery for people to make a living and to get status by imposing unintelligible forms of behaviour onto people. It's a self-perpetuating secret society, and the mess (the name for the table of four in hall at which you eat) is about being initiated into it.
>
> (Barrister and Law Centre worker, 1997)

Helena Kennedy provides a similar account of dining, but also emphasises the particular humiliations which have been reserved for women (1992, pp.38-40). There are few comparable stories of the duller rituals of being articled to a solicitor, though articles serve the same function of acculturation. As Duncan Kennedy argues, for most participants, the fact that the over-riding principle on which the hierarchy appears to be based is generation, develops an allegiance based on expectation: 'training for subservience is learning for domination as well. Nothing could be more natural, and if you've served your time, nothing more fair than to do as you have been done to' (1992, p.61). Respondents recalled being asked at interview how they would relate to support staff and being advised that it was important to keep one's distance (former solicitor and academic, 1997). Others recalled articles being punctuated by a series of menial jobs: parking the principal's car, feeding parking meters, and carrying the principal's bag to court representing typical examples. However, it should also be noted that attitudes to trainees would change with the stage of the economic cycle, and, as we observed earlier, were heavily dependent on an individual 'mentor', an issue which we discuss in the following chapters. Some women spoke of being regarded as cannon fodder, because the supply of labour was so plentiful, whilst others, whose articles occurred at the time of anxiety over 'shortage' in the late 1980's, spoke of firms or principals who operated 'completely meritocratic' procedures.[6]

The process of acculturation is actually begun in the Law School. On the one hand the emphasis is on 'technical', that is Black Letter, law, since one of the primary functions of a legal education is the transmission of a universal form of reasoning and rules which purport to transcend social conditions (Bourdieu, 1987; Collier, 1991; 1998). At the same time, legal training is as much concerned with the production of lawyers as social types who function within a formalised hierarchy and are recognisably legal interpreters. Whilst this characteristic allows the conforming type to consolidate their cultural capital and build relationships which they will later be able to 'cash in', the same process is not always possible for 'deviants', who can feel at odds with the subject itself:

> I really struggled on the CPE (Common Professional Examination). I was the only one who came from a poor black working class part of town, and when I told people they'd always make comments - it got beyond a joke. Then there was the language they used ... I went to an inner city working class school and I could trace everyone and what they are doing, and all those people, my community, are still shocked that I'm doing this, so you alienate yourself from your background, but you're not accepted by the middle class, white legal world either - no one wants you.
>
> (Asian woman Law Centre advice worker, 1997)

One means by which the system of hierarchy and patronage is powerfully communicated is through the media of tutorials and formative assessment; as another respondent noted, 'we certainly are not treated as equals by lecturers. And then some of the male lecturers obviously have favourites - they clearly like and are accustomed to being surrounded by young girls' (mature postgraduate diploma student, 1997).

Other respondents also referred to the maleness of law school culture, and it is evident that this was a characteristic of training for other male dominated professions. For instance in an interesting passage in her account of gender and the medical profession, Witz recounts the objection of male students at the Middlesex Hospital medical school to the presence of female students on the grounds that male lecturers would feel the need to restrain their language. She goes on to cite Newman's (1957) view that the advent of women into medical school ended the widespread practice of the use of obscene jokes and anecdotes in medical training (1992, pp.84-5, though perhaps the practice hung on rather longer than Newman suggested). Similarly, Thornton has identified the way in which women within legal education in Australia were subordinated, through the personification of the law student as male, through sexual objectification at the level of personal relations, and through the 'technocentrism' of the legal curriculum, which projected patriarchal views: 'technocratic law forms a carapace around the partiality of justice so as to disguise the matrix of class, race, masculinity and law' (1996, p.80). Harrington describes how male law professors in the USA used the minutiae of pedagogy, like questioning, institutionalised through a 'ladies' day', to inflict ritual humiliation and embarrassment on female students (1994, pp.41-68).

Our older female respondents had similar stories to tell: a woman who did her law degree at the end of the 1950's said: 'There were six of us in the whole year out of forty. We were definitely there under sufferance. I don't think any of us ever felt a part of it ... The whole university seemed to me to be very anti-women; for instance, I remember the union had a meeting to ban women from it if they wore trousers ... I also remember wearing coloured stockings and being harassed all the way from the law school to the bus stop - a long way - men following me, making remarks like 'why have you got those stockings on?' - it was horrible, gross harassment - like being bullied at school - and I was very angry and upset, and yet it was also what we expected, we were not surprised when men behaved like that because that was what it was like. The other thing was that they saw girls as just there on the look out for husbands, not really serious' (barrister and academic, 1997).

More recent entrants to the profession speaking of the 1980's, still referred to the 'predominance of a masculine ethos in the law department' (general practitioner, 1997). This was held to manifest itself in various ways, ranging from the general atmosphere, and the approach of male students to women lecturers, (as well as vice versa), to the teaching methods and the law itself. One female lawyer, reflecting on her experience of law school at this time, remarked: 'I remember that there were all these down market Yuppy men who were always barging around with sports bags, who seemed to dominate the place, and in particular, I remember a lecture on domestic violence, and injunctions, and they all just kept laughing - it was really horrible' (CAB solicitor, 1997). Another commented: 'One of my memories is of these young men really barracking this middle aged woman law lecturer - just giving her a really hard time, asking lots of silly questions - because, I think, she was a woman and was also rather strange looking ... my other main impression was that there were absolutely no black people ... it was just dominated by white middle class people' (matrimonial lawyer, 1997). For several, the dominant impression was the uncritical transmission of 'this extremely male perspective - i.e. the law - and the continual use of the male pronoun and the absence of any social context' (matrimonial specialist, 1997).

Ten years on, female equality in the student population in terms of numbers has been an established fact for several years; this period has also witnessed a growing diversity of intake in terms of background, accompanied by democratising educational developments such as moves away from black letter law towards skills teaching. These changes were reflected in the views of students interviewed in 1997; for instance there was far less mention of male dominance of the student body. Nevertheless, some of the comments seemed to indicate that many things remained the same. One continuing theme was the hierarchical and mystificatory nature of law teaching; again and again, students complained of being treated 'like kids' and 'patronised'. In remarks which replicate the observations found in Harrington's discussion of law teaching in Harvard (1994), one mature student said: 'on the test which I had done badly in, I just got very scathing comments written on them - nothing helpful or supportive, though, to help me improve ... then in a tutorial I was really slapped down in front of everyone when I was trying to make a point about inequalities; the tutor, he just said "it's no use being politically aware; this is a commercial course"' (mature student on postgraduate diploma, 1997).

Some of the comments quoted above point up what are perhaps the key contributions which the Law School makes to the process of acculturation. Firstly, many Law departments, like the profession they supply, appear untouched by social issues which have been at least superficially absorbed by other humanities faculties, and which therefore generally inform the rhetoric and the selection of staff and teaching methods of these departments. Thus we were advised by a University Equal Opportunities officer that the Law Department in her University had an 'appalling record for equal opps; it's viewed as extremely hard and sexist' (1997). Correspondingly, teaching methods such as the language and examples used, far from being 'neutral', remain resolutely 'politically incorrect'. For instance, in an echo of the experience of one of our respondents of being subjected to salacious details of cases by her principal (cited above), a seminar paper on offences against the person used in one University featured the characters 'Gerald Grope' and 'Miss Nymph O'Maniac', whose relationship ended in a prosecution after the love bite Miss Nymph O'Maniac had willingly agreed to became painful. Though perhaps an extreme example of a style of problem question which is also becoming less common, it is not trivial, in that it epitomises the way in which women are expected to look past the presenting power of relationships to 'the Law'. So whilst some women students had objected to the framing of the scenario and others wished to discuss the sexual harassment issues it raised, the pretence is maintained that these are irrelevant and that the only issues are technical legal ones[7] (Collier, 1991, p.442).

Outside the academy, this aspect of the law and legal processes continues to characterise legal practice, and is exemplified through the imposition of normative masculinity at the point of recruitment. Helena Kennedy describes this approach as characterising women's interviews for tenancies in chambers, typically through the 'rape question' (1992, pp.134-5). Women (including one of the authors) have faced the same question at interviews for articles and for assistant solicitor places. It generally takes the form of an interrogation centring on whether the interviewee is 'woman' (or man?) enough to take on anything the law throws at her, namely violent male clients, including rapists. The underlying principles of the question are that the power relations between sexes are nothing to do with the law, and, that, as legal technicians, lawyers must be able to deal with anything; a further subtext, however, is that women may be unable to display the impartial rationality required in the public sphere because they are likely to be swayed, in representing violent men, by their emotions. Used in this way, at the point of entry to the profession, the question is also a means of essaying women's subordination to the patriarchal core of the profession. Thornton recounts a number of other techniques designed to demean women applicants on the grounds of their attachment to the private sphere (1996, pp.144-5).

As we argued in the preceding chapter, legal professionals are not only the agents who actuate the law; they also live out the attitudes, hierarchies and classifications which law creates: 'There is necessarily a close relationship between any system of law and the experts who operate it' (Baker, 1990, p.177). This symbiosis between law and legal culture is underlined by Bourdieu who argues that the juridical field 'cannot be neglected if we wish to understand the social significance of the law, for it is within this universe that juridical authority is produced and exercised' (1987, pp.815-6). The second way, therefore, in which the Law School contributes to the acculturation of the practitioner as an embodiment of legal reason is in its transmission of a subject which, although clearly politically and socially grounded, is remarkable for the absence of content. Not only is the curriculum generally limited to the six core legal areas - contract, tort and so on, and optional, largely practical specialisms such as evidence, family, consumer - rarely including, for instance, a course on the sociology of the law, let alone women and the law - but the teaching of legal subjects themselves is also unaccompanied by any auto-critiques or input of issues of gender (Bottomley, 1992) or race. As we noted above, Thornton has commented on the resulting 'reduction of social problems to predetermined legal formulae' (1996, p.76), and uses the term 'technocentrism' to capture the centripetal pull of rules rationality and the way in which it disqualifies other forms of knowledge (id.). Feminist critics of the law and legal education have also noted how, in the casebooks which represent the core of the legal curriculum (Frug, 1985), as in the law itself, women appear not as ungendered 'persons', but in their gendered role within the family.

The strength of the recent tradition of feminist criminology, penal studies and jurisprudence, has been to unmask the gendered character of legal processes. As Fredman argues: 'Law is not a disembodied, impersonal force. It is made by legislators and judges and therefore reflects the current balance of power within society' (1997, p.16). We have already considered this point in our discussion of the patriarchal judgments in the 19th century persons cases. However, even today, the law is still permeated by antique liberal notions of male/female attributes and roles, and makes a major contribution to societal perceptions of these. Therefore in confronting the substance of the law, women practitioners are challenged in a completely different way to men. In the following section we will briefly touch on some of the most glaring examples of patriarchal law, as they confront the woman law student and practitioner, and shape the outlook of all practitioners.

The substance and influence of legal education: 'missing pages'

Our woman student respondents were generally struck by what one simply described as the 'sexism of the law', whilst another remarked that it was just what she had expected. Clearly this is the subject of entire books (for instance, see Edwards, 1996); here we will simply highlight some of the ways in which its sexism is most glaringly revealed.

We have discussed above how, in the past century, the common law may be viewed as an embodiment of patriarchy, and arguably this remains the case, as progress in modifying its character through statute has been slow, and partial. Furthermore statute is interpreted and consequently confined (Griffith, 1977) by the spokesmen[8] of the common law, the judiciary, employing common law rules, techniques and discourse. Consequently legal disabilities imposed on women are able to persist even when a substantial advance in their erosion has been achieved as the dualistic thinking which underpins such disabilities continues to characterise the law (Olsen, 1990). For example, whilst formal equality was established as a result of the Sex Discrimination Act and Equal Pay Act, the impact of these statutes has been greatly diminished by the use of a male comparator. Fredman writes: '... the concepts utilised in anti-discrimination law are inherently limited and that is one important reason for the continuation of disadvantage in the labour market ... legislation framed in terms of equality based on a male norm is ... fundamentally limited' (1992, p.121). In this way, the common law has again impeded the social advances represented by statute through a simultaneous adherence both to notions of 'natural' gender differences and an assumption that the commitment to formal equality guarantees substantive equality.

The gendered character of the law is constructed through an inductive process which is based on a complex of assumptions derived from the existing order; as Thayer has observed: 'In conducting a process of judicial reasoning, as of other reasoning, not a step can be taken without assuming something which has not been proved' (1890, p.287; cited in Edwards, 1996, p.1). As in the 19th century, one of the most fundamental of these assumptions remains the essential nature of masculinity and femininity, and their different aspirations and roles. Consequently, Scales has argued that 'the concept of separate spheres eludes all attempts at reform' (1993, p.7); the nature of the public sphere continues to be shaped - both in practice and in law - by the male norm, and women to be largely defined by their reproductive capacity and their subordination to men (Hewson, 1997, p.537). These universal truths then form the basis for construing other general rules, a process which is achieved by, as Edwards points out, 'distinguishing, silencing often, and for ever, equally valid alternative realities (1996, p.1). The body of principles which constitutes the Common Law have thus been selected from a range of possible principles and may therefore be better represented as values. In other words, even today women as students and lawyers are endlessly returned to the situation of the applicants in the persons cases (Smart, 1990, 1992), and confronted by a legal method involving the selective and arbitrary use of 'facts' justified by reference to Common Law 'principles'.

Graycar and Morgan's compendium of studies and cases demonstrates the nature of women's relationship to the law (see too Bottomley, 1996; Smart, 1992). They cite the gendered construction of 'work' and the 'worker' in a range of legal contexts (1990, pp.73-112); for example, the disregard of women's domestic labour underlines not simply women's primary status of homeworker but the entire interdependent status of the public and private realms, and the consequent conception of women's status as archetypically dependent (id). The legal approach to marriage is again indicative of the Alice in Wonderland logic exemplified by the persons cases; as Grigg-Spall and Ireland have argued, although marriage is legally theorised in liberal contractual terms, 'the social practices within marriage are formulated by the courts in terms of masculine authority and female dependence and subordination' (1992, p.127; and see Pateman, 1988, p.166), thereby actively fostering that subordination. Furthermore the marriage contract is not construed as one which is subject to legal remedy, since it was constructed as occupying a private realm 'a domain into which the King's writ does not seek to run' (Atkin, L.J. in Balfour v. Balfour (1919) 2 KB 571). Fredman has commented on the persistence of legal disabilities on married women until late into this century (1977, pp.44-57); indeed, it was not until 1991, in R, 4 All ER 481, that a husband's absolute right to sexual access to his wife was ended.

Correspondingly, although domestic violence, or 'gendered harm' (Graycar and Morgan, 1990) is widespread (Dobash and Dobash, 1980; Horley, 1986) and can be life threatening, scant attention has been paid to it until relatively recently, and the antecedents of this neglect is the common law power of husbands to 'correct' their wives (Fredman, 1997, pp.52-4). The continuing construction of the family home as a 'private realm', embodied in the common law doctrine of interspousal immunity, means that, despite the development of protective measures, there remains a reluctance to endorse civil law remedies. The law's continuing support for private patriarchy is exemplified by the infamous instances of judicial sympathy for men 'goaded' into murdering their wives (for example, Beaumont, 1992, Cr. App R (S) 270; and case of Graham Sherman, Guardian, 28 February 1990). As with sexual abuse and rape, responsibility for domestic violence is frequently explicitly or implicitly assigned to the women themselves who are routinely represented as situated at the whorish end of the whore/madonna dichotomy. Edwards discusses the various myths surrounding these crimes, such as exculpatory factors like alcohol which exonerate the male attacker, and female responsibility: '... decisions made by practitioners in the criminal process support these myths, judges frequently rely on them in their judgment and in decisions to reduce sentence with the result that mendacity on domestic violence is institutionalised in a legally reified form, reproduced by the police, by counsel and by the judiciary' (Edwards, op.cit., p.180). The remarks of Judge Raymond Dean in a rape case in 1988 provide an example: 'As gentlemen of the jury will understand, when a woman says no, she doesn't always mean it' (cited in Mills, 1997, p.10). One of our respondents, a specialist in family law, said that 'even now, few of the male practitioners in this area take domestic violence seriously. You still find the same sexism, the same outdated attitudes' (1997). The role of the legal curriculum in reproducing the legitimacy of such views, either by excluding women's perspectives altogether, or marginalising them in 'feminist legal studies' courses, can hardly be over-stated. As the American Association of Law Schools argued in 1972:

> Unless information on the legal rights and disabilities of women is included in the most basic law course, the nation's law school graduates will continue to have scant understanding of the legal restrictions under which 53% of the population lives (cited in Graycar and Morgan, 1990, p.23).

Underpinning all these instances of the law as a gendered phenomenon is the construct of the reasonable man - the universal voice of the 'Volksgeist'. The palpably false idea of a self-contained 'subject', separable from the constraints of historical time and power relations, remains fundamental to the Common Law and is illustrative of the presentation of a social script which obscures the assumptions on which it is based. As Edwards argues: 'subjectivity, which lies at the heart of the reasonable man, is constituted as universal and rests on particular and highly selective facts. The normative is male ...' (1996, p.3). The reasonable man approach also exemplifies the Common Law project to 'reduce the content of law to single, universal and quasi-scientific rules' (Martin, 1994, p.334). In this, it is entirely at variance with feminist approaches which have not only highlighted the falsity of this attempt at objectivity, but also, by contrast, seek to change the law so that it is able to recognise difference. 'A feminist approach to the concept of the reasonable person brings us back to the public/private dichotomy exposed by many feminist writers ... Those aspects of a person which are considered by the law to be private, such as personality, sexuality, reproductivity, relationships, are thought irrelevant to the process of law. Only public, neutral persons are recognised' (Martin, op.cit., p.353).

It is not only in legal ideology that the normative is male; the normative legal practitioner is also male. However, just as law presents that normative male as the universal voice of reason whose experience can speak for us all, so too workplace culture and working habits are regarded not as intrinsically male and socially constructed, but similarly neutral and largely unalterable; legal managerial culture, like the law, claims to be gender blind. As a result, implicit in the managerial culture of law firms is the social vision of its employees as autonomous subjects, equal before the law, and requiring minimal legal intervention; this is the legal counterpart of human capital theory with its view of preordained separate spheres, leading to differential investments by men and women, different choices as to specialisms, and career paths. Consequently the legal workplace is represented as an arena in which equal subjects will be treated with impartiality, and where such individuals can make certain choices, whilst in reality it is soaked in the prejudices which underpin gendered difference. Furthermore, this perfect market place is construed as a private sphere; the ideal being that of the family firm which requires no outside regulation, no legal intervention.

As we have argued above, the process of acculturation into this worldview, the acquisition of 'habitus', involving depoliticisation and the marginalisation of women's perspective, begins in the law schools, a point which was made by our student respondents. In illustration, one woman commented on the way the issue of provocation had been dealt with in Crime:

> On this course we debated about the battered women syndrome in crime - it came up in the defences to murder and nobody seemed to appreciate what it was about. The students said things like 'Oh Thornton is as guilty as hell - sitting around in her underwear' - they refused to address the issues, which are not flagged up anyway. (Mature law student, 1997)

As a result, when women feel inclined to challenge the substance and operation of legal discourse and practice, they face a powerful deterrent in the culture of the institutions through which the subject is taught and practised. This is the background against which women's increased participation in the profession must be set.

Rapid expansion: 1980 - 1997: a statistical snapshot of the national picture

The entry of women into the profession on a large scale coincided with other rapid and substantial changes, both internal and external: a period of expansion in the demand for legal services (Abel, 1988, pp.166-8), resulting in an overall growth in the number of solicitors with practising certificates; the transformation of the profession into one which was predominantly graduate (Skordaki, 1996, pp.15-6; Burrage, 1996, p.71); structural changes brought about by a greater involvement in services funded by the State (Sommerlad, 1995, 1996), and the transformation of the organisational structure of the profession, with the development of what has come to be called 'mega-lawyering' (Galanter, 1983; Flood, 1996; Hagan and Kay, 1995) - corporate firms with a smaller ratio of equity partners to assistant solicitors. As we noted in Chapter Two, this model of change has been replicated in other jurisdictions. This is demonstrated by the studies of Hagan and Kay (1995) and Thornton (1996), but, as Abel noted, expansion occurred in the UK later than in the United States and Canada, and with much greater rapidity (1988b). Whilst it is problematic to speculate on the causal link between these factors, it is important to recognise that their coincidence means that women joined in numbers a profession which was simultaneously engaged in a complex restructuring. This period of growth also coincided with a rapid expansion in service class occupations, some of which, like the finance and insurance sector in which women formed a major part of the payroll, were increasingly closely linked to the legal profession. Crompton and Sanderson's study of census data shows an increase of female participation in service class employment in the 1970's (that is, before the really large expansion of the 1980's) of 45 per cent as opposed to 16 per cent for males (1990, pp.163-5). The theoretical implications of this conjuncture have been considered in Chapter Two.

Figure 4.1 demonstrates the close relationship between women's participation, professional growth as a whole and the move from an 'apprenticeship' to a 'credentialist' model of training. Women particularly derived benefit from this transformation due to their tendency to outperform men in academic law examinations (Abel, 1988, pp.173 and 476; Lewis, 1996, p.69). Women have generally achieved better results both in Finals and Law Society Finals, now the Legal Practice Course (Law Society Annual Statistical Report 1990, p.33; Halpern, 1994, p.17; Law Society Annual Statistical Report 1994, p.69), and in several important respects their skills appear to be greater than their male colleagues; for example, in the context of legal services and the Single European Market, women's skills and interest in language learning appears to be at a significantly higher level than their male colleagues, as is their interest in European Community Law (Chambers and Harwood, 1990, pp.45-7). However, the superior academic qualifications held by women have not ensured correspondingly successful private practice careers.

Figure 4.1 Qualifications and gender in entry to the legal profession 1880-1985

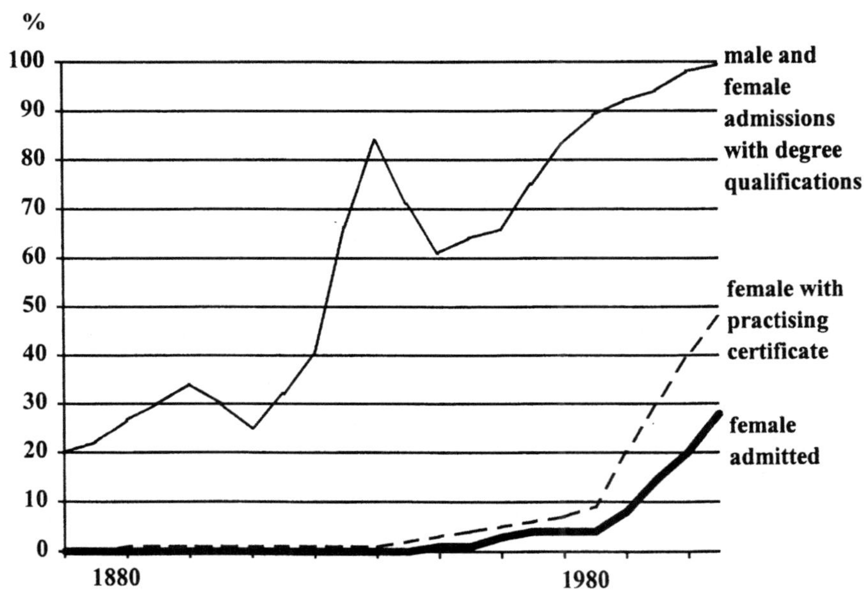

Sources: Abel, 1988; Skordaki, 1996

A range of studies, dating from the beginning of women's more substantial participation in the profession, indicated that women did not experience the same career trajectory as men. Podmore and Spencer (1982, 1982a, 1986) argued that women could be deemed to be engaged in a secondary labour market, with inferior earnings, resulting in part from the fact that they were channelled into areas of work which were professionally regarded as less 'important' (particularly by male solicitors), and that within particular specialisms, men were more likely to be involved in court work (1986, p.40). Their evidence suggested that the 'gender-typing' of work was strongly determined by essentialist views of women's innate qualities and capabilities, and that it was the stereotypical views of men, rather than the preferences of women, which were most influential, even where women might appear to have 'chosen' to work in a particular environment (op.cit., p.46). They also argued that women's progress up the career ladder was impeded by the expectation of male principals that they only intended to work for a few years before having children, and that therefore they were only ever employed as 'cheap labour' (1982a, pp.352-5). These findings were mirrored in contemporary studies of the USA: Rhode summarised these as follows: 'overall, female attorneys in the mid 1980's were less than half as likely as male attorneys to be partners in a firm, earned approximately forty per cent less, and were disproportionately represented in low prestige specialities' (Rhode, 1988, p.1179), and similarly attributed gender-typing to perceptual stereotyping (op.cit., pp.1188-9).

Furthermore, by the end of the 1980's, although women were entering the legal profession in equal proportions to men, large numbers were failing to stay. The Career Structure Survey conducted by the Law Society in 1988 indicated that of women solicitors qualifying in 1977 and 1982, 44 per cent and 26 per cent respectively were working part-time, and 18 per cent and 13 per cent were not working at all (Marks, 1988, p.1). This trend has continued; for example, the Law Society Annual Statistical Report for 1994 revealed that, on the one hand 53.5 per cent of students who enrolled with the Law Society in 1993-94 were women (1994, p.71) and 'women accounted for 53 per cent of new admissions compared to 44 per cent in 1986' (ibid., p.57); on the other hand it is also reported that women's participation rates were consistently lower throughout the age range, but particularly in the 31-45 age band where there was a difference of between 12 and 16 per cent (id., p.8).

The most recent figures available on women's participation clearly indicate distinctive features. According to the Law Society's Annual Report for 1996, women on the Roll are less likely than men to hold Practising Certificates: 26 per cent of women are without Practising Certificates compared to 20 per cent of men, a difference which could be explained by the obviously greater likelihood that women will take career breaks. However it is worth noting that the percentage without Practising Certificates had in fact risen slightly since 1994 (Lewis, 1997, p.11). Research commissioned by the AWS identified clear differences between the reasons offered by men and women for leaving the profession. Women were affected by factors related to child-bearing and rearing, in that 22 per cent mentioned childcare difficulties and six per cent mentioned their determination to put family first. The size of their families was not a significant factor (Bradshaw and Thomas, 1995, p.21). On the other hand women were also influenced by sexism in the profession (13.3 per cent), whilst being less likely to be affected by perceived age discrimination, stress and strain and disillusionment (op.cit., 1995, p.17).

Women are more likely to work outside private practice: 24 per cent of women as opposed to 18 per cent of men work in other fields, and women are particularly strongly represented in accountancy, nationalised industries, the advice services and the health services (Lewis, 1997, p.15). Within private practice, the Law Society's 'Omnibus Survey' found that women still tend to work in a narrower range of specialities than men (on average women would be involved in between two and three areas of work whilst men would be involved in between three and four: (Cole, 1997, p.9). In addition to measuring the spread of activities, the survey also looked at an index of 'specialism'; the concentration of 'time spent' on particular areas of practice. Women were more likely to be specialists (largely, the survey argues because of their lower age profile, as specialism is more common in the younger age band: op.cit., p.12), and in particular, were much more likely to specialise in the less prestigious areas of family law (op.cit., p.14) and probate (op.cit., p.15), though they also specialised in business and commercial work, which is, however, concentrated in the larger firms where partnership prospects are more scarce.

The overwhelming majority of women work as assistant solicitors (65 per cent of women as opposed to 26 per cent of men), and women are poorly represented in the figures for equity partnership at all age levels (Lewis, 1997, pp.17-8) as well as being only half as likely to have sole practitioner status. Although as Lewis argues 'the gap may be exaggerated because greater numbers of women take career breaks relative to men', the statistics on the status of solicitors in private practice by years of experience indicate that women's chances of partnership are not simply delayed, but are permanently impaired.

At each stage of the career path, women's earnings are considerably less than men's as research by the Law Society and the Trainee Solicitors' group has revealed. The Law Society's panel study of solicitors' firms demonstrated that the median earnings of women equity partners were £19,530 less per annum than their male counterparts. This discrepancy was also reflected at salaried partner (a difference of £7,210 per annum in median earnings) and assistant solicitor (£3,000 per annum difference) levels (Sidaway, 1997a). Whilst it was the case that, as argued above, the women included in the study tended to be more likely to work in firms which received a higher proportion of their income from legal aid (and which therefore tend to offer lower salaries), and also tended to be less experienced in terms of post-qualification experience, the earnings differential remained considerable even when these factors were taken into account. As McGlynn points out, this research undermines the human capital argument that salary differentials arise entirely as a result of factors which influence the later stages of a woman's career (1997, p.569). It is evident from the Law Society research however, that the differentials become more exaggerated in later career: whilst at assistant solicitor level women's average earnings are 88 per cent of men's, at salaried partner level they have fallen to 82 per cent of men's, and at equity partner, 63 per cent of men's (Cole, 1997).

A longitudinal study of the graduate law students of 1993 (conducted for the Law Society by the Policy Studies Institute) indicates that women's distinct career trajectory begins with the search for training contracts. Whilst overall, women were as likely to obtain training contracts as men (whereas members of ethnic minorities were not), they were less likely to be successful in the initial round of applications. Once they diverted their applications from private practice, they became as likely to achieve a training contract as men (Shiner, 1997, pp.68-80). This divergence of path makes it difficult to be sure of the situation in relation to earnings during training contracts. Gender does not appear to be a firm predictor of earnings, whilst factors associated with social class, such as parents' occupation, type of school attended, and location of higher education and training did: for example, Oxbridge graduates had better starting salaries (op.cit., pp.91-100), so the fact that gender does appear to make a difference in terms of first destination may be read as significant for subsequent earnings and career trajectory. Another study identified pronounced differences between men and women trainees: Moorhead found that female trainees were paid on average £779 per annum less than their male counterparts, and that there were three women for every two men on the Law Society's mandatory minimum salary for trainees (1997, p.3).

The figures on first destination may be one explanation of the greater numbers of women in non-private practice employment locations. The other explanation, which we discuss in Chapter Seven, is the greater flexibility, and the greater sensitivity towards equal opportunities' issues demonstrated outside private practice.

Concrete statistical data on the extent to which women have been affected disproportionately by the recession is not currently available. However, qualitative evidence is available. In July 1993 the AWS set up a helpline for women solicitors who had been made redundant or were threatened with redundancy because of the recession, as a result of the number of women who had been contacting members of the committee of the AWS with complaints about their treatment by firms. Callers recounted being affected in two ways: firstly, a number of women were simply being made redundant whilst on maternity leave, and secondly, they were being inhibited from taking equity partnerships because of the subsequent loss of rights to maternity leave.[9] During the period of the recession, availability of part-time work and other flexible working arrangements for women appeared to decrease, whilst the number of men in part-time work increased (Sidaway, 1995, pp.77-8).

The data we have reported here offers evidence which supports the notion that women are distributed across the legal profession in a pattern which is distinct from that of men. Hakim points out that patterns of vertical and horizontal segregation are more likely to be identified when detailed occupational classifications are available (1996a, p.150). Although the research by the Law Society offers the prospect of sub-dividing the 'profession' at some future date into more detailed occupational categories which would allow for testing for segregation, it is safer to argue that data on earnings and partnership prospects in areas of law distinguished both by type of firm, and, within firm, by type of work or specialism, indicate that the legal labour market is segmented, and that women are more likely to be found in the disadvantaged segments. Only more sustained evidence from longitudinal studies (like the Law Society's panel study) will allow for the really detailed analysis that could relate these patterns to general change in the occupation. For example, we have seen that women are more likely to specialise in business and commercial work in large firms, but because the development of these large firms is comparatively recent, we do not have sufficient evidence about how their internal labour markets are constructed. Hagan and Kay's work in Canada, which is longitudinal and based on multivariate analysis, would tend to suggest that such firms are constructing a secondary tier of employment for qualified lawyers with little prospect of partnership, and that women are tending to occupy this tier (1995) and this picture is borne out by our interview data.

The experience of our sample

As we have noted above, it was in the late 1970's and 1980's that women really began to enter the solicitors' profession in large numbers, though it was not until 1992/3 that women represented more than half the admissions to the roll (Skordaki, 1996, p.12). Our sample consists entirely of women who were admitted before 1990, when the first survey took place (as we explain in the Appendix, the 1994 cohort is drawn from the 1990 sample). They therefore represent generations of women solicitors who, if their careers had followed the 'normal' pattern, might by now expect to have achieved partnership. The length of time since admission of our sample, compared to the national statistics for 1994 clearly demonstrates the weighting towards greater experience.

Table 4.1 Years since admission of sample, compared to 1994 national figures for women solicitors

Years since admission	1994 (national)* (%)	Our 1994 sample (%)
0-9 years	68.25	39.7
10-19 years	26.1	51
20 years and over	5.56	9.2

**Source*: Law Society Annual Statistical Report 1994

Given the greater experience and age of our cohort, one might have expected a larger proportion of partners than national figures. However, the figures were broadly comparable, which might reflect either a sample selection bias introduced at the point of response (women who were partners might be less willing or able to respond to such a survey), regional variation (women partners and sole practitioners might be more common in the metropolis than the regions), or an age bias in the distribution of partnerships (it might be more common to offer partnerships to women in the 1990's than it has been in previous decades). As far as we are aware, the kind of national and regional data which would allow us to adjudicate between these alternatives does not exist. Therefore some of the quantitative data we discuss in the following chapters, should be read in the context of the possibility that our sample contains an over-representation of respondents who have been disappointed in their partnership ambitions, or never had such ambitions. In order to compensate for this possibility, we took particular care to recruit an above quota proportion of partners amongst the women we interviewed in depth.

Table 4.2 Current position of sample of women solicitors, compared to national statistics for women and men, 1994

Current position	1994 - male (national)* (%)	1994 - female (%)	1994 (our sample) (%)
Equity/salaried partners	59	26	32.3
Sole Practitioners	9	5	-
Assistant/Associates	32	67	67.7

**Source*: Law Society Annual Statistical Report 1994

It is worth noting that the Law Society statistics do not distinguish between equity and salaried partnership: we found that the distinction was a very real one for our respondents, in terms both of remuneration and authority and autonomy within the firm, and several of our respondents expressed the view, both in interviews and in 'open' responses on the questionnaire, that the post of salaried partner was not only gendered, but had virtually been 'invented' to accommodate women, and that the position was purely 'token'.

Our respondents were asked to identify the areas of the profession in which they had practised since qualification, and again some comparison with the national picture is possible, though our figures include all the areas women had practised in (and therefore the column totals more than 100 per cent), and include women who had never practised, whilst Law Society figures include only the current position of those holding practising certificates.

Table 4.3 Women and the different areas of legal practice, 1994

Area of practice	National all solicitors (%)	National women (%)	1994 response* (%)
Never practised	-	-	1.3
Private Practice	83	78	91
Local Government	4.16	5.7	11.5
CPS	2.6	3.9	2.6
Business/Commerce	5	6	7.7
Court System	0.4	0.4	2.6
Teaching/academic	0.125	0.19	17.9
Other	4.7	5.81	10.3
	100	100	

* Respondents could select more than one option: total > 100%

The figures are broadly comparable, and the differences reflect the distinct sampling frames from which the two datasets are drawn: the Law Society's figures being based on the current position of women in practice whilst our regional sample included women out of practice, and previous areas worked in. The greatest area of over-representation in our sample appears to be teaching, but it should be noted that law teachers are not required to maintain their practising certificates unless they teach on the Legal Practice Certificate, and so this area of the profession is undoubtedly under-represented in Law Society figures. The fact that 91 per cent of our respondents had practised in private firms at some stage is to be expected, given that private practice is the logical starting place for most legal careers, and that it is likely that once practitioners have left for another area, such as in-house lawyering in business and commerce, or teaching, they rarely return to private practice.

The samples in both research cycles included women in the three categories of women in practice who had not taken a break, women out of practice (both those taking a career break and those without any plans to return), and women who had returned from a break, as follows:

Table 4.4 Employment history and status of sample, 1990 and 1994

Category	1990		1994	
Women returners	30	(13.2%)	18	(23.3%)
Women in practice	101	(44.6%)	20	(25.9%)
Women out of practice	95	(42.2%)	39	(50.6%)

The variation in the figures between the two dates could be explained either in terms of sample bias or life-course factors. Although it proved harder to identify women out of practice in 1990, their contact addresses proved to be more stable than those of women in practice, many of whom had left firms for destinations their previous employers were unwilling to release: therefore more of the non-respondents may have been women in practice who had not taken a break. However, the skewed age profile of the sample in 1994 might well account for the increased proportion of returners, and possibly, the increased proportion of women out of practice as women either took, or returned from breaks for child-rearing.

Women who had taken career breaks had done so, in each stage of the research cycle, overwhelmingly for reasons associated with child-bearing and rearing.

Table 4.5 Numbers of women in and out of practice taking breaks, 1990 and 1994 (percentage of total sample in brackets)

	1990		1994	
Only one break	31	(13.7%)	29	(37.6%)
Two breaks	18	(7.9%)	19	(24.7%)
Three breaks or more	4	(1.76%)	2	(2.6%)
TOTAL	53	(23.5%)	50	(65%)

There was a tendency to take comparatively short breaks for maternity. Of all the 'first breaks' taken by the unified sample of 1994, 22 per cent were less than six months long, whilst the proportion of breaks less than six months for second and third breaks rose to 33 per cent (and 42 per cent were less than a year). All of those taking short breaks fell into the category of women who either had returned to work or intended to. A number of women in the 1990 sample had returned to the profession after breaks of surprising length: 11 respondents (37 per cent) had returned after breaks of five years or more, and in four cases the breaks were of more than ten years. As we shall argue later in the book, these examples tend to belie the human capital theorists' assumptions about the influence of skill decay on women's careers.

Conclusion

Our summary of the experiences of women today in the solicitors' profession bears out the picture expected as a result of our theoretical analysis in Chapter Two. Whilst the greater levels of participation by women since the 1980's have meant the end of the profession's status as a horizontally segregated occupation, there remains a clear degree of vertical segregation on grounds of gender, in terms of access to senior posts and higher earnings, and a marked degree of internal segmentation, with the work most commonly undertaken by women differing in kind. Women and men appear to have characteristically distinct career trajectories, and this fact can only partly be explained by life-cycle factors. There is some evidence that women are disadvantaged or discriminated against when financial pressure is created by external economic factors or by structural changes in the profession.

The kind of evidence we have used in developing a statistical summary clearly has its limitations. As Hakim argues 'survey datasets never contain information on (these) hidden social processes that have profound effects on women's career success' (1996, p.184). We have therefore complemented the statistical picture by the preceding discussion of the historical legacy of the law as a male-dominated profession, and an account of some of the processes which have supported informal exclusion. In particular we have considered both the role of legal training and the nature of the law in terms of their impact on the practitioner. We have argued that the law adheres to a worldview which, whilst presented as unitary and objective, is constructed upon difference, and the separation and devaluation of women and the private sphere. This characteristic, together with the assumption of having a unique claim to one truth, means that the differences and inequalities it entrenches (of gender and race amongst others) cannot be formally recognised in such a way as would allow for social adjustment with the objective of attaining a more substantive equality. We have then proceeded to argue that this feature of the law is replicated in the professional paradigm - in attitudes, and in ways of working. Since this is combined with the ideology of legal liberalism, the legal workplace is presented as an impartial arena in which equal subjects are free to make their own choices, free from outside regulation. In the following chapters we will examine this claim in the light of our data.

Notes

1 It appears that only one of the early entrants came from a non-legal family (AWS Archive).

2 The experience of a prominent contemporary woman solicitor indicates that little had changed by the early 1990's: 'in 1991, when she became a member of the Law Society's Council, she went to the cloakroom marked "Council Members only". She went in and it was full of men. But it says "Council Members ... where's the toilet for women Council Members?" There isn't one, she was told. The nearest was miles away in the basement. Pembridge refused to budge. She used the men's room until an equivalent facility was provided for women. It took five years' (Weale, 1997, p.7).

3 The practice of shifting responsibility for excluding women onto the client, has, according to our female sample, become a common, and largely unjustifiable, tactic, and is touched upon again in chapter six.

4 See also the experience of women at the Bar: Helena Kennedy (1992), and Holland and Spencer (1992), pp.11-12.

5 In fact this perspective was actually articulated by one senior partner in 1994, when explaining that they had made their only female solicitor redundant in 1991, because 'she was a luxury we could no longer afford' (general practice).

6 It is the tradition of regarding articled clerks as cheap labour which the Law Society has sought to address in reforms to the vocational stage, including the minimum salary and the local monitoring systems for articles introduced in 1985 (ACLEC, 1996, p.133).

7 For a historical perspective on this 'gendering strategy', see Smart (1992).

8 We have used the male pronoun when discussing the judiciary since it remains an overwhelmingly male body: for instance, out of a total of 2,862, 307 members of the judiciary are female, and these are overwhelmingly concentrated in the lower ranks. There are no female Lords Appeal in ordinary, one female Lord Justice of Appeal and seven women High Court Judges as opposed to 89 men (Communication from Lord Chancellor's Department, 18 September 1997). Reform promised by the Labour Party, of the present appointment system, which is characterised by secretive patronage, has

been successfully beaten back by the judiciary; as a result it is estimated that at current rates of appointment it will take around 100 years for the gender balance to equalise (Travis, 1998, p.13).

9 Private communications with Alison Parkinson of the AWS, 23 May 1994; and Judith Willis, who maintained the helpline, 6 June 1994.

5 The Men's Room: Cultural Capital and the Fraternal Contract

Introduction

Based on an analysis of both the data generated by the responses of male lawyers, and the observations of female solicitors, this chapter focuses on the current culture of the legal workplace, and the extent to which it may still justifiably be described as resting on a 'fraternal contract' (Thornton, 1996).

We have argued that a primary cause of the continuing subordination of women lawyers as a category, despite the evidence of their generally good technical credentials, lies in the related constructions of women as domestic and the solicitor as male. Furthermore, we have stressed that, as a result of its personalist or clientelist nature, the profession requires of its members not just technical skills and legal knowledge but also cultural, and, specifically, relational capital (Dezalay and Garth, 1997; Galanter and Palay, 1990, p.768; Hanlon, forthcoming). Consequently the individual solicitor needs to demonstrate the kind of social knowledge and ability which is a sign of eligibility for patronage. This sort of cultural capital can not be accumulated simply through formal study, but requires participation in complex forms of socialisation and 'initiation rites', many of which revolve around masculine culture. As a result, arguably masculinity per se remains *the* core cultural capital of the profession,[1] largely because this in turn assists the professional to build up the relational capital which is vital to a firm's survival.[2] In illustration of this point, we consider the contradiction between employers' claims that their management strategies are guided by meritocratic and impartial principles and the evidence that practices such as networking, mentoring and cloning continue to characterise both private practice and male relationships in the wider legal world of, for example, business contacts and the criminal justice system (Bankowski and Mungham, 1976). This complex of masculine relationships, of which the legal partnership is the most concrete expression, then does not only impede women's inclusion and/or progression, but actively reproduces the sexual contract on which they are based.

It is recognised, of course, that the ongoing restructuring of the profession has resulted in an increasing diversity of types of practice, and that some of these have, in varying degrees, detached themselves from the stereotyped gendering of mainstream culture with which this and subsequent chapters are concerned.

Law and the legal workplace

This focus on the nature of private practice today has been preceded by the discussions in previous chapters of the importance of law in the constitution of the legal professional, of legal culture and indeed of social reality generally. As Foucault has argued, law is a primary tool in the construction of social categories (1980). It is a disciplinary grid which constructs the 'microphysics of power'; of particular significance for women lawyers, perhaps, is law's contribution to the ideology of motherhood (see Smart, 1992; Fegan, 1996). Furthermore, as we discussed in the preceding chapter, the legal discourse in which lawyers have been schooled is designed to socialise them into hierarchical ways of thinking (Duncan Kennedy, 1992), into 'useful and docile bodies' (Foucault, 1979), and is argued to be essentially male (see for instance, MacKinnon, 1987; Fineman and Thomadsen, 1991). Law is concerned with social classifications based on power relations, and is, as such, a primary source of the hierarchical and gendered construction of the traditional law firm. At the same time however, one of the ways law's hegemony is achieved is through its construction as neutral (for example, both gender and race blind) and rational, and we have argued that this ideology is also reproduced in the employers' self-proclaimed commitment to impartiality and rationality in their employment practices.

Two caveats to the stress on the importance of law must now be entered, however. Firstly, it seems that once formed by legal training, and inculcated in such common law ideologies as 'separate spheres' and liberal legalism, substantive law, as a potentially conservative and discriminatory mode of thought and expression, is perhaps of less direct significance for the legal professional than other, informal expressions of masculinity. Just as the law firm requires not only formal legal skills (human capital) but also cultural capital, so too its ethos and practices find expression and succour not only in formal law, but also in the networks of personalist relations which characterise the legal world and which we have discussed in Chapters 3 and 4. This culture of personalist bonds is broadly antithetical to bureaucratic rules and procedures, and, like the common law in the Persons cases, tends to subvert the modernising and equalising potential of anti-discriminatory legislation, which it resists, by-passes or flagrantly breaches in the course of its reproductive process. Illustrative of Bourdieu's observations of the 'legalist illusion' (1990a), which masks the fact that everyday life is largely characterised by non-legal strategies, and by the breaking or bending of rules (Harris, 1996, p.3), we found that a common feature of the legal workplace was a cavalier disregard for formal procedures, and laws, and even, on the part of some practitioners, a fear or dislike of and, as far as possible, a disengagement from, substantive law. When we examine the structure and workings of legal practice then, what we are concerned with is an expression and endorsement of masculine culture which, although at times revealed and reinforced by law, is also expressed in many non-legal ways, and which finds greater resonance with the culture of common rather than statute law. Indeed, we have argued in Chapter 3 that it is possible to theorise the law firm as belonging as much to the private, patriarchal sphere, as to the public sphere (see Bridgeman and Millns, 1998, p.24).

Secondly, it must also be noted that whilst we argue that the legal professional is constructed as male (Smart, 1989; Sommerlad, 1994), and have also posited a tight link between the culture and ideology of law and the culture of masculinity, both of these cultures have multiple faces. Just as the law should be understood not as a static expression of social relations but as a fluid, contested ideology and discourse, so too, masculine culture is not fixed, but similarly contingent. For instance, the masculinity embodied in certain traditional, small town general practices tended to differ, in some respects, from that of the large commercial firms (corresponding, to some extent, to the differing modes of professionalism each type of firm exemplified). It may well be, therefore, that the patriarchal ideology and practice found in the legal world requires a typology, since we encountered a spectrum of modalities ranging from the protective and paternalist, and, at the other end, cultures which exemplified liberal legalism in its most individualist, macho form. Nevertheless, these are simply variations on the essential theme of masculinity, which continues to be characterised by common professional attitudes, networks and practices. Consequently, masculinity remains the core cultural capital required of the legal professional, even though there are a variety of linguistic modalities or markets in which that cultural capital is exchanged and realised.

As a result, even whilst it is being challenged, the existence of what Thornton (1996) has termed the fraternal contract continues to be revealed in various ways; most notably, in the persistent importance of male bonding as a way of doing business, both within and without private practice, in the continuing domination by men of the professional body (the Law Society[3]), in the symbiotic constructions of the lawyer as male and the female as 'other', in the silent, or perhaps unconscious, condoning by the profession of a sexual regime which comprises a spectrum of behaviour ranging from unspoken pressure on women to assimilate through to sexual disparagement and harassment and, finally, in the very structure of partnership.

The fraternal contract and the nature of partnership

There is an organic connection between the nature of partnership, legal practice and the fraternal contract. We have argued that the presentation of law as technical, neutral authority, both masks the extent to which legal rationality embodies patriarchal structures and networks, and also obscures the fact that legal practice is as much about business custom and establishing and utilising clientelist relations as it is about employing legal knowledge and skills (Dezalay and Garth, 1997). This last point is illustrated by the reflections of many of our respondents on their work; for example, one solicitor who had also been an academic was told: 'well you'll be one of the few round here to know any law' (1990), whilst the partner of a general practice commented: 'law rarely rears its ugly head in practice' (1994). A senior corporate finance partner of a multinational law firm said: '50 per cent of the work I do involves a specialist knowledge of the law and 50 per cent is about understanding the business imperatives of any situation ... and establishing good personal relations' (1997). A male property specialist from the same firm commented: 'I like the political aspect to my work; there's very little law involved which is fine, and a lot of policy - lots of negotiations ... It's as much about building personal relationships as anything ...' (1997).

A consequence of the fundamental importance of personal relationships,[4] is that social or cultural capital is crucial[5] both collectively - for the law firm as a cultural entity so that it may accumulate professional credit and safeguard client relations[6] - and, correspondingly, for individual solicitors who must be perceived as having the 'right' cultural capital so that they are able to contribute to, rather than endanger, the firm's professional reputation. However, as Hagan and Kay have noted, legal cultural capital is very vulnerable: 'professional reputations and client relations are fragile cultural commodities ... A result is that the cultural form of legal capital, especially its reputational and relational forms, generates a hyper- (but nonetheless rational) sensitivity to potential devaluation' (Hagan and Kay, 1995, p.30), and they have summarised Gilson and Mnookin's (1985) identification of three major sources of vulnerability as 'the propensity of labouring lawyers to shirk responsibilities, grab assets, and/or leave' (Hagan and Kay, 1995, p.30). Clearly a further source of vulnerability derives from the potential devalorisation of the firm's collective reputation by non-conformist employees; for instance, ones who do not have the social origins, networks, gender or ethnic background 'appropriate' to their firm. Let us now examine these points more fully.

Because it is a formalised personal bonding of individuals, partnership has traditionally proved an effective structure for both constructing relational capital and for guarding against the risks to it identified above. For example, the mechanisms of apprenticeship traditionally ensured the loyalty of the trainee to the firm, in part by promoting its cultural homogeneity (Sugarman, 1996; Burrage, 1996). That patron-client relationships were once the primary mechanism by which professional closure was achieved was discussed in the previous chapter; here we may illustrate this phenomenon by citing the experience of a male solicitor who was articled in the late 1930's: 'I had an entree through my father, who was a client. I was the only articled clerk who wasn't related to one of the Partners. That was how it was done ... it was a question of having someone ... who could act as a sponsor ... it was all done through personal contacts ...' (1997).

Today, although the great expansion of the profession and the development of the degree route have significantly diminished the importance of blood ties, legal partnership is still characterised by patronage and personalist relations.[7] An indication of this and, therefore, of the requirement of individual solicitors that they possess the appropriate cultural capital was provided by the questionnaire responses of senior partners which were characterised by a recurrent emphasis on 'gut feeling' as the main guide to selecting and promoting staff, and the continuing prevalence of 'word of mouth' as a recruitment method. In 1990, for 60 per cent of the firms surveyed this was the most popular way of obtaining staff; in 1994 this figure had declined to 50 per cent.[8] A female equity partner of a medium sized general practice recounted in 1997: 'We have taken on people before now who are known personally to Partners - through the golf club, rotary, etc. - invariably male ... I made the point that if you're going to appoint people, it should be open, done properly by advertising. But as far as my partners (all male) are concerned, the case in question is always a special case ... in the matrimonial department, the partner had written on one application "he plays golf - we'll interview him"'. The same woman then referred to the importance of the 'old school tie', and continued: '... the right school and class background are still important for men, because they have so many applications, you have to have some kind of criteria ... if you don't have the safeguard of clear objective criteria - then you will have criteria such as "he plays golf, went to a school I've heard of" etc.'.

The route to partnership similarly relied, and relies, on patron-client relationships, and, as we explore in the following section on mentoring and networking, solicitors spoke in terms of the need 'for support', or having to be given 'the breaks'. Such support exemplifies the personalist nature of partnerships, for, in their paradigmatic form, these are constructed on a neo-feudal exchange of allegiances (or as Duncan Kennedy phrased it: 'allegiance based on expectation' 1992, p.61). The traditional private practice exemplifies Kennedy's observations on legal training (id.) discussed in Chapter 4: a strictly hierarchical small family business, headed by a patriarchy, in which loyalties are exchanged and long hours extracted from junior practitioners, as part of the test of fitness for the possibility of eventual admission to the senior brotherhood (see White and Jenkins, 1995). Thus, according to a female commercial solicitor: 'People come and work incredibly long hours, market hard both inside the firm and out - because you have to show commitment, and that's the way you get sponsored' (1994).

In the classical paradigm, patronage promotes loyalty, and hence safeguards the firm's cultural capital, and may again be seen as developing quasi-kinship ties, so that it is the 'sons' who inherit the position of the employing 'father(s)' (White and Jenkins, op.cit., p.64). As a result, even the large firms still, as it was phrased in The Lawyer: 'prefer their partners homegrown' (Olive, 1992, p.17). This was how one male solicitor, discussing law firms in Hull in 1997, explained it:

> You can see in the lower echelons of firms which haven't amalgamated - so their tight knit familial structure hasn't been disrupted - the mirror images of the people higher up as they choose assistants. In the firm I was articled to they were trying to find someone to shadow the senior partner; eventually - after years - the right person was found and it's him - the senior partner - only 30 years younger; he's unmarried like him, he even looks like him. He had the same interests, even before he came into the firm, and far more so now that he's been formed by the firm. He even carries the same gabardine over the same arm. I saw them the other day - they could have been father and son. The senior partner was denied the dynastic approach to succession because he had no son of his own, so he's adopted this man - it's very common.

Another male lawyer, a partner in a small general practice in a large town said: 'Good personal relationships are the major factor in our approach to recruitment as well as promotion. You just gravitate towards similar minded people; we have four Jewish and one non-Jewish Partner and we're all male. It's not that we only want Jewish male Partners but we have a lot of interests in common and ultimately I suppose you choose people on that basis, people like you, who will understand where you're coming from, so you get firms with gender and racial homogeneity' (1997).

The remarks of other male managing partners, from across the spectrum of firms, supported this analysis of partnership; for instance in 1994 one explained: 'In the old days it was in the nature of an old fashioned gentleman's club; the questions when recruiting and promoting used to be "were you clubbable?", and then, "is there a business case for this appointment/promotion?" ... if your face didn't fit you wouldn't get partnership' (1994) and whilst this partner (of a very large commercial firm) was categorical that, despite these observations, his firm's practices were now entirely objective and transparent, other lawyers told a different story. A female equity partner at the same firm explained that even though there were now procedures in place designed to ensure greater objectivity in personnel matters, such as official lists of attributes required of candidates for partnership and staff assessments: 'it still, ultimately, comes down to a matter of people's subjective opinions' (1997).

Others argued that nothing had changed but that lawyers had learned to use the rhetoric of equality;[9] for example: 'I noticed an advertisement in our local paper on the lines of "a firm which is striving to be an equal opportunities employer seeks an assistant solicitor". I subsequently bumped into the senior partner of this firm and joked about it, saying "I didn't know you were striving etc. ..." Anyway, he said, "yes, we certainly are - we're very equal opportunities now, as long as they're white, male and under 30"' (male academic, 1997).

As these observations indicate, the personalist nature of partnerships is not only designed to foster loyalty, but is also a form of cultural reproduction, which is in turn a further guarantee of group stability and hence an informal barrier to incomers. At the same time, the resulting conformity to a particular 'brand' of service protects reputational capital. Such homogeneity is hence a crucial aspect of the firm's collective cultural capital and therefore of practice development and client retention, since it is considered that the loyalty of clients may be retained through a firm's familial structure and through their experience of continuity within the partnership, both in terms of the actual personnel of the firm, and also in terms of type. This was indicated by several solicitors from small towns who commented on the traditional allegiances of their clientele: 'here it's old family connections which determine where business tends to go ...' (1994), and a male sole practitioner from a rural area explained: 'People know the firms in this area, and they know therefore what sort of firm it is;

I personally have been with this firm for over 20 years, and this firm has been here for 200. We have traditional clients, families who have been coming to this office for generations because it is their firm, they know and like what they are getting' (1994). Furthermore, even though large firms no longer have these traditional client followings, it is nevertheless important for them too, to develop a 'house style'; as one woman corporate lawyer explained: 'to get taken on by *, you have to have the * look, to be a * (name of firm) sort of personality' (1994).

Obviously, given the traditional masculinity of the profession, and of the majority of its clients in important specialisms such as corporate and criminal law, this conformity is likely to perpetuate both numerical male dominance and the professional masculine ethos (see Mills, 1997); with the result that however excellent women's human capital, it is likely that few of them can possess the appropriate cultural capital (masculinity, or pseudo-masculinity being the core minimum) to be selected above associate level. This persistence of professional closure was succinctly put by a former female equity partner of a large firm: 'Part of the problem with women making partnership is that the face has to fit and the criteria set are fairly masculine' (1997).

As a result, however, the majority of women are now able to fulfil the useful function of transient foot soldiers to the profession. As is implicit in the preceding discussion, partnership ambition is integral to the constitution of the professional, and to the structure and culture of partnership. It is both a test of quality, commitment and loyalty as well as a mechanism for extracting these attributes;[10] thus one woman remarked: 'the criteria for selection of partners are totally unclear. You don't know where you are and they milk that situation for all it's worth ... nothing's written down, you just have to work incredibly hard, promote yourself in the firm and get known ...' (female commercial conveyancer, 1994).

However, the great expansion of the profession in combination with the trend to increase profitability through the employment of a higher ratio of non-partner practitioners to partners (see Coopers and Lybrand, 1996) has made partnership an increasingly unrealisable goal for many; as a male associate in a large commercial firm observed: 'I don't think they expect many people to stay in the long term ... our staff turnover is 25 per cent per annum ... there's a general churning over in law' (1997). This represents a major threat to the classical form of partnership and raises one of the dangers to a firm's cultural capital identified by Gilson and Mnookin (1985): namely, that assistants and associates will leave taking clients with them. The managing partner of a medium sized commercial firm considered the development of the salaried partner position as an attempt to re-work private practice organisation, which he compared unfavourably with the more complex hierarchies characteristic of the corporate world: 'partnerships are very flat structures, and that's an increasing problem, because equity partnership is therefore the main goal for everyone and not everyone can make it; consequently the development of salaried partnerships is desirable because it puts in place another rung in the promotional ladder' (1994) (see also The Lawyer, 5 May 1992, p.17).

Such positions though, were regarded by many of our respondents as 'a sop' and 'a token' (especially since women seemed to be their principal occupants), and equity partnership appears to remain *the* aspiration, especially for men (Halpern, 1994). Consequently, the presence of a large proportion of practitioners who are never in the race for partnership, either because they will ultimately be pushed out, or because their cultural capital will be judged deficient, or because many may themselves not wish to make the sacrifices currently judged necessary to achieve it[11] (Heaney, 1992, p.16), is extremely useful.

The traditional solicitors' partnership is also being undermined by other factors (for instance, see Wall and Johnstone, 1997); nevertheless it is evident that both personalist relations in general and the fraternal contract in particular continue to operate as significant underpinnings of the profession, which in this way retains an essentially pre-modern form. Thus Dezalay and Garth do not only stress the continuing importance of kinship ties: '... law firms are often small enterprises where family ties and an appropriate apprenticeship count as much as academic learning', but also argue that 'the multinationals of law are themselves built on precisely such connections ... They have become machines for producing and accumulating social capital' (1997, pp.111-2). The following reflections of one woman lawyer confirm this picture, indicating that even large commercial partnerships, which have in many ways moved away from the classical paradigm towards a more bureaucratic, corporate structure (Larson, 1977; Paterson, 1996; Flood, 1996; Roach Anleu, 1992), do indeed continue to be complexes of male-dominated personal relations. She had gone from being a partner in a large commercial practice to company secretary of a PLC and found her current working environment far less discriminatory; here she considers the ways in which some of the obstacles to female success are embedded in the nature of partnership:

> Because it's a partnership, there's no one person in charge of promotions, instead, different partners have their proteges, and that's when what I call the gender history - the shared gender understandings - comes into play. In other corporate organisations the overall strategy is the business objective; with a partnership it is too, but the attainment of that objective is more complex to measure. Profitability is key ... and people are valued according to their personal billing abilities. And at the outset someone makes the decision to see if you are someone who is going to generate that cash. But the measurement of individual performance within a partnership structure doesn't depend on measurable objectives ... There are now generally appraisal systems in place in most firms, but I'm not sure how closely these are related to overall business objectives and how objective they are. Partnerships encourage that gender history ... you can see it with mentoring ... most partners are still male and because of the shared gender history most of them feel better about promoting another man (1997).

The American case of Ezold v. Wolf[12] casts an interesting light not only on the systemic indirect discrimination described by this respondent, but also on the contention that it is possible to conceptualise many law firms as private spheres, ideally untrammelled by state intervention.[13] Nancy Ezold sued her employers for denial of partnership grounded in sex discrimination, and won at first instance, the court finding that she had been impermissibly discriminated against by the virtually all-male partnership. However this decision was overturned on appeal, the court finding that the denial of partnership was a business decision and as such entitled to be based on wholly subjective factors. In the absence of direct evidence that the subjective standard was unequally applied, the court held that such decisions are not subject to legal regulation.

Since the internal operations of the professional workplace of both the United States and the UK are characterised by a marginalisation of law and privileging of social relations,[14] this case is of more than mere academic interest. The opacity and subjectivity of recruitment and promotion decisions in this country is neither a secret nor particularly condemned; in an entirely uncritical article in the professional press, readers were advised:

'Given the unusual nature of partnership, which combines the roles of worker, shareholder and manager, it is not surprising that the selection process retains an element of mystery ... The results of a breakdown in the relationship can be extremely messy ... It is likely ... that there will always be a strong subjective element in how partners are chosen. In other words, does your face fit ...' (Olive, 1992, p.17).

The familial, personalist nature of partnerships makes it easier for employers to operate informal, ad hoc procedures not just amongst themselves, but across the board, and to disregard legal and professional requirements to be equitable (Rosenberg et al, 1993; Pringle, 1989), in their determination to exact conformity to partnership norms. In 1990 one of the most striking aspects of the data generated from the responses of our employer sample was their lack of concern with employment law vis-à-vis their own employees. For instance, 38 per cent of the sample stated that they were unaware of the Law Society's guidance on Equal Opportunities, and one senior partner of a medium sized, urban general practice said: 'Whatever may be the equality of the sexes, it still seems to be that women will follow men. Their (the men's) career progresses ... if I'm honest about it and I actually analyse what happens when you are talking about employing staff in the first place ... I ask, are you married/engaged, etc. And you are told you shouldn't ask questions like that. It goes against the ethos of proper methods of employment, etc. It's probably against all the employment legislation as well ...' (1990).

Later on in the research this picture had changed somewhat, presumably because of the implementation in 1995, in the face of some opposition (Sage, 1993, p.19), of a practice rule requiring all practitioners to adopt an Equal Opportunities policy. Nevertheless there was evidence even in 1997 of firms breaking the employment legislation in a variety of ways. According to a male partner of a large town general practice: 'I personally know of lots of women who have been asked questions - and we're talking of current practice - about having children, getting married and so on at interviews, and I know of men who admit asking those questions. Some of them don't seem to even know that they're illegal, and others don't see why they shouldn't ask them anyway' (and see McGlynn and Graham, 1995). Correspondingly many of our 1997 female respondents - from across the range of practices - claimed to have been quizzed about plans for maternity and marriage, or to have been made redundant whilst on maternity leave (and see Ward, 1996, p.24), or shortly after asking about firm's policies on career breaks. This picture was further confirmed by the stories of women who have called the AWS helpline, referred to in the previous chapter, which has been in operation since 1993: 'Calls have come in from all sectors, firm sizes and locations, but the vast majority are from women in private practice whose employers take a cavalier attitude to breaking the law on their own employee rights' (Willis, 1996, p.2).

On the other hand, in the UK greater legal protection is afforded employees who feel able to challenge discriminatory practices than in the USA. For instance in Bamber v. Fuji International Finance PLC (1996)[15] it was found that Ms. Bamber was treated less favourably on the grounds of her sex by the respondents in the way she was afforded access to opportunities for promotion, training and other benefits. The tribunal considered that there could be no explanation for failing to promote her other than prejudice. Nevertheless, the discriminatory practices and structures characteristic of partnerships, discussed in this section, rarely result in legal challenge. This must be in part because, in addition to facilitating discrimination, the personal structure of many firms makes it correspondingly hard for women to challenge discriminatory cultures, practices and decisions; for instance, writing about sexual harassment in law firms in the United States, Mucciante found that 'women are not often likely to object ... because of the fear that they will alienate a mentor' (1991, p.15). This was also a finding of the Reynell report on the UK legal profession; even though 49.5 per cent of the women surveyed felt they had been subjected to sex discrimination, 20 per cent to workplace bullying, and 29.6 per cent to sexual harassment, 'the majority did nothing. Some moved jobs ...' (Reynell, 1997, p.19). Our research only uncovered three women who had taken action because of discriminatory treatment. One, a former employment specialist with a City firm, recounted how, following a period off work as a result of a still-birth, the firm to which she had, in her words, 'given seven years of my life ... working 11 hour days and marketing', attempted to manoeuvre her into resigning when she became pregnant again. When she made it clear that she was prepared to resist this 'the reaction of the employment partner was to go berserk, because I was clearly raising sex discrimination and the possibility of constructive dismissal. There was a showdown during which they revealed how outraged they were at the idea of me making *legal* allegations against them

… other Partners weren't even speaking to me because of this, and even now, if I see some of these people they cut me dead …' (1997, her emphasis).

Thus one result of the fact that workplace relations are not, despite the rhetoric of classic contractarianism, in actuality so much contractual as personalist, means that anger is the likely response if a solicitor tries to use legal rights to combat discrimination. For instance this was how a black woman lawyer described the reaction of her employers (a large general practice) when she took them to an Industrial Tribunal: '(The head of my department) … was obviously so angry that I had actually dared to use the law against them …' (1997). Consequently recourse to law may produce ostracism, both within the firm, partly because colleagues are, in the words of this woman: 'too scared to support you openly' (and see Smerin, 1995, p.6), and in the wider professional world. In this way, the personal networks of professional society represent powerful deterrents to a formal defensive challenge: 'Legal practice is a small world. Threats that if a woman attempts to assert her rights she will receive no reference are common … in one case a woman was told by an independent local employment lawyer that if she fought, neither she nor her solicitor husband would have jobs in the area' (Willis, 1996, p.2).

As these stories indicate, another way in which the nature of partnership is revealed is in the language used to discuss personnel issues. Indicative of working environments characterised less by bureaucratic procedures than by personalist relations which revolve around loyalty as much as the cash nexus, reactions to, for instance, resignations, requests for maternity leave, wages, or promotions were frequently expressed in emotional, rather than formal, terms. One such term, which frequently surfaced, was that of 'betrayal'; for example, in her discussion of a colleague's application to return from maternity leave as a part-timer, a female equity partner said: 'my fellow partners regard it as a betrayal, which is how it was also put to me when I left *' (1997). A male practitioner connected such reactions to the web of relationships which made up the legal world, and to the significance of such relational capital: 'leaving and changing jobs is seen as a serious betrayal because of all the importance attached to … (client) networks … I've got a very good friend still at * (name of former firm) and he gets into trouble if he associates with me' (1997). Nor was the following description by an assistant solicitor of her boss's reaction to her pregnancy atypical: 'After an initial friendly reaction, he completely excluded me and by the end wasn't talking to me at all ... it's very common - it's the idea that you've let them down and that the firm owns you ...' (1994).

The suggestion of ownership expresses the neo-feudal nature of partnership, which was obliquely referred to by one commentator when, in a discussion of the prevalence of sexual harassment within the profession, she spoke in terms of such 'behaviour (being regarded) as normal or "droit de seigneur"' (Dyer, 1994, p.18; and see Pringle on the master/slave element underlying bureaucratic relations, 1989, p.90). An even more striking example of this approach to the employer-employee relationship is provided by the evidence that firms have suggested to pregnant solicitors that they should have an abortion (Willis, 1996, p.2).

Finally, other commentators on the links between the structure of partnerships and barriers to women emphasised the fact that law practices were small businesses (and see Johnson, 1989 on the employment practices to which small businesses tend to be susceptible). For instance, in the 1994 survey some firms which had generally appeared favourable to women and open to employing them as returners, claimed that concrete measures were 'impractical for small businesses'.[16] The senior partner (of a medium sized commercial firm) contributed to this argument about tight financial constraints and also explained that issues are personalised to a degree in partnerships in a way that they are not in limited liability companies: 'the problem is that within partnerships, women's pregnancies are not just hidden in the balance sheet as in larger organisations - it's a problem of small businesses. We are in business to make money and as partners we work harder than assistants, and if you're working harder for less you resent it - so there is open resentment of our female partner who is taking maternity leave - for me there will be a personal cost of around £40,000 as a result of her pregnancy; it was put on the agenda at the partners' meeting and we said openly "we can't have this as a small business"' (1994).

Some employers referred to a range of constraints on partnerships which limited their potential manoeuvrability; for example the managing partner of a medium sized, small town general practice explained: 'What you've got to appreciate is that this is a small business ... it's a different organisation from, say, a local authority where people can slot in and out easily ... we run a tight ship ... we do not have the capacity ... therefore to give career breaks … we don't carry a surplus staff … also our clients know us personally, so we must have continuity' (1990). Similarly a male equity partner of a general practice emphasised the small scale of his partnership both in terms of the numbers of staff, and the tightness of office space: 'as Partners you live in and out of each other's pockets, the offices are small, there's only a few of you, you can't have major differences … you must have good personal relationships' (1997), whilst a woman who had been an equity partner in a small firm said; 'you have to be so close - in effect I was married to five men' (1994).

These last comments leads us into the homosociality (see Collier, 1998) blending into behavioural distortion, which tends to result from such closely bonded personal cliques, especially where there are either no women of comparable status, or they are in the minority (see Kanter, 1977; Hearn and Parkin, 1995). Many of our respondents provided examples of this; for instance a woman recounted her experience of general practice: '* (name of firm) gave me a lump sum not to go back! From a colleague point of view I was never accepted; it was very male and they had this social thing going - lots of after hours drinking to which I was never invited, and they would play boyish pranks on each other … I was just completely excluded' (1994).

A particularly striking account of this informal social closure was given by the male office manager of a four partner, small town general practice which was all male, apart from the support staff:

> When I came here - with a background in retailing - I got a feeling of a very male working environment, and that they were reluctant to bring women in. I suppose they were quite sexist and said things like 'we don't want women stepping on our toes' … I think also they like discussing men's things … swearing … joking … also they've said 'they have a lot of emotional problems though, don't they women' … I'm working on them and they're quite young - in their 30s/40s … their wives work … but it's a man's world and if we had a female partner I think it could be a problem … could upset things because they've got a close working relationship at the moment (1994).

This picture was confirmed by a female solicitor who had trained with this firm, but had then left a few months after qualifying:

> the partners weren't that old but they were very conservative ... sort of 'oh my God, women have got into the profession - help!' and 'but I suppose we better get one'. They all used to belong to all these male only things - Round Table, Masons, etc. By the end I just didn't want to be there. They kept all the good cases and gave me bits and pieces - I was excluded - just cheap labour ... they used to go out drinking together. It was a boy's club and they just didn't really want me there. (General practitioner, 1997)

In summary then, a partnership may be viewed as a web of relationships which, in part because the profession is historically male, remains largely male both in composition, and in ethos. The common practices and culture through which these relationships are then realised and reinforced will be examined in the following sections.

Mentoring, cloning and male bonding and the nature of partnership

A central feature of cultural capital is that it involves the value judgments of others; thus it is crucial that a Partner recognises and values an employee's cultural capital, because promotion remains largely a matter of patronage and sponsorship. In their questionnaire responses in 1990 and 1994 employers implicitly refuted the charge which is frequently levelled against them of engaging in the mentoring of males, claiming to appoint and promote on merit alone; in short, as Hagan and Kay have remarked, legal employers are human capitalists (1995, p.12), whose proclaimed value rationality is purely that of business. However, clearly the assessment of what constitutes 'merit' must be a value judgement, and as we discuss below, will contain elements of assessing whether the mentee will 'fit in'. Furthermore, in interviews the personalist nature of partnerships was generally acknowledged, and the practices of mentoring and networking frequently referred to by both the partner and non-partner respondents cited in the preceding section.

The kinship culture of partnership is actively expressed in the organisation and deployment of power through instrumental and social cliques (Rosenberg et al, 1993), and in the practices of mentoring and networking. In the words of one woman: 'You have to be pushed forward, helped if you want to get on. I mean you have to have a mentor, a patron' (female academic, 1997). The significance for professional success of patronage, in combination with the maleness of the profession, has led some to advocate the development of female mentors.[17] For instance, the (male) senior partner of a medium sized general practice wrote: 'It's a traditional profession which is still very male dominated and reliant on networking and "who knows who". Women must learn these games and develop their own to counter them' (1994). However, since in substance such 'games' constitute one of the principal exclusionary mechanisms employed by white male professionals against outsiders, it would appear far preferable to work towards the exposure and eradication of such insidious discriminatory forms of bonding, and the culture which sustains them. In any event, as Laura Cox has noted: 'mentoring rarely works for women … it is no substitute for the development of more flexible policies and procedures in chambers and solicitors' offices' (1997, p.18).

When we consider the practices of mentoring and networking, we are not talking of a formal system, in that they rarely take the form of open, bureaucratic procedures (which could thus be open to challenge). Sometimes the assistance and sponsoring *is* concrete and overt, but more often it is simply that the careers of some are favoured, as opposed to, and often at the expense of, others, through the mobilisation of the web of relationships which comprise partnerships. Such assistance generally takes the form of work opportunities, for instance types of cases given, training offered, support for individual practice development initiatives, and so on, and its significance becomes particularly apparent at the promotion stages of a career, although the process frequently begins during articles.

Clearly, assisting individuals with their careers is not necessarily discriminatory unless the criteria upon which decisions to mentor are based, are opaque and subjective and favour one group over others. As we have argued above, because of the maleness of the profession and the pressure within partnerships for cultural reproduction, this is precisely what tends to happen. As a result the great majority of our female respondents considered mentoring and networking to militate against the inclusion/promotion of women, since the individual favoured was far more likely to be male than female.[18] For instance one woman (an employee of a large commercial firm) in commenting on the absence of transparent procedures and criteria for achieving partnership, both of which enhance the importance of obtaining a sponsor, said: 'Men are more likely to get the opportunities, or are more acceptable to the partnership anyway than women' (1994). Another remarked: 'To succeed you have to work hard and have excellent legal skills, but you also have to get on with the Partners, and they're nearly all male. So it's a male culture that you have to penetrate in some way' (1994). Others endorsed this cultural perspective; 'it is a very male culture ... there seems to be this male affinity, male bonding. You could see that most of the partners did get on best with other men. What's more, as a result, this male culture was self-perpetuating. I experienced it personally' (academic, 1997).

One male solicitor made it clear that he consciously engaged in this office culture: '... during my office time a fair amount of it has to be spent maintaining relationships within the firm' (1997), whilst the female company secretary quoted earlier commented on some of the difficulties for women in making such relationships: 'normal topics of conversation between men and then between women are different - they operate on a different wavelength. There is a gender history to these different social interactions which is inescapable. You see it now with little boys learning to talk about football ...' and she emphasised again that these shared, gendered understandings had a particular significance in law firms: '... being put in a position where you can contribute to the overall profitability of the Partnership through billing is crucial, and that's where you see the difference between the sexes - i.e. through mentoring, promotion - it's only after you've been promoted and are able to bill in your own name that you can really succeed ... The chance to shine is not often available and often depends on a fluke - hitting it off with a Partner who has good work to distribute' (1997).

As this woman remarked, the 'shared gender history' is frequently expressed through the common discourse of sport which is one of the key markets in which male bonding and hence mentoring occurs: 'with a typical cross-spread of men you have to talk about football or rugby ...' (male solicitor, 1997). Sporting interests indicate that the man will be, as one woman argued, '... one of the lads - you know it's all about sport - so he (a sporty newcomer to the firm) will make it' (1997). Another woman (also from a large commercial firm) argued that both sport and mentoring remained important keys to male success: 'It's definitely still much easier for men - even mediocre men - to succeed. You need a mentor, and men get sponsored more often. We've had a new guy start here and the partners are saying that he's got the right potential - he's six feet tall, plays Rugby Union for * - and now they're saying that they've got this new, dynamic team - meaning him. In fact he's just average, but the corporate team like him - he's clearly one of them' (1997).

Additionally, sport is an important forum for making contacts. A male practitioner explained its role in his landing a traineeship with a large multinational firm: 'I had a friend whom I played hockey with who was quite a senior partner at * and fairly early on I asked him about … articles. I got an interview and was offered articles … when I hardly knew the difference between civil and criminal law … I don't think I would have succeeded at a more formal interview' (1997). Interestingly, the senior (male) Partner in the corporate department of the same firm asserted, in 1997, that the recruitment of trainees was an entirely meritocratic procedure, undertaken by an outside body of consultants, however, as is evident from this account, such practices, precisely because they tend to be informal, and because they are so embedded in the personalist culture of the profession, generally survive the implementation of formal procedures and systems. For example, a female equity partner in another large firm explained that when it came to promotions the system of individual partners sponsoring a particular candidate had been retained, so that 'you can't get away from individual value judgments, although now a proposer has to write a proposal justifying their choice of candidate' (1997). Another woman, speaking of her time with another large commercial practice which had also instituted systems with the stated aim of overcoming discriminatory personnel practices, said: 'I think in fact that at * the process of selection for promotion was entirely arbitrary and favoured men - for instance the 'system' of promotion to partnership in the mid-30's (assistant solicitor, 1994). A woman who had worked at the same firm testified too to the continuing importance of mentoring in such firms: 'One partner at * was very nice, but in a very paternalistic way and if you worked with him as a woman you knew you wouldn't get on because he wouldn't push you forward at partners' meetings, give you good work and so on' (academic, 1997).

This picture was confirmed by an equity partner of an all male five Partner general practice: 'when we choose someone, either as a trainee or a solicitor, or promote someone, we have to get on with them, so I suppose we choose people like us, who have the same interests' (1977), and the managing partner of a large commercial conglomerate acknowledged that '... there are problems of male sponsors appointing people in their own image ...' (1994). In fact this tendency to cloning was alleged by a management consultant to be even characteristic of large City firms, supposedly in the vanguard of the bureaucratisation of working practices: 'Even when they have procedures in place, these don't necessarily result in the appointment of more women, because often such firms are very inward looking and there is essentially a reproduction process when it comes to promotion; after all, the legal workplace is very conformist, very concerned with the suppression of difference and the cultivation of particular manners and styles of conformity'(1994).

However, this routine privileging of the male at the expense of the female is not simply an aspect of the male relationships which dominate private practice. In addition to the strong likelihood that men rather than women will be mentored within the firm because of their overwhelming predominance amongst the professional elites, their shared 'gender history', and the simple equation of maleness with professionalism, the fraternal contract in its wider ramifications is also sustained by the male networks which continue to flourish outside the firm and which further bolster the position of men. For being 'in with the lads' does not just mean the lads within the firm, since patron-client relationships are also characteristic of the wider networks in which lawyers participate - and currently must participate - as part of their professional lives, and which are similarly harmful to women's career trajectories.

Such networks provide a major constituent of the value basis of the profession, expressed by one woman as 'the camaraderie between men'. A former City lawyer talked of 'the maleness of it all which really does discriminate against women - part of it is that it's still men who make the rules, form the patterns of how it's done - partly it's the maleness of how business is done - whilst drinking in bars - probably even making deals in the gents' loos' (1994). Another used the term 'male club' both to refer to one of her former firms as well as to the wider business world in which its practitioners had participated. The following section will consider this male club.

Male culture, mentoring and practice development

It is evident then that the personalist culture of partnerships, and the resulting practice of mentoring, form part of a wider system of clientelistic relationships which are crucial aspects of professional life. That this has long been characteristic of legal work is illustrated by the discussion of personalism in Chapters 3 and 4 (and see Birks, 1960, pp.275-6). Both male and female respondents testified repeatedly to the continuing vitality of such relationships. Two examples from opposite ends of the spectrum of practices serve as illustrations. An assistant solicitor in small, rural, general practice said: 'there's still a lot of old school-tieness - I mean old boy's school-tieness - in the profession - you know, having a public school background, men sticking together, background socialising; you've got to be able to participate in all of that, play golf with the client, work on your clients by moving on the social side' (1994). Similarly, a male practitioner from a large commercial firm described a typical working week in the following way: 'I'd say that I would work two kinds of days; one 8am till 6pm, and another 8 till 2am, but the billable work is mainly done 8 till 6, and you're often marketing in the evenings ... three or four nights a week and then two or three times you have to go out for long lunches ... building relationships with clients ... there's huge pressure to get on with clients' (1997).

Since engaging in these relationships is increasingly acknowledged to be a core lawyering activity (Leigh-Kline, 1998, pp.60-61), it frequently involves the firm in a formal capacity. Such official marketing encompasses a wide range of sponsored events including seminars, lectures, business lunches, cocktail parties and cricket matches, and is generally called practice development (PD[19]). However, the term practice development is also used in connection with the after hours socialising/networking in which professional males have traditionally engaged. Such activities, hard to identify as social or work, are nevertheless also regarded as key to building up and maintaining cultural capital, illustrating the seamless linking of different forms of male bonding. The resulting confusion between work and business emerges in the comments of one woman who defined practice development as 'socialising with people in order to get their business - it's about making friends' (commercial conveyancer, 1994).

These points are further illustrated by the description by a male respondent of the sort of practice development he was engaged in:

> There's a lot of entertaining, a lot of drinking ... You have to make the client feel that they've had a really good evening, a really fabulous time that they'll remember. Most men go to get drunk, have a laugh, pick up a woman. They go on trips to places like Newcastle, Amsterdam, Barcelona and the aim is to get drunk and pick up a woman ... If you let your hair down with someone, you know you can trust each other. If you've gone to a club, got drunk, fallen over and one of you has tried to get off with a woman, and maybe hasn't succeeded, then there's more trust ... (Former insolvency practitioner, 1997)

He then went on to explain that such trust was essential to building the male networks on which much legal business still appears to depend, and was related far more to the personal bonds established in this way than to legal skills, because these meant that a reciprocal relationship was established as clients: 'trust you to look after one another. It's not about trusting your expertise in law, that's lower down the list. ... trusting you to see them all right is a higher priority' (see Granovetter, 1985; Hanlon, forthcoming).

This man's comments also reveal the fact that the 'camaraderie' established by such activities is indeed largely male, for it is evident that the markets in which relational capital is invested and exchanged (practice development) remains extremely male in all its aspects, from the nature of and forums for many of the events to their culture. For instance, many commented on the heavy drinking involved: 'all these functions are very alcohol related' (1997), whilst some linked this to an increasingly macho tendency: 'you have to be able to drink an awful lot over a long period of time - it's very competitive' (1997). Others emphasised both the nature of the activities and the kind of male behaviour it appeared to engender: 'There are often problems for women because of the types of events; for instance there was one where the clients were taken go-karting, and after a while the only woman there dropped out because the men were getting so competitive' (former equity partner, female, 1997).

There are numerous different forums in which practice development takes place, some of which are formally male exclusive, and many of which involve sport.[20] Some socialising was specifically built around individual partner's networks, and that this was generally the case in more rural areas was indicated by many solicitors; for example, according to the (male) senior partner of a two-partner, small town general practice: 'many local solicitors see it as important to belong to the Round Table or the freemasons and also possibly to be active in a local political party, as well as cross entertaining with other professions and would make all this a continuation of their habitual, social life, for instance, playing golf ...' (1994), and another, a (male) sole practitioner, explained: 'in a country area, the choice of solicitor, if not linked to existing ties, is then generally made through recommendation or personal contact made in a social environment - so it's important to be active in the community' (1994).

Partners in large commercial firms presented the process of practice development as far more scientific, however other respondents from such practices referred to similar processes: 'My (City) firm had 30 partners and what happens is that every partner has contacts - belongs to various associations as well as to informal networks - and these generate events nearly every night, that they know about, are involved in/invited to as a result of belonging to these networks ... for example, some exhibition, a cocktail party, or seminars followed by drinks ... you would go along, as a team, to these ...' (female employment specialist, 1997). And whilst the male corporate partner of one international commercial practice denied that informal social links remained a factor at all in generating business for firms such as his, and placed more emphasis on practice development in the form of seminars, this account was contradicted by other practitioners from the firm. For instance, a former insolvency practitioner (male) from the same firm said: 'In the insolvency department at * about 15-20 per cent of the time was spent in attracting clients/marketing, but it was about 50 per cent of the importance ... The insolvency world in * is a very small one - there are about 40-50 accountants practising in insolvency - a set pool - and you've got to get out there and make friends, build links ...' (1997).[21] Similarly, the senior (male) partner of another major commercial firm commented: 'I think there's still a huge amount of business done at football and rugby matches, days out at the races, etc.' (1994).

In fact the growing acknowledgement by many that the capital of social relations (Dezalay and Garth, 1997, p.125) is as important as legal ability (see Leigh-Kline, 1998, p.61) appears to be resulting in its professionalisation, so that it is becoming officially incorporated into the area of legal skills. Consequently it is now the subject of articles in the professional press, and an area of concern and interest to educationalists (Stebbings, 1994) and to legal consultancies. An illustration of this, written by a director of a communications and design consultancy and former Head of Communications at the Law Society, is quoted at length because it provides an excellent example of what is expected of many lawyers today. In an echo of Dezalay and Garth's argument, the article is summarised as 'More law firms now recognise that social skills of their fee-earners can radically impact on the bottom line':

> Firms regularly ask for training to hone their interpersonal and presentational skills to secure a piece of business for which they are competing ... I recently dealt with a project ... (which) involved a young partner in a City firm whose legal skills were excellent. The culture of the firm was to socialise with important clients, sometimes moving seamlessly from a business meeting to drinks and dinner. This worked well in cementing working relationships and was congenial for all but the young partner. He operated efficiently in the work environment but when bottles were uncorked he made excuses and left. He found it hard to make the necessary small talk around which relationships are built, and generally behaved in a closed manner - an attitude that could prove an obstacle to career advancement and the ability to win and retain clients for the firm ... It became clear that the young partner was not fully engaged in the *legal* process. (Stapeley, 1996, p.38, our emphasis)

The significance placed here on practice development, reflecting in large part the increased competition for clients, was confirmed by many respondents, both partners and employees, so that 'ability to get clients' was frequently cited as one of the most important criteria for partnership (and see Epstein, 1981); in the words of a former practitioner (male) with a large commercial firm: 'To be the most valuable ... you have to build up your own client base, so you have to be very active in practice development. ... For instance, you have to ring people up ... invite them out, get involved in lunches and dinners, and with local groups like the Round Table or the Rotary Club ... generally be active in the sort of environment where you meet fellow business people' (1997). A woman partner from a general practice explained that it was also about fulfilling a role in the community: 'to make partnership - you need to get to a stage where you have a profile amongst people and get asked to do things and those jobs show that you've broken through the ceiling - joined a sort of elite from whom public figures are chosen. It's part of becoming part of a circle within which influential people meet' (1997).

In fact many solicitors expressed the opinion that socialising and networking were as, if not more, important than legal competence. A male academic and former solicitor said 'I often say to students, for instance when we're looking at interpersonal skills, "it doesn't matter if you're the worst lawyer in the world, you'll be made partner if you bring in work through the door"' (1997). Another man (a solicitor from a large commercial firm) endorsed this view, and expressed a positive dislike of the formal legal side of his work. Another illustrated the point by explaining that the higher you rose, the less law you did: 'Marketing, getting and keeping clients is the most important thing, so that's what you have to show when you're aiming at partnership - women are often the fee-earners who do most of the technical, legal work' (1994).

As this last comment reveals, men are perceived as being more likely to be able to succeed in this arena than women. As a result, according to many of our female respondents, average legal skills are acceptable in men, providing they fit in and can therefore be seen as also having the qualities to attract clients; in the words of a former female equity Partner, speaking in 1997: 'I can think of someone in my department who has just been made partner, mostly because of his work getting abilities which is a result of going out for drinks with the lads. So he's not a brilliant lawyer, but he fits in, and he's got a client following and that's the rationale for making him a partner' (1997).

In other words, the qualifications lever may facilitate women's entry, but will not necessarily assist in overcoming informal barriers, one of which is the male culture of the solicitor's world: a vital component of solicitors' cultural capital is their ability to participate in this male culture, so that they must either be male or acceptable pseudo-men.

Male bonding - business or pleasure? The integration of the public with the private

'He found the work stimulating and rewarding, but he was less certain about the way in which it encroached upon his private life. While he continued to go home at the end of each day, he could continue to believe that he had an alternative life elsewhere ...' (Stapeley, 1996, p.38). These last remarks by the consultant cited earlier highlight another facet of the informal male networks which emerged from our data, and which illustrate how the sexual contract works in practice: the, as she said, 'seamless' integration for men of the private and the public spheres, of friendship and of business. As a former employee of a large City firm observed: 'the men lived the partnership - that's their world - their friends and their business contacts - it's all connected' (female academic, 1997); or, to paraphrase Lomnitz and Perez-Lizaur (1987; cited in Dezelay and Garth, (1998) p.124), it appears that the personal and professional lives of the male solicitor find their raison-d'être in each other. This was commented upon by another woman who contrasted men and women in this respect: 'I think women tend to separate friendship and business. I would rarely discuss business with a friend but men do on social occasions. In my general experience men do tend to generate business from friends - my husband does - it's a completely different attitude' (female salaried partner, 1994). Another woman whose husband was also a solicitor made a similar point: 'My husband has regular nights out with business associates ... they're sort of social occasions, not strictly P.D. events' (academic, 1997). Of course, the merger for professional men of many of their leisure pursuits with their business activities is both facilitated and justified by women's servicing role and men's exemption from responsibility for the domestic sphere (Seron and Ferris, 1995); thus one woman commented: 'working long hours and all this socialising ... it's all an excuse to avoid child care'[22] (female equity partner, Legal Aid practice, 1994).

A male practitioner with a large commercial firm, who identified himself as an outsider, also commented on the essential congruity for many men of work and leisure: 'To be a successful solicitor - to make partnership - you have to really commit the whole of your life to it - social life, everything - family life - it all becomes secondary, not only because of the long hours demanded, but because of the psychological framework which exists here. If they go to things at weekends they're always looking at people as potential clients - in other words, all other aspects of life are integrated into work life. Lots of solicitors, for instance, go to sporting and other leisure events with clients. The majority of their time in fact is spent pushing and promoting the firm ...' (1997). Explicit adherence to such open-ended availability (a point which we will return to in Chapter 7) is correspondingly crucial (and in this way male bonding and the notion of commitment functions together as powerful exclusionary mechanisms): 'A friend of mine went to a client do in * and took his wife and there she was saying "N... and I put work second" and N... was horrified because this was in front of a client, and the partner said "that may be your way N... but it is not the * (name of firm) way"' (male commercial lawyer, 1997). Another man explained how his life was affected by the need to network: 'I went to a colleague's stag do and it was all clients. The pressure completely absorbs your whole lifestyle - I'm out three or four nights a week ...', and it emerged that this meant that every Friday night he went out drinking until the early hours with colleagues and clients - 'with the lads ...', even though the relationships with these people never 'get beyond business ... no way do they become real friendships ... yet it's still about bonding, which you can then pick up on the next week or later' (commercial specialist, general practice, 1997).

A further facet of the integration of the private sphere with the world of work was illustrated by the following account of the wife of a solicitor who was aiming for partnership:

> I now have to do some practice development with my husband as his wife. For instance there's a murder weekend coming up at * Castle. It's a venture between my husband's firm and a firm of accountants - a joint entertaining thing for a combined set of clients. I don't really want to do it ... but it would be a bad mark for my husband if I didn't go. I think it may be a test as to whether they make him a partner. In other words, I think that if as a package we perform in the right way it will be in his favour ... I mean if we say the right things, wear the right clothes, use the right knife and fork, are generally acceptable, fit in ... I don't relish being there all weekend with clients and all us ladies having to do cookery demonstrations ... but I don't think I really have any choice about whether or not to go - it was clearly a three line whip ...
> (Academic and former practitioner, 1997)

The men's room

Some male solicitors,[23] with comments reminiscent of those of the female company secretary on the 'gender history', stressed that the male bonding which is such a central feature of most practice development is also sustained by a common discourse. As she observed, a prime example of this is provided by sport. According to one man, whilst making professional contacts is often achieved through 'golf, playing rugby, football, cricket ...', it is also the case that even at non-sporting events, because the 'majority of business clients are male, and because you have to engage in small talk ... you have to talk about football or rugby or cricket or whatever ...' (planning lawyer, large commercial firm, 1997).

However, other men spoke, unprompted, of the unifying bond of sexist language, which they alleged was characteristic across the spectrum of practices. For example: 'Law is still very male dominated. You see that in lots of ways. For instance, if you go into the solicitors' room at the Magistrates Court it's still a virtually all male preserve, even in a town this size. If women do come in they have to adapt to the laddishness of it all. There you hear really crude sexist banter, but then you also hear all these really racist remarks, some of which are also very sexual. For instance, I've heard people saying about their black clients "I bet he's got a really big nob" ... And of course it's also part of this shared boys' culture which involves other parts of the criminal justice system too, for instance with coppers as well, because they're really bad like that too' (equity partner, general practice, 1997). Other men made similar observations; for example: 'If you go into the advocates' room it's very male dominated both numerically and also because it's like a boys' school common room. They're all telling each other dirty jokes and being fairly obnoxious ... groups of male solicitors gather there and that kind of talk is rife ... boys looking out of the window at, and commenting on, whatever woman is passing in a very sexual way - building site culture ... the clients can be like that too ...' (associate solicitor, 1997).

A black woman from the Crown Prosecution Service also referred to sexist behaviour and language, and argued that it was to be found generally in the profession: '... the atmosphere at the Magistrates Courts is less like a men's club than it used to be. There is still all this sexist and racist banter though. For instance I was sitting in * no. 1 court and one of the men made a stupid, sexual joke about women, but I just ignore it or sometimes even join in ... I think the thing about the legal profession is that there's also a lot of stereotyping of women. For instance I often hear derogatory remarks - often about older women too' (1997).

Both women and some men made it clear that this sort of culture was also to be found in large commercial firms; for example, 'I have overheard conversations ... crude discussion of female solicitors ... of women in general' (male commercial lawyer, 1997). An example of such discussion was provided by a woman from a multinational firm: 'you hear the male fee-earners talking about all the female trainees - they do it quite openly. Generally discuss their appearance; I even heard one lawyer once say "I'd like to give her one"' (1997). Another commercial lawyer (male) remarked: 'Most men are sexist. Why do I say that? because I perceive that to be the case ... often it's very intangible, but it's also because there is always sexist conversation amongst men' (1997). Interestingly, some respondents, both men and women, also considered that the laddish culture epitomised by the crude sexism of some forms of practice development and by the discourse described above, was flourishing rather than receding:

> I remember one male partner ... he was always talking about sex, drinking, etc. What's more that particular very laddish culture - of which he was an exponent - is taking over ... it seems to be taking over from the old, more gentlemanly style of male culture ... and these very aggressive commercial firms which pioneer this type of thing - they're not ashamed of this laddish culture - even though some of its manifestations are disgusting ...
>
> (Female academic and former practitioner, 1997)

Conclusion

According to Jack and Jack, 'in subtleties of custom, structure and decorum, law is still a man's game' (1989, p.935), and, following the work of Rosenberg et al (1993), we may view the legal culture we have discussed above as both characterised by masculine values, (whilst professing its essential neutrality) but also, consequently, operationalised so that these values are actively reinforced, and alternative values excluded. As a result the majority of women, as the perceived bearers of these alternative values, are excluded from the professional elites and generally restricted to areas which have been constructed as compatible with such values.

Furthermore, as Epstein argued many years ago, it may be that rather than the resulting occupational segmentation being eroded, there has occurred instead a perceived need to mount ever more effective boundaries against female intruders, magnifying sexist behaviour so that it functions as an effective mechanism of exclusion (1981). Arguably therefore, there is a link between the apparent accentuation of masculinist culture and the networks which sustain this, and the incipient sexualisation of the workplace (Pringle, 1980; Hearn and Parkin, 1995; Filby, 1992; Adkins, 1995); both may be viewed as aspects of a response by the male profession to an increased female presence and competition. Perhaps the increased commitment which is generally demanded may be similarly viewed as, in part, a form of closure; for instance the explanation put forward in 1994 by the managing partner of a large commercial firm for the culture of long hours did not focus on client demand, but rather on the machismo of certain male solicitors: 'the people in that department - company - are over endowed with testosterone ... greed is good, lunch is for wimps'. Hence, rather than feminisation, are we witnessing masculinisation of the profession? In the chapter that follows we will consider this question further through a discussion of the impact on women of the professional culture and structure which we have examined above.

Notes

1. This is not to deny the evolution of markets which now specifically require the cultural capital of femaleness, or ethnicity. Despite the emergence of these niches, the profession as a whole continues to require white maleness. The discussion below reveals the narrowness of acceptable maleness.
2. The long-standing importance of building up personal ties in order to attract clients is commented on by Birks, in his discussion of the profession in the first decades of this century: 'Membership of the local council, charity committees and sporting clubs, or even becoming a church warden are activities which may prove professionally profitable' (1960, p.275). For Granovetter (1985) such ties enable individuals to establish order in their market activities.
3. In September 1997, the Law Society council had 11 women members and 59 men.
4. And see Morison, J. and Leith, P. (1992) who similarly argue that the informal, social relations which underpin the life of a barrister are more important than technical legal skills and knowledge.

5 'More than legal technique, therefore ... social capital ... is essential' (Dezelay and Garth, 1997, p.112).

6 An illustration of this is provided by a 1997 survey carried out by Legal Recruitment Consultants, which took as its starting point the views of employees on corporate image; 82.1 per cent considered that their firm enjoyed a high reputation (Reynell, 1997, p.8).

7 Similarly, a study of sex equality at the Bar and in the Judiciary revealed both to be characterised by patronage and discrimination (Holland and Spencer, 1992).

8 See Campbell, 1989, p.7 on the inequitable and inefficient nature of this approach to staffing.

9 This point has also been made by a woman practising in the City (Richardson, 1991, pp.25-6).

10 The following remark by a female associate was typical: 'People here know I'm not aiming for partnership and it is seen as a character weakness ... they think you can't be motivated enough' (1994).

11 This female assistant's view was quite common: 'I don't think many women in this firm have partnership aspirations because it would be exceptionally difficult to balance partnership with children' (1994). Others emphasised their desire to have some quality of life; some stressed that they *did* have partnership ambitions but not in their current firms because of the price that would be extracted.

12 Ezold v. Wolf, Block, Schorr and Solis-Cohen, 983 F 2d 509 (3d Cir. 1992).

13 O'Donovan (1985, pp.29-30) has argued that the workplace, as a part of the public sphere, has been subjected to extensive legal regulation in contrast with the private, domestic sphere. But in the general failure of such regulation to re-shape the world of employment to allow for the equitable participation of 'carers', the private sphere may be conceptualised as extending into this area of civil society. Hence the private sphere may be viewed as constituting not just locations, but social relations (Bridgeman and Millns, 1998, p.24).

14 Studies of the profession in all the common law jurisdictions reveal a picture which appears to be virtually identical with our findings; e.g. on the USA, see Brockman (1992), Foster (1995), Kaye (1988), Gross (1990), Epstein et al (1995), Rhode (1991).

15 Miss H. Bamber v. Fuji International Finance PLC (1996) IT No. 28081/94/LS D5268. Other cases have found inflexible working patterns to be discriminatory; for instance, see Robinson v. Oddbins Ltd. (1996) Discrimination Case Law Digest No. 4224/95.

16 The justification for these claims was somewhat undermined by the fact that the survey also revealed even smaller firms in the same city, with similar practices, which did have in place practices such as career break schemes and part-time working. Another small practice which was prepared to act on its stated commitment to equal opportunities commented: 'if people are worth having, it's worth giving career breaks' (1994).

17 For instance, this is recommended by some American lawyers; see Roberta Cooper Ramo (1997). It has also been advocated by the organiser of the Women's Lawyers Conferences, Margaret McCabe.

18 Similarly, less than half of Reynell's respondents considered that opportunities for advancement extended to all fee-earners, and over a quarter of the women surveyed felt

restricted in the work they could handle, a third were dissatisfied with the extent to which they were involved in business development, and 23.8 per cent of them felt they had insufficient client contact (1997, p.10). See also Heaney (1992) reporting similar findings by The Lawyer survey of women partners.

19 Referred to in the USA as 'rainmaking'.

20 This is interesting given the connections frequently made between sport and law; for instance see Menkel-Meadow (1989a). Jack and Jack have argued that 'competitive sports supply the first stage of prelaw training' (1989, p.935).

21 It is of course important to emphasise again the differences between types of firm and areas of law. Clearly practice development will hardly feature at all for some solicitors, whereas for others, such as insolvency practitioners, lavish corporate entertaining appears to be an important part of their work. However building relationships remains extremely significant for all lawyers, and a matrimonial specialist from an urban legal aid practice said that even her firm routinely engaged in entertaining, for instance of CAB workers.

22 We shall return to this issue below, in our later chapter on Commitment.

23 This seems an appropriate point at which to emphasise once again that whilst we are talking in terms of categories, we do not assume all women, or, in this case, all men to share these characteristics or views. Several of our male respondents quite clearly dissociated themselves from many of these forms of male bonding and discourse.

6 'She's All Right for a Bird': The Accommodation of Women

> ... in terms of the profession generally, I think that the more women you have, the greater the threat to the male hierarchy - so the more hostility there is - and even less inclination to make any accommodation.
>
> (Male partner of a general practice in a large town, 1997)

> Women today in the profession? ... the firms need them, because there's so many qualifying now and often they are the better candidates, we see that, and they look good, so they wheel them out at corporate do's etc. ... young women are accepted as long as they ... have the figure and the looks - all that is really exploited by some firms. My niece, she worked for a top City firm and walked out - said she didn't want to be forced into behaving in that mode. For instance she had been sent off to the Middle East on one of their big cases and said her role was partly to look gorgeous all the time.
>
> (Female academic and practising lawyer, 1997)

The proportions of law students who are now female and the quality of their credentials (see Lewis, 1997) has forced the solicitor's profession to admit them in growing numbers during the last 15 years (Roach Anleu, 1992, p.403). One result has been the claim, made by both men and women, that gender bias is eroding and that the remaining obstacles to women are mainly related to the nature of legal work, clients' demands and female biology. It is therefore argued that it is the market which requires that women assimilate, and which prevents the profession from modifying its working habits and structures, and that it is a matter of individual choice whether women are prepared to adapt in order to meet these demands and hence succeed or follow the dictates of their biology (Rhode, 1988).

The question of the immutability of working patterns (Mossman, 1994) and of unconstrained choice (Menkel-Meadow, 1989a) will be directly scrutinised in the following chapter on career breaks and commitment. Here we are more concerned with the implications of the 'equality model' and the proposition that overt gender bias is disappearing. We will also focus on the way in which the culture and practices discussed in the previous chapter, in their discriminatory impact on women who are attempting to replicate the male career path, belie the depiction of the legal workplace as a neutral environment composed of autonomous individuals.

In fact, the current nature of legal work, whilst clearly in part driven by external forces, is also a product of the same factors which perpetuate direct sex discrimination and the development of gendered, internal markets (Cockburn, 1991). Far from a neutral construct, it is shaped by culturally male behaviour, which is in turn dependent on the asymmetrical gender power relations characteristic of wider society which legal ideology and discourse continues to construct in terms of male breadwinner, female homemaker. In other words, the shape of current legal practice is both a manifestation and reinforcement of the public/male and private/female dichotomy which the law constructs and protects.[1] As we have noted in Chapter Four, rather than bringing about changes, women's entry into 'is public sphere has generally necessitated their conformity to this construct of legal work. However, it has not resulted in parallel requirements of males to alter their behaviour in the private sphere (Baxter, 1992, p.245; Morris, 1990, p.500; Gregson and Lowe, 1993); an issue that will be discussed further in the following chapter. As a result, in general, women's professionalism remains contingent (Kaufman, 1984, p.354), undermined by the persistence of views of them as primarily responsible for domestic responsibilities (Baxter, 1992). Consequently their conformity has not ended their role as a disposable, transient workforce and/or the practitioners of less prestigious specialisms (Halpern, 1994, p.60; and see Carter and Carter, 1981). Women's chances of attaining, and retaining partnerships are not only reduced by the way in which legal work is currently conducted, but also by these internal labour markets and by the persistence of indirect and direct discrimination, both of which phenomena therefore operate as mechanisms of closure.

However, as Anderson and Tomaskovic-Devey (1995) and Halford and Savage (1995) have argued, patriarchal workplace culture is not static, but continually shifting as it is challenged, eroded and reshaped. This point is especially relevant to the legal profession, which has been undergoing a transformation in recent years, resulting in an extremely varied demand side,[2] and producing for women a similarly variable picture of career possibilities and barriers. At the same time, female (and male) lawyers have been drawn from wider social groups than was previously the case. As a result, as we noted in our introduction, there is a developing concern with labour market studies which 'homogenise' women by taking gender as their primary focus (for instance, Bottero, 1992). This concern echoes that expressed in feminist studies in general that the category of female itself is problematic and not uni-dimensional (see for instance, Spelman, 1988), whilst for some it is no more than a discursive construct which is continually evolving (Smart, 1992). Such concern may appear especially pertinent to this book since our focus on the maleness of professional culture, and on 'women's' subordination would appear to exemplify this type of un-nuanced approach which is rooted in a binary essentialism. We have nevertheless contended that such an approach is justified on several grounds. For instance, the evidence of the persistence of gender bias requires a broad overview.[3] Secondly, the homogenisation of women by the law is paralleled in the profession. The reification of gender, and the construction of stereotyped and unidimensional categories of lawyer, and of men and women, is a primary characteristic of professional culture; indeed the professional project required a strong degree of uniformity of type in order to achieve and retain status.

Nevertheless, it is clearly important to once again underline the patterned nature of women's experiences which our research revealed; for instance, we did not only come across women who were extremely successful in male dominated specialisms, but also niche practices which appeared to be either equitable, or dominated by women. But, although it should always be borne in mind that some women have made some significant gains, it also appears that in some sectors of the profession female participation has been accompanied by an accentuation of the masculine culture discussed in the previous chapter, and a parallel sexualisation, and, correspondingly, devalorisation of women's cultural capital (see Pringle, 1989; Collinson and Collinson, 1996; Collier, 1998; Filby, 1992).

The following discussion then represents, to an extent, a generalisation of women's experiences, largely based on the situation in commercial firms. This is justified in part because they are the major employers of women solicitors. Moreover, whilst they may be viewed as representing an extreme in terms of patriarchal culture - as one woman observed: 'all big firms have the reputation of being real hard nosed bastards, if you're a woman with children you don't have a hope in hell with them' (salaried partner, large town general practice, 1994) - we would argue that they may be viewed as paradigmatic of the new approach to women solicitors. Our research findings indicated the existence of a similar pattern and discourse of employment throughout the different variants of legal firm; thus an experienced woman associate in a large urban legal aid practice said: 'at the end of the day, this sort of firm is just the same (as the big commercial firms). Look at this one - there are three of us women here, all with lots of experience, highly qualified, good reputations. In the last partnership round, not one of us were even considered; there are ten partners and they are all male. And they didn't even have the excuse that we have children, aren't committed, etc. My son is grown up' (1997).

'Women are simply the better calibre candidates'

Since the late 1980's a key element of the Law Society's promotion of equal opportunities' policies and practices has been the appeal not only to principles of equity but also to 'good business sense'. This is also the position put forward by other commentators who stress, for instance, the quality of many female practitioners (Simmons, 1996, p.27), the benefits of retaining expensively trained staff (for instance, McGlynn and Graham, 1995), and the value that will accrue to a firm through having a progressive image ('Comment', Solicitors Journal, 1989, p.983; Richardson, 1991). The responses of employers in all three surveys appeared to indicate that these arguments in favour of employing women had been largely accepted; women were praised for the excellence of their qualifications (Lewis, 1996), and for qualities which are deemed specifically female such as 'meticulousness' (1997). One senior partner explained that all his professional employees were female because the 'female applicants were simply more able' (1994), whilst another wrote: 'they are capable ... most women are professional, direct and efficient ...' (1990). The office manager of a small, rural general practice, in illustration of the tendency of 'tokens' to over-achieve (see MacCorquodale and Jensen, 1993), said that he was looking for female employees because: 'a lot of men need a good kick up the backside to do a job whereas a woman is determined to get a result - she has a mountain to climb because they don't get as many advantages as men and so she'll work her backside off because she knows she's being watched ... they're also more pro-active, innovative' (1994). Finally, a male partner implied that 'the realisation that women make better solicitors than men' would eventually overcome the 'major obstacles to the progress of female solicitors' (1994).

These responses were also reflected in the statistical data generated by our 1994 survey of employers. In an echo of the national trend, women were sometimes preferred as trainees to men, especially by the larger firms: overall 68 per cent of the trainees taken on by the respondent employers were female. The gender balance at assistant and associate levels also favoured women. In 1994, eight out of 20 firms which responded had *only* female assistant/associates, and three firms employed more women at this level than males. However at partnership level, again mirroring the national picture, the ratios were reversed, with female partners standing at only 13 per cent of the total. For example, all four professional employees of a medium sized commercial practice were women, while its partnership consisted of two (salaried) female partners and ten (equity) male partners. One large commercial firm had 49 female practitioners at assistant/associate level and 43 males, and 21 female trainees as compared to 12 males, but only two female partners out of a total of 36.

Male partners who were interviewed tended to be very conscious that the small numbers of female partners could appear to be indicative of sex discrimination and generally raised this issue themselves. Various explanations were proposed; for instance: 'I don't think women are disadvantaged but I'm sure they'd say something different because of the breakdown of partners. I see it as their immaturity if they do resent it' (senior partner of medium sized general practice, 1994).

However the majority of employers favoured the human capital explanation for the gender disparity.[4] The following account by a senior partner of a multinational firm linked sociobiological explanations with an argument about the length of time women have been participating in the profession:

> ... if you asked me how many women partners we have here that would be the wrong question, because it goes back to how many women were entering the profession ten years or so ago and wanting to pursue a long term career. Now however more than 50 per cent of law students are women and that percentage flows through into our younger assistants ... however, if they want to break off their careers to have a family ... then it is harder ... if they keep going and combine the role of mother with succeeding in a high pressure business environment then it's very difficult ... then there's the problem that they have to have flexibility about how long they work. The job does involve very long hours ... I don't think there are any barriers which are internally imposed by male chauvenists but there are barriers which are practical ... (1997).

This firm had eight women partners out of a total of approximately 80 but roughly equal numbers of women and men at associate level and below. Given that the Partnership stage of the 'normal' career path is reached about 5-7 years after qualification, and since women have been qualifying in almost equal proportions to men since the late 1980's, the argument that women have not been participating in sufficient numbers for long enough to be eligible for partnership is now palpably untenable. A diametrically opposed interpretation of the figures, and one that was put forward by some employers, would be that they constitute evidence of the proposition that discrimination is now generally taking place during a woman's career trajectory, rather than at the point of entry; as Rosenberg et al have argued: 'the apparent willingness of employers to hire women does not necessarily mean that they will be treated equally' (1993, p.422; and see Grint, 1992, p.220).

Women's perspectives on their position

Whilst many women endorsed the emphasis on the obstacles to women resulting from the nature and demands of private practice work, they also, in implicit contradiction of the 'women friendly' views expressed by many employers, considered that, on the whole and in varying degrees, the legal profession was characterised by male bias. For instance in 1990 51 per cent of women respondents in practice expressed the opinion that there was discrimination against women, whilst more commented in the 'open' questions, on the persistence of barriers to women. The remarks of one respondent summed up the general feeling: 'I have encountered a general prejudice against women in the inability to accept them as intellectual equals, and outdated social attitudes' (general practitioner).

Furthermore, the optimism expressed by some in 1990 that prejudice would diminish over time and with increased female participation, had evaporated later on (for example, see Robert Walters Associates, 1992, cited in The Lawyer, 25 February 1992, p.1). Seventy-two per cent of female respondents in 1994 considered that negative attitudes towards women were common in the profession, and successive women remarked, both in the 'open' comments part of the questionnaire and in interviews, on the deterioration in the position of female practitioners, following the recession. One woman wrote: 'Whatever progress that had been made has been largely wiped away by the recession. Women's working and maternity rights, etc., and general opportunities will always be dictated by the current economic climate', whilst another said 'I think part of the reason why women were doing well in the 1980's was because of the shortage of staff. I think we are now dispensable'. The following observations capture the mood of most women respondents in 1994: 'women are still being used as better paid legal executives in many firms' (a female equity partner in a medium sized general practice), and 'women are still second class citizens'.

The interview sample of 1997 tended to be similarly negative about the position of the majority of women. For example: 'we're still there to be patted on the head - still in the junior ranks'. Others elaborated on this by claiming that women's function was to work as 'the back-room girls' and 'the volume producers on a daily basis ... we nearly all work as associates/ assistants ...' and, similarly, this was one woman's interpretation of the increasing willingness to take on women trainees in large numbers: 'As an articled clerk at * you were cannon fodder ... I think it was part of the idea of articled clerks as slave labour that they tended to be female and all the partners male' (commercial lawyer). Others reflected on their relatively lowly status despite their experience and qualifications: 'I'm definitely way behind where I should be' (in-house lawyer). Similar pessimism about the prospects for women solicitors has been reported in two recent surveys (Young Women Lawyers and Kim Tasso, cited in Veares, 1998, p.2).

The position of women: employer neutrality or bias?

The perception of many of the female respondents of their position as generally subordinate and of the links between this and prejudice is supported by both a range of theoretical perspectives and tangible indicators of discrimination. For instance, we have already considered in Chapter Four the national statistics on the lower rates of pay women tend to receive and the small numbers of women at the higher levels of the profession (for example, see Daniel Bates, 1995; Sidaway and Cole, 1996). However, in this chapter we are more concerned with the qualitative, somewhat intangible obstacles to women's career progression (see Spurr, 1990; Lentz and Laband, 1995); we wish to explore the systemic, indirect discrimination discussed in the preceding chapter from the perspective of our female respondents, drawing on theoretical insights discussed in Chapter 2.

Gender stratification theorists are united in their refutation of the proclaimed neutrality and rationality of the labour market. Instead both markets and the 'skills' they reward are argued to be socially constructed (Gaskell, 1995; and see McGivney, 1993) and intrinsically linked to the gender, race and class characteristics of those who Thornton has termed 'benchmark men' (1996).[5] As we discussed in Chapter Two, some studies have proceeded from this base to an examination of the exclusionary mechanisms which have been utilised to close professions, or segments of professions, off to women (Witz, 1992; Crompton and Sanderson, 1990). A related proposition is that horizontal and vertical segregation is a result of the existence of dual or multiple, gendered labour markets: as Podmore and Spencer observed in the early 1980's, women in male dominated professions operate in an opportunity structure and internal labour market which is different to that of men (1982; and see Roach Anleu, 1992; Legge, 1987). Correspondingly, other theorists have focused on the gendering of particular jobs, and the differential rewards such jobs produce.

Commencing with the increasing numbers of female employees, employers tended to claim that these are indicative of their impartiality, and of their motivation by a purely economic rationale: 'anyone of whatever sex, race or creed is welcomed where we perceive a profit being made' (senior partner, medium sized commercial firm, 1994). By contrast, for women the predominance of subjectivity in personnel matters was a continual theme; for example, with regard to recruitment, a woman partner of a small general practice explained: 'here it depends on what you are applying for; if you are a matrimonial lawyer, you'll get selected and interviewed by the matrimonial Partner and he wants someone like him' (1997). An academic lawyer, who had responsibility for assisting students with finding traineeships, said: 'The women now, especially the more mature ones, are generally much more able than the men we get ... but the firms are still generally looking for the young company man - sort of 2:1 candidate with a reasonable accent who is keen to get on, plays football on a Sunday and will generally be part of the team - I say that because that's the sort of student who gets the interviews and the jobs, even though, as I say, the women are often brighter and more hard working' (1997).

Instead, perhaps employers' claimed impartiality should be viewed as symptomatic of lawyers' self image as intrinsically fair. As one woman partner said: 'You wouldn't get far with the idea of sexism because they tend to see themselves as gender blind' (1994). Thus the acknowledgement that 'word of mouth' and 'gut feeling' survive as a popular means of obtaining staff, is not necessarily perceived by employers as potentially discriminatory: 'We have an equal opportunities policy in place because of franchising. The senior partner thinks he treats everyone the same anyway, so you have to point out to him that if you're giving your friends jobs (as he does), then that isn't equal opportunities. He says something like "I hadn't thought of it like that"' (female equity partner of small general practice, 1997).

In support of women's perceptions, despite the trend towards employing large numbers of women at a junior level, we encountered employer concern about potential gender 'imbalances', and this was especially the case at the higher levels. For instance, in 1994 several recruitment agencies advised that some of the larger firms had expressed anxiety about the increases in female solicitors and reported that many were specifically asking for male practitioners in order to 'even the numbers out'. The managing partner of one large firm said that the (female) partner in charge of recruitment was worried about how to ensure that there was 'balance between the sexes ... whether I like it or not, some clients like a male solicitor, and most of our clients are men', and a female equity partner (in a large commercial firm) reported, in 1997, that when recruitment above trainee level was discussed in partnership meetings, 'They've said things like "we want a reasonable balance between men and women, so we don't want too many women". In fact it's clear that for them a balance equals a preponderance of men, because at the time this was said there were already more men; I can remember saying ... that even if we recruit one more woman, we will still have less women than men ...'.

Conversely, women focused on the imbalance between the large numbers of women at the lower levels of the profession and the tiny percentage at partnership level, since they perceived this as a true indicator of employer fairness. The remarks of many contained the idea of partnership as a fraternity, and a common claim was that the few women who become partners had had to emulate and be better than their male counterparts, and yet were still tokens. One commented: 'Because I work for the CPS I deal with a lot of firms and all of them have nearly all male partnerships, whilst the majority of assistants I would say are now women ... they wouldn't want lots of female partners ...' (1997). Another woman, who had been an equity partner, but who felt she was hounded out by the male partnership following a short illness, recounted how, when she asked if they had found a replacement for her, was told, 'no, because all the applicants are women and we don't want one; we want a man who will fit into things here' (1997).

The route to partnership and internal labour markets

An illustration of the social construction of both jobs and skill is provided by the explanation for the desire to maintain male numerical superiority at the top which was suggested by a senior partner. In 1990 he considered that a major deterrent to the employment or promotion of 'too many' women was the damage it did to the credibility of firms: 'When I get letters from solicitors, I look at the list of partners. The stronger firms still only have one or two, I don't want to use the word token women, but one or two women on the list. I mean just take one firm ...' mentioning one of the largest and, reputedly, most progressive * firms, 'you will find four (female partners) out of 25'.

This same man (now an Industrial Tribunal chairman) endorsed these views in 1997: 'when I get partnership lists I do still look at the numbers of men and women on them ... I think it remains true that too many women on a list ... will affect the impression of strength of a firm. For example, if you're going to be in the top commercial league, i.e. one of the major financial firms which tend to have 20 partners or more - then you wouldn't want to have too many women ...'.

Indications that deeply embedded, stereotyped notions of female attributes continue to operate beneath the surface rationality of the legal labour market emerged even more explicitly from other responses; for instance, 'women tend to be more conciliatory and better at emotional things than men' (male partner, 1994). Female respondents too voiced the 'cultural feminist' perspective (Cain, 1990),[6] that is, the perception that there are specifically 'female' characteristics,[7] but were often also conscious that however favourably phrased, 'female' traits were generally likely to be viewed negatively (Jack and Jack, 1989) and that it would be therefore advisable to acquire a degree of 'maleness' (Gross, 1990). A commentator from the AWS lauded 'the feminine characteristics of compassion, vulnerability, mercy, empathy, intuition and passivity' and bemoaned the fact that they 'are repressed and demeaned' (Golden, 1997, p.5). Other women similarly noted the general devaluation of essentialist 'female' qualities and denied that these should preclude them from entering 'male' specialisms. For instance: 'the actual law involved in insolvency is quite technical and there's no reason why men or women shouldn't do it equally well' (1997).[8] Another woman made the same point: 'I can negotiate a lease as well as any man; and I can be aggressive in a reserved way' (1994). Other women refuted the need to be aggressive even in the traditionally adversarial courtroom scenario. One woman focused rather on the disadvantage which resulted from a deficit of stereotypical masculinity: 'They think you've got to be aggressive in a very male way ... it ... damages your chances of getting anywhere' (criminal lawyer, 1994).

However, there is inevitably a link between the ascription of essentalist female traits and assumptions about natural, gendered roles and functions. As Foster has put it: 'The legal profession follows society's role dichotomies' (1995, p.1649), although we have rather emphasised the role of legal ideology and discourse in shaping the social script, and, in turn, the outlook of practitioners. The result is that, in the words of a female equity partner: 'in private practice ... there are still enormous preconceptions about women's roles' (commercial firm, 1997). Such assumptions, in combination with other aspects of professional life like the heavy work ethic, then 'militate against taking women on in the first place, because people don't expect them to be able to make it'[9] (male equity partner of a legal aid practice, 1997). Furthermore the concomitant anthropomorphism of legal specialisms, has resulted in certain departments, especially corporate and insolvency, being characterised as aggressively male and 'sexy'. 'There's a lot of machismo in the law; there's a real thrill connected with doing a big deal - lots of drinks after deals - and some departments are seen as very glamorous - sexy' (female commercial lawyer, 1994). Another said: '... certain areas of the law still seem to be reserved for men - e.g. banking and corporate finance - there's a laddish atmosphere there and women are simply not welcome ... so you just don't find women articled clerks doing certain types of work and that must be the result of direct discrimination' (in-house lawyer and representative of AWS, 1997).

Even though women are now breaking into traditionally male preserves (see figures in Chapter Four), this gendered construction of the law, in combination with the ascription of stereotyped characteristics to women, leads in turn to continual questioning of women's competence to do certain (usually more prestigious) work. One result, as described in Chapter Four, is that women seem to tend to self-select into less hostile specialisms (Halpern, 1994); as the woman last cited went on to observe: 'you also get women not opting for (very male) areas of the law'. A female criminal lawyer commented: 'Crime is pretty macho both on the part of the practitioners and of course most of the clients are male ... there's a perception that to get on you have to be as tough as the men' (1994); and: 'when I first went into insolvency I was the only woman in * (name of large town) doing it and they thought I was completely cracked. I went for an interview and was asked how I would cope as a woman at a creditors' meeting when it gets very heated' (former female partner, 1997). Similarly, one woman reported being asked (in 1993) how she would deal with 'tough male barristers'.

Correspondingly, despite the growing challenge to the system of internal, gendered labour markets, the perceived complementarity between femininity and other legal specialisms persist: 'I genuinely think women are better at (matrimonial law) because they are better at dealing with the emotional side' (female lawyer, 1997).[10] As a result, at times the cultural capital ascribed to women is specifically valued, because a firm requires, for instance, a matrimonial or conveyancing lawyer: 'there is prejudice against women ... on the other hand ... there is positive discrimination for them, for matrimonial lawyers ... ultimately we're talking about profits and good commercial sense' (equity partner of small town, mixed practice, 1994). However, such 'female' specialisms are not prestigious,[11] and consequently one explanation frequently put forward for the difficulties of women making partnership was that they tended not to be in the 'sexy' specialisms - particularly corporate - from which most partners were drawn. Thus the male senior partner of a medium sized general practice wrote in his comments on the major obstacles to women's progression 'being expected to work in "sensitive" or "feminine" areas of law' (1994). This rationale is clearly circular, in that, conversely, 'sexy' specialisms are unlikely to be female. Whilst the prestige of a department is connected to its profitability and hence to the economic climate - so that insolvency was highly important during the recession - it also relates to its personnel: as in other sectors of the labour market it appears likely that the 'feminisation' of a specialism will lead to its devaluation (Bradley, 1989). This point was made by two of our respondents. A male equity partner had switched from doing commercial work to family because he preferred it, arguing that it was one of the most complex and challenging of specialisms: '... the commercial lawyers say to me "why is someone like you doing family law?" ... because it is a female ghetto and I think that may be the reason why it is not sufficiently highly valued, whereas commercial of course is very macho and *the* specialism' (his emphasis; medium sized commercial/ general practice, 1997). And according to a female practitioner: 'A lot of women work in residential conveyancing and over the last few years it has been very much devalued and I think this then means that even less men work in this area' (female associate in large commercial firm, 1994).

A further vindication of Epstein's warnings of the dangers of the 'difference' approach, was provided by the comments of some respondents on the ultimate incongruity of 'female' traits with professionalism: 'there used to be a question mark over women being tough enough' (former equity partner of large town, medium sized general practice, 1997). The remarks of others revealed expectations that women could fulfil an essentially domestic role at work: 'I don't see any reason now to distinguish between a man and a woman ... there's certainly no intellectual argument against women. I'm sure some women would run very good practices, on a good housekeeping basis, probably a tighter ship than some men' (managing partner of a small town general practice, 1990). There are echoes of this evaluation in the experiences of one woman of her traineeship: 'I was frequently sent out on errands - for instance, to buy presents for partners' wives, to pick up the dry cleaning' (academic, 1997), and a female partner recounted how one of her male colleagues treated her 'like a cleaner. I am his joint marketing partner ... and he frequently gets me to organise all the functions - I am sure that this is deliberate' (salaried partner, medium sized general practice, 1994).

It therefore appears to remain the case that whatever a woman's credentials, it is likely that the focus will be on what is perceived to be her essentialist femaleness as much as on her professional skills and, further, that this ascription of stereotyped qualities will probably impede career success. However, as we argued in the previous chapter, another key to partnership is obtaining a mentor. The ascription of domestic and caring roles and qualities to women and the perception that partners must be 'tough and aggressive' (male partner, 1994), substantially reduces women's chances of being mentored for partnership. A woman with partnership ambitions noted the homology between stereotypical professional masculinity and the archetypal partner, and the corresponding incongruity between 'femininity' and partnership: 'the typical partner here is very male and very ruthless - I don't have the personality to make it here' (matrimonial lawyer, large commercial firm, 1994). Similarly a male solicitor commented that certain legal specialisms, such as commercial and crime, were 'very macho and you have to comply ... for instance for commercial you need to put on the posh accent and be rough/tough and wear the red braces - all right that was very '80's, but it's still there' (partner medium sized commercial/general practice, 1997). This perspective was recently endorsed in an AWS Newsletter which commented that: 'The masculine characteristics of strength, domination, power, aggression, logic ... toughness and lack of feeling are glorified (in the profession)', and noted that such personality traits are prerequisites for career success (Golden, 1997, p.5). Correspondingly it is presumed that the workers who do not merit or want sponsorship will generally be women. One employer wrote in 1990 that 'it is generally accepted that most women will not, and don't want to, progress as far as men', and a female commercial lawyer (who was aiming for partnership) argued that: 'men have this attitude that women can either be completely aggressive, aspiring to be a man, or a passive little woman, and not really serious, working hard and hoping they won't get chucked out, but never in the running for a partnership' (1994).

The route to partnership and the role of mentoring: the female perspective

Partnership exemplifies those aspects of professional culture which are so hostile to women: 'what you're showing when you're aiming at partnership is the ability to get and keep clients - that's what partners do mainly and women are often the fee-earners who do most of the work and certainly the backbone work ... at the end of the day, I think a lot of women take the decision to have a different type of life whether or not as a result of the obstacles they might face, or as a result of the general legal ethos' (general practitioner, 1994). As a result, some women consciously eschewed the conduct which was perceived as important if a solicitor was to be considered for partnership and were primarily viewed as good workers: 'women, I think, are seen as reliable back shop workers' (commercial lawyer, 1990).

However, just as many women are now challenging the occupational segmentation of the profession, so too, many expect to have long term and successful careers. In the words of one woman who began practising in the 1950's, 'women today expect to get further; they're no longer content with second best' (1997). This difference between the generations was reflected in our data; for instance, 29 per cent of the women solicitors in 1994 who were in practice had partnership ambitions. Moreover, the proportion of women who had returned who still had partnership ambitions was even higher at 40 per cent.

Nevertheless, most women also demonstrated a realistic perception of their chances of reaching the top. In 1997 one woman said that although she still wanted to be a partner, she didn't think it was possible in her current firm (a large commercial practice) both because of the hours demanded and also because of a general prejudice against women. Others spoke of the consequent improbability of receiving support; for instance, 'I don't feel I'm not a partner just because I'm a woman, I feel it's because I've had children ... and because of the sort of personality I am. I haven't pushed myself forward with the sole aim of becoming a partner - which is what you have to do - you have to get sponsored and men are more likely to do this, and to be sponsored' (matrimonial lawyer in large commercial firm, 1997). Another said: 'There is clearly informal mentoring here and in most firms and the people who do get on do have people supporting them - people in authority. People can't get on without someone higher up supporting them, and I'd be surprised if women got the same opportunities across the board as men ...' (woman partner, 1994).

However mentoring does not only maintain male numerical and hierarchical predominance and reward and hence reinforce the stereotypical male characteristics referred to above. It also requires a complementary differentiation and devalorisation of (most) women and of 'female' characteristics. The practice is not therefore just of significance for individual careers, but must be viewed too as an expression of the 'resistance by the (male) club' (Brockman, 1992); that is as part of a process whereby the routine favouring of male professionals as a category is predicated on the ghettoisation, relegation and ultimate deprofessionalisation of women, as a homogenised category. In other words mentoring is an example of professional closure in action.

This process may begin at the training stage; one woman explained how she had been articled (in the mid 1980's) to a medium sized general practice and how, for, she thought, paternalistic reasons, 'certain areas of work were kept back from me - I wasn't given the choice because they felt it wasn't suitable ...' (1997). A woman taken on in the late 1980's by another medium sized general practice along with a male trainee, stated that whereas he was encouraged, she was treated as cheap labour: 'the male trainee was sent to the * branch office because the two solicitors there were men and because the opportunities were greater. He was offered a job after articles and I wasn't. Also I spent most of my time in conveyancing; I wanted to also do private client, tax planning, etc., which would have given me more career possibilities, but I wasn't given that chance, or indeed any encouragement - yet I had far better qualifications' (former female equity partner, 1997).

Other women also linked mentoring with internal labour markets, as career paths in terms of specialism were generally controlled by the male partners: speaking of her experience in articles in the mid 1980's with a large commercial firm in London, one woman claimed that training specialisms were allocated 'by individual partners on the basis of their personal preferences'[12] (1997). The following comment by another woman trained in the early 1980's was echoed by many others: 'I qualified in 1985: I did my articles with * (a large commercial firm), and then left - I was told directly that there was no future there for ladies because they had babies. It was made very clear that as a woman you were just not considered seriously and this was also reflected in the chances I was given during articles' (academic lawyer, 1997).

The following, typical account, illustrated how this process of blocking could continue throughout women's careers: 'At * (large commercial firm) I was working with this man who had the same qualifications as me and was just one year more qualified, yet I was made to assist him. The partner of our department quite clearly placed me below him in the pecking order. All the cases went to him - I was just the back room girl' (commercial lawyer, 1997). As a result women generally had to make it crystal clear that they were totally committed to the male norm - that either they were not going to have children, or that children wouldn't affect them - and also had to be better and work harder than men in order to be sponsored. Since few women can do this, the circle is completed, and men, as a category, can be mentored and women restricted, and the ideology of partnership reward retained, along with its synonymity with masculinity, for, in the view of many employers, most women either would not want to, or would ultimately be incapable of being, groomed for partnership anyway. For instance, one woman said: 'How do women become partners here? They have to do 150 per cent more than the men, and may still not get promoted' (female commercial lawyer, 1997). Another woman observed: 'A mediocre man could make partnership if he worked long hours and was in with the lads ... I know of men like that ... but a mediocre woman couldn't'[13] (academic and former practitioner, 1997).

Nevertheless, despite the fact that patronage is ultimately more, or at least as, important as credentials, professional credibility depends on the depiction of the workplace as guided by a philosophy of theoretical liberal legalism in its rhetorical commitment to the idea of autonomous individuals, each making their way on the basis of merit. This denial of the interconnections between the professional paradigm as male and the continuing importance of mentoring in private practice was spelled out by one woman partner: 'There's a lot of lip service paid to equality, that is, it is claimed that it is the merit of the individual which counts and that no one is promoted purely on their gender ... but this actually means equality in the light of existing criteria which are themselves defined by reference to the "good, 100 per cent male candidate"' (female company secretary, 1997).

Practice development and partnership: women's point of view

According to one woman: 'Legal practice is a service industry; you have got to get on with the client' (salaried partner, 1994). Urry (1990) has underlined this importance of the social interaction involved in service work, and this aspect of legal work is particularly prominent in practice development. Furthermore, as we discussed in the previous chapter, the construction of personalist networks, both within and without the firm, are crucial to attaining promotion: '... to get partnership you have to market hard, cultivate connections, put yourself about a lot ...' (former practitioner and academic, 1997). As we also discussed above, this is an area of legal work which tends to be particularly problematic for women (and see Kim Tasso, 1998, cited in Veares, 1998, p.2).

Whilst firms place great importance on marketing, many women spoke of a lack of assistance, and even hindrance, from employers in this arena. For instance, 'there are still male only events - lots of dinners and golf days, etc. There have even been events like that which have involved my clients, and which I would therefore have attended as a matter of course had they not been men only' (commercial conveyancer, 1994). Other women recounted similar stories: 'Yesterday was *'s golf day ... it wouldn't cross their minds that there might be women who would play golf ... or that there are women who wanted or could have used the opportunity to entertain their male clients in some shape or form, who wished they had been invited ... other forms of entertainment exclude you too - for example sportsmen's dinners - women don't get a look in there - and of course this exclusion has a really adverse effect on women's careers' (leasehold specialist, 1994); another said: 'One of the main partners here - in his early 40's - he loves taking over * restaurant for the main client dinner and no females are ever invited - male trainees of three months can go, but no women. My clients attended, so it looks really bad for you. One of his excuses was that the speaker was too blue' (female associate, large multinational firm, 1994).

A former equity partner in the same firm had had a similar experience in 1996: '... it was a stag dinner. I didn't know these sorts of thing still existed - all male affairs to which women aren't invited. One was held at a cricket club and * had sponsored the dinner and each department took a table, including mine, and so I invited half a dozen guests and was all set to go when, the day before, I realised it was a men only dinner and had to ring my clients and say that they should go with my colleague because I wouldn't be able to go. Following this I did say to one of the senior partners that they shouldn't be sponsoring this sort of thing - but he just didn't take it on board' (1997).

This refusal to recognise the discriminatory impact of such exclusionary events is clearly highly significant, especially given that the firm in question is a very large commercial practice which is currently taking on as many women trainees as men and which, we were advised by one of its senior partners, has a working party on women's career development and invisible barriers to their success. As Weber has argued in connection with the American bar, such exclusions undermine women's professional status: 'One form of belittling behaviour is the tactical exclusion of women from the "fraternity of fellow lawyers", the message is that women do not naturally belong in the company of their male counterparts' (1990, p.901).

However, in addition to placing obstacles in the way of women successfully participating in some of its corporate entertaining events, the same firm then raised the problems women sometimes encountered with practice development as a rationale not only for not promoting women, but also for not taking too many on as assistants or associates:[14] 'In partnership meetings they have said that they don't want too many women ... I got their gist which is that they don't want more women than men above trainee level ... because of the client base and the entertaining that was required' (female partner of large commercial firm, 1997).

Women from other firms recounted similar problems; in the same way, difficulties with practice development may be cited by firms as one reason for getting rid of women: 'in terms of credentials, I am far and away the best, and also in terms of managing staff, but in other ways I never fitted ... now they want a man to replace me because he will fit into that culture and can join things like the Rotary and the masons' (former partner of medium sized general practice, 1997). Another former equity partner recounted how her male partners had 'decided they would have to get a young man to take over the commercial department from me - a man who could infiltrate the commercial echelons of * better than me because he was a man - so he could join the trade clubs, round table, 40's club, etc. - all of which involve social gatherings out of hours - and some of which are male only' (1994).

Other respondents argued that whilst there is a professional tradition of allocating responsibility for obstacles to women's professional development onto clients, this is a misrepresentation; for instance one woman said: 'my point was that the way you succeed commercially is through your performance in meetings, at share take overs, etc. - that's where you impress clients ... and how you get and keep clients ... I don't think socialising after hours does get you much business, I was always very successful without any of that ...' (female commercial lawyer, 1994). Instead, most of the problems are perceived as originating with the firms themselves: 'my clients were always more sympathetic and accepting than the firm was' (conveyancer, 1994). Another said: 'They have an idea of what the client wants, which is a stereotype, and many clients are in fact more forward looking than the law firms' (commercial lawyer, 1997).

Apart from the instances cited above where firms damaged women's standing with their clients by excluding them from practice development events, many solicitors also alleged that women were less likely to be supported in their marketing efforts by their firms: 'We did a lot of work for * and all the reports to * had to go out in this male solicitor's name (no more qualified than me) and I was never invited to client do's with *. Then I did manage to make my own contact with * and had a chance to entertain them, but the partner wouldn't give me any money for it, even though it was good practice development' (commercial solicitor, 1997). That this woman's experience was not untypical is illustrated by the following remarks of a male commercial lawyer: 'women are seen as having a short career span; at the moment I can spend money on practice development and when I say "look there won't be anything coming back from this for a while", the senior partner will say "it's all right because it's a ten year development plan", but they wouldn't spend all that money on someone who's going to leave after only five years - which is the perception with most women' (1997).

This is not to deny the very real difficulties presented to women by the male culture of the public sphere: 'the actual law is very technical and presents no problem for women, but PD is the other side to it, and it's seen as going down the pub ... it's very male dominated' (female insolvency lawyer, 1997). Many solicitors underlined the connections between career progress and marketing and linked success in the latter to the overwhelmingly male nature of the clientele: 'men can succeed partly on the basis of the business they bring in. Men find it easier to bring the business in ... most of the big clients are men anyway - most of the business type places to meet are male dominated - e.g. the gold clubs ...' (general practitioner, 1994). Another spoke of 'the Round Table mafia - all the business men in an area belong and that's where contacts are made and business done, and of course women can't belong to it and there's no alternative forum ...' (in-house lawyer, 1997). This woman went on to delineate the connections between these problems and occupational segmentation and the devalorisation which employers are then able to make of women's cultural capital: 'So women are kept in specialisms like Legal Aid - women can deal with the smaller clients, who just walk in off the street ... and then of course such work becomes devalued because women do it'.

A former salaried Partner in a large commercial firm was equally clear that practice development was principally about building up the relational capital which is the stuff of the fraternal contract: 'whilst I approached PD events as an exercise in getting business, and would therefore bring up the subject of business, what they were looking for in a law firm was something different. Those events weren't necessarily overtly about business at all. I think now that my approach just didn't fit easily ... these events were really about doing/getting business through social networking, through making friends ...' (company secretary, 1997). Another woman confirmed this interpretation, and her comments also highlight the differential links for men and women between the public and private spheres, so that the dependence of this culture on domestic servicing permits men's participation,[15] whilst simultaneously hampering women's: 'practice development means getting on with clients ... and it's harder for women because it involves making friends often with men, and because women have less of those types of forums - golf club, Round Table, at which you meet people and because of the home commitment - you don't want to be hanging around at work' (academic and former City solicitor, 1994).

The experiences recounted above are symptomatic of the complex of obstacles that shape women's participation in the male legal community. The vital importance of 'relational' capital means that just as for men, for women successful networking skills are valued as highly as legal expertise. As a result, the response of some has been to argue for the emulation of men in this sphere; for example it was recently advocated in the Law Society Gazette, citing tips issued by the Woman Rainmakers Interest Group of the American Bar Association, that women 'learn to play golf and how to bet' (Willetts, 1997, p.18). However, the core function of much networking as an arena of male bonding places virtually insurmountable barriers in the way of most women really succeeding in it, whatever skills they acquire. For most women therefore, fitting in with the 'old boys' club', is inevitably beset by difficulties, and may also be viewed as a test (see MacCorquodale and Jensen, 1993); hence the implied criticism in this man's comments on a former colleague: 'there was this female partner who wasn't ladsy - a good technician and quite sociable, but relied on her skills ...' (general practice lawyer, 1997).

In this way practice development exposes the paradox at the heart of the 'equality model'. On the one hand, in order to achieve professional success, women must generally perform like men. However many professional networks remain exclusively or predominantly male not so much as a result of historical accident, but because their function is to allow men to bond (Collier, 1998), raising the question of how such male dominated events have accommodated women. In Adkins' opinion 'men are constructed both as a more powerful group of workers than women, and as having power to harass, sexualise and appropriate women's sexual labour, because of the gendered relations of production' (1995, p.155), and, as Filby has argued, 'sexuality is constructed as a separate and defining characteristic of women: in organisations ... sexuality is where women are ... the customary association of masculinity and rationality allows male sexuality to remain unspoken and yet dominant' (1992, p.24). It may be argued that these various features of the exploitation of female sexuality are especially apparent in the area of practice development. The socialising and entertaining involved in much work revolves around particularly stereotyped gendered role playing and the generally insecure and ambiguous nature of women's professional status is inevitably accentuated in such (generally, largely male) forums, thereby placing an unspoken obligation on women to play a sexualised role: '... when you're with the men (at a corporate marketing thing) you laugh, flirt a bit - I'm used to that' (academic and former tax lawyer, 1997). In fact, as Stanko (1988) and Cockburn (1983) observe, such 'compulsory heterosexuality' is compatible with male bonding, encouraging it to take place. Thus, on the one hand, as we argued in the previous chapter, the core cultural capital required in the networking arena is masculinity; at the same time, a woman's value for these events may be her sexuality; or as one woman suggested: 'To succeed you have to be an attractive female boy' (commercial lawyer, 1997). Another summed up the difficulties confronting women in the following way: 'in that male dominated entertaining life, the odd attractive woman is a good thing. But you don't want too many women because then the event would take on a different feeling' (female commercial conveyancer, 1994).

Sexual cultural capital and marketing

It is therefore arguable that the relationship between labour market segmentation and the stereotyped attributions on which this is based is revealed with particular clarity by the different forms of cultural capital imposed on, and required of, men and women - especially in the market of client relations. This view is echoed in several studies of women in service industries, and especially traditionally male dominated ones, which have also stressed that women's accommodation has been achieved by 'the implicit use of sexuality as a commercial or organisational resource by management ...' (Filby, 1992, p.25; and see Hearn and Parkin, 1995; Pringle, 1989). As a female academic lawyer commented in 1997, when asked to reflect on her time as a tax lawyer: 'Men and women bring different things to their work. I think men have drinking and male things, playing golf, rugby whatever, in their favour - so they must be able to participate in all that bonding - but women have fluttering their eyelashes, laughing and touching - all of those ways of relating to men'. Another woman said: 'I think if women are nice to look at, that's certainly valued by employers' (1994). Whilst according to a male planning lawyer: 'A lot of male clients would like to have a young, pretty female solicitor looking after their interest because most of them are sexist ...' (1997). Similarly, a male criminal lawyer noted the unenthusiastic response with which many clients had greeted female lawyers in the 1980's, but that 'they were quite acceptable if they were pretty' (1990).

As a result it was claimed that at times, for some employers, the primary cultural capital of some female employees lay in their sexuality: for instance a male senior partner commented: 'If you look at the Law Society Gazette, if these big firms do appoint one or two women to top positions, they'll photo them in photogenic ways - they're always very attractive - and this is then used to show off the firm' (1990); and an academic lawyer said: 'I know women students who've gone from here to firms where they've been required to attend certain types of meetings - with big corporate clients - where it's been obvious to them, because they were pretty and sexy, that they were partly being used to please clients; I don't think it's that uncommon ... * (a medium sized general practice) was notorious for that; they had no male trainees at one stage and took stunningly attractive women instead - all male partnership, though of course' (1997). That sometimes partners' personal preferences, in connection with female trainees, appeared to have sexual overtones, also emerged from the remarks of another academic lawyer, who had trained with a large City firm: 'There used to be jokes about who the recruitment partner was in a particular year, because of the appearance of the women recruits - they'd say you could tell who he was because one year you'd get a swathe of blonde ones, but then the next year, a different partner and you'd get a swathe of brunettes - so the women were clearly chosen partly on the basis of the sexual preferences of the particular male partner' (1997). Another female academic, formerly a practitioner in a large general practice, said: 'Women ... being treated as sexual objects in law firms seems to be especially bad in London, with the big firms ... all that corporate entertaining stuff - the women are often being treated as little better than - well, prostitutes really. Their role is like that in many ways' (1997).

The following account endorsed this view of the sexualised role many women seemed to be expected to play at marketing events:

> ... there are events nearly every night ... and you'd decide as a team, on a particular function (to go to) ... the culture of such events is very male dominated and a certain amount of flirting goes on ... No one in words explicitly says that you must go out and flirt but you are going out to market the firm, its services, to make friends in that very male business world in order to encourage that other person - generally male - to send you work so if that means they pay you attentions that you don't want, then you just have to grin and bear it. There were incidents where I'd feel uncomfortable, but then I'd feel 'what the heck - it's just part of professional life for a woman' ... you'd try and dissociate yourself from it.
>
> (Employment specialist, City practice, 1997)

Similarly, a woman equity partner who was emphatic that her professional style was to 'appear neat, professional, non-frilly ... you downplay the stereotyped feminine image' nevertheless reported having to suffer male attentions: 'you have to put up with clients kissing you ... The sort of age group who do it would be about 55 ... part of showing that it's a semi-social occasion ... I don't like it, but you just think "oh well"' (1997).

As a result a common complaint by women concerned the potential ambivalence of practice development situations: 'It's difficult to do PD if the person who I'm trying to cultivate is male - there's always a feeling of ambiguity in a situation where I'm having to ask a man out to lunch ...' (1997); and: 'clients don't know whether to treat you as a woman or as a professional' (commercial lawyer, 1994). One woman explicitly linked this problem with the persistence of double sexual standards: 'A lot of PD involving the opposite sex is about flirting, and it's more socially acceptable for men to be active in that area. Women feel uncomfortable, being so forward' (academic and former tax lawyer, 1997). Another woman seemed to feel that her unease was her problem: 'It's probably me, but I find going out one to one with a man difficult because it's never quite clear if the meeting is supposed to be business or personal. I was invited out recently by a surveyor and was unclear about his intentions. You have to be very careful about what you're saying' (commercial conveyancer, 1994).

However the following comments of a female equity partner, a mature and confident woman, expressed similar concerns: 'I've never found it easy inviting Building Society managers for lunch. I think it's difficult ... there are various potential problems with Practice Development for women - possible misunderstandings ...' (1997); and another woman summed up the problem in the following way '... the thing is that PD is all about bonding, and so the question is, are they looking for something extra ...?' (commercial conveyancer, 1997).

The deprofessionalisation of women which both results from, and reinforces, the focus on women's corporeality and the sense that it was something which women are largely powerless to resist, was commented on by many women; for instance: '... I have seen people flirt, but I don't know whether that's responding to unspoken expectations as to how they should behave at these sorts of events. Though let's face it, there's always a lot of drink at these do's; everyone drinks and then that affects behaviour; there have been some really over the top things here' (commercial conveyancer, multinational firm, 1997).

Another woman alluded to the connections with the essential incongruity of femaleness and normative professionalism: 'some men have this attitude that you're a woman principally, not a professional ... and then that ambivalence is exploited. I think the partners definitely think it's a bonus if you're an attractive young girl; then they want you to be out there, because they think you'll get the clients in. So in that sense you get to front things rather than being just the back-room girl ... it's quite blatant. I have actually heard partners say things like: 'she's attractive, let's have her by the door'' (corporate lawyer, 1997). So, while traditionally male solicitors have portrayed themselves as 'wise counsellors' and 'men of affairs' and viewed their authority as deriving as much from being 'men of the world' (male partner, 1994) as from their legal expertise, by contrast, women's authority is contingent (Thornton, 1996) and undermined both by their sexuality and perceptions about their career span: 'you're both the attractive front woman who is a major factor in getting the work in, and the back room girl doing the basic slog' (female associate with large commercial firm, 1994). As a result, one woman commented: 'Playing this complaisant sexual role - smiling, flirting - is a way of advancing ... and yet at the same time you won't be taken seriously in that role, even though you're doing what is wanted of you as a woman' (female employment specialist, City practice, 1997).

Professional closure: sexual disparagement and harassment

The ambiguity surrounding the female professional is of course fostered by the sexual regime which also operates within the law firm (Thornton, 1996). The focus on women's corporeality manifests itself in a variety of, often contradictory, practices ranging from the imposition of a dress code (see McGlynn and Graham, 1995) designed to obscure women's sexuality (Longrigg, 1998, p.3), to disparagement and harassment. Evidently, quite apart from the pressure to play a sexual role at marketing events, the combination of a hierarchical structure dominated by men, and a culture of deference,[16] are likely to produce social relations of domination which include sexual objectification (see, for instance, MacKinnon, 1987). The observations cited above that when women are recruited this may be sometimes, in part, as a result of their looks as much as of their quality as workers were endorsed by others, some of whom linked this sexualisation to subsequent mentoring: 'I felt you had to be really attractive to succeed ... those who were attractive got the attention of male partners ... so one way to succeed was to be very attractive, flirt, make up to the partners, etc. - who would then help your career' (1997). Another told the following story:

> by the second year of my articles, we were all insecure about whether we would be kept on because of the recession ... my supervising Partner, with whom I worked closely, was happy with my work, so, at the Christmas do I expected that when he picked a trainee to dance with it would be me. But he didn't; he picked the trainee who had the reputation of being the most attractive. You see every year one of the girls is picked out and labelled as the most attractive; you hear all the male fee-earners talking about all the female trainees. (Academic and former commercial practitioner, 1997)

An account of similar behaviour, evocative of the 'master-slave' relationship (Pringle, 1989) included a description of what appeared to be virtually obligatory after-office hours socialising on Friday nights during which the power/sexual relations became explicit: 'the male partners would get quite drunk; sometimes it would get quite out of hand. All the secretaries had to go' (female solicitor, describing a large town general practice, 1990).

One woman pointed up the forcible ascription of sexual cultural capital to women, and alluded to the resulting de-professionalisation: 'as a woman you were being clearly assessed on your physical attributes rather than your capabilities as a lawyer - I didn't like that' (academic, 1997). A Local Authority lawyer alleged that her appearance had been a major factor in her success when she had been younger: 'In retrospect, I feel that in my 20's/30's I won all those housing cases mainly because of how I looked then. Law is a cabaret - that's a very important part of it all; the appearance is vital and goes with the dramatic delivery' (1997). Another woman said: 'I never flirted at all, but that was very much part of the culture, that was how women were expected to behave. People did it in different ways; there are scales of flirtation. For instance some women did it by acting like a silly woman - playing up their vulnerability. Others used blatant physical signals' (commercial lawyer, 1997).

MacCorquodale and Jensen (1993) argue that a sexual/sexist culture may also be viewed as a device to test loyalty, to see if the incomer will 'play the game', and if she can be, as one of our male respondents said 'one of the lads'. This interpretation was borne out of the remarks of several women; for instance; 'there is all this racist and sexist banter all the time - you have to be able to take a joke - I think you can be too P.C. about these things - it's just the culture - just a joke - I usually join in, sometimes, I suppose I may even initiate it' (black female CPS lawyer, 1997). Another woman said: 'People aren't blatantly sexist and in fact they are quite nice people and you have a laugh, but it's just that the sexism is underlying it all ... but you're expected to take it all' (assistant solicitor, general practice, 1994).

As a result, failure to accept the culture in such good spirit may result in exclusion, as a male solicitor made plain in this account of a technically able insolvency practitioner who wasn't 'ladsy': 'she came in for a fair amount of ridicule really, she's recently been sacked as a partner. She just didn't fit in with the insolvency world, and she picked up this ridicule - it wasn't anything serious like harassment, I'm not even sure she was aware of it. People would say things like "look who's coming over to join us" if she came over to their table ... The Senior Partner didn't make any allowances for her, in fact it was always very clear that he wasn't very keen on her. They've taken on a man they see as more suitable' (1997).

Some respondents claimed that some women had achieved career success by engaging in the culture. For instance, a male respondent made the following comments about a former colleague who had become a partner: 'She was very talented, worked very hard, had no children ... Her behaviour was also very flirtatious - both with the partners in the firm and with the business clients - and it seemed to go down well' (former practitioner and academic, 1997). However, generally, the sexual objectification of women must serve ultimately to further undermine the professional status and authority of the female lawyer and to reaffirm stereotyped gender identities and hence relations of domination. For whereas a sexualisation of workplace culture may bond the male workers, and participation enhance their status, it is likely to have the reverse effect for women. Indeed women pointed out the pitfalls of engaging in such behaviour (though also making it clear that they often had little choice).

Furthermore, as the accounts of male solicitors (cited in the last chapter) of sexist behaviour clearly illustrate, despite the increase in an egalitarian rhetoric, disparagement of women persists. A female criminal lawyer wrote in 1994: 'I feel very disillusioned with my profession. I am a good advocate - I get good results - but I have to put up with so much rubbish - put downs from male colleagues'. The following remarks of a male criminal lawyer tended to corroborate her perceptions, although also underlining the need always to bear in mind the variations in behaviour resulting from different organisational cultures: '... crime tends to be macho on the part of practitioners and of course most of the clients are male ... until last year this firm was dominated by women - so here sexist talk is unusual. Having overheard conversations (between male lawyers) - I mean crude discussions of female solicitors - of women in general - I guess the culture of other places is very different ... and in the advocates' rooms at the courts, you always get that kind of talk' (1997).

Various respondents also referred to an 'undertone of disparagement of women lawyers' (1997). One black woman lawyer linked her experience of being put down both as a woman and a black, working class person with the resulting pressure to be better than her 'orthodox' and, correspondingly, more acceptable colleagues: 'as an outsider - if you do law they really make you pay for it in every way ... It's a brotherhood of male white middle class able-bodied people ... as a black, working class woman therefore I feel I constantly have to prove myself - I feel you get nowhere because you don't fit, and then if you do get somewhere, then you're told it's simply because of being a black woman' (Law Centre worker, 1997). Some lawyers who did nominally conform to the norm were also, however, aware of these prejudices; for instance, a white male barrister and Law Centre adviser commented: 'Women and the legal profession? There's still a lot of prejudice I think. The other day Judge * said to a woman solicitor in chambers, but in the presence of her client and other lawyers, including myself, "How on earth did you get this order? You must have fluttered your eyelashes at Judge *"'. This man then went on to draw connections between such behaviour and the law itself: 'Law of course is replete with examples of prejudice against women, amongst others ... I can think of many cases, including ones I have personally dealt with, where the remarks of the Judge are very anti-women ... so it's not surprising perhaps that you find discrimination in the profession' (1997).

Some women stated that their authority had been clearly undermined by their own firm. For instance a female commercial lawyer reported: 'Partners will tend to talk to clients before they allocate them a solicitor and I know they sometimes say things to clients like "she's all right for a bird" - I've had that reported back to me on more than one occasion. Also colleagues have said things like "you've done really well for a woman" (1994). Another woman claimed that her career at one firm had been blocked because she had refused to conform to what she perceived to be sexualised expectations of female behaviour: 'This senior partner - because I was a woman and he didn't like me - I was not attractive enough and didn't play those games - he was always putting me down - in front of people - sometimes in front of clients too' (female commercial lawyer, 1997).

However, arguably physical sexual harassment is the most effective way of undermining women's professional status and is also the clearest expression of professional hostility towards female colleagues (see Lentz and Laband, 1995). As Collinson and Collinson have argued: 'women's entry into non-traditional work appears to intensify the likelihood, nature and extent of sexual harassment' (1996, p.51). The hidden nature of this form of discrimination and the willingness of the legal profession to condone and trivialise it has been highlighted by the forcible exposure of a candidate for the presidency of the Law Society: '(The Law Society council) didn't take (Eileen) Pembridge seriously when ... she pointed out that the then deputy vice-president, City solicitor John Young, had a reputation for groping women. He was in line for the presidency ... they said: "Yes, we know about it but it's his turn". Their attitude was: "yes, but it's only women" ... (they) wouldn't get John Young to stand down' (Cunningham, 10 July 1995).

Furthermore two recent surveys report high rates of sexual harassment in the profession.[17] Responses to a questionnaire in 1995 indicated that 35 per cent of women had reported an incident (McGlynn and Graham, 1995, p.12), and a 1997 report found that 40 per cent of female assistants claimed to have suffered from sexual harassment (Reynell, 1997, p.19). Similarly, of the female law students recently surveyed by the Young Women Lawyers Group, half believed sexual harassment was a problem in the profession (Veares, 1998, p.2). We however have no quantitative data on its incidence amongst our questionnaire sample since the surveys commissioned by the Law Society did not include a question on this subject. In any event, as we discussed in the previous chapter, there appears to be an understandable reluctance to formalise complaints in general against employers, including complaints of this nature (and see Smerin, 1995, p.6; Mucciante, 1991, p.15 and Dyer, 1994, p.18). Nevertheless, the experiences recounted by some of our women respondents appeared to amount to sexual harassment even though they were not labelled by them as such; as we have discussed above, the sexual tinge to some of their work relations appeared to be taken as almost inevitable, even if it was unwelcome. Other women had also been subjected to behaviour which was not conducive to any other interpretation. For instance: 'at one of my meetings with the senior partner, he asked me to sit on his knee - he patted his knee and said "come here". I laughed and tried to pass it off, and left the firm shortly after that' (general practitioner, 1994).

One response to the sexualisation of work relations, and the concomitant deprofessionalisation of women, has been an explicit eradication of 'feminine' characteristics. Indeed, as we discussed earlier, this form of assimilatory behaviour has been the traditional response of female practitioners to the unidimensional male model of lawyerdom (Jack and Jack, 1989). The following section will discuss various aspects, including the pitfalls, of this tactic.

Assimilation: 'you have to fit in with the culture ... you have to be one of the boys, and it's even hard for white women to manage that'

Whilst niche firms, some of which consciously espouse different modes of practice, are emerging, and some women are opting for sole practice, in general the conservative and closed nature of the profession ensures that most solicitors - male or female - can only participate by assuming the 'habitus' appropriate to the 'field' - by assimilating to a greater or lesser extent to the norm. Evidently, this pressure to assimilate stems from the fact that the profession was traditionally single-sex, and that the lawyer was indubitably constructed as male (Sommerlad, 1994). As we have argued above, defence of this symmetry between masculinity and legal professionalism has also proved to be an effective mechanism of closure; one female lawyer with a large general practice said 'no concessions are made, you have to conform, work very hard and be just like the men' (personal injury lawyer, 1990).

Since the legal workplace remains so clearly the domain of males (Foster, 1995, p.1646), and hostile to any inclusion of the traditionally female private sphere, assimilation translates into emulation of the stereotypical male norm discussed above. As a result, women lawyers have long tended to aim for a form of equality which suppresses sexual difference. Moreover, just as the male norm as representative of neutrality and reason continues to be a largely unchallenged tenet of legal discourse, so too, participation on such terms has fostered the process of 'miscognition' (Bourdieu, 1987), making it difficult for many women to truly question the current construction of private practice. There is therefore the tendency we noted above, despite recognition of the persistence of male prejudice, to attribute many of the difficulties facing women onto the nature of the work; for instance: '... the further one gets one realises how hard one has to work and there is no reason why those at the top should reduce the number of hours that are needed to work for us newcomers. So I don't think it's a question so much of women being stopped or of a glass ceiling, it's more just what is required in terms of the working culture' (salaried woman partner, large commercial firm, 1994). This is a theme to which we shall return in the next chapter.

As we saw in Chapter 4, demands for equality without special treatment was the approach adopted by 19th century feminism, and a common tactic was to remain single in order to be able to participate in the public sphere. This was the course generally followed by the very first women solicitors in England and Wales, and their identification with their professional status rather than with their gender meant that some refused to be even interviewed by researchers for a history of the AWS (retired solicitor and researcher on the AWS project, 1997). Later entrants also followed this path; for instance, a woman who qualified in the 1960's said: 'we modelled ourselves on the men ...' (academic, 1997). Whilst this attitude continued to predominate amongst our female interview sample, many phrased it rather in terms of being 'gender neutral' and 'asexual'.

Mimicry of the male model is therefore understandable given the process of acculturation discussed in Chapter 4, and in the light of the pressures emanating from the profession. As one woman commented:

> I constantly come across the feeling that I'm supposed to behave like a man, not just a man - a white, heterosexual, middle class man. If I behave as though I'm one of them I'm perfectly acceptable even though I'm a woman. But as soon as I start behaving differently, which I do for all sorts of reasons, then I become less acceptable and my credibility as a solicitor isn't accepted by other solicitors or even barristers. I find it less so with clients because clients are much more tolerant than other practitioners.
>
> (General practitioner, small town, 1990)

Clearly there are degrees of assimilationist behaviour. As we discussed above, it appears to be evident to many women that success depends - generally[18] - on the eradication of stereotypically 'female' characteristics (Jack and Jack, 1989) as they are likely to lead a solicitor into the decidedly 'unsexy' female ghettos of, for instance, conveyancing, and since all the qualities which appear to be really valued in the law are culturally male. Some women will therefore pursue an extremely 'macho' assimilationist tack, especially if they are aiming at partnership. A woman academic, when reflecting on her old general practice firm, commented: 'There is a female partner there with children ... but she was like a man really; she behaved and was treated like a man. It seemed to me that she always presented herself as a man in order to make clear that being a woman was in no way a handicap'. Similarly a female equity partner in a general practice said: 'I do know women lawyers who aren't so different from archetypal male lawyers - I'm thinking of the career minded, grey suited, long hours working, profit conscious type of lawyer ...' (1994).

As this last woman indicated, one way in which female lawyers have presented themselves as men is through their dress: 'women are supposed to dress in a certain way ... women who wear suits are perceived as business-like and up for it. Some dress more like men than the men with sober suits and matching trousers ... The image is really sober' (female lawyer, large commercial firm, 1997). According to others: 'Some really look like men'; and 'How you look is undoubtedly very important'; and 'women tend to fall into the "classic/aggressive" mould, dressing in smart, tailored clothes, having a "sensible" haircut, not wearing any/much make up ...'. Another said: 'My approach was that you had to wear a dark suit so as not to stand out from the men. I certainly felt that was the way to get on at * - to be an honorary man' (female equity partner, 1997). Generally such masculinist dress codes designed to mask women's corporeality (Thornton, 1996; Longrigg, 1998, p.3), are voluntary, although sometimes they are imposed by firms; either way, they rarely include wearing trousers. This results in an irony which replicates the more general problems which women lawyers encounter in trying to establish their professional identity (Cockburn, 1991). As Clare McGlynn has commented: 'women solicitors were desperate to try to fit in with their men colleagues, and thought they could do this by dressing conservatively, but to do so, and to fit in, they have to wear skirts, which of course automatically marks them out as different' (private communication, 1997). The tactic of emulation has also been subjected to critical scrutiny by employment lawyer Denise Kingsmill, who advocated that 'women ... make their own impact ... women lawyers may have resorted to a male style of dress for defensive reasons. They have felt - largely because they were made to feel - that they were accepted in the profession under sufferance and that by dressing as honorary men, they might not draw too much attention to the fact that they were not actually male' (Bawdon, 1994, p.34; and see Gross, 1990, p.295, for parallels with the USA).

Another mode of the assimilationist approach has been that of the traditional separatist tactic - remaining single and/or childless (see Drachman, 1989 for a study of this in America; also, Rhode, 1988). This career plan, which has been observed in other occupations, remains characteristic of the legal workplace too (Podmore and Spencer, 1982) and will be discussed further in the following chapter. A former City lawyer commented: 'One or two young women had made the decision not to have children and were making it clear and were in effect saying "you can treat me like a man"; it was clearly a factor in them achieving partnership' (1994). One woman who had adopted this tactic commented: 'aspirations? To maintain equity partner status by working full-time plus and postponing child bearing - otherwise one is not taken seriously as a woman' (1994). The remarks of another woman illuminates the differential obligations for men and women flowing from the sexual contract: 'It's interesting that a successful man ... has usually got to be married and have children; that's seen as part of being a successful man. For women, the reverse is true. I have a friend in London ... who has just had to put relationships on the back boiler; in fact she thinks she will never get married. It's the price such women pay' (former practitioner and academic, 1997).

A further aspect of assimilation is the perceived need to do better than the norm (Caplow and Scheindlin, 1990, p.423). Described by Porter as 'fearful perfectionism' (1997), MacCorquodale and Jensen have related this characteristic to the high visibility of women lawyers, as incomers and as a minority group, generating a great pressure to achieve: 'Tokens' actions have symbolic consequences in that they are seen as reflecting on the whole category of "women"'; mistakes, shortcomings, and personal lives become public information and their non achievement characteristics, such as physical appearance, tend to eclipse performance' (1993, p.583). This was a theme for many of our older female respondents; for instance one woman commented: 'I often find women have to come on terrifically strong - frequently more assertive than men - as if they have something to prove' (rural general practitioner, 1994). A former high-flyer with a very large City firm recounted how in the 1980's women felt: 'it was very important to play by the rules, and be better than the men; you were taken as representative of all women, so it was vital not to make a mistake' (1994). This pressure may have decreased at the more junior levels of the profession in proportion with the increased numbers of women. However the continuing paucity of women at the top evidently means that such pressure to over-achieve and conform remain for women partners. The consequent need to prove yourself as just as committed as men - and committed to a way of working which is extraordinarily demanding - can result in a Stakhanovite approach to work for those who are particularly ambitious, so that if the woman does have children these do not represent any impediment. For instance in 1991, the professional press reported on one such woman in an article entitled 'Solicitor tops working-mum league':

> Hatten Wyatt & Co partner Anna Turnbull Walker 40 has been named as "Working mother of the year" for successfully combining a career as solicitor with the demands of 3 children ... nominated for the award by her husband ... As well as being head of the criminal dept at the firm, she is a duty solicitor and can be called up at any time day or night. She starts work at 7 am each day, goes home at 3.30 pm to be with her children, often returning to the office when they are in bed. (The Lawyer, 15 October 1991, p.3)

Some of our respondents told a similar story; for example an equity partner of a medium sized general practice wrote: 'I work as many hours as my domestic life allows. I often work in the evenings after the children have gone to bed, and often at weekends ...'. Despite this gruelling regime, she went on: 'My working arrangements have been altered to my wishes and I couldn't ask for anything more - but this is due to me not having a proper maternity leave and working extremely hard, even days after giving birth' (1994).

In addition to the practical and emotional problems that this model of success is likely to present to most women (or indeed any carer engaged in the double shift), assimilation can give rise to other difficulties. Even in the paradigmatic, large commercial firms, cultural capital is not a fixed property, nor is its currency publicly available, with the result that women can never be sure what it is they are aiming at. One male practitioner argued that there were two distinct routes to success for women: 'some females get on because they fit into the male scene. They become very dry and pushy - even more business like, detached or whatever than the men. Others succeed by being - it's not really overtly sexy - that would be too cheap - but it's about playing the men - and this gets that type to the top - they get to first or second base with the clients too by using their femininity

- you see it especially with PD - they have to be excellent lawyers too of course. In a way it's like the women have to be more cardboard cut outs than the men - there's these two ways of doing it - they either seem to have to be really plain, not necessarily unattractive - just in the way they present - and asexual - or very feminine. But then if you look at the women who don't go for it, or aren't bothered, who opt out of the race, then they can be normal, they can afford to be themselves' (male equity partner, commercial/general practice, 1997). The observations of the managing partner of a large commercial firm similarly emphasised the strategic significance of women's distinctive sexual cultural capital: 'being female can be used as a very effective weapon in negotiation, because finally clients have to like you, to build links; for instance, * (name of female partner) is very feminine, attractive, knows it and uses it ... I don't mean in a cheap way, but she uses her skills including her gender skills to practise more effectively as a lawyer ...' (1994).

It therefore appears that as many legal workplaces have become sexualised arenas, simple emulation of the male may no longer always be sufficient. This was borne out by the comments of our female respondents which tend to indicate that the two types of practitioner - pseudo male or feminine - may not necessarily constitute separate, distinct routes to success. As Cockburn has argued, and as we noted in our discussion above, the concept of gendered difference is ambivalent, so that shifting roles are demanded according to the setting. Thus Cockburn has noted that it is 'a continual problem (for women at work) to know when to hide their difference from men and when to assert it' (1991, p.160). So, if women *do* use their sexuality this may mean they are considered 'cheap', or not taken seriously. Similarly if they are perceived as 'tough enough', this may be condemned, even though it is a criterion for success (and see Gross, 1990, p.295). The danger was expressed by the personnel officer of a large commercial firm: 'if women succeed, they're regarded as honorary men - but that has a penalty too because they are then seen not to be feminine enough' (1997). A female lawyer commented on the differential valuation of qualities such as toughness according to gender: 'The firm had a couple of bad experiences with the two women partners - they had chips on their shoulders - very ruthless - though of course quite a lot of male partners too, their personalities are pretty unpleasant as well - I suppose it's just likely to be more exaggerated and unacceptable, more noticeable in women' (matrimonial lawyer, large commercial firm, 1994).

Other women made a similar point: 'men have this impression that women are soft and gentle, and if you don't fit that stereotype, then you're labelled aggressive, even though in actual fact it's jut that you're assertive' (female commercial lawyer, 1997). Another woman observed: 'There's a perception that men can be middle of the road, but as a woman, you're either perceived as a complete walk over or a complete tyrant - there's no happy medium' (1994); and another: 'Stereotypes abound - you're either too soft or too hard ... In reality I don't think women are harder than men, it's just that if they're tough that's how they're labelled' (1997). One consequence was that even if women made partnership, they might find that they were subsequently ejected. The managing (male) partner of a large commercial firm explained that the firm had been forced to do this with one of their women partners - because 'she tried to be a man - it didn't work' (1997). A woman observed: 'I think men find the ambitious women more difficult to deal with ... they may be more likely to make Partnership but they then fail at it because of personality problems - even though really their personalities are like those of male partners' (commercial lawyer, 1994). As a result, extreme emulation of the male norm may not work anyway; one woman commented: 'They expect you to have the same attitudes, responses, motivations as men which is wrong and can cause fundamental problems ... but if you do behave as a man would, then you *may* succeed - but it's no guarantee' (commercial lawyer, 1994).

A further problem with opting for a strong assimilation strategy is that the symbiotic relationship between the sexual and employment contract means that only a limited number of such honorary men may be absorbed either on a long term basis, or into the higher strata of the profession. The participation of large numbers of women as elite members of the professional workforce would require radical changes in professional culture, and such changes would challenge fundamental patriarchal relations - both in the profession and society generally.

Moreover, because men remain representative of the norm (Dex, 1987) at the top echelons of the profession, the cultural capital of individual women who are able to succeed at this level may be enhanced by their rarity value. In the words of a management consultant: 'these days there may be a virtue in a woman representing the firm and this approach may be contagious ... for example, some firm will say we've got to have a woman - that other firm has got one - it becomes a matter of PR, of image' (1994); or, as a woman who became a commercial lawyer in the 1970's and then an equity partner, said: 'my firm like the novelty' (1994). As a result women as a category, rather than as exceptions, cannot penetrate this elite. This then leads some successful women to consciously differentiate themselves from their gender; indeed, this is likely to have been fundamental to their pattern of assimilation. As a result, some women are perceived to emulate the male solicitor in an extremely aggressive way. For instance, a prominent member of the AWS recounted the following encounter: 'I had a conversation the other day with a woman partner from * (name of large City firm) - unmarried - no kids. She said "what is this AWS for?" - very aggressive. I said "don't you think the position of women in the profession is different?" She said "I resent all these women partners of mine - they go off on maternity leave - they leave early and draw the same money as me"' (in-house lawyer, 1997).

Furthermore, this necessity for such women to distinguish themselves from the general category of women means that it is questionable whether such exceptional women are likely to mentor other women. As Menkel-Meadow has written: 'to the extent that women are promoted individually in small numbers to a largely male-dominated institution, their performance as "tokens" will be highly conventional and is not likely to lead to innovative behaviours and practices, resulting in an even smaller chance of bringing about organisational reform' (1989, p.310). These observations were endorsed by one woman's comments: 'women who do make it often accept the culture and become great exponents at it ... it's a real pity that these women perpetuate it all when they get there - "I made it without any special favours, so you can do it in the same way" syndrome' (academic and former commercial lawyer with a large City firm, 1994). Other women alluded to the 'queen bee' phenomenon:[19] 'some of the worst prejudice came from women partners who have stayed single and who seem to resent those who want it all - as they see it' (assistant solicitor, large general practice, 1994).

Whilst it was clear that many of the female partners amongst our respondents *were* committed to helping female colleagues, this was problematic; one female equity partner observed: 'it would be very difficult to raise these sorts of equal opportunities issues at full Partnership meetings; they're very formal - 80 people sat around a table, and only eight of them are women' (large commercial firm, 1997). Moreover, the significance of personalist relations at the top of the profession, as in other parts, is likely to mean that the voices of successful women are rarely heard anyway. As Foster argues, women partners may be considered 'mere tokens ... isolated from a male majority seeking to preserve its own identity' (1995, p.1654).

As we have discussed above, both men and women have little choice but to conform to the dominant model of private practice; however, as Christine Littleton has argued 'under the assimilationist approach ... women merit equal treatment only so far as they can demonstrate that they are similar to men. The assimilation model is thus fatally phallocentric. To the extent that women cannot or will not conform to socially male forms of behaviour, they are left out in the cold. To the extent they do or can conform, they do not achieve equality as women, but as social males' (1987, p.1283). Hence assimilation has defused the potential for change represented by the increase in women lawyers, since it means that the male professional paradigm has been largely unchallenged. Furthermore, because female participation has generally been on the profession's terms, assimilation has not prevented the devaluation of values or attributes which do not correspond to the dominant culture, the emergence of occupational segmentation, or the sexual objectification of women. On the contrary, arguably it has contributed to an accentuation of professional machismo. As Rosenberg et al argue with regard to women who unreservedly emulate the male model: '... those women who play the careerist game may unintentionally reinforce those aspects of organisational and professional culture that encourage men to believe they can control women or drive them out through discrimination and sexual manipulation' (1993, p.431). Foster makes a similar point: 'Those who achieve full assimilation usually do so only by becoming part of the majority's status quo, thus participating in and perpetuating a discriminatory system' (1995, p.1654).

Conclusion

In this chapter and the preceding one we have attempted a broad overview of the profession, and tried to consider the interrelationship of 'the discrimination, disparagement and harassment' (Rosenberg et al, 1993, p.417) which results from the construction of the lawyer as male, and the female as domestic, and the connections between these behavioural manifestations of exclusion with the personalist structure and culture of the profession.

The dominant impression of the eight female law students and trainees we interviewed in 1997 of the world they were about to enter, summarise, in many ways, the picture which emerged for us. A black Muslim woman said: 'I see the profession as a white middle class closed place where only people who are part of that can go into it and who then protect their own interests ... I see the Law generally as very male and unapproachable'. The following comments make a similar point: 'getting in all depends on the contacts and background you have, not on your talent. That's clear from who has got training contracts here'; and 'my impression of the profession is of a very closed world ... I've met a lot of lawyers, from university, through my husband ... there's a sameness about them ... they've all been cloned ...'.

By contrast, the response by employers to the charge that there exist glass ceilings to female career progression, located in the classical discourse of contract theory, is the argument that occupational segmentation of any kind is not a consequence of structural discrimination or professional culture, but rather a rational preference on the part of the discriminated. In 1994, one woman summed this up as: 'if you can't stand the heat, get out of the kitchen' (personal injury lawyer). The general perception in 1997 was that the professional workplace had become an even hotter place. The intensification of masculinity which many of our respondents alluded to has been prompted in part by changes in the wider society. Whilst some noted a change in the rhetoric, and some hoped that things would improve when the older generation of senior partners went, many others made it quite clear that some of the most hostile men were quite young: 'the irony is that the younger partners are generally not parents and so they have no idea - I feel they think I am earning a second wage' (salaried partner, general practice, 1994); and: 'I experienced less opposition from the more senior partners who maybe had daughters who were trying to make it, and more from men of my generation - in their 40's - who were going to, or had made it precisely because they had wives at home and thought us having two incomes was unfair' (former City lawyer,

1994). This may suggest that male hostility is indeed a form of closure, a defensive reaction to what is perceived as unfair competition, which, rather than dissipating over time, may simply diminish for the individual in question when they no longer feel so threatened.

In any event, it is also clear that, in addition, and connected, to the cultural barriers we have explored, there remains overt prejudice against women; as the equity partner of a medium sized general practice commented: 'Nothing would be said about appointing women as equity partners with regard to things like maternity, though I think there would be a nudge or a wink. But I honestly feel that if you had the right candidate it would be OK, for instance, we had our first Jewish partner recently, and some partners said the clients won't like that, but stuff it is my attitude, and it's the same with women' (1994).

Notes

1 The requirement that women conform to culturally male behaviour appears to be a characteristic of most previously male dominated professions; for instance a recent report on accountancy found that women were obliged to adopt 'macho working patterns, and, in particular, long hours, and a "boys' club" mentality' (Jackson, 1997).

2 It is therefore necessary to distinguish between, for instance, the firm specialising in Legal Aid work, although such a practice must be further broken down into, borrowing McConville et al's categories (1994), radical, classical and managerialist types; the corporate firm, engaged in 'mega-lawyering' (see Galanter, 1983); the High Street general practice; the sole practitioner.

3 Young has argued that acknowledging the reality of social groups does not 'commit one to reifying collectivities. Group meanings partially constitute people's identities in terms of the cultural forms, social situations and history that group members know as theirs, because these meanings have either been forced upon them or forged by them or both' (1990, p.44).

4 By 1994, however, there clearly had emerged some, mainly small and predominantly Legal Aid, firms which were consciously egalitarian in their practices, and as a result there was a spectrum of opinion in the sample about the position of women. Fifty per cent related the large scale withdrawal of women from the profession to children, however 35 per cent went on to relate this to the ethos of the profession; one employer spoke of firms' 'inflexibility on hours'.

5 Again, comparisons may be made with other professions; for instance, see Biklen on the cultural construction of what it means to be a teacher (1997).

6 Which broadly includes Gilligan (1982), Fineman (1991) and West (1991).

7 See Pierce, 1996 for an example of such stereotyped valorisations and Epstein's critique of this approach, 1991.

8 Gross, in her discussion of women and the law in America, makes a similar point about legal work in general 'There is nothing inherent in lawyering that requires that one adopt the traditional (male) model of lawyering', 1990, p.295.

9 Although, as we argue elsewhere, the presumption that women will have a truncated career span appears to operate as a positive incentive to recruit them for the 'legal factories' which require a large ratio of employees to partners.

10 This perspective also informed a recent article on a female P.I. lawyer in which it was claimed that the work was as much emotional as legal, and that as a result women were more suited to it (Nicolson, 1995, p.30).

11 This is despite the fact that, as a male senior partner observed, one of the classic 'female' specialisms, family law is arguably one of the most difficult: '... because there's so much discretion for the courts so you have to really know the case law ... and also it brings in so much other law - property law, trusts, crime, contract ...' (1997).

12 Although this woman, an equity partner with a commercial firm specialising in corporate tax, persuaded the partners to reverse the decision by 'making a fuss'.

13 As we suggested in Chapter Four, in our discussion of the remarks of the more successful early entrants, it may well be that it was in part their exotic and rare quality which made some of them more attractive to this brotherhood as potential mentees than became the case as the proportions in which women have entered increased, thereby clearly marking them out as competitors.

14 Given that, as we have already explained, the same firm was one of the largest employers of female labour at the trainee stage, this fact would indicate that women trainees are primarily valued as cheap labour and/or their sexuality.

15 This exemption from domestic labour therefore amounts to social capital (Seron and Ferris, 1995) or gender privilege for men (Williams, 1990).

16 Many solicitors commented on the subservience expected from trainees and juniors. A mature entrant to the profession, a former academic, described how he was constantly given menial tasks to perform for his principal (like re-parking the car) so that he would 'know his place'.

17 A recent investigation of the problem at the Bar described sexual harassment as 'prevalent' there too (Hewson, 1995, p.626).

18 Although as we noted earlier, some occasions or situations appear to require women to adopt extremely feminised forms of behaviour.

19 See Helena Kennedy, 1992, pp.60-2, and McCabe, 1995, p.483 on the Queen Bee syndrome at the Bar.

7 The Meaning of the Career Break: Human Capital, Cultural Capital, Social Capital

Introduction

> Pregnancy is seen as a major inconvenience by employers ... (it is) important to have open policies which negate the need for women to make individual deals. (Practising solicitor who had not taken a break, 1990)

> My last interview contained the inevitable 'when are you planning to have a family' question. (Commercial lawyer, 1994)

> My view of career breaks? Partnership prospects plummet. Women returners are given less prestige jobs and pay. This is bound to have an effect on confidence. They are expected to behave as if they didn't have a family and still work very long hours. Employers should recognise the enormous experience available to them if they are prepared to meet women returners half way. (Woman in general practice who had never taken a break, 1994)

> I was well in favour before I became pregnant but was then made to feel that I had let the firm down. On my return I was grovelling around for typing after four months leave. Working part-time you're always left with the feeling that he's doing you a favour even though in fact it's the reverse.
> (Returner to general practice, 1994)

> Domestic chores? ... The ultimate responsibility for domestic life - for the planning and organisation rests with me ... my husband tends to have responsibility for mending locks ... that sort of thing ... It's a traditional gendered division of labour. (Company secretary, 1997)

As these remarks indicate, the 'career break' is a crucially significant factor in women's subordinate position in the solicitor's profession, intimately related to three forms of capital: human, cultural and social. On the one hand a vital contribution to male dominance at work is made by the continuing assignment of the bulk of domestic duties to women (Market Assessment Publications, 1996; Murgatroyd and Neuburger, 1997), including even highly successful lawyers engaged in a 'full time plus' career. On the other hand, the career break and its accompanying ideological baggage serves to devalue not only the returner, but women in general, for whom marriage and maternity, and therefore ultimate relegation to the private sphere (Pateman, 1988), continue to be viewed as their destiny. At the same time, despite these essentialist views of their female employees, employers generally remain committed to the ideology of individual choice, and have failed to take concrete steps to facilitate any combination of caring responsibilities and work (O'Donovan, 1985, pp.29-30). The rationale offered for this approach by human capital theory, and the critique of it made by gender stratification perspectives form the theoretical basis for this chapter's discussion of the career break.

By a career break, we mean the decision to take time away from a specific firm, or a legal career in general, in order to have a child or to undertake some other form of caring responsibility. In the discussion that follows we will distinguish between different types and lengths of break: clearly, both the stage in a career at which a break is taken and also the duration of a break are likely to be determining factors in a woman's subsequent career pattern. Our own sample of respondents reflects a range of different experiences of interrupting a career. However, we shall also argue that the effects of these latter factors can be over-emphasised. Firstly, the 'break' has an iconic significance at least as important as its supposed practical effects, in that it facilitates the perpetuation of an ideology of women's unreliability and lack of commitment to paid work. Secondly, the effects of longer breaks can be mitigated by a range of human resource strategies, and therefore where women are adversely affected by having an interrupted career, we should see this as a commentary on the demand side of the labour market at least as much as on the supply side.

Marriage bar, baby bar

The historic significance of childbearing as a disqualification for employment is exemplified by the marriage bar, which formalised men's right to both women's sexual services and their domestic labour. The processes of the achievement of women's franchise, and the ending of their formal exclusion from public office reflected the readily accepted distinction between single and married women, which continued, de facto, throughout the middle years of the century (Cohn, 1985; Walby, 1986, pp.171-2; Bradley, 1989, pp.211-3; Grint, 1991, p.85). Even organisations such as the BBC, which initially accepted the equal rights to employment of married and single women, were to change their policy - in 1932 they decided to dismiss married employees (Holdsworth, 1988, pp.71-2). The effect of the marriage bar, as Hakim points out, was that it reinforced the sexual division of labour within marriage, 'institutionalised the marriage career and discouraged young women from investing in qualifications and careers' (1996, p.125). As a consequence, women's working careers during this period tended either to be continuous for unmarried women who worked, or continuous on either side of a single break for childbearing and rearing (Hakim, 1996, pp.140-4).

This pattern has changed with the erosion of the marriage bar in the post-War era, with women taking more and shorter breaks; 'discontinuous employment has expanded in absolute and relative terms, at the expense of continuous employment and the home-making career' (id.). Instead of the complete barrier constituted by the marriage bar, childbearing, and its associated career breaks, now represent the major obstacle to career development (EOC, 1995; Figes, 1994).[1] Thus, McGlynn has argued that in effect the formal marriage bar has been replaced by the informal 'baby bar' (1996, p.229): pregnant women are increasingly encountering discrimination at the workplace, which is being legitimated by the courts as justified by 'sound business reasons'. Instances of specific discrimination were vividly reported to us by our respondents.

However, the issue is more complex than might be suggested by simply considering instances of pregnancy-related dismissal and unsympathetic attitudes to problems of childcare (Market Assessment Publications, 1996). It appears that the traditional view that marriage itself did (and should) reduce both a woman's 'availability' and her need for an independent wage, persists and can therefore also affect her prospects. In this way the social meanings of acts such as marriage remain as important as any practical difficulties for employers presented by the need, potential or actual, for a variation in working patterns; thus one male senior partner commented: 'How may obstacles to women lawyers be overcome? Impossible unless they are going to neglect other areas of their lives' (general practice, 1994). We will therefore also argue in this chapter that the normative judgements which underlie the treatment of pregnant women are an integral part of a conceptualisation of womanhood in general, which consequently predisposes employers in the legal labour market to view the careers of all women as having limited horizons.

Career breaks, motherhood and the glass ceiling

As we noted in Chapter Four, the results of a recent survey by the Law Society, amongst others, have confirmed the continuing existence of a glass ceiling for women solicitors, preventing all but a few from progressing to and then beyond salaried Partner level (Sidaway, 1995, p.80; see also, Abel, 1988; Nott, 1989; Reynell, 1997). It is commonly asserted that such 'ceiling effects' in professional women's careers are most closely connected with career breaks and there is a large body of evidence which supports the existence of this inter-relationship, both across professions and also internationally (for example, see Walters, 1994; Murray, 1987; Menkel-Meadow, 1989; Brannen and Moss, 1991; Caplow and Scheindlin, 1990; Holland and Spencer, 1992). The consequences of breaks are often related to both the negative impact on career development of deviating from the so-called 'golden pathway', a metaphor for the normative career pattern modelled on the experience of successful men (Davies and Rosser, 1987; Itzin 1995b, p.260), and also to the problems associated with the frequent requirement by women with young children for reduced or flexible hours of work. For instance, Colgan and Tomlinson (1991) have identified a full time uninterrupted working life as essential for career progression (see also, Abdela, 1991; Dex, 1987; Hughes, 1991; Molyneux, 1986; Steele et al, 1990).

Moreover, the weight of the literature argues that the negative impact of career breaks is specifically related to maternity. Okin has described the workplace as constructed on the 'systematically built in absence of mothers' (1989, p.127; and see Fineman, 1992, p.309). Workers who take career breaks for purposes unrelated to maternity do not necessarily incur the same penalties (EOC, 1995, pp.13 and 19; Innes, 1995, pp.179-82; Coleman, 1996, p.321). Thus Newell has commented on the deleterious influence of motherhood per se on earnings and status (1993: 276), whilst Curran speaks of the 'stigma of motherhood' (1988, pp.345-6): the fact that there are few jobs for which being a mother is seen as being an advantage, whilst, conversely, men achieve a labour market advantage through both marriage (Seron and Ferris, 1995, p.1) and fatherhood (Curran, 1988, pp.345-6).

Our own data supports these findings, and demonstrates that breaks associated with childbearing generally result in significant career changes, and that these changes are frequently involuntary: as one woman wrote: 'a career break can suggest to employers that you are dispensable and I know of several cases where people have been made redundant whilst on maternity leave' (in-house lawyer, 1994, and see Willis, 1996). Hence, of the women in our 1994 sample who had taken a break, 73 per cent reported changes of employer, 86 per cent reported changes in their hours and their pay, and 55 per cent reported a change in the kind of work they undertook. Fifty-two per cent of the sample who had returned to work reported that it had been under conditions worse than they had hoped, with particular difficulties experienced in finding any job at all with suitable conditions (42 per cent). In both 1990 and 1994, women who had returned emphasised, in the open sections of the questionnaire and in interviews, the effect of a return both on their status, and on the view which employers and colleagues had of their long-term prospects. This was often linked to their preference for working part-time: for example, one woman had felt forced to accept the view of her colleagues that part-time work debarred her from access to the more prestigious face-to-face work with clients. We should also note the ambiguity of the term 'part-time': we will examine below the fact that many part-time women solicitors work hours which would be thought of as 'full-time' in other occupations.

The responses of other women support the contention that the glass ceiling is related to motherhood per se. Even when no, or a minimal, break has been taken, and even where there was no reduction in hours worked, becoming a mother could have a detrimental effect on a woman's career.

One female solicitor explained that she had taken only three months maternity leave but that 'this was sufficient to produce differences in the subsequent pay reviews - not for the better; my experiences of return have been depressing and exasperating but illuminating' (1994). It is generally considered that this phenomenon is linked to the need of mothers to give extensive proof of their commitment to the professional labour market (see Hantrais and Walters, 1994). However, as we indicated above, we argue that this in turn must be connected to the construction of womanhood and the ideology of motherhood (see Fegan, 1996), and is therefore also related to a number of other factors, involving the effect that their changed status has on women's cultural capital.

Approximately a quarter of the returners in the 1990 and 1994 cohorts explicitly linked a decline in their status and prospects to a more general suspicion on the part of the employer of the commitment and loyalty of women with domestic responsibilities (see Hochschild, 1989). This view of the attitude of the profession towards breaks was also confirmed by non-returners: in the words of a childless, full-time female solicitor, breaks for children are 'catastrophic in terms of status' (matrimonial lawyer, general practice, 1994; and see Bawdon, 1996, p.24; and for comparison, Hagan and Kay, 1995). Many full-time and all part-time returners indicated that they had experienced significant downgrading in all aspects of their work; for example, a woman who was on a break from practice, but had previously been a part-time returner, stated that if she were to go back she would want: 'recognition by colleagues that you are a professional even though you only work part-time' (1994). Furthermore, loss of status could be permanent; according to a full-time returner: 'it is very difficult to change from being a woman returner to someone with a career who has ambition … once a returner, always a returner' (general practice lawyer, 1994).

For others, the refusal of private practice to make any accommodation for women with children (Garlick, 1990) had resulted in their complete withdrawal from private practice.[2] In 1990, 19 per cent of the sample of women out of practice had no intention of returning, 44 per cent had mixed feelings and four per cent had not considered the possibility.[3] Of those completely withdrawing from practice, a small minority felt they had not achieved enough post-qualification experience to enable them to return, some had returned and found the pressure too much to cope with, and the remainder were pessimistic about the possibility of finding a flexible employer - a sentiment which was shared by many of those who expressed mixed feelings. In 1994, 47 per cent of women out of practice stated that they had no intention of returning (see also Mossman, 1994, p.67).

Human capital and rational preference theories of the break

The perspectives of our (overwhelmingly male) employer sample contrasted sharply with those of the female respondents, the majority adopting either a human capital or preference theory perspective. As Hagan and Kay observe:

> these theories have scholarly origins, but they also have lay variants and followings in the profession itself ... Human capital theory derives from the field of economics and finds some of its most ardent followers among the 'human capitalists' who manage law firms (1995, p.12).

As we have seen above, human capital theory argues that variations in, for example, occupational status, specialism, pay and opportunity are attributable to differences between individuals' skills and credentials (for instance, Caplow, 1954, and Becker, 1980; and see Stuart, 1998, p.30). The efficiency gains to be made by partners in a family from a division of labour are held to result in men and women respectively specialising in market and domestic work, leading to a free rational choice to invest a concomitant amount of time and money in each sphere. Consequently, it is argued, women are disadvantaged in market work through their human capital deficits (Becker, 1985; 1991). As we have argued in Chapter Two, Catherine Hakim's theory of 'women's heterogeneity' in the labour market is modelled on a similar binary opposition between 'market career' and 'marriage career' women (1995; 1996).

Thus, for most employers, differentials between male and female professional lives were held to be primarily explicable by reference to the attitudes, qualifications, attributes, and biological characteristics of women themselves. Consequently they located all, or most, responsibility for occupational segregation with women themselves (see also Menkel-Meadow, 1989). Specific causal significance was attributed to maternity and career breaks in response to the suggestion that there existed a glass ceiling in the profession; for instance the explanation for women's lack of progress that 'women bear children; men do not' was typical. Implicitly, and frequently explicitly, therefore, the consensus was that differential career paths were a result of a mixture of nature and choice. In particular, women's choice to have children was held to lead ineluctably to certain consequences; hence, one employer explained that women had 'difficulty with long term planning caused by lack of ability to give total commitment to the career' (general practice, 1994).

We have commented on the weaknesses of this explanatory model earlier, but it is particularly important to subject it to a critique in relationship to maternity breaks, because of the key link they form in the theoretical chain of 'human capital' reasoning. The 'human capital deficits' which it is argued result from career breaks for reasons of maternity, can usefully by considered under three headings: skills, confidence and commitment deficits. Absence from the labour market is argued to produce a decay of existing skills, which may be exacerbated by a failure to invest in training to learn the new skills demanded by the way in which the character of the work may have changed during the woman's absence. Confidence deficits, which may be closely linked to skills deficits, are the consequence of a woman's belief that she can no longer function efficiently in the workplace as a result of the isolation imposed by child-rearing, and the external perception that child-rearing is a 'low skill' or 'no skill' activity (Hochschild, 1989; Brannen and Moss, 1991). Commitment deficits allegedly result from the woman's divided loyalty between her two spheres of activity, which are held to produce either a reluctance to make the additional human capital investment necessary to progress up the career ladder or alternatively a decline in willingness to conform to employers' requirements in terms of patterns of hours or other conditions of employment.

Preference theory, or the 'chosen spheres' model, focuses less on women's credentials, and rather on their life patterns, and resulting attitudes and career choices. Hakim has argued that motherhood causes a displacement of women's primary commitment from their careers onto the domestic sphere (1996a). From this perspective, female solicitors become mothers by choice, and then do - and, implicitly, should - exercise a choice either not to undertake waged work, or to work less hard, or in less prestigious specialisms, and consequently occupational segregation is a result of such choices (Brannen, 1989). As a result, it is argued, employers' largely hostile reaction to this labour supply is entirely rational and, furthermore, rooted in a social orthodoxy both about the inherent rightness of the current organisation of the profession and, correspondingly, about the place of mothers with young children.[4]

This explanatory model of women's subordination in the professional labour market, and the determinist sociobiological foundation on which it rests, has several weaknesses. Before moving on to a detailed critique of its component parts, it is worth making a few points about its presumptive framework. The first issue is the focus of human capital theory on only one side of the labour market - the supply side. We stressed in Chapter Two the importance of an explanatory model which meshes both sides of the labour market, and argued that a concentration on the supply side to the exclusion of the demand side, whilst presented as an impartial depiction of the natural, or rational order, is in fact ideologically driven. Newman reinforces this point with her depiction of a 'vicious circle' of culturally exclusive practices which deter women from seeking senior management positions in public sector organisations (1995, p.24).

Employers represent their workplace practices as economically rational. However, this position is refuted by the wide variation we found in patterns of working (also revealed in the trade press), and employers' views on the benefits and disbenefits of specific modes, such as part-time working. Whilst the needs of distinct niches in the legal labour market might differ, views vary on a more idiosyncratic basis, both between and within firms. Many firms have found flexible arrangements in the workplace both possible and desirable; indeed one City firm has now instituted a part-time partnership scheme (Chambers, 1997) - yet this was generally rejected out of hand as impossible by similar employers in our sample. Furthermore, even some of the most convinced opponents of flexible arrangements for women in our study were prepared to consider them in the cases of male colleagues who had retired, but still wished to do some work. In some City firms, senior partners have also institutionalised a system of 'sabbaticals'. Moreover a range of evidence suggests that models of 'acceptable working patterns' are sensitive to the 'long waves' of economic cycles. During the period of anxiety over the 'demographic dip' and the skills shortage (Wharam, 1986), there was a rapid increase of interest in flexible working patterns, not simply amongst academics (Rajan and Eupen, 1990) but also amongst employers (Curnow, 1989), an interest which appeared to evaporate on the advent of the recession (Skordaki, 1996, p.34). One woman wrote: 'whatever progress had been made were largely wiped away by the recession. Women's working and maternity rights will apparently always be dictated by the current economic climate' (former City lawyer, 1997). We will deal with the causes and consequences of inflexible working in greater detail later below.

Other women solicitors in our sample expressed their awareness of the dubious rationality of workplace demands, and rejected human capital explanations for their professional marginalisation. Instead, they generally focused on examples of active bias on the part of employers, or on features of the profession which are inimical to women in general. The following observations were typical: '... women are not taken entirely seriously or treated fairly' (part-time returner, general practice, 1990); 'Having a baby is still generally considered to be the end of one's serious career' (residential conveyancer, 1990); 'I think there is still a lot of discrimination against women in the legal profession' (commercial conveyancer, 1994); and 'women don't get the same opportunities as men' (academic and former corporate lawyer, 1997).

Women identified the prevalence of the 'separate spheres' and human capital ideologies as an underpinning rationale for discrimination; for instance:

> they'd say things like 'We've put all this money and time into you and then you'll have babies and never come back'. It seems to be the financial aspect that upsets them most of all. I can think of other remarks like 'we pay you and then you piss off and never come back'. That also justifies them treating you badly and not making you partners and so in the end you begin thinking, 'all right then, I will just leave'.
> (A representative comment, made by a commercial conveyancer, large urban firm, 1994)

In this way, the human capitalist view achieves a status of 'reality'; the prevalence in the workplace of beliefs which are shaped by the conventional social script becomes, as we see in the last quotation above, a key element in the calculative rationality of women and men obliged to make decisions about career paths. So the fact that the (male) specialist in the workplace, in this division of labour, will have higher earnings is not just an immediate issue for the couple concerned, nor simply a fact of life: it is a determining factor in an ongoing process of gendering of jobs. Similarly, the dominant ideologies of motherhood and of the world of work combine to reinforce the employers' claim that a working culture which is visibly predicated on domestic servicing is necessary; for instance: 'many women see themselves as not having the right to take time off to have babies ... it causes too many problems' (full-time returner specialising in criminal law, 1990). The consequence of this rationality is that the inflexibility of workplaces' conditions of service, the long hours culture, and the principle of 'availability' so characteristic of the solicitors' world, are therefore erected as insuperable 'natural' obstacles rather than barriers which are socially constructed.

By contrast with human capital theory, gender stratification perspectives refute the proclaimed neutrality and rationality of the labour market, thereby rejecting the possibility of unconstrained choice (Hartmann, 1979; Davies and Rosser, 1986; Itzin and Newman, 1995). Instead they are concerned to expose the ideological nature of the current construction of work and its relationship with the private sphere. For instance, Brannen and Moss point out the profound effect that the traditional view of gendered responsibilities and parenthood has on the way in which resources are made available to support the care of children. They argue that it not only legitimates the general failure on the part of both government and employers to make any contribution to childrearing, but also means that women often find it difficult to obtain support in the private sphere - from social networks, and even family (1991, pp.251-2). At the same time it justifies the retention of working patterns shaped by men's access to women's domestic support (Wajcman, 1996). Seron and Ferris, in their analysis of the comparative positions of male and female single and married attorneys in New York, refer to the resource made available to male married attorneys by the assumption of responsibility for childcare by others as 'social capital', and demonstrate that this social capital is generally unavailable to women (1995). Consequently women tend individually to bear the responsibility of working out and resourcing solutions. The following sections will consider our data in the light of these competing approaches.

The skills deficit: is it real and is it important?

Both the 'material' of legal work, and the technology applied to it has been the subject of intense and rapid change over the past decade (Galanter, 1992; Flood, 1996; Wall and Johnstone, 1997). One might therefore anticipate that the problems of skills decay and skills obsolescence likely to be experienced by women returners would be particularly pronounced in the solicitors' profession. However, in general, we found this not to be the case. In comparison to the 'confidence' deficit discussed below, far fewer women mentioned the skills deficit, and where they did, it often seemed to act as a proxy for a confidence deficit. Although 53% of respondents in both 1990 and 1994 cohorts identified up-dating themselves in legal developments as a difficulty, it was one that they found it relatively easy to overcome swiftly.

There are various reasons for this. First of all, we have briefly alluded before to the extent to which the business of legal practice is *about* law may be over-stated. As Wall and Johnstone demonstrate, much of the new technology which has made the 'legal' side of legal work more accessible is under-used by solicitors; in particular, where on-line up-dating databases were available in firms, they were only used by a small minority of lawyers (1997, p.104). Wall and Johnstone argue that this may be a function of the work of solicitors being more concerned with giving advice about legal procedure than the law itself. Other commentators have argued that a comparatively small amount of a solicitor's workload relies on 'legal knowledge' (Carlin, 1962; Abel, 1998, p.13), and this view was endorsed by several of our respondents. For instance, a senior partner stated that the role of a solicitor was to be 'a wise man - a man of affairs - a counsellor, rather than a legal expert - that's the role of barristers' (1994); and an assistant solicitor in a corporate firm said: 'most firms operate like businesses not professions ... I suspect partnership means more work on the business side of things and less law, which would suit me. I don't really like the law - I've just been off to the library for half an hour and I find it boring. I haven't really got the patience or the care for it' (1997). Furthermore, whilst a number of firms in both 1990 and 1994 mentioned up-dating courses when asked about the kind of training with which returners should be provided, none of them mentioned a skills deficit as a likely handicap, and all those firms which had actually employed a returner reported very positive experiences.

In response to a general question in 1994 on the key changes affecting the profession, employers did underscore technical and market-driven change, and identified retraining in this area as very important, but applied this to the profession in general, and did not single women out as having a particular need. For example, whilst all senior partners responding in 1994 believed, quite naturally, that compulsory general updates would be essential for anyone whose break had lasted longer than five years, only 10.5 per cent (2/19) believed that retraining in the woman's specialist area of law would be necessary. One woman who had returned in the 1980's and was now an equity partner argued that brief courses for women returners could supply most of the necessary updating:

> There are courses for them and we know that it's possible for people to retrain, so a few years out needn't be a problem. I know personally from being off for five months that you are rusty when you come back and that you do need an update and also a settling in period. On the other hand, it's true that you need updates anyway; so to get back you probably need confidence boosting most of all. (1997)

A recruiting partner for a medium-sized small-town firm argued that it was the firm-specific skills which were most important for practice, and it was a willingness to adapt and learn which would be a more important indicator for him in making recruitment decisions:

> I don't expect them to have done a course in computer this that and the other or high tech something or other. To my mind you can over-train people. If I was looking for somebody, I'd be looking for somebody who's competent to do the job, the law and the procedure that they're doing in the area that they're going to operate in. When I say they learn the rest on the job, they come into a firm like this and they soon find out how this firm works, how our accounts department works. Because in other words you could overtrain people, you could have them going on courses for all sorts of things. (1994)

Another element in this attitude displayed by employers towards training for returners, may be that they do not envisage such employees as undertaking highly 'skilled' work. Furthermore, it may be that it is not in their interest for women returning to the kind of gendered work roles made available to them to achieve a level of skills which is more generally marketable, and which will move them out of the firm internal labour market. Among the qualities of women returners commented on by employers who had employed them were their 'loyalty' and their 'gratitude',[5] even though their terms of employment were often inferior.

Finally, conceptions of skills decay and obsolescence are predicated on the capacity to define skill levels objectively, apart from the social systems which construct the meaning of the term 'skill' (see also Curran, 1988, p.337). A substantial literature exists identifying the way in which 'skills' are socially constructed (for a summary see Grint, 1991, 188-98), but our observations on the construction of the legal labour market have already made it clear that the notions of 'desirable attributes' deployed by employers in their hiring and firing policies are profoundly gendered, and are detached from the notions of technical legal skills which are used to underpin the profession's claims to special status and rewards (Sommerlad, 1996). If, as we have argued, a woman's career trajectory is rather influenced by her access to cultural and reputational capital, then the factors which operate in the cases of individual women returners are more likely to be those such as the extent to which their employer gives them access to 'fronting' work with clients; the extent to which reputational capital in a particular sphere depends on gendered 'private activities', and access to the social capital, which Seron and Ferris argue gives unlimited access to 'professional time' (1995).

The confidence deficit: a private or public problem?

A loss of confidence has been confirmed in the general literature on women and the labour market as a powerful factor affecting women's successful re-entry to work after a break, and this has been the foundation of much work on returner training (Payne, 1991; Rees, 1992; McGivney, 1993; Sommerlad and Sanderson, 1997). The responses of our own sample confirmed that it was an important issue: in response to a closed item listing possible barriers to returning to practice, 44 per cent of the 1990 sample (Sommerlad and Allaker, 1991, pp.51, 104), and 58 per cent of the total 1994 sample identified confidence as a 'potential deterrent'.

The issue of confidence is more complex than it might at first appear, however. In the human capital model, it is closely related to skill decay, and in the case of the law, the combination of skill decay and rapid occupational and technological change might be anticipated as the most significant factors. However, loss of confidence may be constructed by the more general social neglect and isolation of parents of pre-school children, or by an anticipation of the labour market's view of mothers' transmogrified capacities. Differing explanatory models of the loss of confidence have substantially different implications: whether to locate policy remedies in supporting women, or transforming employers' views of them, for example. Hence we attempted to achieve some precision in understanding the exact character of the loss of confidence.

In contrast to the numbers citing a general loss of confidence, a lesser proportion (30 per cent in 1990) identified specifically 'loss of confidence as a solicitor' as a deterrent. Furthermore, of the 39 women in the 1994 sample who were currently out of practice, seven mentioned loss of confidence as an issue in response to an open question about barriers to returning to work. The following is a representative selection of their comments: 'my confidence has evaporated'; 'I now feel I lack confidence, and so much has changed with computerisation of the office procedures and the new terminology in the law'; 'I'm lacking in confidence, it's difficult to know how to get going - I think I've left it too long'; 'a career break affects confidence almost immediately, and prospects if it lasts longer than six months'.

Three out of the 18 women returners in the 1994 sample also mentioned loss of confidence, though two of them associated this with the problems of having sole responsibility for childcare and the conditions under which they were being obliged to work; 'my confidence is shattered - I'm constantly tired because my child does not sleep at night' (associate solicitor, returned after a three month break, 1994). Even women who had not yet experienced a break anticipated that low self-esteem would result; three out of 21 in the 1994 sample identified this as a problem though two of these specifically associated the projected loss of confidence with the loss of status which they felt would inevitably accompany a break. This issue was also highlighted in both 1990 and 1994 by the results relating to the training which was perceived as important for returners. As reported elsewhere (Sommerlad and Sanderson, 1997, p.56) the training which was most closely associated with anticipated loss of confidence, such as up-dating in new technology, was seen as more significant by the samples of women out of practice and women who had not taken a break. Women who had actually returned saw these areas as comparatively less significant, and more easily surmountable, thereby implicitly contradicting the human capital view of confidence loss as related to skill decay.

The responses in both stages of the research cycle emphasised the importance of the length of the break. The significance of this factor, however, must be set in the context of the fact that law firms have little attachment to even modest 'retention' policies, such as those which involve keeping employees on maternity breaks in touch, and offering re-entry training and flexible hours. Those of our respondents who had experienced more sympathetic employment policies had found the process of returning to be much easier. The experience of Nordic countries where family policies are more positive, indicates that a substantial difference can be achieved in retaining women employees (Hantrais and Letablier, 1996, pp.134-5: see also a range of policy reports relating to UK contexts: Curnow, 1989; Association of Personnel Managers, 1990; Rajan and Eupen, 1990).

The reluctance to make any concessions to the private sphere extended to a failure to take up any of the opportunities offered by the 'information revolution'. There were no accounts by any working mothers of attempts to make use of faxes, e-mail or home computing facilities to improve contact or continuity. One woman had been refused the facility even of a lap-top, as the partners 'could not see the point of spending all that money' (part-time returner, 1997), and another salaried partner spoke in 1994 of 'people in other firms who asked for capital equipment to work at home, and that met with much more resistance than a reduced working week for a reduced salary' (female corporate solicitor). As another returner commented in 1994 'what is tragic is that, in a world where technology could help so much, the profession is extraordinarily reluctant to help women (and men) work outside a minimum core of hours, in the home, using computer/fax links'.[6] This perspective is echoed in Mossman's criticism of similar inflexibility in Canada (1994, p.67).

The confidence barrier, once overcome, appeared to be relatively short-lived, and did not represent the kind of permanent 'disability' which might have long-term effects on a woman's career. One woman working in general practice found that she was able to adjust rapidly: 'I was anxious that I wouldn't be competent - I did suffer a loss of confidence, but I soon realised that I still knew as much as colleagues, and in fact, having taken a returners' course with the AWS, I knew even more, because I'd had an update' (assistant solicitor, general practice, after a long break, 1994). The account of another woman, who had returned part-time to a branch office, before moving back to the headquarters of a large commercial firm, indicates that organisational insensitivity can be more damaging to confidence than anxieties about professional ability:

> I had no retraining before I came back. I did find things difficult. Firstly, the * office was not well served in terms of professional developments, and didn't really keep us up to date. I found it subsequently difficult when I came back to A*, having been away three years, partly because I was treated as if I'd only been gone a very short time and would therefore be familiar with everything, yet everything had changed - aspects of the culture of office procedure, and I didn't know about it, but was expected to, and that was very undermining. So my problem was not so much about skills or up-dates - nor even confidence initially, because I immediately got a client back who wanted me, thought a lot of me, so that immediately boosted by confidence. So what really caused me problems was the fact that people in the A* office do things differently now - so I don't quite know how I'm supposed to do things. For example, you now have to have a staff pass. I haven't got one - I don't think it's deliberate, I think it's just inefficiency and the fact that they assume I'll have one, but it makes me feel like a non-person. (Commercial conveyancer, 1997)

So confidence, which is so often treated and described as a personal problem, is intimately connected to the way in which the organisation functions, and, we would argue, the way in which organisations are gendered. Like 'commitment' and 'motivation', 'confidence' is a relative state that can only be meaningfully interpreted in conjunction with an analysis of the work and workplace about which women might feel more or less confident.

This is clearly indicated by instances of women who felt positive about their abilities before they returned, but who subsequently found their confidence being undermined by the attitudes of colleagues and the inflexibility of working arrangements. Consequently, part-time returners experience particular problems. Whilst the confidence of some was evidently sustained by a belief in their own ability to practise successfully and to maintain good relationships with clients, they found that 'in general the office was just not geared up to meet the needs of fee-earners working part-time' (part-time returner to general practice, 1990). Others similarly commented on a lack of support from the office: messages were not taken or passed on promptly, a part-timer's typing might slip down the scale of priorities.

One respondent in 1994, who was pleased with her return to work, and expressed satisfaction with her own level of confidence in her ability, found that the attitudes of male colleagues exacerbated the stress which resulted from the dual pressures of her situation:

> It is clear that my partners consider that my wish to work part-time is something like 'afternoons off for golf'. They feel it is a bit stubborn to insist on it - and that in practice I have afternoons 'off'. In actual fact I stay at the office in term time till well beyond my 'half-time' - racing back to get a six year old and a ten year old from school. Then my second shift begins and lasts a further six hours. There is little understanding of the unsung pressure of such a routine from my employers.
> (Returner to general practice; back in work for five years, working an official twenty hours, but actual thirty hour week)

As these last comments indicate, a further element in a returner's loss of confidence stems from the overt devaluation of both the work and skills required in caring work. The following remarks of a personnel officer for a large commercial firm were echoed by many female respondents: 'some of the men are openly sarcastic about females in general, and are especially resentful about maternity leaves which they seem to regard as holiday; they will often make comments like "why should they just be able to go off and have babies"'. Yet some of the skills involved in caring work - interpersonal and organisational skills - are precisely those which are now identified as crucial for legal work (Bell and Johnstone, 1998). For instance, a male job-sharer commented: '... while looking after the children I have had to learn the time management principles known to every childcarer. Applying these to my work has made me more efficient' (New Ways to Work, 1994, p.4).

In all three cycles of the research, women returners mentioned the constant questioning of their commitment as a persistent irritant which undermined their confidence. Low self-esteem would often stem from the fact that certain work was held back from them: as a part-time returner who specialised in commercial property noted, this could affect career prospects as well as confidence:

> The guy I work for - he wouldn't involve me in things because I'm part-time - on principle. In the past, before, he did involve me - fronting a case for him, dealing with the client and so on. On most cases he wouldn't now, though, say that I'm back - so I just do back room work and I only front with the one or two clients who know that I'm back. It's of enormous significance being kept out of the clients' view because that's what you want to progress - you must have a profile with clients to go anywhere. But you will only generally get those opportunities if you're full-time. (Commercial conveyancer, 1994)

However we found evidence that this treatment was accorded to full-time as well as part-time returners; for instance, a woman who subsequently achieved equity partnership with a different firm found that when she initially returned (on a full-time basis) to the firm with whom she had worked before the break 'certain areas of work were kept back from me - I wasn't given the choice because they felt it just wasn't suitable - for example I never got to do personal injury and industrial injury work - for a * Trade Union because the legal executive would go down there for three days at a time and they felt that my husband wouldn't like that' (1997).

The 'commitment deficit': rationality or ideology?

The connections between the professional mode of working and domestic support are clearly revealed by the unwillingness of either employers or colleagues to accept manifestations of split loyalty (Hochschild, 1989). Unsurprisingly, therefore, 'commitment' was named by virtually all employers in both surveys as *the* principle criterion for selection for employment and for partnership. It was also the principal 'problem' identified by firms in the employment of women returners (though not by firms which actually had employed returners). Furthermore, the central importance of commitment to professional inclusion and progression was confirmed by women in practice, returners and non-returners, and women out of practice, in all of whose responses the term repeatedly surfaced. For instance, a returner argued that 'there should be understanding that just because you have children does not mean that you lack commitment'; and a woman in practice noted that 'a request for a career break is seen to be a lack of commitment' (non-returner, 1994). Another practitioner, who, similarly, had never actually taken a break herself, observed that career breaks are viewed as 'a sign of a lack of commitment (the death knell) …'.

The continuous need to demonstrate commitment also clearly affected employee behaviour. For instance, many women argued that it was necessary to obtain promotion or partnership before having children, because even if only a short maternity leave was taken, the perception of increased domestic commitment would inevitably harm any career prospects. Part-time returners reported working regular and extensive overtime, partly because of pressure to prove their commitment; thus one commented: '… I am taken by those with whom I do not work closely to be giving less than a full commitment to the firm'. Another explained: 'it is very easy to feel that you have to do a full-time job in part-time hours …difficult not to feel guilty about being part-time and feel as though you have to prove your seriousness about the job by over-committing yourself' (1990).

As we noted above, Hakim's work on women's employment (1995; 1996; 1996a) has given academic respectability to the employer perspective on commitment and choice. Rather than viewing occupational segregation as solely a consequence of structural discrimination, she argues that it 'has been reconstructed in the late twentieth century to provide separate occupations and jobs for women following the marriage career, which allows only non-committed contingent work and non-career jobs which are always subordinate to non-market activities' (1996, p.450; our emphasis), and: 'criticisms of labour market discrimination as unfair and unjustified often rest on claims that … women workers are just as committed, dedicated, hard-working and productive as men', and proceeds to argue that in reality there exist significant gender differences, which emerge particularly clearly with part-time workers: '… the commitment of a part-time worker to a part-time job is not equal to the commitment of a full-time worker to a full-time job. At the minimum, the two levels of commitment differ in degree, and arguably they differ qualitatively as well' (1995, p.434).

A critique of 'commitment'

An initial point to make about the notion of commitment, and one to which we shall return in considering our evidence, is that in the discourse of both employers and economists, it is not a measure of output, either in terms of the quantity of 'product', in this case the amount of useful legal services delivered, or in terms of the quality of the product. As a concept, therefore, it is unable to embrace the fact that many women argue that their dual focus on domestic and work spheres obliges them to make efficiency gains in each, to cut out elements of workplace culture which are unnecessary, and oriented towards social satisfaction or political and/or demonstrative functions (preening and display). We would argue that in this context, measures of commitment are in fact measures of conformity, and ways of displaying 'availability' to the firm. We would also argue that research evidence on the gender differences in the type of commitment displayed by women professionals would tend to indicate that women's commitment might be more oriented towards the quality of work.

Hakim's initial measure of work commitment is unidimensional, and based on a single question concerning desire to work in the absence of financial necessity, the so-called 'lottery question' (1995, p.435). Arguing from data which actually proves little gender difference between full-time workers, she claims that the demonstrated gender difference between the total populations of men and women are significant in looking at gendered attitudes to work. It could be contended that the findings are at least equally significant in measuring men's commitment to home, but clearly this aspect of the relationship between private and public spheres is accepted as a given. It is particularly interesting that in her subsequent full-length treatment of 'women's heterogeneity', Hakim looks at domestic labour, and in this sphere as well adopts the male standard as a core rationality. She notes that 'single women spend 50 per cent more time on domestic work than single men, an average of three hours a day instead of just two', but rather than use this data to draw conclusions about men's 'commitment' to domestic work, or their standards of hygiene, she concludes that 'this suggests that one-third or more of the time spent on housework by women consists of optional extras, that is consumption work' (1996, pp.48-9).

Several of our respondents applied the same logic in reverse to the difference between the amount of time they spent in the office compared to their male colleagues. An equity partner specialising in corporate tax reported the comment of a male colleague that it was not possible to be a mother and give 100 per cent to a job, and went on to argue that:

> in fact, almost any per cent would be at least as much as the average partner actually puts in. By that I mean I really pack in the work in the hours available. You have to make the time count and be ruthless about things that you don't do, because you're not prepared to spend all the hours that many men put in - of course you do if the client really needs you to, but if it's just a question of having been out for a long lunch and then not really getting on with it in the afternoon - generally being a bit dithery - then I don't do those sort of things. (1997)

The same respondent also recounted the difficulties she had experienced in attempting to have meetings run more efficiently. Her views on the superfluity of some of the time spent in the office were echoed by a part-time salaried woman partner at the same firm (a large commercial practice), who amplified this perspective by pointing out the function that this time fulfils in terms of office politics (and see Bass, 1998, pp.28-9) and the personal networking, which we have identified as being a key aspect of the framing of the profession as essentially male:

> There's a culture of being around, and talking about who was in late, who left early and so on. But a lot of it is just about being seen to be around - it's down to office culture and politics. I think though that the office culture can be a powerful network, especially in a big department where there's a lot of jockeying for position, because you need to get on with partners who will be able to further your career. But women don't have time to engage in all of that. (1997)

The 'surplus' time that men spend at work, in other words, is not 'consumption time', as Hakim argues women's 'surplus' domestic labour is: it is time spent in the personal accumulation of cultural capital. As we discussed in Chapters Five and Six, some of this cultural capital has currency in the firm's internal processes, and may be tied into reciprocal relationships which are work-related. As one male insolvency practitioner put it: 'during that office time a fair amount of it has to be spent on maintaining relationships within the firm - obviously if you're in a big firm and you're on friendly terms with 200 solicitors it's easy and quicker to clear up any tricky points with a quick phone call' though he added 'quite a lot of time is spent chatting - too much probably' (1997).

Some of the other time which is spent with clients but is not billable is, it is argued by those involved, concerned with the cultural capital of the firm, though some of the senior partners interviewed in 1994 and 1997 were sceptical about the real value of long lunch hours, go-karting and hospitality boxes at football grounds. Given that an individual's personal cultural capital is so closely tied to the firm, then this 'surplus time' is a key to personal advancement: as one male planning specialist at a corporate firm, who had no partnership ambitions noted: 'the ultimate way of getting praise at * is through bringing in new clients' (1997). Whether the kind of marketing which we described in Chapters Five and Six really does generate new business is difficult to test, but what seems clear is that the belief that it does serves to generate a social system and culture which creates a form of 'commitment', measured in terms of quantity, rather than quality of work (and see Wajcman, 1996), which impairs, and is used to justify the impairment of, the prospects of women. This state of affairs is clearly not unique to the solicitors' profession: French notes the way in which the 'long hours culture' in the management of public service organisations is used to challenge the 'competence' of women who can not, or choose not to, participate in it (1995, p.61).

Hakim's work relies heavily on the views of employers about the 'instability' of women part-time workers, views echoed by employers in our research, and fails to examine the way in which these same attitudes are crucial determinants in the career decisions of employees (see also Newman, 1995, p.25). Our research provides clear evidence that employers' views result in a deterioration of working conditions and career prospects, which in turn contributes to women's so-called 'employment instability'. Women who had returned to work in both the 1990 and 1994 cohorts, and who had changed employers, had done so in the majority of cases because of either the failure of their previous firm to demonstrate any flexibility at all in working practices, or the women's anticipation that the firm's general attitude would be hostile to them.

Conversely, the extent of male employment stability, though well attested in Hakim's national figures, may not be as great at some stages of a solicitor's career as it once was. One specialist in a large corporate firm argued that in fact many firms did not expect staff to stay on a long-term basis:

> Our staff turnover is 25 per cent per annum. Why? Partly, I think because there's a general churning over in law anyway. You have to move job to increase your salary; my salary hasn't risen significantly recently because I stayed here. There's no recognition for good, devoted service. So the pattern is to move every two years and up your salary each time. (1997)

Commitment: an alternative approach

A striking feature of the discussion of commitment is the general failure to define it. As we argued above, the use of a single measure fails to encompass the quality of commitment offered by employees, which may also be gendered. A more exhaustive analysis of the concept than that offered by Hakim relates it to the 'unique constellation of (professional) traits' (Kaldenberg et al, 1995, p.1359). Kaldenberg's study of dentists has approached the concept in terms of behavioural and affective commitment. Behavioural commitment is interpreted as the investment of a 'limited resource (money, time) ... in pursuit of an end' and is found to vary according to gender, largely because such an investment may be 'credited to several different ends' (op.cit., p.1372), so that the male work role is also perceived as an aspect of the familial role whereas in the case of women, such a work role is perceived as competitive with their ('natural') familial role. This was also a finding of Seron and Ferris's work on law firms in the USA (1995).

In contrast to behavioural commitment, affective commitment represents a 'moral involvement to abstract principles'. The research of Kaldenberg found that 'females are spending less time doing professional work than men, but tend not to differ from them in their attitudes about work. Likewise, females show less behavioural professional commitment than men, but do not differ from men in affective commitment' (1995, p.1373).[7] The female respondents to the survey did tend to articulate a more generalised, altruistic notion of service and of commitment to the client; the following explanations for the choice of law as a career were representative: 'It's a people job - I wanted to help people' (general practitioner, 1997); and 'Men have this status thing in their heads ... I'm more interested in the client' (conveyancer, 1994). Similarly a recent Policy Studies Institute survey of law students reported that women were more concerned than men about the value of legal work to the community and that conversely men were more interested in their potential salary and the status of the job (Halpern, 1994, pp.59-60). Moreover, Marsden, Kalleberg and Cook argue on the basis of their work in the USA that there is no gender dimension to 'organisational commitment', the loyalty that an individual displays towards the immediate employer; 'when job attributes, career variables and family ties are simultaneously controlled, the authors find that, if anything, women tend to exhibit slightly greater organisational commitment' (1993, p.368). Whilst for Carrier, assertions about the impact on career involvement and aspirations of caring responsibilities are largely rooted in gender-role stereotypes (1995, p.344).

Finally, in an illustration of Marks' study of the stresses induced by multiple roles (1977) which noted that commitment in one field did not inevitably produce a lesser commitment in another, the majority of female respondents did not accept the orthodox construction of commitment as a finite quality. Most part-timers surveyed viewed themselves as just as committed as their colleagues. Given the obstacles of returning to practice (which frequently include the need for lengthy and expensive retraining), the generally lowly pay, status and prospects on return and the problems of combining domestic and work responsibilities - generally without the back-up of a 'wife' - it could be inferred that the commitment to, and interest in, work exhibited by a returning solicitor must match if not exceed that of the full-time solicitor who has never taken a break (see also, Hagan and Kay, 1995, pp.153 and 185; and Epstein et al (1995) p.423). Indeed, far from such a work style representing a lack of commitment to a career, 40 per cent of such returners stated that they still aspired to partnership. This conclusion is confirmed by Hagan and Kay's findings, especially with regard to women who return to full-time practice (id.). They found that role diversity in fact enhanced rather than diminished 'life experience', and that 'women who have children and continue to work full-time in private practice do not lose their commitment to their work, and they are often more satisfied with their work and happier with their personal lives ...' (op.cit., p.187; and see Chambers, 1989; Carrier, 1995).

The results of our study amongst others (Brannen and Moss, 1991) indicate that participation in the public world requires such exclusion of the private during the hours worked that rather than domestic commitments taking precedence over, and thereby reducing, professional commitment, the reverse is frequently the case. Many women returners claimed that such were the demands of work, and such was the pressure to demonstrate commitment, that to participate at all as a professional meant a continual relegation of the needs of the family: 'the extra hours were severely detrimental to me and to my daughter and eventually caused me to leave altogether'. As one woman who had eventually left practice for a teaching career argued: 'what's so unfair - which we all say - is that if anything gets sacrificed when you're working, it's not your work, but your children. I think that those men and childless women don't in practice work any harder or have any greater commitment than women with children - but they make the rules' (1997).

Employers who had taken on women returners frequently claimed to view them (and indeed women in general) as more reliable and consistent: for example, 'women work shorter hours but get a lot more done in those hours' (senior partner, general practice, 1994). The commitment of women 'part-timers' could also be evaluated by comparing the 'official' working hours with the actual hours worked. The 23 women who described themselves as working 'part-time' in 1994, (which included hours up to 35 a week), all reported working regularly in excess of the official hours, for amounts varying between five and 15 hours, so that some women working 'part-time' were in fact regularly working 50 hour weeks. Moreover, nine of them worked in the evenings at the office at least sometimes (five at least once a week), and sixteen worked regularly at home in the evenings, and 'sometimes' at home at weekends. There were in fact no statistically significant differences between part-timers and full-timers in terms of additional hours worked.

'Commitment to work', we would therefore argue, is a flawed and deeply ideological concept. Until it embraces measures of output (quality and quantity of work undertaken) as well as input (hours worked), and until measures which are predicated on imagining a gender-neutral division of domestic labour (like the 'lottery question') are abandoned in favour of a more qualitative comparison of men and women's respective commitments to both home and work, research in this area should be read with great caution. Nevertheless, the concept of commitment is extraordinarily powerful, so that even those women whose practice of working extensive overtime we have just described, would frequently accept the notion that their status meant that they could not demonstrate the same commitment, and so could not expect the same rewards as full-timers:

> It's a basic fact that women give birth to children and then take prime responsibility for childcare and therefore can't give the same sort of commitment. That's where I'm coming from and I accept that because of that I can't make partnership because I can't put in the number of hours.
> (Associate solicitor, with three children, six months after returning from her last break, 1997)

'Choice': the real rationality of 'rational preference'

The conception of women's labour market position being the product of their own 'choices' is deeply embedded in human capital theory, and was crystallised in US law in the case of EEOC v. Sears, where the presiding judge agreed with the Sears case that 'men and women tend to have different interests and aspirations regarding work, and that these differences explain in large part the lower percentage of women in commission sales jobs' (the higher graded jobs) (EEOC v. Sears Roebuck & Co 628 F Supp 1305 (1986)). Hagan and Kay point out that whilst Becker acknowledges discrimination as a factor in differences in gendered labour market outcomes, it is regarded as theoretically separate from the issue of career preference (1995, p.13). Our respondents clearly indicated the way in which awareness of inequalities in gendered outcomes was closely linked to career choices, which may in themselves be theoretically distinct from career preferences. Just because a woman has 'chosen' a job, it doesn't mean it's the one she really wants. As we have noted, women who have taken a break increasingly retain their partnership ambitions, whilst expressing the view that, in a difficult economic climate, they are 'lucky' to have been able to obtain flexible working conditions, even on a reduced salary, and with poor prospects. Similarly, as we noted above, if the underpinning ideology of the labour market is to identify males as the prospective high earners, then women may 'choose' to sacrifice their ambitions, but not abandon them. Although some recent research (Hardill et al, 1997) has begun to challenge the orthodoxy of male dominance in dual-career households (Edgell, 1980; Gregson and Lowe, 1993), we found that among our respondents, women were more inclined to subordinate their careers to male partners.

Thus a solicitor who had been a highflyer in London with one of the largest commercial firms in the country explained how she had come to leave:

> My husband and I both worked very long hours - regularly till 8.30pm - and I think in the long term he was likely to do better than me, not because he's better qualified or brighter, but one of you has got to make the sacrifice, and be prepared to be home by 7pm and it's generally the woman because they know that men will get the breaks and will therefore be more likely to make it - so we had an unspoken deal - I don't feel resentful. (1994)

Another respondent, from 1990, phrased it more pithily - 'my husband is a "high flyer" and two high flyers and a family just don't mix'. A childless woman who had moved into teaching had made the same decision with her husband on the basis of his prospective greater earnings; 'we took the decision that when I came here he would move on and work hard so he earns far more than I' (1997).

However, it is not simply the earnings differential which constrains women's choices. The demands of the profession in terms of working hours and availability were seen as representing a quality of life which was incompatible with any genuine commitment to childcare (see Market Assessment Publications, 1996), and ultimately difficult to sustain even without caring responsibilities (Chambers, 1997). A former equity partner at a corporate firm, who decided to leave for a part-time position at another firm at the end of her maternity leave described her decision in the following terms:

as an equity partner, the partnership does provide for six months leave and for people then to come back: but I think those provisions might just as well not be there, in that they certainly didn't expect you to take the six months leave because if you were serious about your profession, you wouldn't take six months off ... I suppose at the end of the day I have made the decision to leave - I've decided I don't want that lifestyle. If I'd stayed I would have had to have carried on as if nothing had happened, working 8 until 7 every day, and I just wasn't prepared to do that. (1997)

The majority of women who had taken breaks in our sample clearly did maintain their commitment to sustaining a working career, but were divided over whether they accepted the constraints on their freedom of manoeuvre and their prospects.

Similarly, the notion of individual choice must be contextualised by the fact that the cult of lengthy working days depends on a gendered division of labour in the private sphere. Women's choices are therefore further constrained by the continuing resistance of their male partners to take on domestic responsibilities. It was striking how many women (as in Brannen and Moss's study (1991)), including some of the most successful, claimed to bear the main responsibility for domestic labour; the following accounts were typical:

I have three children - twins who are nearly two and a four year old. I have a nanny three days a week. The division of domestic labour between me and my husband? He's better than most I know but I do 95 per cent of it - in the evenings and at weekends. I think it's just women's lot. Men assume that you will take responsibility ... so if you don't do it, it doesn't get done. He's better than most - he doesn't disappear for days on end to play golf like many; at least he's supportive ...

(Female salaried partner in large commercial firm, 1997)

and:

My husband doesn't play any part at all in looking after the children, I do it all ... so I have to be part time. (Commercial solicitor, 1994)

And a salaried partner whose husband bridged the gap in the early evenings between the departure of the nanny and her arrival commented: 'It does cause friction and I have to do everything at the weekends - that's my punishment' (1994).

In fact eliciting the character of women's choices may only be possible by providing the challenge of a 'counterfactual' question: Brannen and Moss's concept of 'congruence' is useful in evaluating the extent of 'fit' between a woman's ideal and actual working status and conditions. So, for example, many of our sample of women out of practice in 1990 had maintained partnership ambitions whilst many returners had an ideal view of their diminished status as part-time workers being a temporary condition. Conversely some women felt that they had been obliged to undertake a commitment at work greater than they really would have wished, some because they were single parents, and therefore needed the money in order to pay for good quality childcare; others because it was the only way of achieving job satisfaction. A lack of congruence between women's ideal and actual conditions may therefore indicate a considerable lack of flexibility in the demand side of the labour market, rather than either unrealistic ambitions or lack of ambition on the part of women.

This argument may be supported by looking at evidence concerning the extent to which women use a strategy of job-changing to achieve what some American theorists (Polachek, 1981) have described as 'compensating amenities', that is, exchanging remunerative advantages for benefits which provide a better accommodation with family life. Estes and Glass found that in North America women in fact attempt to maximise both family accommodation and financial reward, but the extent to which they are able to realise this goal is affected both by the extent to which they have managed to achieve substantial human (or cultural) capital before the birth of their children, and the characteristics of employing organisations (1996, pp.428-9).

In contrast to human capital and rational preference theorists, we would argue that, whilst women's experiences of maternity and a break from a career do make them different from men who are able to concentrate full-time on their career in the knowledge that they have domestic support, what is more important is that they are *perceived* differently. This perception is, of course, in turn connected to the assignment to women of the sole responsibility for parenting. However, even if the family issue continues to be constructed as the mother's, rather than a parent's, problem, many of the supposed practical difficulties of employing women with care responsibilities are still less problematic than they are generally represented as being. Nevertheless, women who become parents are regarded as having taken a path which leads away from higher rewards in the profession. Their ascribed cultural capital is discounted, and any retained aspirations to career progression are seen as anomalous. We identified a number of elements in the construction of this anomalous status.

Corporeality

Thornton cites Kristeva's theory of the 'abject', the 'peculiar repugnance and horror associated with bodily functions' as helping to 'explain the gross discomfort experienced by men of law when confronted by the non-erotic materiality of the female body in the public sphere' (1996, p.231). Thornton goes on to argue that it is the contradiction between the eroticised embodiment of women and the materiality of the state of pregnancy which male lawyers find so difficult to deal with (op.cit., p.232). The experiences of our respondents served to confirm this representation.

We have already referred to the sexualisation of much of the work associated with practice development in previous chapters, and the use of female sexuality as a resource is not confined to this area of work. The social interactions characteristic of legal work also involve the use of women's emotional labour (Hochschild, 1983) - hence the tendency of employers to view women as ideal for matrimonial work. However in illustration of Young's argument that 'the civic public must exclude bodily and affective aspects of human existence' (1986, p.66), one of our respondents noted that despite the eroticisation of the employment sphere, discussion of personal and domestic matters remained taboo:

> Are there open criteria for promotion? You've got to be sexy at the time. I use the word 'sexy' because it's just part of the jargon - part of the parlance - a way of describing 'in' work. It's probably because we're all so busy, we've almost unsexed sex; everything, including sex, is now totally related to work - you stay here all hours, take work home with you, etc., and as a result we've brought something which belongs in the private world into the public. Everything merges into everything else. On the other hand I wouldn't dream of

> talking about my private life to a partner because they're not interested and I think they would feel that if, for instance I spoke of a problem I was having at home, it was a sign of weakness - they'd feel it meant I wasn't handling whatever it was well. (Commercial specialist, corporate firm, 1997)

A childless woman who had worked in a large City firm observed: 'there's certainly a clear cut off when women have children ... women were looked down on when they had had maternity leave ... they found it very difficult to cope with pregnant women walking around the office' (1997). A woman from a similar firm explained how her pregnancy had been seen as inappropriate for aspects of her work that involved client contact:

> My Partner said to me 'you can't address a seminar in this state - it's not pleasant to look at'.

This appeared to be a common, though not invariable, reaction; for example another woman explained that the general attitude in her firm had been:

> you're a pregnant woman - we've got to hide you. I was very annoyed, but another part of me wasn't surprised because there had been a salaried partner who had been pregnant and was completely marginalised, and who hadn't told people until at least five months and then had spent all her time trying to cover it up. If you wore a dress that clearly showed you were pregnant that wasn't acceptable - it was seen as unprofessional - comments would be made. (1997)

The same respondent also referred to 'the look' which indicated the unacceptability of pregnancy, a clear illustration of the 'symbolic violence' discussed by Bourdieu, and cited in Chapter Two.

However, we would argue that, powerful though the revulsion towards the corporeal is, unless it conforms to a form of acceptable sexuality set by male bosses, it also confirms and justifies a range of other essentialist views of women. Many women spoke of the need during pregnancy to work even harder, and to show no sign of weakness, since this would confirm the view that women collectively could not 'cope'; as a former City lawyer observed of her maternity leave: 'No concessions were made and I didn't ask for them ...' (1994). Several women recounted tales, sometimes of colleagues, sometimes of themselves, of working right up until the birth of their children, and returning within weeks. One such account of work in a City firm also indicates why some women have adopted this tactic, since otherwise maternity would probably signal the end of a highflying career:

> At my level I felt that there was no distinction made between men and women, though at the higher level there were women who'd left because they couldn't manage the maternity arrangements. Those who stayed didn't take long off when they had their babies. There was a famous case while I was there of a female partner who went into labour in the office, finished the report she was working on in the office, in labour, then got a taxi to the hospital and was back at work within two or three weeks of the birth. Her handling of the birth was not uncommon; there was a general need to disrupt things as little as possible.
>
> (Equity partner of large commercial firm, 1997)

In fact, for women, any intrusion of the private into the public world can be regarded as an essential weakness: our informants included women who had experienced miscarriage and stillbirth and had had to suppress both the physical and psychological effects in order to maintain their position. An associate solicitor specialising in commercial conveyancing expressed this point vividly:

> One thing that's been very marked for me is that since I've lost two babies ... after the last one, I rang and said that I wouldn't be in the next day and then returned two weeks later - since then no-one has said anything - at Partner level, that is. Nobody in that period after said to me 'Are you coping?'. That is the distinction I think. You're in a male dominated environment and personal things, however tragic, are ignored. I had an appraisal for the year recently, in the course of which this still birth had occurred, so I got visibly upset at this, when I had to review the previous 12 months but I couldn't say I couldn't handle it. I had to try and hide it and they didn't even acknowledge that I was upset ... that's the distinction. You are just expected to get on with life and they don't want any mention of it. Similarly with any other personal problems ... private life is completely excluded - though men can talk about their own problems. (1997)

We will return to this issue of the exclusion of the private world from the world of work, in the specific sense of the domestic private world in a subsequent section.

Available property

As we have argued in earlier chapters, the profession carries the legacy of working relations which are based on structures of patronage and hierarchy, where debts of loyalty are accumulated and then called in. These personalist systems are internal as well as external: senior partners expect to be able to call on employees at will, and several of our respondents cited the practice of calling departmental meetings at weekends. A specialist in corporate tax, and an equity partner, described the continual pressure to make concessions in her domestic arrangements: 'part of the difficulty I have is to refuse to come in at weekends to Heads of Department meetings - I say no and they don't like it, though they usually end up saying that they understand. You're supposed to be married to the firm in some ways, and I don't like to feel that I'm for ever having to say no to many of these extra demands on my time' (1997). As a result, some women considered that marriage per se had a negative effect on how they were perceived (Glover found the same in her study of teachers and white collar workers; 1994, p.95).

Open ended availability, which can be seen as a synonym for 'commitment', is consequently a fundamental device for bonding within the firm, and for testing loyalty, and this is a major factor in the exclusion of people who manifestly have outside commitments (Hochschild, 1989). This is exemplified in Chambers' account of the development of a 'flexible work scheme' for partners at a major City firm: 'we found ... that many lawyers regard flexible working as a non-starter. The very nature of partnership, they say, requires all the partners to pull together, with equal commitment. The part-time partner contravenes the philosophy, the spirit, of partnership' (Chambers, 1997, p.22).

This approach is of course reinforced by the increasing demands by clients in a range of sectors for 24 hour availability (id.), and by the need to engage in competitive entertaining (the practice development described above in this chapter and also in Chapters Five and Six) to attract clients.

However, as we discussed above, the continuing trend for women to assume the lion's share of domestic obligations may preclude them from participating in such work to any great extent. Furthermore these obligations are in part a function of the understanding that their husbands/ partners have no such obligations; indeed if they are professionals they are likely to be freed up precisely in order that they may network (Seron and Ferris, 1995). In this way, the identification of commitment with total availability represents 'gender privilege' (Williams, 1990) since it justifies the release of male lawyers and their male clients from sharing in domestic duties, thereby (generally) ensuring greater success for men's careers (Hagan and Kay, 1995, p.18).

'Availability', or what Seron and Ferris describe as unlimited access to professional time (1995), therefore fulfils both a practical and an ideological need, and can be regarded as forming an element of an employee's symbolic capital. For women returning after a break, their lack of availability changes the way they are perceived. A former equity partner recounted the following experience:

> I remember a conversation that I had, before I got pregnant with one of the Senior Partners about a mother of an eight year old child who was a partnership candidate. He said that he couldn't see a woman with children becoming a partner in insolvency. It was clear in his eyes that the fact of having a child precluded her from being a partner because she couldn't do evening entertaining of clients - she wasn't totally available. (1997)

Furthermore, the need to demonstrate availability is arguably complicated for women not just by their potential or actual commitments in the private sphere, but also because of the implicit or explicit use which some firms make of their sexuality (for parallels in other service industries, see Filby, 1992). It is apparent that it is not just pregnancy, but in fact any kind of attachment that can be incompatible with some of the sexualised roles described above in the section on practice development; in addition several women in 1990, 1994 and 1997 mentioned the fact that they were expected to be 'married to the firm'. One successful City solicitor described the effect of her actual marriage:

> When it began, I didn't immediately stop going to functions, but perhaps I didn't smile as much and I would make excuses and leave earlier. And then I would just not go to some things. None of this was received very well, because you're putting your life before the firm. Suddenly they stopped including me. For instance in a marketing meeting; then I was not invited to a series of seminars. I wasn't actually told 'you're no good', I was simply excluded ... Before when you're single it's assumed by the firm that they can do with you as they feel. (Associate at large corporate firm, 1997)

The private-domestic in the public realm

As we have argued earlier, the notion of the 'private realm' is gendered: whilst men do business through the quasi-private 'men's club' (see also Thornton, 1996, p.241), the private domestic world is set in such contradistinction to the public world of employment, particularly in the law, that it is frequently made clear to women that to succeed, they must proceed as if they had no private responsibilities - that is, as if they were men. This will normally involve the employment of full-time domestic help, or, as we have indicated above, on very rare occasions, a shift in primary caring responsibility to the spouse or partner. An equity partner remarked: 'My husband and I have always shared domestic chores; I think that's been a major factor in my success. In the early stages though we would both say that what we needed was a wife' (general practitioner, 1997).

Where working arrangements institutionalise the intrusion of the private world, through part-time working or job-sharing, there is a concomitant decline in status, as one job-sharer claimed: 'even if we resume normal full-time jobs, I don't think either of us could get over the stigma of being job sharers - they call us "the Mums". And there's always a question mark over whether we can do important work. For example one partner came down and said to our partner "this is a big job - can they do it - are they up to it?"' (commercial property lawyer, 1997).

As we noted above, although the embodiment of women lawyers is eroticised, there is a contradiction between this element of the personal being present in the workplace, and the public image of the lawyer, the neutral technocentrism identified by Thornton. As an academic and former general practice lawyer argued:

> Showing emotion would be frowned upon. You had to show that you were entirely detached. Talking about your personal life would be a problem; you were there to do a job. No one was interested in babies, and families. If you went out for coffee with the boss, there could never be any personal discussions. In fact, as a result conversation was really difficult. He was so professional and focused, he wouldn't even say 'hello' to you in the street.
>
> (1997)

None of our respondents mentioned having attempted to breast-feed a baby at work, as some of Thornton's had, and indeed hardly any of them had ever taken their child into work. One equity partner commented on the adverse reactions when she had had to take her four month old baby in: 'If I had to I would sometimes bring * in, which made everyone feel bad' (1997), and it is reactions like this, or fear of such reactions which prevented most women even contemplating doing this. The consequence was a good deal of stress and anxiety which, because they were generally the primary carer, women reported over the common difficulties of illness, unreliable childcare and school holidays.

We would argue that the repugnance demonstrated for the private sphere also reflected the domestic arrangements and prejudices of individual male practitioners. That is to say, that where individuals endorsed a strict division between public and private spheres in their own life, they were that much more likely to object to the intrusion of the private in the form of a working woman with domestic responsibilities. This could be described as the 'what's my wife doing in the office?' anomaly. For example an equity partner in a general practice in a medium-sized town described the discussions held in her firm on the development of a maternity policy, which followed a merger with another firm. In spite of the fact that she didn't plan on having a family herself, she had argued that the firm should have a policy: 'I was very shocked by the reaction of one of the middle-aged men who said "well if you choose to have a baby you must take responsibility for looking after it" implying that I should give up my job. When I protested he said "You could always have an abortion"' (1994). On another occasion the same solicitor was approached by another middle-aged male partner, who in spite of their parity of status, 'summoned' her to his room: 'he said "I've been reading the staff minutes and I see you've got your secretary pregnant ... I mean the firm's got her pregnant again". I said that women were entitled to have babies, and he replied "well she's got one already and you know my views about women working, they should stop at home with the kids"'.

A male equity partner in a small town, medium-sized general practice was quite clear about the issue: 'We are a very old fashioned, traditional firm ... clearly there is prejudice against women ... and in the profession generally ... there is even more prejudice against women of child bearing age ... the view taken by some older solicitors is that they don't like women working and the clients won't like women dealing with them' (1994).

A corollary of this hostility to mothers working was an exaggerated concern for the 'mother's role': So the senior partner of a medium-sized general practice responded to a question about how obstacles to women in the profession could be overcome by writing 'impossible unless women are going to neglect other areas of their lives, or other duties' (1994). Women returners reported expressions of concern for the problems of fulfilling a dual role being used as a rationale for a range of decisions which would adversely reflect on their careers, such as restricting access to client work, transfers to different, less prestigious legal work, or even the refusal to guarantee a return to work at all.

An equity partner in insolvency practice spoke of the way in which fellow partners communicated their own views as to how she ought to manage the responsibilities of childcare: 'though they're not that old - mid-40's - they're very old-fashioned in that they think women with children should be at home washing nappies. These views did come out in some conversations, but particularly surfaced when I decided I would leave' (because of the firm's attitude) 'then it became clear that they genuinely think I am going to stay at home with the baby. They said "Oh you'll enjoy being at home with a baby" it wasn't malevolent, but rather paternalistic' (1997).

Conversely, as we indicated above, other male colleagues refused to recognise breaks for maternity as in any way serious, and would make their feelings clear with expressions on resentment. For example, one part-time associate solicitor reported that 'after my return I was made to feel that I was trying to "have my cake and eat it"' (1994); and, according to a female equity partner of a large town practice: 'the reasons for career breaks are often belittled' (1997). Unsurprisingly, several women referred to the fact that few of their male colleagues seemed to spend much time with their families. One woman recounted how her boss, who she described as 'virtually living in the office', had told her that he made a practice of not getting home before the children's bedtimes and that if he ever saw that their lights were still on 'he would drive around the block a bit until they went out' (commercial conveyancer, 1997).

Adherence to the view of domestic labour as naturally female (and consequently low skill) also means that men who differentiate themselves from some of the characteristics of male professionalism by displaying an overt regard for domestic responsibilities are likely to be regarded as deviant and less than professional. One such male respondent was an equity partner and criminal specialist of an extremely busy two partner general practice in a small town. Since the birth of his son (now aged twelve) he has chosen to work part-time, yet remains one of the town's most sought after criminal practitioners, thereby proving the feasibility of such arrangements. The predominant reaction, however, of the overwhelmingly male legal community of the area is that 'it is OK for a woman to be a part-time, but bizarre for a man' (partner, general practice, 1994). In 1997 the part-time partner reported that his state of virtual professional ostracism continued.

An obvious consequence of men and women's different career trajectories is the fact that many women who return after a break will find themselves in positions junior to men substantially younger than themselves. This raises issues of authority: on the one hand women return with an enhanced authority in the domestic sphere, and as we have seen above, what they would argue are enhanced organisational skills, whilst on the other they may have had to accept a work role which is below their proven ability and their actual capacity. Therefore it could be argued that their achieved authority is in conflict with their ascribed subordination; again, a related point is the change that often occurs in women's perceived sexuality following maternity, and ageing.

The inflexibility of working practices: extent and consequences

In this section we discuss the practical responses of employers in the solicitors' profession towards women taking career breaks. Our sources of data here are the comments of the firms themselves, and reports by women of the behaviour of firms and other employers. The data from firms is obviously open to suspicions of sample bias, particularly in 1994, when the response rate was very low (see Appendix). It appears likely that firms participating in the survey are those most likely to be favourably inclined towards issues associated with equality of opportunity. The more hostile firms are likely not to have bothered to have completed the questionnaire.

This suspicion was confirmed by triangulating the response profile with women's reports of the attitudes of firms. Therefore, where we provide data on the responses of firms to particular proposals in relation to supporting women returners, these will give an unrepresentatively positive view on the part of the profession. Most of the data used is from 1990, when the response rate was acceptable, but before the recession had drastically affected employment in the profession.

We have already extensively discussed the way in which employers endorsed the human capital and separate spheres explanations of women's drift from the profession: 26 (40 per cent) firms in 1990 attributed the cause, at least partially, to the women themselves. However, 12 firms (19 per cent of the sample) placed at least some emphasis on employment practices and showed real insight into the problems faced by women in pursuing their careers, whilst thereby generally accepting that women had the primary domestic role. 'Failure by most firms to offer working hours suitable to those with family commitments' was a typical comment from this group, whilst others referred to lack of career progression as a potential factor in causing women to leave. Sixteen responses (25 per cent) attributed the cause (either wholly or partially) to other external factors such as the lack of adequate childcare provision by the state, women being attracted to alternative careers, women taking the major responsibility for the domestic burden and women placing the careers of their partners first. Eleven firms (17 per cent) failed to acknowledge a significant loss of female personnel at all and eight (two per cent) firms could offer no comment on the reasons behind the loss of female solicitors.

Employers' views on female wastage were clearly influenced by both their own experiences and also by knowledge of the experiences of others, in that where they heard of an individual leaving the profession for purely personal reasons this was often used to infer reasons for the loss to private practice of women solicitors in general. Similarly, there was a tendency to over-generalise from a single negative experience of women returning, or being employed part-time: 'we had a bad experience a few years ago, and our view is "never again"' (senior partner in a medium-sized firm, 1994). It might be suspected that in some cases, the problematic experience might be confirming (as well as caused by) already existing social attitudes. The structure of law firms, with the absence of bureaucratic constraints commented on above, means often that women's destinies are decided by the chance of who happens to be their significant line manager. For example one female assistant stated:

> The position of women in the profession is a reflection of women's position in society generally and the way they are treated varies tremendously in line with the personal attitudes of the men they are employed by. (1994)

There was a marked reluctance on the part of firms surveyed to view the issues of recruitment and retention in more generalised strategic terms, and this failure corresponds to 'the piecemeal and individualised approach' to the problem highlighted by Danielle Ross (1990). This compares unfavourably with corporate strategies adopted by certain other employing groups during the same period of time, such as many of the clearing banks. A major rival employer, the Crown Prosecution Service, also claims to have developed a policy to adapt working practices to a range of needs (Mills, 1997), in the form of flexible working patterns and retainer schemes. These policy initiatives may not, however, have emerged simply from the more bureaucratic and public policy orientation of the organisation, but rather to meet a recruitment crisis. As a commentator remarked in the professional journal: 'the desperate days at the Crown Prosecution Service during the recent recruitment crisis of two years ago meant that they combated the problem by creating one of the best staff programmes in the field. This is particularly true for women and ethnic minorities' (Gillies, 1991, p.13). On the other hand at least one of our respondents claimed that this policy was not always favoured in the CPS's regional management structure, and that its upper echelons were male-dominated. Moreover, the same respondent also argued that over time, as the pressure to reduce costs mounted up, flexibility was decreasing, and conditions were becoming less favourable to women.[8]

Less than 20 per cent of the sample of firms (only 12) attributed the loss of women to inflexibility on the part of employers, and this calls into question the level of support they might offer to women, and it is useful to recall that 50 per cent of the women who had not returned to practice cited the type of work available, and 28 per cent unsuitable working hours as the predominant deterrents deriving from the profession. There was, therefore, a clear mismatch between women's experiences and needs and employers' perceptions of their own policies.

Other commentators have stressed the general need for the profession to adopt policies and practices which will assist rather than impede women's careers (and see Chambers, 1997). This was the emphasis of the United Kingdom Inter-Professional Group's recommendations (1990, p.7), whilst the Association of Solicitors Personnel Managers pointed in 1990 to the lack of childcare facilities, career break schemes and returner schemes and noted that the widespread failure to augment statutory maternity pay did not encourage mothers to return to work (1990, p.5).

Twenty-six (40 per cent) firms of those surveyed in 1990 stated that they made 'special provisions' for employees with children. For the most part (20 firms), this consisted of implementing flexible working hours. These arrangements were often restricted to female secretarial and administrative staff however. Firms were also asked if they would consider the adoption of a number of specific ways of assisting employees with children.

Table 7.1 Policies to assist parents

Figures give the number of firms willing to consider each suggestion (1990) (respondents could select any number of suggestions).

	All Firms	2+ Partner Firms
Flexible working hours	40 (62%)	33 (66%)
Home working	24 (37%)	21 (42%)
Job share schemes	20 (31%)	20 (40%)
Assistance with childcare	13 (20%)	11 (22%)
Combine with other firms to provide childcare	26 (31%)	22 (44%)

So firms were at least willing to consider practices which would assist working parents, but the most popular option appeared to be that of flexible hours. When asked if they would be willing to offer specific assistance to women returners 43 (66 per cent) of firms indicated that they would. Twenty-four firms (37 per cent) further indicated that they perceived a need for special arrangements to be made for this group of employees. Again, flexibility in working hours was considered the most viable option, though 55 per cent were also prepared to fund re-training.

Firms were also asked how they might use a woman returner on a work placement basis, as part of a refresher course, since this idea was most popular with women returners and was integrated into the course developed by Manchester Polytechnic (now Metropolitan University) in 1990. Many did not understand our use of this term, but 30 (46 per cent) firms gave vaguely positive support to such a scheme. However, unfortunately, others ruled this out as a possibility. Two of the senior partners interviewed were particularly concerned about issues of confidentiality and continuity.

In practice, the extent of employer flexibility could be quite unpredictable: one woman who had already experienced two successful breaks with the same employer was told on the third occasion that her job would not be available on return. The following account from a woman who had been a partner but eventually moved to another firm part-time, exemplifies both the pressure involved in attempting to conform to the male norm and the constrained character of the choices women exercise. After a caesarean birth, she returned to work within three months because 'if I didn't see my clients for six months they would have gone somewhere else'. When her daughter was a year old, she realised she could not carry on:

> At the time we were having a lot of angst in the partnership - one of the partners had become quite strange and wanted to hold lots of Partners' meetings which were going on until 10pm every week and what with that and work (I was working 9-6) generally … it got too much - I realised I was going to be ill - not seeing my family - so many other things to do - shopping and so on, and everything seemed to be the firm. I think the partner singled me out to do more than I would have done … I don't know if it was to prove something or punitive in some way … I'd decided I'd have to leave because I knew they wouldn't let me stay on part-time. I told them and they were horrified. Then the Senior Partner said they didn't want to lose me and would I stay on part-time. He said they needed me and asked what would be my ideal, so I said a three-fifths working week, and I also said I would have to have assistance because of the nature of my clients. It would have been possible but the other partner said he wouldn't agree to me being a part-time partner - I'd have to leave and be an employee. Then he said if I was going to be part-time I couldn't run the commercial department and they'd have to get a young man to take over. (1994)

She left and joined her husband's firm part-time in a neighbouring town, taking many of her clients with her. Several of our interviewees had had similar experiences of trying to match up to the male model, becoming ill and then looking for a move to work which would allow them to keep their health. This experience was not unique to women with children. Two women without children who experienced an acute illness found their colleagues similarly unsympathetic, and were obliged to change jobs.

As we have noted throughout the book, but particularly in our earlier section on commitment, contemporary developments in the profession have created a demand for a workforce which is constantly available, and as Seron and Ferris have noted of the USA, the self-employed sector is particularly 'greedy' (1995). Hence even those firms which were willing to tolerate a lower level of availability, would not contemplate part-time partnerships. It was clear therefore, as our female respondents indicated, that even where firms were prepared to offer flexible working arrangements, this meant being locked into a secondary market, for as we discussed above, commitment as currently understood is generally incompatible with a lower level of availability. Thus a managing partner of a general practice wrote: 'partnership is a full-time plus occupation, demanding total commitment' (1994). Moreover the requirement to work full-time plus is not confined to partners; in the words of one respondent: 'the view is that a professional has to be on a 100% call' (1990), and, according to another, 'people tend to think that in order to do the job properly you have to be contactable by clients all the time' (1994). As a result one woman explained that her department (corporate) had a reputation of doing completions at 4am - 'we will work all night' (1994).

The phenomenon of 'expanded professional hours' (Seron and Ferris, 1995) in the UK profession has been widely commented on in the professional press, with some commentators arguing that young solicitors in the UK work harder than any of their European counterparts (Law Society Gazette, 17 May 1995, p.1), even though transatlantic commentators have argued that yet more will be demanded in the global market for legal services (Rose, 1996, p.8). Another respondent noted the reciprocal and reinforcing nature of this culture with that of the corporate clients: 'part-time partnerships should be possible but not here. You have to look at the clients we serve as well. They wouldn't contemplate part-time Partners because they work like that (i.e. long hours) too and they expect it from the solicitors. Most of the clients are men ...' (1994). Another woman described her (large commercial) firm as a 'beast that requires total devotion ... there's no room for nice considerations like family' (1994). The 'nature of the job' is therefore used to justify complete inflexibility (a phenomenon common to other 'senior' positions in public and private sectors (Itzin, 1995a, p.148)).

Exceptional women - how to take a successful break

Our respondents in all stages of the research cycle included women who had managed to establish a successful career up to and including equity partnership, either before or after having children, though it was considerably more common for equity partners to have achieved this position before maternity. It is worth looking at some of these 'success stories' in greater detail, since they provide us both with evidence to test theoretical positions on the reasons for women's subordination in the solicitors' profession, as well as offering ideas about how support for women's careers can be developed.

A key element that women identified as being important in their success was access to 'social capital' (Seron and Ferris, 1995). This normally, unavoidably, involved the employment of full-time domestic help - in other words, shifting the responsibility to other women, as 'housewife substitutes' (Wajcman, 1996, p.626). So, for example, a woman who had taken a 12 month break in the 1970's some time after achieving partnership in a medium-sized urban firm, and continued as a partner up to and beyond a partial retirement, cited the 'availability of permanent and loving childcare in *my own home*, without having to look for outside nursery care' (her emphasis), the childcare consisting of 'a domestic help and trained nanny who doted on my daughter and who herself had an extended family living nearby who would always help out in day-to-day care' (1990).

As we discussed above, a re-negotiation of the domestic division of labour seemed to be far rarer, but did occasionally occur. A highly successful equity partner with a corporate firm shared domestic labour with her husband, who was not a solicitor, and had the support of a nanny from 8.30 in the morning to 6.30 in the evening: she took the 'shift' in the morning before the nanny arrived, but because she had to work until at least 6.45 every evening, her husband took the evening shift. A salaried partner commented in 1994 on the need for domestic back up in the form of outside help and a supportive husband. She had a live-in nanny, 'and a husband who doesn't work such long hours. He finished at 5pm every day so he bears a lot of the childcare burden in the evening'. By 1997, this woman had left private practice for a position as an in-house lawyer in industry, and though she had achieved greater autonomy, she still depended heavily on domestic support, as she worked similar hours, 'both my children are at school now and we have an au pair. My husband takes responsibility in the evenings as he still generally comes home earlier than me'. Other women reported employing 'fleets of nannies and domestic help' (City lawyer, 1994).

Whilst several women referred to the importance of a supportive, or 'understanding' environment at work, among colleagues and employers, it was not always clear what they meant by this. One woman who took her break after achieving partnership in the 1970's referred to the 'goodwill' of her partners, and this was evidenced by the fact that she remained a partner even whilst absent from work. In other instances it appeared to involve some fairly minimal concessions in terms of working hours, for instance, responding to a reluctance to attend weekend meetings by 'saying that they understand' (equity partner, 1997). The same woman argued that her position was comparatively favourable 'because it is at least accepted that seeing your children is something a woman ought to want and be able to do', yet she still described a schedule involving nine and a half hour days, weekend work and the occasional evening of practice development.

Several women mentioned the importance of achieving partnership and the accompanying reputational capital before taking a break (see also Itzin and Phillipson, 1995, p.83), so that the terms of return could be negotiated in the knowledge that they would represent a loss to the firm. For example the retired equity partner quoted above argued that 'the only key to the problem at the moment is for the woman to establish her worth and her value to the firm *before* taking a career break so that they *want* her back and are prepared to make the adjustments which are inevitably necessary' (1990, her emphasis). Other women spoke of their success in returning as being a function of their 'rarity value' (corporate tax lawyer), or because clients were particularly attached to them: one respondent in a City firm spoke of returning to work three weeks earlier than planned because she was worried about losing a particularly important client to a male colleague. The same woman believed that the reason she had not 'made partner' was that 'I don't think I timed my children properly. I should have delayed my first child - I think if I was up for partnership it was when I had my first child' (1994).

As we discussed earlier, a corollary of the establishment and maintenance of reputational capital was the need to minimise any career break, so that contacts with clients could be picked up as smoothly as possible, and the assertion of an 'undamaged' status could proceed smoothly:

> When I had my children (now 14 and 17) I stopped two months before the birth and went back three months after. Because I was always intending to go back I never built up a separate home life. I wanted a child, not a baby, so I never felt I missed out - I was very lucky though in that the firm I worked for was nine to five. (Equity partner, medium-sized firm, 1997)

A woman equity partner who had decided not to return to her former firm had done so on the basis that 'to have continued I would have had to pretend that I hadn't had a baby, I would have had to put in all the hours I had before, that is 8.30 in the morning to 7.30 at night, and evening entertaining and weekend work' (1997).

As we have already indicated, the majority of our respondents worked in the corporate commercial sector, where we had assumed that these kinds of pressures would be most severe. However, one of our male respondents working in the legal aid sector argued that if anything the pressure was even greater in this area of work because of the major cuts in legal aid funding:

> None of the female solicitors or partners here have kids ... the only solicitors with kids at this branch office are men. If such women had kids - they couldn't do it. And if they took time off and then returned - I think their positions would be diminished - whatever their previous reputations. They couldn't work less hard and earn less money and maintain the same status - their reputations would inevitably suffer. (1997)

Clearly, the maintenance of a successful career combined with continuing domestic responsibility requires exceptional organisational ability, and a supporting infrastructure: we noted above the way in which part-time workers bemoaned the difficulties they experienced with support staff. One successful part-timer, who worked in her husband's general practice, commented on the combination of her own organisation and commitment, and the support she received from the office:

> In fact though I don't do this job on just three days a week. I work a five day week but not always in the office - most clients know that they can get hold of me any time, and I have an excellent secretary - and she'll ring me at home - it works through a combination of extremely organised home and work life. We

> have a live-in housekeeper and other excellent support, and I've always been prepared to do whatever necessary to do my job. (1994)

Whilst many other women took work home, worked late at the office in the evenings and undertook occasional weekend work, this was a comparatively rare instance of a woman conforming to a pattern which Seron and Ferris found to be quite common in New York: the professional home worker (1995, p.40). As we have noted above, firms in our region appeared far more reluctant to support work from home. Consequently, for women who did not have the same kind of approach, or office support, it was even more essential to ensure that their organisation of both spheres was watertight.

Women at all levels of practice argued that those who succeeded by making equity partner, and achieving substantial reputational capital, were 'exceptional' women: as one woman said 'How do women become partners? They have to do 150 per cent more than the men' (part-time commercial conveyancer, large commercial firm, 1997). A former salaried partner who had moved in to industry, described the only woman who had become an equity partner in her former firm in the following terms:

> The woman in * who has achieved the highest degree of success is extremely well organised. She is an excellent lawyer, she also has training and administrative responsibilities. She is fantastically efficient and intelligent. She now has a child - but was promoted before she was either married or had children, which may be relevant. (1997)

Another part-time associate at the same firm described this same equity partner as being able to 'hold her own against any man in the firm and she is respected for that' (1997). Several women referred to the need to be 'that extra bit special' as a woman.[9]

As we discussed above, it was also clear that however successful they were, women felt that they generally maintained primary responsibility in terms of the overall organisation of the domestic world and childcare, particularly in emergencies, and therefore had to be capable of absorbing considerable stress. As we have already argued, this stress is the necessary consequence of the inflexibility of working hours and the exclusion of private concerns from the public world. Research on the social work profession indicates increased stress on workers of either gender with dependent children, but that the highest levels of stress are to be found amongst women (Ginn and Sandell, 1997). Our sample of men was not large enough to allow generalisation about their experience of stress related to domestic commitments, but women's responses suggested that the gender effect in the law might be more pronounced. A part-time associate solicitor argued that:

> People do still work in the basis that everyone has some domestic back-up and it's therefore so difficult when our nanny is ill - we have an agonised argument about who should stay - it will depend on who has the most important meetings - it's all very fragile. And women really worry about all this; I'm not sure that the men do. (1997)

The fact that women retained background responsibility for childcare, even when at work, was also reflected in the fact that several of them mentioned feelings of guilt about absences and the effect that high pressure working life had on their relationship with their children. Clearly a capacity to absorb or manage this kind of guilt was an important aspect of the success of these women. An equity partner at a family firm looking back on the stage when her children were at school remembered:

> I do feel terribly guilty about my child's first day at a new school - I read something she had written about mummy being very bad tempered because she was late for work. (1997)

These emotions were echoed by our longest established equity partner in notes on her 1990 questionnaire: 'feelings of guilt when leaving for the office in the morning and when I was late home and later (in particular) when I was late picking her up from school'. A woman who had moved from being a salaried partner in 1994 to an in-house lawyer in 1997, modified her views about her relationship with the children as they got older. In 1994, when the children were three and five, she felt she was 'not desperately torn between looking after the children and being at work. The kids seem happy and cheerful and I don't think they are suffering by my being at work'. By 1997, with both children at school, she appeared rather more doubtful: 'I'm very conscious that I would like to go home and collect them from school - but that would render the job impossible and I love the job and had I wanted to do a part-time job, no doubt I would have found one … I'm conscious that I'm doing less for the kids in one respect but comfort myself that we do things at weekends and that they seem to be fine'. In many ways, therefore, these women are still generally imprisoned by the conventional social script (see Fegan, 1996 on the ideology of motherhood). They are exceptional, not just in their abilities, but because they succeed despite the fact that such success rarely alters their domestic role, or the general view of women.

We noted earlier in the chapter that, as Seron and Ferris argue (1995) the 'greedy' organisations tended to be located in the areas of the self-employed private sector where extensive availability to clients was the norm, and no systematic approach had been taken to meeting those demands. As one might expect, therefore, for some women the route to a successful career lay in moving to a more bureaucratic form of organisation, in the form of the Crown Prosecution Service (CPS), or a position as an in-house lawyer for a major industrial concern. One in-house lawyer (IHL) argued:

> Things are better, though, I think for women in big organisations because they have got clear maternity policies - written down - most people in small firms are trying to argue for what they can get - they're on their own. Most big companies accept that equal opportunities are a fact of life - there are lots of women who are high up as IHL's. (1997)

Another woman had moved to a position as IHL because of the 'wider focus in terms of the content of the job', though an additional reason was the anticipation that 'moving into industry and creating for oneself a sole client' would enable her to 'work on a more regular pattern', and although she worked a similar number of hours to those at her previous firm, she argued that she still had total autonomy, 'so if there's a child's doctor's appointment, for instance, then I can go' (1997). An alternative strategy for finding a more comfortable environment is to set up as a sole practitioner, but the only respondent to attempt this had done so out of desperation and had not found the strategy successful in terms of reconciling home and work:

> I left * and Co in 1986 to have my third child. When I said I wanted to return to work (about April 1987), he advised me that my job was no longer available. I took legal proceedings against him and he settled before we actually reached the Industrial Tribunal. As I felt very bitter (I had worked for him for seven years) I did not want to work for anyone else for the moment. I therefore set up on my own and I found this difficult as I only wanted to work part-time and I very quickly became busy. I did not enjoy this situation and on July 2nd this year I was taken over by * and I am now their employee. (1990)

That these strategies have a broader appeal than simply to the women whose responses we report is demonstrated by the figures reported in the Law Society Annual Reports, which demonstrate that women are more highly represented than men in local government, the Crown Prosecution Service, industry and commerce as reported in Chapter Four.

However, a key lesson to be learned from a close examination of the careers of these successful women is that there is no recipe which guarantees a successful return from a break. The passage of time, or the changed numbers of female recruits to the profession, may affect over time the way a firm views the prospect of supporting a woman's career break. For example, the returner who in 1990 expressed the most positive view of opportunities within the profession was a 60 year old woman who had, some time after achieving partnership, taken a break in her late thirties and then returned to the same firm where she remained as a partner, eventually going into partial retirement, and reducing her equity share accordingly. She was widely known locally, and had been president of the local Law Society. She attributed the continuity in her career to 'goodwill on all sides'. During her year's absence she had received her share of the profits with a deduction for the employment of a locum who subsequently became a partner. She returned full-time, but when her daughter reached school age, in the mid-1970's, she was able to reduce her hours and her equity share pro-rata in order to be able to meet her daughter from school. Then when her daughter was able to go home by train, she reverted to full-time working. The firm would therefore appear to be an early model of how to support the development of women's careers. By 1994, however, when we interviewed a senior partner at the same firm, it was apparent that the transition from women's occasional to routine entry to the profession had put the matter in a different light. The woman described above had died by then: the male senior partner referred to her as representing 'an excellent role model for anyone of how to conduct a practice, but she set a standard that was difficult to follow'. He then spoke of the personal cost to him of the pregnancy of colleagues, stating (perhaps in ignorance of the way in which her predecessor's leave had been arranged) that the current woman partner who had taken maternity leave had cost him personally £40,000, and described the consequences:

> We're in business to make money and we work harder as Partners and if you work harder for less money then you resent it - so there was resentment of her. It was said - openly - we can't have this as a small business ... it reflects on the degree of generosity of arrangements we might be able to make in future.
>
> (Managing Partner, male, 1994)

In contrast to the recommendations of our women respondents, his expressed preference was for women to have their families before they became partners, a strategy which we have noted as being unlikely to meet with success, even if it is likely to prove more economically beneficial for the firm. His views were clearly widespread amongst the male partners, as they were mentioned by a female assistant solicitor working in the same firm as one of the reasons for her disillusionment with the firm. Though she acknowledged that the firm had employed women at associate level, she felt that it was much more difficult for them to achieve partnership, and cited a previous woman partner who had been advised not to return after having a child. The effect was that:

> All the women who joined around my time seem to have gone now anyway, there's only one woman left who's in line for a partnership. The women just get fed up with it all. (1994)

She had left the firm after failing to gain promotion, and joined a law-related insurance organisation before having a child, since she thought a bureaucratic institution would be more supportive of maternity rights. She was disappointed in this hope and eventually moved to working part-time in a small four partner firm on a day rate. This series of linked histories demonstrates that for women, it is not the case that a pioneering woman can blaze a trail for others to follow. Each case becomes a special case, each inclusion is achieved on individualised criteria and creates no necessary precedent for other women. By contrast, the 'bad example', the woman returner who 'didn't work out' does form a precedent, and helps to reinforce generalised criteria of exclusion.

It also appears likely, that for large numbers of firms in the small to middle ranges in terms of size, the economic arguments against supporting maternity breaks work powerfully on partners: and it must be recognised that the economic disbenefits to firms of employing women given the low level of state support are real. Consequently, as women represent a greater proportion of the profession it may be harder for them to achieve partnership in the smaller firms if they wish to have families, unless they are prepared, as some of our respondents were, to renounce partnership benefits. As we have noted elsewhere, such firms appear increasingly 'risk-averse' in relation to the employment of women (although they may be prepared to employ returners, once they have had their children). We would argue that this is a far greater determinant of the nature of the labour market than the supposedly risk-averse nature of women (see Hakim, 1996, p.183).

The degree of change in attitude over time also reflects the particular stage of the economic cycle: one returner referred to a particular firm who had accepted her back on a part-time basis in 1990 because 'they couldn't get hold of enough solicitors for love or money'. Other women employed by the same firm in 1990 and 1994 also spoke of their 'helpful' approach, though qualifying this by noting that they had a 'dreadful maternity policy - you just got statutory entitlement, but helpful in the sense that they ferried work to and from my home for me and said that I could come back full- or part-time' (1994). Subsequently, however, another associate solicitor who became ill after returning to work from a break was made redundant and told that this was partly because in the recession, part-time working was no longer an option.

Furthermore, the extent to which the elements we have identified as contributing to success will apply may vary within firms. This variation may reflect the different culture of legal specialisms, such as those explored in Chapter Five, or the idiosyncrasies of the partners who head particular departments. We have noted in several case histories the influence of individual men in blocking women's progress, or resisting attempts to obtain flexible working: acting as gatekeepers rather than mentors. The women who had accumulated considerable cultural capital with their clients and within their firm were less dependent on the quirks of individual men: nevertheless, their cultural capital was not an absolute shelter, and could be subject to erosion as their status as mothers overshadowed their status as lawyers. We emphasise again therefore that the examples of successful women serve, if anything, to underline the point that women are admitted to the senior ranks of the profession on the basis of individualised criteria of inclusion, but excluded on the basis of collectivist criteria. By contrast, men's 'normal' career path is seen as leading to partnership, and the qualifying behaviour is modelled on a male norm. As the most obvious source of differentiation by gender, motherhood appears to play a key role in marking the point of divergence, when women tend to occupy a role as secondary factors of production.

Conclusion

The issue of how women solicitors, who have invested considerable time and resources in accumulating human and cultural capital, are accommodated by the employing firms in the profession once they have children, requires a fresh perspective. In many ways, the prime organisational principle of the modern law firm, the accountability of staff through a system of 'billable hours', an earnings targets, lends itself ideally to flexible working. One woman referred to her large corporate firm as being an umbrella for a collection of autonomous self-employed lawyers who simply paid a fixed proportion of their earnings to the firm that gave them shelter, resembling, in a sense, a retail franchise. Within this structure, there is no logical impediment to employing women on a fractional, or pro-rata, basis, providing they provide the firm with a fixed proportion of their earnings. However, not only have we found that this flexibility is unavailable to those who wish to work part-time, but also that those who wish to continue to work full-time must not only be exceptional in a range of senses, but must also deal with a variety of attitudes on the part of employers and colleagues which express a diminished view of their capacities. As Hakim has argued:

> the current focus on low earnings as an indicator of discrimination has distracted attention from the fact that career women confront far more discrimination than secondary workers because they compete as equals with men but are often treated as uncommitted secondary earners.
>
> (Hakim, 1996, p.209)

Consequently, we have argued against the classical human capital view that it is the life events associated with childbirth themselves which affect women's careers. Rather, it is the ideological significance of the difference which employers perceive and then ascribe collectively to women which is more important in downgrading women's prospects. This collective ascription of women as unreliable and uncommitted is inscribed into employers' overall view of women's position in the labour market. This in turn is filtered through the prospects which women perceive for themselves. Consequently, the way in which we construe the idea of women's 'choices' needs to be reconstrued, as Henwood has argued in the context of the engineering industry (1996).

Historically, women solicitors have exhibited a belief in the impartiality of the legal labour market and have demanded equality of treatment rather than 'special favours'. To this end they have heavily invested in human capital; their experience of legal practice, however, reveals that while their entry has wrought changes in the legal profession, the patriarchal discourse of professional work and sex roles has remained fundamentally unchanged. In classical liberal discourse, the relationship between capital and labour is represented as resting on free contracts between rational, sovereign individuals; and commitment and choice are essential components of this apparently neutral discourse. But commitment is generally construed as unconditional loyalty to the employer, and in the legal labour market this tends to mean rigid conformity with a professional model which is based on an absolute exclusion of other commitments. On closer examination it can be found to indicate a way of life in which in fact the public and private worlds are in fact almost entirely integrated for the male, in that commitments in the private world, social, and at times domestic, serve the public.

In comparison, the archetypal female career can rarely achieve such complementarity, but will generally be characterised by charges of a commitment deficit. However, the construction of women's professional behaviour as indicative of a lack of commitment, and as representing an exercise of free choice rests on several dubious presumptions. For instance, it accepts, of course, the distinction between, and separation of, the labour market and the domestic relations which sustain participation in that market. Secondly, it assumes and naturalises a dominant domestic role for the woman, following childbirth, whatever her stated preferences. Thirdly, the employers' views of the qualifying conditions for labour market participation are treated uncritically. Finally, this explanation of women's distinctive career trajectories is predicated on the neutrality of 'commitment' and 'choice'. In fact, as two of the key concepts which articulate the relationships between individuals and the labour market, they are charged with the values and ethos of the profession, and rest, in turn, on wider societal expectations as to gender roles, which turn on the assignment of all responsibility for childrearing to women.

Notes

1 This has also proved to be the case in more highly centralised economies such as those of the former German Democratic Republic (Trappe, 1996), where there existed a major commitment to supporting women in work.

2 The work habits and generally misogynist culture of private practice which militates against the participation of people with caring responsibilities were also cited by childless women as reasons for leaving the law; many female respondents spoke of the 'skewed priorities' of workaholic Partners, of the 'inhumanity of the workplace' and their determination to achieve 'quality of life' (see also Mansnerus, 1993). Similarly, childless women were revealed to be highly conscious of this feature of legal practice, and this has also emerged in national studies. For instance, Daniel Bates (1996), found that just under 73% of their respondents believed that their career would be (or was being) adversely affected by motherhood, and a recent article in the trade press reported that 'maternity benefit is still a sensitive subject. It is virtually never raised at interview' (Ward, 1996, p.24).

3 (n=95).

4 Although we are currently seeing an attempt to overturn the orthodoxy on the place of mothers with young children, as the Labour government institutes its campaign against single mothers on benefit.

5 Correspondingly, a recurrent comment of returners, especially those who had obtained part-time work, was that they were 'lucky'.

6 The profession's reluctance is not only 'tragic', but also clearly discriminatory, given the willingness to spend large amounts on other aspects of practice, such as practice development.

7 Similar findings were made by Brown, Curran and Cousins (1983) which, utilising the distinction between expressive and intrinsic rewards to test commitment, found both types of employment orientations equally present amongst both men and women.

8 It is indeed clear that the 'colonisation' of the public sector by managerial values derived from the private sector (Power, 1997) is leading to an erosion of those attributes which made it a more hospitable employer for women.

9 In her study of professional women who successfully combined high status job with family responsibilities, Carrier cautions that in her sample 'partnered women with children and a full-time career may represent a select group of "survivors" with unusually high levels of ambition and career orientation' (1995, p.355).

8 Conclusion

> I am unable to see what the danger is that is to arise from admitting women to be solicitors ... It is very ... probable that the women who are to benefit by this reform will be disappointed in the result, because I fear that their place in the profession is likely to be that of dull, drudging, subordinate clerks in solicitors' offices.
> (Lord Sumner, speaking in the debate in the Lords on the Solicitors (Qualification of Women) Bill, Lords Debates, Hansard, XXIV, 27 February 1917)

> This is not a Bill to compel you to employ women as solicitors. Nobody need employ a woman even after she is qualified ...
> (Earl of Selbourne, speaking in the debate in the Lords on the Solicitors (Qualification of Women) Bill, Lords Debates, Hansard, XXIV, 27 February 1917)

In this book we have reviewed the progress of women in the solicitors' profession in the 80 years since these predictions were made. We have also attempted, through our treatment of the results of our research, to erect a theoretical framework to support the analysis of the processes through which women are positioned in the profession. In this conclusion we will review the principal elements of this theoretical framework, and its relationship to our research evidence. We will then look at the question of how this analysis might inform those concerned with the strategies of achieving greater equality within the profession. Studies of gender inequality are vulnerable to two contrasting criticisms. On the one hand, the charge may be levelled that the analysis is bleakly determinist by locating the source of inequality at such an impenetrable depth of the social structure, that it provides no resource for action for change (Chambliss, 1997, for example). On the other hand, a work which attempts to provide a prescription for change is likely to be rapidly overwhelmed by events, and is also open to jibes about 'policy-oriented research' (Hakim, 1995). We have attempted to use theoretical insights to explore the respective merits of some suggested policy strategies, without attempting to provide endorsements of a particular strategy.

The whole project of exploring women's position in the legal profession is itself vulnerable to criticism: compared to the difficulties experienced by lone mothers losing a large proportion of their state benefit, or women working in the low-wage sectors of retailing or manufacture (or as clerks or legal secretaries in solicitors' offices), women solicitors are clearly a privileged group. However, we hope that the discussion in the preceding chapters demonstrates that there are two key reasons for pursuing this project. Firstly, the pioneers attempting to obtain entry into the law, like those attempting to gain entry to medicine, were genuinely engaged in a struggle over legal as well as economic and social status. The persons cases concerned women's rights to participate in full in public life, and the depth of opposition to women's entry to the profession expressed throughout the struggle in the courts and parliament bears witness to the importance attributed to the issue by those wielding political and juridical power. Another reason for paying attention to the experience of women solicitors is precisely their greater access to resources frequently unavailable to other women. They have been able to use their educational success to exert pressure on 'the qualifications lever' which opens up primary external labour markets such as the professions. They also have access to social capital through their ability to purchase domestic servicing which should enable them to escape the descent through the employment market which overtakes so many women after bearing children. An examination of their experience, privileged in terms of class and status, therefore allows us to focus more closely on the gender-related aspects of their position.

The solicitors' profession: labour market and social field

In Chapter Two, we identified labour market theory as providing a useful tool for the evaluation of historical patterns of change in the profession. In particular, theories of segregation and segmentation allow us to evaluate the apparent phenomenon of feminisation which appears to have characterised development in the profession since the mid-1980's, and which the data from our research seems to corroborate. For instance, the

1994 breakdown of staff showed that 68 per cent of the trainees taken on by our employer sample were female, and that the percentage of female partners had nearly doubled from 7.4 per cent of the total in 1990, to 13 per cent in 1994, and several of these women had made it to the top in 'male' specialisms. Furthermore, the profession today is increasingly heterogeneous, with the result that it may be argued that it is no longer valid to describe private practice culture as characterised by a gender hierarchy.

However, despite the evidence that 'women and the workforce have changed ... (w)hat still have to change are the work*place* and men', (Marks, 1990, p.362, her emphasis). Female respondents from across the spectrum of practices argued that the glass ceiling remains in place for women,[1] and by 1994 only 12 per cent of the sample made any positive observations on women's position in the profession; a recurring theme was that women were 'second class citizens', and not taken 'seriously'. Many considered that those who had made it not only had to be better than their male colleagues but had also been admitted as 'tokens'[2] (see MacCorquodale and Jensen, 1993).

The apparent contradiction is resolved by looking at the way in which women's career prospects and salary levels are distinct from men's, as is their tendency to be concentrated in particular segments of the profession. We examined the evidence of this differentiation in Chapter Four and noted that support for our respondents' views comes from several recent surveys (for instance, see The Hansard Society, 1990, pp.43-51) which reveal the persistence of inequities throughout the profession. Alternatively therefore, it could be argued that the comments of Lords Sumner and Selbourne have been largely vindicated by the general resistance by private practice to women except as 'the volume producers of "day to day" business' (female general practitioner, 1994), and by the continued adherence to the discriminatory masculine culture we examined in Chapters Five and Six. This culture is predicated on the ideology of female domesticity; a situation which is not radically challenged by the establishment of a few niche firms, or by women setting up as sole practitioners.

Consequently our data and those of other surveys (for instance, Reynell, 1997; Sidaway, 1997; McGlynn and Graham, 1995; Ross, 1990) have led us to reject the notion that feminisation of the profession,[3] in the sense of profound and lasting cultural change, has taken place since the large scale entry of women (see Menkel-Meadow, 1989, for a discussion of what 'feminisation' might entail; and Porter, 1997, who argues that women do 'handle power' differently). On the contrary, by 1994 the majority of our respondents were expressing disillusionment,[4] arguing that, despite a rhetorical commitment to equity, the situation had actually deteriorated during the 1990's. Women contended that because the recession had solved the 1980's recruitment crisis, they could now be treated as a disposable, transient workforce (Breugel's reserve army of labour, 1979). Some women specifically connected this to the conventional social script, so that, if married, they were held to be earning a component wage (Caplow, 1954; Tolfree, 1990): for instance, 'they are targetting women (for redundancy) on the basis that they are two income families' (1994). At the same time, alternative working patterns were generally no longer tolerated, and where they were available, carried a price in career terms.[5] In fact some women (and a few men) argued that there had been a backlash (see McCabe, 1995, p.483), and that, in common with other areas of life, increased competition from women and a fear and loathing of feminism (Cockburn, 1991, p.165; Collier, 1998) has rather stimulated an overt *masculinisation* of private practice.[6] The excellent credentials of many women, their willingness to work extremely hard, and their growing resistance to the stereotyped roles which the profession has prescribed for them is perhaps one reason that its ethos is becoming increasingly characterised by a new, and sometimes aggressive, masculinity or 'laddism' (see Collinson and Collinson, 1996), aspects of which we considered in Chapter Five.

Seen in the light of the theoretical analysis of patriarchy and the professions discussed in Chapter Two (in particular the work of Witz, 1992), the experiences of the women in our sample may be seen as reflecting a response to women's usurpationary strategy involving the introduction of new processes of social closure. We have argued that this is based on the application of individualist criteria of inclusion, simultaneously with gendered collectivist criteria of exclusion from the highest levels of the profession, the most important of which is the malleable concept of 'commitment'. In our discussion, however, we have tried to develop an account which goes beyond attributing women's experiences to individual acts of discrimination: whilst individual agency is important, we have argued, with Bourdieu (1987), that it is the properties of the social field in which agents are located which structure that individual agency. We also argue later in this conclusion that it is to the potential for transformation of the properties of the social field that we must look in order to evaluate strategies designed to achieve change in women's status in the profession.

Bourdieu designates the field within which women solicitors work 'the juridical field' (1987), and in Chapters Three and Four, we have argued that the field was historically structured so that there was an interrelationship between the discourse and ideology of law, the general position of women in society, and the culture of legal practice. In this way, the juridical field is intimately bonded with other social fields. We have argued that these fields combine and react upon each other to constantly reproduce asymmetrical power relations between men and women, both in the workplace and in society at large. In particular, we have argued that the historical roots of private practice as an exclusive brotherhood and its constitution as a business founded on personal networks with colleagues and clients, is a primary cause of women's location in a secondary professional market. Furthermore, as we have sought to show in Chapter Five, this historical legacy remains a formative influence on private practice and on the behaviour of its individual actors, both male and female.

Firstly, we have briefly considered the role of law in the constitution of female subjectivity (Fegan, 1996) and, relatedly, in the construction and maintenance of 'a rigid line of demarcation between two analytically distinct spheres of public and private: the former ... designated the world of men, the latter the world of women' (Thornton, 1986, p.5). Drawing on the discursive and ideological support thereby provided by the Common Law (see Fredman, 1997), the male professional culture was powerfully resistant to women's entry. After it was finally forced to concede their formal admission, the tenacity of this culture, for instance in terms of the personal bonds through which it operates and the unpredictable and discretionary nature of its response to incomers, combined with the ideology and discourse of separate spheres to create major difficulties for women in either entering in large numbers or progressing far (Mossman, 1990). Although, following the admission of Carrie Morrison in 1922, the solicitors' profession ceased, formally, to be exclusively male, in practice it remained men's work, and this characteristic was of course important in its continuing high status.

In Chapter Four, we identified the way in which this cultural legacy was equally formative of women's responses to the situation. In particular, the 'naturalness' of the gendered roles which it prescribed and reinforced, militated against women entrants challenging either the professional ethos or working practices. The practical results of this acceptance of both male working patterns and gendered roles in the private sphere are discussed by Drachman in her study of early female lawyers in America: 'the first view was the separatist approach which reflected the 19th century notion that professional women had to separate career and marriage by remaining single. The second view was the Victorian attitude, which reflected the notion that women had to sacrifice career when they married. The third view was the integrated approach which reflected the notion that women could have both marriage and career' (1989, p.231). Clearly the first two views represented the least challenge to the professional culture, and until recently they have represented the predominant response of women solicitors.

Moreover, the habit of assimilation was further encouraged by other factors. Firstly, the inculcation into women lawyers through legal training of a deeply discriminatory culture which nevertheless masquerades as neutral and rational, inhibited resistance (see Fineman, 1990). Such resistance might be construed as evidence of precisely the emotionality and irrationality which legal discourse deemed natural female properties, and could thereby emphasise the essential ineligibility of women to be lawyers; as a result, for the most part, these pioneers were urged to work without 'bringing sex into your practice' (Cott, 1987, p.232, cited in Menkel-Meadow, 1989a, p.299). In this way, the Common Law could imprison female practitioners within its dualistic logic and its essentialist view of their gender. Because the law proclaims itself to be intrinsically fair and impartial, and the legal workplace exemplifies and daily trades in these supposedly autonomous values, participation on nominally equal terms (see Lahey, 1991, p.4) is all that women practitioners can (and could) demand. At the same time, an acceptance of the masculine character of lawyering meant, ironically, that the minority of women lawyers could share in the status that engaging in such masculine work brings.

Secondly, the need to have familial or clientelistic bonds with male lawyers in order to be able to obtain employment in the first place (Milford, cited in Skordaki, 1996) meant that, until the recent expansion, most women lawyers shared the conservative background and world view of their male colleagues. As a result, the earlier generations of women lawyers, have, of necessity, been generally complicit in the exclusionary professional project. Assimilation was also fostered by both the isolation which was the experience of the first women practitioners, and by the professional ethos of individualism. This early period therefore produced no 'collective alternative point of view' (Skordaki, op.cit., p.14): no tradition of public challenge by women lawyers to the dominant professional paradigm[7] - for instance in terms of dress, patterns of speech (such as use of the word person, rather than man), and working practices. As Mossman has written of the first generations of Canadian women lawyers: 'By accepting maleness as the standard for being a lawyer ... women who became lawyers did so on the understanding that their acceptance as lawyers depended on their conformity to such a standard. In this respect, the admission of women to the legal profession ... challenged its exclusivity for men, but not its male exclusivity' (1990, p.88).

Even after wide social changes had begun to produce both more substantial numbers and different types of female solicitors, their low visibility and generally isolated and truncated careers helped ensure that the public image of the lawyer remained resolutely male (and white and middle-class), and, correspondingly, the working habits and ethos of the profession unchanged. This, in combination with the profession's readiness to generalise about the deficiencies of women as a collectivity on the basis of individual 'deviance' or 'failure', meant that women felt on probation, reinforcing the tradition of conformity. In fact, as the various generations of our female respondents observed, it generated a form of super-assimilation: a necessary determination to both emulate men in every possible way and even outperform them.[8] Kaye has therefore termed this second period (just prior to the massive influx of women) the 'superwoman stage, a time when women lawyers coming into firms were intent on conforming to - even outstripping - the standards that had been set by the men ... on standing out as lawyers but never as *women* lawyers' (1988, p.121; her emphasis). The comments of one of our female respondents who had worked in a major City firm for 15 years, starting at the end of the 1970's, illustrate this phenomenon: 'I think I was the first in my department to take maternity leave so I felt it was very important that I made it work ... there were lots of stories current like "we had a woman back and it was disastrous". So you felt you had to show that it needn't be like that … I think it's a generation thing; now I'd be much readier to say things and make demands, but at the time it was a question of "don't rock the boat"' (1997).

The challenge to the classical paradigm: the rise of the mega law firm and the role of women

The preceding discussion has emphasised the continuity of the solicitors' profession as one built and maintained around fraternal bonding, and a functionally and expressively male culture. Our account has also, however, attempted to underscore the fluid nature of the professional project.

In particular, the linked phenomena of rapid expansion, structural change, and the admission of large numbers of women represent a challenge to the classical patriarchal paradigm of the solicitor. The scope of change, leading to an increasingly diverse pattern of forms of association, legal specialisms, and relations with organisations external to the profession, has created a more kaleidoscopic image of 'the lawyer', and women's greater presence has increased the potential for both individual agency and the emergence of a collective women's voice. This is signalled by the activities of such groups as the Young Women Lawyers and the AWS. Moreover, women's increased prominence and the persistence of inequities are receiving considerable publicity, in both the trade and national press. Overt discrimination, though clearly still practised, is nevertheless resisted by many individual women and, currently, officially condemned (see Law Society News Release, 7 July 1997, p.1).

Our analysis of this transformation has been designed to highlight the complexity of change in the field. Although women's entry into the profession is intimately bound up with the rapid expansion in the provision of legal services, it is difficult to argue a direct causal relationships between the two phenomena. The expansion, particularly in the commercial sectors and in legal aid work, and the accompanying processes of rationalisation and concentration have created a more diverse range of professional settings. Correspondingly, there has been an alteration in the structures of value in the social field of the profession, so that the qualities of the ideal typical solicitor are more diverse, and the value of the cultural capital which women and men bring to the legal labour market is more varied and less predictable. This has two consequences: in certain settings women's employment prospects may be superior to those of male competitors, though as we have argued, this may be precisely because their long term career prospects are regarded as circumscribed by their presumed reproductive role. Secondly, because the social script determining the value of cultural capital continues to be written by men, and yet is not 'published', it is difficult for women to plan either their career, or even their day-to-day behaviour, since qualities (such as their sexuality) which might attract market rewards in one set of circumstances may have the opposite effect in others. The over-riding determinant of value, we have argued in Chapter Seven, is the ascription to women of an ultimate role in the private/domestic sphere, and the application of gendered expectations about parental responsibilities to the entire employment and life cycles of all women.

The professional transformation has resulted in a considerable increase in fee targets and, consequently, in working hours, which all firms have been subject to in recent years; the great influx of women lawyers has largely coincided with these expanded work demands, so that in practical terms it is harder than ever to combine caring responsibilities with working as a solicitor. It is perhaps unsurprising therefore that what Kaye has described as the third stage of female lawyering has been characterised by the tendency for women to examine 'the hard won prize' and 'weigh ... it against the rest of life' (Kaye, 1988, p.121).[9] The combination of a greatly increased and more socially diverse female presence and the resistance by growing numbers of them to the current structure and ethos of private practice, is thus an important feature of the more general challenge to the classical paradigm of the Master Craftsman. As a result, although more than 70 years have passed since the first woman solicitor was admitted, it is really only now that the profession is having to confront the problems of 'integrating men and women in the practice of law' (Mossman, 1994, p.64).

A further feature of the recent professional restructuring, and one which is intimately connected to the increasing visibility and confidence of women, has been the development of 'mega-lawyering' (Galanter, 1983; Nelson, 1988; Galanter and Palay, 1991). Whilst it appears that the hiring of women by smaller, more traditional firms often continues to be dependent on patronage, one of the contributions by these 'mega' firms to the ongoing transformation of private practice has been their willingness to employ women in equal or even greater numbers to men, and as a result this book has particularly focused on the experience of women in such practices.[10]

The emergence of the mega legal conglomerates, has, of course been accompanied by corporatisation and bureaucratisation (Larson, 1977; Paterson, 1996; Flood, 1996; Roach Anleu, 1992a). At the same time, in addition to bureaucratisation, other factors such as the large numbers of partners in such firms and the growing importance of being seen to have a commitment to equal opportunities have led to more open policies on recruitment and promotion and, apparently, an erosion of personal influence. Nevertheless, both our respondents and other commentators (for instance see Wallach, 1992) have considered that many of the trends to greater equity are more apparent than real. For instance Filby in his discussion of sexuality in service industries has argued that 'despite the huge investment in management development, organizational design and so on, every day management at the sharp end is typically ad hoc. Private theories and initiatives, hunches, prejudices, "taken for granted" and by the same token discriminatory practices, are given wide operational scope' (1992, p.38).

We noted in Chapters Five, Six and Seven the fact that the essentially self-employed nature of practitioners and the consequent responsibility of departmental partners for the profits of their department means that personal influence remains paramount in these large firms. We have therefore argued in that beneath the surface of bureaucratic rationality (see Pringle, 1989), the networks of personal bonds retain their vitality, both within the profession as a key to success,[11] and amongst the wider business community as a source of business. The ability to participate successfully in these predominantly male relationships, to build up relational and cultural capital, is crucial for career success (Heinz and Laumann, 1982; Dezelay and Garth, 1997; Mills, 1997), even though the real value of such forms of marketing was questioned by some of our respondents (including partners). Moreover, as we discussed in Chapter Six, one way in which some women have been incorporated into these networks is precisely through a determination of their 'difference', by a focus on their corporeality (Filby, 1992; and see MacCorquodale and Jensen, 1993, p.585). Founded in the stereotypes which underpin the sexual contract, the sexuality of such women, as the property of the firm, can be brought into prominence and exploited - both in order to maintain male authority (Hearn and Parkin, 1995) and as a resource in the market of client relations. On the other hand, the masculinity of other networks has meant that women have been largely excluded from participation in them at all.

Ultimately, the mega law firm, like the traditional general practice, is still characterised by a male dominated personalist culture which is rooted in the ideology of separate spheres, and which continues to effect a form of closure. The exclusionary nature of this culture is also revealed by the way in which it enables men in power to determine the nature and value of individual women's cultural capital, and to do so both by reference to a male norm and to stereotyped qualities of women as a collectivity. Women as a category therefore remain trapped in a gendered and devalued role as outsiders which, despite bureaucratisation and the rhetoric of equal opportunities, and the fashion for working parties on women's advancement, it is hard for individuals to escape from, whatever their individual human capital.

So what is the significance of the large scale employment of women by the mega firms? On the one hand, it appears evident that gendered inequalities (as expressed for instance in earnings and status) are most likely to occur where there is the widest possible range of discretion for those in power to produce unjustifiable differentials, and in this sense the breakdown of the gentlemen's profession and the emergence of the bureaucratised large firm may represent a step forward. Indeed, several employees claimed that the ethos of these large firms was 'sex-blind; as long as you work all hours, it doesn't matter what sex you are' (female commercial lawyer, 1994). On the other hand, many respondents described them as extremely 'macho', in both their practices and ethos, requiring employees to be particularly aggressive and assertive. We therefore found that whilst a commitment to economic rationality meant that the large firms took on women in equal numbers as trainees, they would be required to conform to working habits which are modelled on the parody of maleness described above - not just in terms of working patterns, but also in the sense of adopting 'male' behavioural traits. However, at the same time the expectation that they would fail, or not 'stay the course', meant that, as we noted in Chapter Six, this requirement to act as surrogate males did not necessarily evoke equitable treatment by employers.

Of course one of the characteristics of the mega law firm is the great increase in internal specialisation and stratification (Galanter, 1983), resulting in the emergence of legal workers who are distinct from the ideal of the 'mastercraftsman', in that they generally enjoy neither the autonomy nor the status which derives from 'competence in the whole field' (Larson, 1977, p.231). For Thornton, the development of the mega firm is consequently a positive impediment to cultural change: 'bureaucratisation is a gendered phenomenon. Hierarchical ordering leads to superordinate positions becoming masculinised, with subordinate positions becoming feminised, in accordance with the conventional social script' (1996, p.271). Whilst this appears to imply that elite posts were previously more open to women, a view for which there is no material basis, we would agree that the evidence suggests that women are frequently being incorporated into large firms as Lord Sumner's 'subordinate clerks', or, according to one respondent: 'as slightly better paid legal executives' (1994). The concentration of reputational and cultural capital in these huge firms has generated the need to maximise profit producing potential through the employment of large numbers of assistant solicitors to service the reputation bearing Partners (Hagan and Kay, 1995) and it is in order to fulfil this servicing role that many women are taken on, as highly specialised assistant solicitors.[12] It may therefore be argued that many women lawyers are viewed as a different form of labour from the start (Chambers and Harwood, 1990, p.48) and, consequently, that mass female participation neither necessarily signals a change in culture, nor has produced one. Our discussion in earlier chapters, and our remarks above concerning personalist relations, makes clear the tenacity with which the male monopoly over reputational capital is retained, the continuing importance of male networks in building and safeguarding this capital, and the links between these factors and occupational segmentation and segregation. If, therefore, the development of mega-lawyering has involved the emergence of a disposable legal proletariat (Derber, 1982) whose primary function is to service the master-craftsmen partners, then women appear to be positioned in that role.

Conversely, the very discretion and variability which continues to overtly characterise smaller firms, in combination with, at times, a rhetorical commitment to 'being a professional, rather than just running a business' (male equity partner, small general practice, 1994), involved an adherence to neo-feudal and paternalistic ethics, with the result that such employers could be more willing to retain women staff. These practices spoke within a discourse of loyalty; for instance, 'A lot of firms ... buy and sell labour, but we haven't got to that stage yet' (male equity partner, general practice, 1997). Despite this assertion, it is also evident that the commitment to a more gentlemanly style of practice combined with hard economic realities, such as the desire for continuity in order to keep clients, to give a further impetus to being prepared, at times, to retain women. Similarly the difficulties for smaller firms of attracting skilled labour in the first place could mean that they might welcome women returners, following their rejection by their former, corporate employers, and were, sometimes, even prepared to offer them flexible working conditions.[13]

Separate spheres and the continuing resistance to change

We would argue therefore that whilst the emergence of large legal 'factories' has allowed for the employment of generally childless women in large numbers and on a more equitable scale, this professional restructuring has not been accompanied by an eradication of the profession's masculinist and exclusionary cultural legacy. The ideology of separate spheres, which underpins this culture, survives and justifies the continuing relegation of the majority of women to a secondary labour market. It is evident that the current organisation of work, the open-ended access to 'leisure-time', the prevalence of men only activities, expressed in the concept of commitment, are all constructed upon, and in turn reinforce, gender inequalities.

Mossman has argued that as a result, many women lawyers will experience all three of Kaye's stages[14] during the course of their working lives (1994, p.76), and this was illustrated by the remarks made in 1994 by a female salaried partner with a large commercial firm who had two small children and therefore worked the double or 'second shift' (Hochschild, 1989): 'my generation came in thinking they could do anything and that all the options were open to them. A lot of women are now finding that it is just too much because the structure which one accepted when one was 28 or 29 of working very long hours was ok until one had to try and match it up with something very different ... now a lot of us are in our thirties and see a different reality'.

As is implicit in this woman's comments, it is not simply that the social script ordains that women should follow a particular route and possess particular characteristics. Studies (for instance see Hochschild, 1989; Brannen and Moss, 1991; Market Assessment Publications, 1996; Wajcman, 1996) have shown that even high earning professional women bear a disproportionate amount of responsibility for the domestic sphere, and, as we noted in Chapter Seven, this appeared to be the case for most of our respondents too; as a result such women have to be 'supermothers' as well as 'superwomen'. Furthermore, as we have argued, the naturalisation of the gendered status of this burden then both acts as the rationale for male domestic irresponsibility and makes possible the lengthy working days, revealing the essential complementarity of the private and public spheres (Pateman, 1988). The symmetry between the workplace and the domestic sphere is revealed with particular clarity by after hours practice development, and in this way the lengthy working day and after hours socialising represent 'gender privilege' (Williams, 1990), for the social capital represented by women's domestic labour (Seron and Ferris, 1995) allows men to achieve greater career success (Hagan and Kay, 1995, p.18). The likelihood of such success then in turn reinforces dichotomous career patterns in heterosexual couples.

The apparent acceptance of domestic work as 'naturally' female by many successful women may perhaps be connected to an implicit recognition of the maleness of their professional work. A disturbance of male/female roles in the private sphere would challenge the masculine character which is essential to high status work, and in this sense threaten their own status (see Henwood, 1996). Adherence to the view of domestic labour as 'naturally' female (and also not proper work (Grint, 1991, p.40)) similarly, therefore, explains why, although employers can now accommodate women who abdicate this responsibility either through remaining childless or by employing other women as domestic supports, it cannot conceive of men having significant domestic responsibilities. Thus one woman commented: 'Men solicitors still seem unable to promote their own participation in the family and would still give some sporting commitment as an excuse for being absent rather than assert men's right to participate' (NUJ equal opportunities officer, former general practitioner, 1997). As we noted in Chapter Seven, we found that men who do deviate from professional norms in order to share in domestic responsibilities (for instance by always leaving work on time) are likely to be stigmatised.

Endorsement of the 'rightness' of male irresponsibility in the private sphere then perpetuates, and justifies, the culturally male ordering of the public sphere (and hence the long hours, and male bonding) (Seron and Ferris, 1995), as well as the devaluation of the private sphere (Fredman, 1997, p.413). Consequently one woman argued: 'It would be helpful if work was not considered as *the* major life commitment for everybody. As long as men are considered not fully committed unless they appear to be working long hours and taking minimal holidays, then women who have to go home on time will lose out - even if they work full-time. A more family centred work style with paternity leave and an insistence on taking full holiday leave and an understanding that *fathers* may stay at home if a child is ill - would work wonders for women' (woman out of practice, 1994; her emphasis).

Commitment and choice in social closure

We have argued in Chapters Six and Seven that women solicitors have experienced a transformed and revitalised form of social closure. The combination of circumstances which restructured firms and opened up the labour market, at the same time that women were able to use the qualifications lever to transcend the long-standing formal obstacles to admission, also diluted the strength of the personalist bonds on which employment opportunities had been based. However, one response to the resulting influx of women has been to develop the idea of 'commitment' as a core criterion for successful participation in the profession, and 'lack of commitment' as a primary explanation for women's absence from the top level of the professional hierarchy.

Women's exclusion from these positions is based on assumptions made about their collective attributes: these assumptions are rooted in a human capitalist approach to the 'natural' division of labour which continues to provide the parameters for the profession's view of women in general. Both the individual decision-makers and the institutional arrangements in firms appear to be built around the notion that the careers of all women are ultimately bounded by child-bearing and rearing, and the domestic servicing of a male partner. Whilst, ironically, it may be these very assumptions that make women's labour appealing to many firms in the first place, they remain attractive employment prospects only as long as they do not represent a challenge to both the fact and the mode of the construction of partnership as a male activity dependent on domestic servicing.

As a result, the resistance by many women to this destiny and the growing popularity of the 'integrated approach' (Drachman, 1989, p.231) has not prompted the profession in general into any form of self-examination or deviation from culturally male behaviour,[15] but rather, as we noted above, may be a factor in an intensification of such behaviour. Even though the large firms could afford to lead the way with experiments with alternative forms of working which would facilitate the combination of parenting and a career, they have largely failed to do so (but see Chambers, 1997). Instead, we found a tendency on the part of such employers to declare that the profession was now largely equitable, but that the market imposed working patterns which meant that women would have to 'choose' between children or a career; in other words, between 'men's work' and 'women's work'. As Fredman notes (1997, pp.198-9), the law itself, continues to endorse the human capitalist view that it is acceptable that the market should determine the limits to women's rights in maternity provision, both in respect of pay and remedies, as cases like Ministry of Defence v. Cannock ((1994) IRLR 509 EAT) demonstrate.[16]

Furthermore, as we have observed above, it appears that despite the professional obligations of many top women lawyers, they have generally failed to bring about a renegotiation of domestic responsibilities. The continuing lack of commitment of men to the private sphere, which we have argued should frame the debate over women's commitment in the public sphere, is a crucial part of the profession's construction of an entire ideology around the need for total availability and, consequently, a working week which, ultimately, has no limits.[17]

Correspondingly, the male professional model, societal expectations and the privatisation and individualisation of childcare combine to place the major responsibility for social reproduction on to individual women. Furthermore the law itself functions to construct and reproduce these features of parenting so that women's predominant role is represented as natural and immutable (see Fegan, 1996; Fredman, 1997, p.414).

Hagan and Kay have argued that the adoption by law firms of a human capitalist approach reinforces the emphasis on individual choice, which is in any event a keystone of liberal legalism, and encourages firms to take little or no action to solve the 'problem' of work and family (1995, p.180). Consequently, as we noted in Chapter Seven, the assignment to women of all responsibility for their career paths was a common feature of employers' responses (cf. Allen, 1988 on the medical profession). In reality there are, in general, only two 'options' open to women as they get older: either to accept a subordinated role rooted in cultural notions of appropriate femaleness or to conform to a male working pattern (Harrington, 1994, p.33).

Hagan and Kay also comment on the 'role of constraints' (in particular lesser opportunities for promotion) 'in shaping choices made by women' (1995, p.180). The effects of discriminatory cultures are then intensified by the general absence of alternative working patterns, so that failure to conform to the masculine model usually means that women with caring responsibilities are forced to leave altogether: by 1994, less than ten firms in our sample (and this included no large firms) had made any adjustments to the full-time plus pattern of work working pattern. Furthermore, where adjustments had been made, they were generally gender specific, with the result that women who take advantage of them find themselves on what the Americans term the 'mommy track' (see Kingson, 1988). As we discussed in Chapter Seven, this usually requires women to 'downshift' into a spectrum of lesser positions, with the consequence that they may become locked into a secondary and in some ways less professional market which is a cul-de-sac in career terms. It has therefore been argued that this represents no real choice: 'when an option is exercised almost exclusively by women and has rarely if ever been used by an attorney later elevated to partnership, it is not a true option for those who wish to climb a firm's ladder of success' (Harvard Law Review, 1996, p.1377). Moreover, what may initially appear to be a step forward ultimately serves to reinforce traditional societal roles, including the professional norm (Dickens, 1992), whilst the work of 'caring' remains simultaneously sanctified and devalued. Recent judgments demonstrate the law's reluctance to challenge inflexible patterns of working: as Fredman notes, the absence of a male comparator for women wishing to claim the right to jobshare has recently led to the rejection of a complaint of discrimination (British

Telecommunications plc v. Roberts EOR No.70 (1996) p.53, cited in Fredman, 1997, p.191).

Adjustments to working patterns also tend to be made on the basis of the valuation of the woman's cultural capital, and represented as concessions to her as an individual (Ross, 1990). Consequently, this option does not only highlight that antithesis of employee choice: namely, the persistence, even in bureaucratic contexts, of individual employer discretion. It also demonstrates the flexibility of closure mechanisms: as we noted above, when it suits the profession, individual women are condemned, their future careers pre-determined by their membership of a gender; however on other occasions, where, in order to amount to meaningful choices, concessions like career breaks or flexible working need to be made to all women, as a class of workers, women are treated as individuals. Evidently, until such concessions are made to all male and female employees, as of right, and without the current accompanying stigmas and penalties, the male standard in the workplace remains in place, and there is no true choice for anyone.

We have argued that the second option of super-conformity to the male model is as dependent, again, on subjective and sexist valuations by men as it is on the credentials of the individual woman. For women to overcome the practical and attitudinal barriers which the profession has erected literally superwoman qualities appear to be required, involving - frequently - the neglect of a private life. Even when women indicate that they are prepared to agree to this Faustian bargain, the exact terms of which are rarely made clear, but which are evidently rooted in the sexual contract, other elements of professional culture, such as the fact that it can only accommodate a limited number of women, mean that they may still not necessarily succeed.

Transforming the properties of the field - alternative approaches to the struggle for equal status

Alongside his analysis of the power of the juridical field as a conservative ideological force, Bourdieu has identified the significance of differentiation within the field resulting from both the entry of new social groups as practitioners, and the expansion of the field to reflect the increased power of dominated groups in the social and political fields (1987, pp.850-1). However, the inclusion of these divisions and struggles within a field unified by its acceptance of its independence from the social field has limited the impact of this differentiation: 'The private partisans of autonomy and of the law as an abstract and transcendent entity find themselves defenders of an orthodoxy.[18] For the cult of the text, the primacy of doctrine and of exegesis, of theory and of the past, are coupled with a refusal to recognise the slightest creative capacity in jurisprudence, and thus with a virtual denial of social and economic reality and a repudiation of any scholarly grasp of that reality' (Bourdieu, 1987, p.851).

So whilst the formal inclusion of women into the ideology of liberal individualism, through the legislation of 1919, is fundamentally incongruent with the maintenance of patriarchal relations in the private sphere, and the resulting male privilege in the workplace (see Hochschild, 1989; Brannen and Moss, 1991), the contradiction is resolved by dressing an endorsement of normative gendering of domestic and work roles and values up as universal abstract principles. Nevertheless, the tension between the rhetoric of freedom and choice and the reality of sexual hierarchy has been accentuated by the increasing participation of women in the labour market, and the incremental process of legislative and ideological development of 'equal opportunity' in the public sphere which has accompanied it (Crompton 1994, pp.126-7). Like Crompton, we found that this contradiction was perceived and resented by our women respondents, and added to this resentment are other factors, specific to the legal profession, which appear to indicate that now is a propitious time to try to effect a fundamental change to the ethos of private practice.

Along with other authors, however, we question the efficacy of measures which locate the source of the problem at the level of individual exchanges and interactions: both the perpetrator and victims of 'acts of discrimination' are enmeshed in sets of socially validated assumptions about legitimate behaviour, and also in the networks of personalist relations which underpin the more formal transactions which are taken to characterise the labour market. Consequently strategies which are designed to transform the properties of the social field which is the legal profession are more likely to have a lasting effect than those which aim to transform the prospects of individuals. Fredman has argued that 'real change requires far more radical intervention, in which legal forms are complemented by wide-ranging social measures opening the door to balanced participation by women in paid work and facilitating balanced participation by men in family work' (1997, p.415).

The basic issues of both policy and practice which would facilitate women's equal participation in the workforce, and humanise the workplace, have been well rehearsed in a range of publications (see for instance, Berry-Lound, 1990; Wilkinson, 1994; New Ways to Work, 1993; The Hansard Society, 1990[19]). There is a consensus that a broad range of practical initiatives are required in order to bring about structural changes, so that male exclusionary practices are countered. Others contend that without a transformation of the organisation or firm itself, little will change (Cockburn, 1989), and identify the need for policies and practices 'to be underpinned by a strong corporate philosophy that can serve to overcome attitudinal barriers (Rajan and van Eupen, 1990, p.29).

In the pages which follow, we explore a number of imagined transformations which might impact on the career destinies of women and men solicitors. Inevitably, such descriptions can take on an exhortatory tone, and veer between recommending a massive cultural change beyond the reach of policy, or small scale adjustments which are limited in impact, and easily ignored. We have tried to concentrate on issues and policies which will have an effect on the way in which actors perceive the possibilities of legal practice. A starting point is with the character of the Law itself. Fredman argues strongly that in spite of its weaknesses, it is important to use the power of positive law in the pursuit of equality (1997, p.387, ff.). One of the problems implicit in this approach however is the fact that the juridical field is characterised by, and depends on, the 'invisibility' of personalist relations, over which formal bureaucratic relations are inscribed as on a palimpsest.

To render these relations visible, it is necessary to reconceptualise the role of law, and to initiate actions based on that reconceptualisation. Duncan Kennedy has cited the work of Robert Hale on the effect of law as a distributive system, which determines the relative resources available to different social groups (Kennedy, 1993, pp.83-125). This is not simply the product of the fact that the intervention of the law in specific situations (as in the persons cases) directly deprives groups of resources, but also of the fact that the law, by its failure to intervene in other areas, endorses the maldistribution of resources. In support of this argument, Kennedy cites

Hohfeld's concept of legal permissions; 'it is clear that lawmakers could require almost anything. When they require nothing, it looks as though the law is uninvolved in the situation, though the legal decision not to impose a duty is in another sense the cause of the outcome' (1993, p.91). The effect of non-intervention in the legal workplace is accentuated by the character of the transactions concerned, which appear as a myriad of individual interactions rather than a systematic exercise of dominance by one group over another. Similarly, Kennedy specifically applies the model to gender relations in general, and points to the way in which the relative bargaining power of men and women is 'affected by hundreds of discrete legal rules' (1993, p.104).

The invisibility of male dominance is therefore one property of the field, and along with other commentators, we would argue there is a strategic role for 'making "men" visible as a category and calling them to task for their domination of positions of power, wealth and influence' (Bacchi, 1996, p.153). One strategy for this goal might involve the pursuit of existing individual legal remedies, as in the case of the two lawyers, Josephine Hayes and Jane Coker who have initiated sex discrimination claims against the Attorney General and the Lord Chancellor respectively (the Guardian, 7 February 1997, p.3, and 21 February, 1998, p.7), on the basis that appointments to government legal positions had been made through an 'old boy's network' which excluded women. This approach depends on accumulating evidence about inequalities of treatment, or supporting an inference about inequality of treatment through analysis of inequalities of outcome. Where the dominant mode of organisation is the patriarchal private firm, we have argued that this militates against the visibility of this kind of evidence. Correspondingly, autonomous organisations of women lawyers, and the bureaucratic structures responsible for professional self-regulation, both of which transcend the boundaries of firm organisation, offer the potential for bringing discriminatory practices and outcomes into the light.

In previous chapters we have noted the controversy over the character of bureaucracy, with some feminists arguing its status as an intrinsically patriarchal mode of organisation, whilst on the other hand there is evidence to suggest that bureaucratic procedures act as a restraining influence on discriminatory practices. As the professional regulatory body, the Law Society offers the only option for bureaucratic restraint over the profession at large, both because of its function as an 'umbrella' organisation for the varied practices which make up the profession, and because of its ability to initiate policies. One commentator on discrimination against women in the profession reported that 'the president of the Law Society, Tony Girling, has expressed his "shame" at the levels of pay inequality in the profession' (McGlynn, 1997, p.569). Substantive change may depend on the Law Society transforming its broadly human capitalist, laissez-faire approach into a role which involves giving a moral lead, and taking a proactive, interventionist stance. Thus McGlynn has argued that whilst the 1995 practice rule which mandated all firms to adopt an anti-discrimination policy was welcome, it 'should only be seen as a first step towards a fuller equal opportunities policy' (id.). In this way, it could be possible to colonise both the primitive backswoods and the ultramodern frontiers of the profession either on the basis of 'human resource' or 'equity' arguments (for a parallel argument in terms of the public sector, see Newman, 1995a), though we will discuss the limitations of the 'business case' below.

Women respondents in both 1990 and 1994 also envisaged a role for the Law Society. Their suggestions ranged from exhortations such as: 'give us the respect and support we deserve' to practical suggestions like 'set up or encourage returners' courses'; 'reduce fees for practising certificates and lower insurance premiums for part-timers'; 'increase female representation on Law Society bodies'; 'lobby government for tax relief on childcare'; 'publicise examples of employers' good practice' and 'educate men'. Arguably, the logical starting point for the Law Society would be with internal reform; as one of our female respondents suggested, an allocation of places for women could be made on Law Society bodies, and in particular on the Council.[20] A co-ordinated strategy would involve as a central feature an open commitment to equality and to bringing about cultural change, and such commitment could be signalled by urging firms to join Opportunity 2000. Newman has indicated the importance of building alliances in initiating effective change (1995a, p.276): the leverage exerted by autonomous women's groups like the AWS and Young Women Lawyers is increased by alliances with statutory bodies like the EOC and sympathetic elements in the Law Society bureaucracy, the function of these alliances would be both to promote policy packages, and to sponsor monitoring procedures.

Policies which encourage either a juxtaposition or a sequencing of employment as a lawyer and family life could include the introduction of varying levels of practising fees and insurance premiums, the development of returner programmes, and the production of information packages for firms and for employees - for instance guidelines on retention, details on how to set up working from home, and alternative billing systems. The Law Society is also capable of fulfilling an educative role, drawing on the sort of systematic, regular research currently conducted by its research department (the Research and Policy Planning Unit). An example of information packages designed to challenge myths about the feasibility of alternative working arrangements (and their suitability for women rather than men) is offered by the American Bar Association, which provides advice and sample policies for law firms on alternative work patterns, parental leave and sexual harassment (see ABA, 1990).

However, as various commentators have pointed out (Hagan and Kay, 1995; The Hansard Society, 1990, p.49), reforms designed to promote retention (without career penalties) and genuine equality in recruiting, pay and promotion are likely to be ineffective unless there is a parallel establishment of efficient machinery to monitor their implementation by firms. In part this results from the material reality that some of the concrete measures that are needed - such as the provision of career breaks - would be extremely problematic for small law firms, especially given the increasing financial pressure under which so many of them are now operating (Coopers and Lybrand, 1996). Nevertheless, programmes of reform need to be clearly aimed at stimulating employer initiatives and changes in order to counter the dominance of human capital perspectives among firms.

Furthermore, as we have discussed in previous chapters, the most supportive and least discriminatory employers in our sample were represented by some of the smallest firms; the difficulties they may encounter simply underline the need for action at a wider level, and does not mean that nothing can be achieved at the small firm level. Indeed the principal obstacle to change at the professional level comes from the mega-law firms, and this is highly significant given that they represent the professional elite and are therefore influential both in the profession and in civil society. The processes of rationalisation and concentration which such firms are engaged in mean that there is bound to be a search for a second class workforce, and unless they are obliged to re-evaluate their current attitudes and working patterns, it is highly likely that women will continue to be ascribed this role, both because they are a differentiated group which does not entirely belong to the public sphere, and because they are newcomers. This link between the dynamics of capitalist production and developments within the profession, and the harmonious relationship between the need to extract surplus value and the hierarchical culture of private practice must ultimately represent one of the most formidable barriers to achieving equity between men and women. The task therefore is clearly formidable; as Barbara Mills, former Director of Public Prosecutions, reflecting on strategies which she has undertaken to effect a change in culture at the Crown Prosecution Service, observed: 'This is a very long-term problem. Legislation, public awareness, media attention, all of these things are part of trying to change these attitudes. I view it as being a case initially for equality … But in fact as well as that there is a business case for this, because do you really want to train your women employees and then lose them?' She goes on to assert that such innovative practices also work 'beautifully. It is the initial problem of people having to think in a slightly different way … It just needs a bit of forethought and a bit of management …' (Mills, 1997, p.9).

However, as McGlynn has argued, the 'business case' for equality has its limitations which include 'its defence of the status quo, its concentration on voluntary action, its subrogation of equality to a means by which to achieve the end of improved economic performance, and its inability to deal with some of the pressing causes of discrimination against women' (1998, p.112). Where it is possible for firms to construct a business case *against* equality, it becomes difficult if not impossible to retrieve the principled stand which sustains a long term strategy. Consequently McGlynn has argued that the Law Society should not only support the implementation of the Equal Pay code but adopt a practice rule requiring its implementation (1997, p.569). Effective implementation involves a confidential system to facilitate individuals bringing complaints against employers (McCabe, 1995), and the imposition of a requirement that law firms provide the Law Society with information on matters relevant to discrimination. Such information could then be utilised to produce a register of firms, which could be publicised in the trade press, so that access to women as supply of secondary labour by precisely the firms which could afford egalitarian personnel policies may be cut off if they are used exploitatively. The monitoring process could also involve direct penalties, so that discriminatory firms could be (temporarily) barred from granting trainee contracts.

Local Law Societies are independent of the professional body; nevertheless, the Law Society could investigate ways in which some of the above policies - for instance those designed to facilitate the retention of employees on parenting breaks - could be co-ordinated, or partly fulfilled by them, so that small firm employees are not disadvantaged. For example, a major feature of effective retention strategies involve keeping the employee in touch with the profession; the Law Society could explore whether local societies could be persuaded to play a role as local information and contact centres, as well as sponsoring returner training (Sommerlad and Allaker, 1991). The function of these policy initiatives would be to increase the cultural capital of women solicitors by institutional acknowledgement of their value, and to increase the availability to them of social capital. However, in order to effect a systematic re-evaluation of women's cultural capital, policies which involve a more direct intervention in the training of lawyers, and the management of their workplaces, also need to be addressed.

Commentators on the UK legal profession have remarked on the increasing significance of the role of the State, not simply in providing exclusionary shelter, but also in representing a major client as the purchaser of legal services through the Legal Aid budget (Abel, 1988; Abbott, 1988). This therefore provides the State with a major lever for initiating professional change, not least through the Lord Chancellor's advisory committee on legal education (ACLEC, 1996). The increasingly high profile being given to 'skills' in higher education (The Times Higher, 14 November 1997, p.4) provides the opportunity to import the notion of cultural change in relation to gender issues into the curriculum of legal education and training.

The potentially significant role of ACLEC (1996) in sponsoring innovation in the curriculum of legal education and training, is paralleled by the Law Society's considerable influence over the composition of legal training at both degree and LPC level. This could be utilised to propose the incorporation of a gender/race awareness course either as part of a 'law in context' module, or as an aspect of the new skills input on degree, and as part of professional updating (McCabe, 1995).

Evidently firms themselves need to be at the forefront in effecting reform, and a female equity partner of a medium sized general practice made a variety of suggestions as to practical changes which she considered they should be implementing: 'Job sharing on a regular basis. Outwork by computer (drafting can be done as well at home as in the office), fax at home, an understudy to oversee things in the office; teamwork' (1997). Obviously, at the micro-level, adoption by employers of the sorts of policies discussed above in connection with the Law Society could do much to initiate a change in corporate culture. Firms could also make an overt commitment to the development of a more equitable culture by becoming members of Opportunity 2000 (McGlynn, 1997). In terms of practical measures, large employers could consider providing workplace nurseries and/or child care vouchers. However, more importantly, firms should clearly jettison traditional notions of appropriate career paths and the adherence to long, office based days and examine new approaches ranging from alternative billing arrangements to part-time working at all levels. As Barbara Mills has observed: 'we just have to break this long hours culture. We have to recognise that in fact flexibility for individuals is something which can positively improve morale and output. It doesn't mean you have a fall-off in work at all' (1997, p.8).

Such a re-evaluation of current structures and work norms would involve discarding the current reliance on fee targets as a measure of performance, where quantity tends to be a proxy for quality, and a move towards a more genuinely flexible assessment of the quality of individuals' work. Systems known as value billing and fixed-fee billing have been proposed as more equitable and sophisticated indicators of the quality of work; value billing is a 'subjective method that takes into account the complexity of the matter, the experience and reputation of … (the lawyer), and the results achieved in addition to the time and labor involved … fixed-fee … (involves breaking) down large projects into smaller components … and charging a fixed fee for each task' (Harvard Law Review, 1996, p.1386). Correspondingly, firms should reconsider their position on part-time work, and make this available wherever possible to both men and women, without stigma (Sachs, 1993). It should therefore be made quite clear that the route to partnership can be either full or part-time, and is based on open and neutral criteria. Similarly part-time equity partnerships, resulting in a proportionate profit, should be available - again to both women and men (New Ways to Work, 1993, p.8; Chambers, 1997).[21] A strong argument in favour of such arrangements is that, contrary to the usual objections to part-time partnerships, these would be cost effective, since if they were freely available, women would be less likely to delay maternity till achieving partnership (Schwartz, 1992, p.188 cited in Harvard Law Review, 1996, p.1382). The implementation of a more flexible work structure should have the effect of humanising the workplace, and thereby making it more compatible with obligations and activities in the private sphere for both men and women. In line with this approach is the suggestion that employers consider adopting a 'mixed-compensation package consisting partially of money and partially of time ... this model has been tested and found feasible ...' (Harvard Law Review, 1996, p.1389).

What are the grounds for hope that firms might prove responsive to these kinds of policy suggestions? In addition to the fact that for over a decade women have comprised around half of law graduates and new practitioners, there is the dissatisfaction that practitioners, both women and men, are increasingly expressing about the current workaholic culture of private practice. Perhaps even more important than either of these developments, however, is the fact that the profession is already undergoing a massive upheaval, so that mainstream structures and norms are no longer accepted as the only ways of operating in legal practice. Private practice is currently, in Hagan and Kay's words, 'a contested domain' (1995, p.179; and see Mossman, 1994, p.173). Furthermore, the profession's claim to operate on the basis of economic rationality and neutrality and fairness makes its culture vulnerable to immanent critique. Rhode has commented: 'In the long run, failure to mitigate work-family conflicts will prove expensive to all concerned. It cannot but help increase turnover, impair recruiting, compromise job performance and jeopardize the health and well-being not only of women, but of all care-takers as well as their families' (Rhode, 1988, p.1206). However the importance of professional self image makes an equally compelling economic case for reform.

Our discussion has noted the fact that it is the relationship of the juridical field to broader social fields which provides a major obstacle to change, with the idea of the 24-hour firm gaining ground in specialisms as far apart as criminal law and international commercial practice. However, it is also the advocacy of change in wider civil society which offers in turn the prospect of a response from the legal profession: policies which aim to transform professional culture alone are insufficient. As we have argued in earlier chapters, the law itself plays a major role in constructing, conveying and reinforcing gender stereotypes; in a circular process, gendering is then continued in the legal workplace which utilises traditional male/female identities and roles in its maintenance and justification of strategies of exclusion (Barrett and McIntosh, 1982; Walby, 1990). There is thus a continual interchange between the public and private spheres. What is needed therefore, are intitiatives which do not only seek to effect a transformation of professional culture and the 'gendered structure of wage labour' (Williams, 1990, p.356) in general, but also to challenge the ideology of mother/fatherhood which currently constitutes what both genders experience as reality (Fegan, 1996). In particular, we would argue that the transformation of mothering (and caring in general) into a genuinely valued, visible and socialised occupation known as parenting, is fundamental to both achieving deep-seated professional and cultural change (see Hochschild, 1989) and to making different career trajectories a matter of unconstrained individual choice - for both men and women. Hagan and Kay have cited the case of Brooks v. Canada Safeway (1989) in which it was stated that 'raising children is a contribution as much or more than a choice', and that consequently the business community should shoulder some of the costs currently borne by individual women (1995, p.190). It is clear that unless policies are implemented which address the current privatised[22] and individualised nature of childcare, and the notion that it is women's sole responsibility, anyone engaging in childcare work will be penalised in that their careers will be blocked and, if they remain in the labour market, they will end up doing the 'second shift' (Hochschild, 1989). At the same time, the culture of lengthy hours and male bonding will remain characteristic of the workplace, predicated on access to the social capital represented by women's (devalued) domestic labour.

An argument for this sort of macro-level, and multi-pronged approach clearly raises questions of initiatives at the highest levels, which is evidently more problematic than working for small-scale, practical reforms. On the other hand, the need for cultural change to underpin practical policies has even been articulated at government level. The following strictures by the Department of Employment echo many of the points made by our female respondents: 'employers must recognise that women can no longer be treated as second class employees'; the comments go on, however, to endorse women's responsibility for the domestic sphere: 'They will need women employees and must recognise both their career ambition and domestic responsibilities. This will involve broadening company training policies, much more flexibility of work and hours and job-sharing, to facilitate the employment of women with families and help adapt to their needs' (1988, p.8).

However, five years later a similar message was phrased in gender-neutral language, apparently recognising that such changes would need to be available to both men and women: '... employees will increasingly be looking to employers to offer them different patterns of working which will allow them to achieve a satisfactory balance between work and other responsibilities, especially the family ... to enable them to have the best of both worlds, and to give of their best in both worlds' (Michael Howard, 1991, cited in Steele and Peach, 1993, p.1).

These pronouncements were made by a government more generally associated with an ideological commitment to patriarchal relations in the private sphere and in particular within the institution of marriage, and correspondingly disinclined to use public policy to 'impinge on the private life of individuals' (Hantrais and Letablier, 1996, p.132). The stance of the incoming Labour government on childcare and work appears to indicate an enthusiasm for policies which support the juxtaposition of working life and caring responsibilities: in the instance of lone parents,[23] perhaps an over-enthusiasm.

Of course this is not to deny the considerable obstacles to effecting cultural change, at both a professional and societal level. Despite the great increases in dual earner households (Hardill et al, 1997, p.314), and the fact that the notion of a 'new man' has been current for more than a decade, men have proved extremely resistant to a renegotiation of domestic labour (Hochschild, 1989; Brannen and Moss, 1991; Grint, 1992, p.37; Elliot, 7 October 1997; Murgatroyd and Neuburger, 1997). Furthermore it is evident that changes in this sphere, and in discriminatory cultures, cannot be achieved through legislation.

A characteristic response to the issue is to assign a major role to the State (as does Mills in the extract cited above). We have already discussed the potential here in the sphere of legal education. Rhode too argues that: 'the state should institutionalize substantive rather than formal commitments to gender equality and expand its enforcement responsibilities' (1994, p.1200). For Brannen and Moss, the Swedish state provides a useful model, having adopted an integrated programme based on an explicit recognition of the principle of gender equity, which addresses a range of areas from child care and education services to a 'programme of employment rights which include flexible parental leave, paternity leave, leave to care for sick children and the right to work part-time in an existing job ...' (1991, pp.261-2). However, as Hantrais and Letablier have noted, across Europe national policies for combining family life and employment have varied widely in their emphasis and intention (1996). Some countries (Portugal, for example) emphasise equal rights in employment and encourage a model of 'juxtaposition' of family life and employment, without providing any state support for childcare, whilst others (Germany and Austria) provide state support for a sequential ordering of childcare and employment. It is Nordic states which have provided most support, in terms of parental leave provisions and childcare, for the reconciliation of family and working life, though as Hantrais and Letablier point out in a cautionary note, this has not necessarily produced indications of gender equality in terms of salary levels or division of domestic responsibility (1996, p.127). The significance that these authors draw from this variation is the difficulties that result from attempting to impose a policy template on a cultural base which is hostile to the principles on which the policy is based (op.cit., p.188). This certainly needs to be borne in mind in examining prescriptive policies in the UK legal profession, where, as we have identified, the culture is so hostile both to state intervention of any kind, and to supportive policies towards the private sphere in particular.

We have argued that a strategy which supported women in the legal profession would involve a multi-faceted, co-ordinated programme which would include measures dealing with childcare provision; initiatives to bring more women into public bodies, especially the judiciary; and codes of practice, with procedures for monitoring and enforcement, covering working patterns and career structures for public employers. Similarly, the adoption and implementation of such codes could be made mandatory for any employers entering into a contract with the state: the kinds of contract compliance provisions which were not uncommon in the late 1970's and early 1980's, but which have since fallen victim to 'backlash' political initiatives. There is scope for strengthening the positive action permitted by S.47 of the Sex Discrimination Act, and also to improve current equality law, for instance remedying its ad hoc and piecemeal nature, and reconsidering the standard of the male comparator. Finally, the publicity given to recent research has strengthened the case for a re-evaluation of the contribution of domestic labour to the national economy (see Grint, 1991, p.40; Murgatroyd and Neuburger, 1997): it is this re-evaluation of the significance and distribution of domestic labour which will ultimately have the most marked effect on women's cultural capital and their career destinies.

Postscript

Menkel-Meadow argues that there are basically only two kinds of reports on the issue of women in the profession and that both are characterised by the assumption that women's participation is beneficial: 'in the optimistic version because discrimination that excludes over half the human race is unjust; in the pessimistic version because the participation of particular kinds of people (i.e. mothers) might be socially useful not just for mothers but for changing institutional workplaces' (1989, p.295). She goes on to argue that women's participation may be 'transformative' of legal practice.

Our rationale endorses all of these positions, which may be considered mutually inclusive. Exclusion or marginalisation of people from a profession which plays a vital, constituent role in the formation of culture and policy because they are unable to conform to an extremely rigid version of white, middle class masculinity is not only unjust to the outsider majority, but also of great significance for the cultural and political life of a citizenry. Carol Smart has argued that women should cease to look to law for solutions, and speculated whether, instead, women should be responding to the law through 'resistance rather than calling for more law - even law based on agreed feminist principles' (1991, p.155). However, women cannot escape the impact of law on their lives, both in terms of decisions made across a variety of fronts from employment to criminal matters, and also, underpinning all of these, in terms of its major contribution to the reproduction of gendered identities and male/female power relations. Consequently Fegan has argued that law's role in creating and maintaining dominant ideologies requires challenge at both the substantive and conceptual levels (1996, p.187). We would argue that the challenge must also be mounted at the practitioner level. To ignore the concomitant need to reshape the profession is to apparently accept the law's claims to disembodied truth.

On the other hand, should a focus on the subordination of women practitioners form a particularly prominent part of the challenge to the law's contribution to the formation of social reality? Firstly, it has been argued that not only is the profession now so diverse, but women are 'making it' in far greater numbers with the result that this sort of focus is no longer valid. However, we argue that professional strategies of exclusion and marginalisation are still most visible and all encompassing in terms of women. It is the profession's continuing reification of gender which requires its 'reification' in academic commentary (Menkel-Meadow, 1989). Secondly, a focus on the current sexual hierarchy which remains characteristic of mainstream private practice is important because it is both dependent on, and part of the challenge to, the conventional social script, which is itself powerfully conveyed by the law as a natural state. If such a focus can assist in fracturing the current monolithic masculinity so that it is obliged to allow for the accommodation of carers (both female and male), this should then, in turn, permit the entry of other types of difference and thereby constitute part of a more general assault on law's discursive and ideological contribution to social inequalities. Change in this labour market is part in turn of change in the wider juridical field, and part of the wider process of breaking the sexual contract and reconstructing social reality.

Other proponents of the development of a new legal practice have concentrated not so much on the need to challenge the claims to universality and neutrality which constitute law's legitimacy, but more on the current quality of legal practice. Women's experience as outsiders, and as mothers, would, it is argued, make the legal process less competitive, and produce greater sensitivity to clients (Rhode, 1988; Menkel-Meadow, 1994 cited in Harvard Law Review, 1996, p.1379a). The excessive work demands which currently characterise the profession have been argued to have a negative effect on all lawyers, and hence on the quality of their work, because it means that they become 'so isolated that they lose the sense of the texture of their life or their ability, as lawyers and as human beings, to respond to people's and society's needs ... the hyper-technician, honed down and homogenized by the bureacracy ... will not have the human capacity to solve the legal problems of the twenty-first century' (Fox, 1989, pp.962-3). Similarly Okin argues that it is a cause for general concern that 'those who rise to the top ... are among those who have had the least experience of raising children' (1989, p.127), arguing that as a result such people are less well equipped to make important social decisions.

We would endorse this approach. As currently constructed, the public sphere, because it has banished the ethic of caring (even in its traditional professional form, with the advent of the new business ethos), requires characteristics which are currently equated with masculinity. Whether such characteristics are socially or intrinsically gendered is too complex an issue to discuss here. The more important point is to argue for the construction of a new type of humanised civil society in which the current apartheid between the private and public spheres is destroyed and, consequently, caring and homemaking work ceases to be privatised and devalued, so that employers and the state are obliged to take a proactive role in facilitating citizens, both male and female, to participate in such work.

Ultimately moreover, these arguments for a different kind of professionalism, distinct from the current representation of the lawyer as a neutral technocrat (Thornton, 1996), are related to our contention that changes in legal practice must form an integral part of any challenge to the current nature of the law. The Rule of Law rests upon the popular belief that the law is neutral and objective. The dissonance discussed earlier between the persistence of patriarchal relations and the ideology of equal opportunity finds its counterpart in the problems faced by an unrepresentative elite in its formulation and reproduction of 'common sense'. The Rule of Law requires both a deconstruction of the law's current claims to represent the truth, and, as part of the process of reconstruction, lawyers must become more representative of an increasingly pluralist and fragmented society. If the professional monolith is splintered so that it is able to accommodate women on truly equal terms, this will be a first and vital step towards similarly accommodating other forms of difference.

Notes

1 This finding is replicated in surveys of other professional women; for instance see *Working Women* (Market Assessment Publications 1996).

2 One woman said 'why do I call them tokens? because there's still so few of them, and that's the way it seems set to stay' (rural general practitioner, 1994). Another woman pointed to the fact that the new position of salaried partner (which she called a 'token, a sop') was generally occupied by women (and see Sidaway and Cole, 1996, p.16).

3 As we have noted previously, this picture of hostile workplaces and endemic discrimination is evidently also characteristic both of private practice in other jurisdictions (see, for example, Kaye, 1988) and of other professions (see Coe, 1992).

4 This must be contextualised by reference to the nature of the sample which by 1994 contained only women who had been admitted for at least four years, and who had therefore experienced many of the barriers we have discussed in this book; on the other hand, as we noted above, their negativity is echoed in numerous other studies of professional women.

5 Our data on this is confirmed by a study of equal opportunities in the legal profession, conducted early on in the recession, which reported that the Law Society considered that whilst 'the recruitment crisis in the late 1980's did encourage some firms to introduce measures such as flexible working arrangements ... this momentum has declined' (Hurstfield, 1992, p.14).

6 Despite a reluctance by women lawyers to describe themselves as feminists; cf. Rhode, 1988, 1205.

7 Skordaki similarly notes that membership of the same social, ethnic and class background militated against the development of any feminist separatism, but also points out that this did not apply to all the early women entrants - for instance, Carrie Morrison and Mary Sykes were both radical (1996, pp.14 and 37).

8 'The old stereotypes that women are less rational and more emotional undoubtedly contribute to the requirement that they have to play longer and harder to earn the right to compete on equal terms' (Jack and Jack, 1989, p.937). For further parallels with the USA, see Rhode, 1988, pp.1202-5.

9 Some have argued that this resistance of many women, especially once they become mothers, to the workaholic model may bring about a general change which would benefit all lawyers (Pexton, 1990; Nott, 1989).

10 This has also been the focus of many other commentators (for instance, Kaye, 1988). Menkel-Meadow has endorsed this approach partly because 'it accepts and assimilates to conventional sociological and popular cultural notions of what is important' (1989a, p.307); others have pointed to the linkages between the elites of these firms and wider societal and political power (Harrington, 1994).

11 The parallels between the accounts of women lawyers and those of women in other professions are striking; for instance, a study of business elites links women's need to work extra hard with a failure to devote time to 'organizational politics ... Men are good at office politics and women suffer as a result' (Davidson and Cooper, 1992).

12 A common anxiety expressed in interviews with female assistants and associates employed by the large firm was that they were becoming too specialised; for instance, 'I am now into leasehold even more than I was before - I am extremely specialised in that I am working for one big client almost all the time and that's bad ...' (1997).

13 Several female respondents recounted how, having been forced out from a large corporate firm as a result of maternity, they had found a far more sympathetic employer in a smaller, 'less prestigious firm'. This picture which our data presented echoes that of the Law Society Panel survey which reported that the highest percentage of female equity partners were to be found in 2-4 partner firms (Sidaway and Cole, 1996, p.15). It appears therefore that whereas at the start of their career women are more likely to find a place in the large firms, if they wish to subsequently take a break and/or deviate from the norm, for instance by requesting shorter hours, they are likely to be discarded. Conversely, women may not be taken on, unless they have personal contacts, by smaller firms when they first enter the profession, but may subsequently find a niche in such firms following their rejection by their larger employers.

14 Pioneer, superwoman and examining and weighing up the 'hard won prize' (Kaye, 1988, p.121).

15 Again, this appears to be a cross-cultural phenomenon; for instance see Sachs, 1993, p.62 on a similar failure by the legal profession in the USA.

16 This market orientated approach has also characterised European Law, see for instance Case C - 342/93, Gillespie v. Northern Ireland and Social Services Board, decided February 1996 NYR.

17 This is illustrated by advice which has been given by American lawyers on what modern commercial clients require: 'Foreign lawyers should be available 24 hours a day (and) become friends with their clients ... if they want to be instructed by US corporations ... John Wright of City firm Warner Cranston, who attended the session ... thought it was now the norm for English firms to go that extra step for their clients' (Rose, 1996, p.8).

18 See Alfieri (1991, p.121), on this phenomenon amongst 'poverty lawyers'.

19 For practical strategies for change relating specifically to the legal profession, the American and Canadian literature is particularly useful, and we have drawn on it for many of the proposals in this chapter. For instance, see Rhode, 1988; Kaye, 1988; Harvard Law Review, 1996; Mossman, 1994. The AWS has produced various guidelines on specific areas, such as 'Guidelines for Part-Time Working', n.d.

20 There are 75 places on the Council in total; in September 1997 five were unfilled, 59 occupied by men, and 11 by women. Given that it has frequently been alleged that representation on the Council is decided by 'Buggins turn' (Smith), it would be difficult to mount the usual merit argument against such positive action.

21 Chambers (1997) has reported that the scheme to permit part-time partnerships at Linklaters has so far had very few takers. We would suggest, however, that this is rather a demonstration of the tenacity of the full-time plus culture, and that change will only come over time and as a result of the sort of package of measures we are proposing above.

22 Although, whilst childrearing is privatised, for instance in that there is little state support for it, as Fegan observes, one of the ways in which motherhood is devalued is by its representation as a 'state enforceable duty rather than as a life choice involving personal commitment' (1996, p.189).

23 As Mossman has pointed out, it is essential that any solutions are neither based on assumptions that women will bear such responsibility nor on an idealised, and prosperous two parent nuclear family (1994, p.75).

Appendix: A Description and Discussion of Methods

In much of the literature concerned with research into women's position, a rather spurious dichotomy has been manufactured. On the one hand, some social scientists such as Hakim (1995, 1996) and Hammersley (1992, 1994), argue that 'feminist research' has conflated processes of enquiry and of politics, and in extreme cases, has abandoned rational discourse. Whilst they argue that adherence to a positivist rationality and perspective on methodology is not uncritical, we shall argue that in some cases, their inattention to the 'construct validity' of many of the concepts and categories used in positivist research on women does mean that the 'results' cross the boundary from 'the truth business' (Hakim, 1995, p.448) to ideology. This is particularly true in the case of the ideas of 'choice' and 'commitment', which we have already questioned. On the other hand, some feminist writers on methodology appear happy to abandon any claim to 'truth' of an independent kind (Stanley and Wise, 1983). It is not uncommon as a consequence of the critique of traditional epistemologies at the heart of social science for women writers to be particularly critical of quantitative research, and regard it as having little to offer in debates which are concerned with social processes. For example, in the introduction to her illuminating study of women lawyers in Australia, Margaret Thornton justifies the rejection of a systematic quantitative approach using questionnaires in these terms: 'useful quantitative data may be obtained in this way, but it is not going to convey very much about the space behind the representations without according the scholar considerable leeway for creative interpretation' (1996, p.4).

This approach appears to us to be equally partial (and see Maynard and Purvis, 1994). Questions which concern women's position in the labour market must be dependent on access to the kind of systematic and soundly grounded empirical information provided in Hagan and Kay's study of

Toronto lawyers (1995). Their work demonstrates that an appropriate treatment of quantitative data can indeed support complex inferences about processes. In particular, the use of a longitudinal 'panel' methodology, is one of the few ways of reliably accounting for the way that changes in the wider economic system, and in the internal structure of the profession, affect women's position in the labour market, or rather the complex webs of labour markets with which they have to interact.

We do however, have to accept that there are certain kinds of issue that are difficult to examine with a quantitative methodology alone. Both 'gender' and 'profession' are social constructions to which actors attribute a wide variety of meanings. Women's fate in the labour market therefore depends to a considerable degree on issues of perception. Women are involved in complex 'readings' of what the profession in its different manifestations is like before they make career decisions, and these readings can be subject to both gradual and cataclysmic 'shifts' as a result of career or life events. Similarly employers make their labour market decisions based on perceptions of constant elements or changing demands of the 'legal services market': they also, as we found, have fixed perceptions of gender and gender destinies, and the proper relation between the public and private worlds. For these reasons, some of the processes involved in the labour market are only susceptible to study through methods like interview and case study, as researchers with perspectives as diverse as Crompton and Sanderson (1990) and Hakim (1996) argue. One does need, however, to exercise proper caution in the process of generalising conclusions from data which have been drawn from samples which are prone to bias. We have tried to acknowledge all the limitations of our data as appropriate in the text. Hakim points to the importance of sample selection bias in working on women's work orientations (1996, p.84): for example, if we were to base our work entirely on the perspective of women in practice who had taken a career break and returned, we might over-estimate the extent of the demand side barriers to women's participation in the legal labour market. Similarly, if we were to draw our data largely from women at the younger end of the profession (who are numerically dominant), whose partnership ambitions could not reasonably have come to fruition, we would be likely to understate the demand-side inhibitions to career progression, as most of these women would not yet have experienced them. Similarly, opportunities and inhibitions or barriers are not evenly distributed through all the internal labour markets which characterise the profession. A topography of these different markets would be a worthwhile subject for a substantial research project, but we have to acknowledge that our findings are dominated by the experience of women who are working in, or have worked in, the larger corporate firms.

It is the common experience of social scientists who work with a qualitative methodology that at some stage their work will be described as supported by 'anecdotal evidence'. The underlying implication is of a lack of care in sampling respondents, and a selective treatment of data. The best response to this is to be as transparent as possible about the means of data collection and analysis, which we attempt below. Another exhortation, however, which is frequently made to those who research the experience of marginalised groups, deserves a fuller answer. Even sympathetic commentators will make the point that the data should be treated as 'women's perceptions of how they have been treated' and not as 'facts'. The epistemological point is indeed a difficult one, and perhaps it would be wise to qualify accounts of women's experiences as consisting of 'social' or 'phenomenological' facts in order to satisfy the positivists. However it is curious that whereas so much caution is exercised over the credibility of women's accounts, there is little equivalent incredulity about employers' accounts of women's 'unreliability', 'lack of commitment' or 'lack of motivation or ambition' (an issue which we have taken up in Chapter Seven on career breaks with our critique of Hakim's data on 'commitment'). Our interview method was intended to get women to concentrate on the factual description of their experiences initially, and seek their reflections later, and our experience was that it was often only in recounting factual experiences that our respondents began fully to identify their significance.

The initial research, undertaken in 1990-91 was based on both quantitative and qualitative methods, consisting of four postal questionnaire surveys, supplemented by follow-up interviews and other sources of appropriate qualitative data. The follow-up study in 1994 was designed to fulfil two functions: to update the descriptive information on the respondents to the 1990-91, in effect to conduct a longitudinal comparison of the experiences of this cohort at two points in time; and to provide greater depth to the understanding of individual women's experiences. We decided not to repeat the 1990 exercise in toto and introduce new members into the cohort, but rather to limit the sampling to respondents from the 1990 survey. The implications of this procedure in terms of sampling bias are discussed in the section on sampling below.

Questions - senior partners

The labour market obviously includes other elements of 'demand' such as local government, local industry and education, but these were deliberately excluded from consideration in this study.

Eight main research areas were generated for the employers and were the basis for specific questions for the senior partners' questionnaire.

- Indications, either in the existing gender balance of firms, or in the attitudes that were expressed towards women in the profession, or in the training or working arrangements for women returners, that firms had no interest (or a limited interest) in this sector of the labour market.

- Distinctions between firms in terms of their perceptions of a problem of recruitment and retention and the related problems of female staff.

- Relationship between any such distinction and other attributes of the firm, such as size or degree of specialisation or area.

- Characteristics of firms indicating that whilst they had a demand for the labour of women returners, this was confined to particular niches, for instance in terms of area of law (e.g. matrimonial work) or level at which they are employed in the firm (e.g. only at assistant solicitor level).

- Firms' perceptions of the retraining needs of returners - how would this supply of labour need to be modified to meet firms' needs?

- Whether firms interested in this area of the labour market used recruitment procedures which would give them access to it.

- Whether firms were interested in women returners but nevertheless unaware of, or hostile to, conditions of employment which might prove more attractive to women returners.

- Whether firms were prepared to provide substantive support, in terms of finance or changed working conditions to the process of reintegrating women into the legal market.

Research questions - women solicitors

The 'supply' side of the equation provided a more varied population which was sub-divided into three groups according to their career experiences. In the first study, women out of practice (WOPS) who were the main target group of the study, since they represent the current pool of unused labour. This group was presumed to be highly differentiated, including those who had trained, practised, left and did not intend to return, and those who had every intention of returning, as well as those in a state of uncertainty. Secondly, there were women in practice - returners (WIPSR) - those women trained and working as solicitors who had at some time had a career break, and, finally, women in practice - non-returners (WIPSN) - women trained and working in the profession with no previous breaks from work (except on a strictly temporary basis). This group initially appeared a less promising source of information since it might contain women who had no intention of taking a career break, and whose views might change radically if faced with the prospect. However the research demonstrated that many of these women did intend to take a break at some point, and therefore might be embarking on temporary or permanent absences from the profession at a time when it was predicted that there would be severe recruitment difficulties. Their views and expectations were therefore essential in examining the implications for long term strategies of human resource management in the profession.

For the 1990 survey, three separate instruments were developed for the three groups of respondents, since it appeared that the areas of overlap on questions would be relatively small, and a lengthy instrument with alternative routes might risk lowering the response rate. As was the case with the senior partners' group, a number of research areas were generated from which to develop questions for the three questionnaires designed for each women's sample.

- Any differentiation in the samples in terms of long-term career ambitions.

- Any differentiation in the samples in terms of experience of, and reasons for, career breaks.

- Issues related to working conditions which might affect a decision as to whether to return to work.

- Samples' attitudes to the profession which might affect their decision to return.

- Attitudes related to concrete experiences attributable to gender (e.g. inappropriate specialisation, perceived lack of prospects, etc.).

- Proportion of the sample perceiving any form of training as being a necessary pre-requisite to re-entering the profession.

- Areas of training provision seen to be most significant.

The development of the women's questionnaires was supported by discussions with local women solicitors who discussed the draft formats with the research team. For the 1994 study, a difficulty was immediately presented by the likely change in status of a number of respondents, e.g. women who would have returned to practice since 1990 (WOPS to WIPSR) and vice versa. Consequently the three questionnaires were rationalised into one instrument with questions re-worded to become as far as possible applicable to all three sub-sets of the research programme. Whilst this avoided the possibility of an individual receiving an inappropriate questionnaire, it rendered some of the time series comparisons difficult because of major or minor differences in question format between 1990 and 1994. The revised instrument was piloted with a small sample, and amended.

Sampling

The women out of practice proved to be the most difficult sample to develop. In the early stages of research, only a handful of retired women solicitors had been identified, but the Law Society then provided names and addresses of women solicitors in the Yorkshire areas who were known not to be holding a current practising certificate; this eventually proved to be the source of many of the 'WOPS' sample. Sub-division of the practising women solicitors, also identified through Law Society records, also proved to be a difficult and lengthy task; each individual woman solicitor identified as practising in the catchment area was contacted by telephone and asked to categorise herself as either a returner or non-returner for the purpose of questionnaire distribution. This exercise occupied the research associate full-time for several weeks, and the smaller scale of the follow-up survey precluded the repetition of this painstaking process in 1994, rendering the rationalisation of the questionnaire structure even more essential.

Questionnaires for the 1990 survey were sent to 100 per cent of the women identified as belonging on the sampling frame. For the smaller-scale 1994 survey, the sampling frame consisted of the respondents to the 1990 survey, and questionnaires were sent to 50 per cent of the women on this frame, on a random basis. This will have had two clear effects: firstly, institutionalising any sampling error in the 1990 exercise, and, secondly, ensuring that the age structure of the 1994 sample would be unrepresentative of the population in the area. In terms of the aims of the follow-up survey however these effects were not thought to be of importance.

The process of self-classification described above resulted in some ambiguity as to what length of absence would constitute a career break and hence a 'return' to work. Subsequently it became obvious that some women with similar experiences in terms of length of break had allocated themselves to different categories. For the employers' survey, enquiries were made of all large firms to ascertain which partner should be approached to complete the questionnaire. Smaller firms and sole practitioners were also telephoned with a further personal request to complete the questionnaires.

Response rates

In addition to the factors affecting response rates discussed above, it emerged during the follow-up study that a large number of respondents in the 1994 employee cohort had changed firm or address, or left practice altogether, and again the timescale of the research did not allow for these individuals to be traced. The response rates are summarised in the following table.

Table A.1 Questionnaire response rates, 1990 survey

Figures express number of questionnaires sent and received for each sample.

Sample	Number Sent	Number Received	% Response
Senior Partners	118	65	55%
Women out of Practice	202	95	47%
Women in Practice (Returners)	52	30	58%
Women in Practice (Non-Returners)	162	101	68%

For the 1994 survey, senior partners were surveyed on a 50 per cent basis, using the 1990 respondents as the frame. Selection was stratified in order to gain a balance of firms. The response rate on this occasion was 20/32 (62.5 per cent).

The 'women's' sample was aggregated for the 1994 survey, and sampling was on a random 50 per cent basis from the respondents to the 1990 survey. The response rate overall was 78/113 (69 per cent), though there was some variation in the response rates for the sub-sets from the 1990 survey: whereas WOPS represented 42 per cent of the 1990 sample, they represented 50 per cent of the 1994 sample; the proportion of WIPSR had risen from 13.2 per cent to 23.1 per cent, and the proportion of WIPSNs had fallen from 44.6 per cent of the 1990 sample to 27.4 per cent. Cross-tabular analysis demonstrated that this was not a function of change in the circumstances of the respondents, as movement between the categories equalled out. Responses to telephone prompting of WIPSNs through their previous known employers indicated that large numbers had left their previous employers, and contextual data indicates that this may well have been through reasons of redundancy.

Sampling biases

The four 1990 samples were subject to a number of known biases as follows:

- As discussed above, those women most likely to respond to the 'WOPS' questionnaires would be those most likely to be considering a return, particularly given the channels of publicity used which would be particularly accessible to those women who were still in close contact with the profession.

- Responses were not received from a number of major firms in A* which represent the employers (both current and potential) of a large proportion of local women solicitors. The problem of gaining a response from firms in relation to this kind of topic is common to other research in the area (Nott, 1989; McGlynn and Graham, 1995).

- As previously stated, because of the self-classification system used to distinguish between the 'returners' and 'non-returners' of those women in practice, a few women with approximately the same length of break allocated themselves to different groups. However this was an inevitable consequence given that our research was largely concerned with the psychological impact of a break, which will not necessarily relate to length of absence.

- The women in practice (WIPSN) sample may be biased in that those women most likely to reply might be those considering a break in the future and/or possibly those women with particular 'grievances' against the profession. However, given the high response rate from this group (68 per cent), it is unlikely that these biases are present to any great extent.

For the 1994 survey, we must add the additional sample bias discussed above, in terms of the over-representation of WOPS in the sample, and the skewed age distribution resulting from the decision to measure change within the boundaries of the 1990 sample. These factors are of some significance given that 70 per cent of women with Practising Certificates have been in practice less than 10 years (Annual Statistical Report 1994, p.10), and that participation rates of women solicitors, measured by maintenance of Practising Certificates remain above 70 per cent up to the age of 60 (Annual Statistical Report 1994, p.8), though women are proportionately less well represented in private practice (78 per cent of women as opposed to 85 per cent of men).

However, the sample of Women in Practice (WIPSR + WIPSN) appears to match the characteristics of women in the population over the country as a whole. Whilst 31 per cent of the population of women solicitors are either partners or sole practitioners, and 68 per cent are assistants or associates (Annual Statistical Report 1994, p.12), 32.5 per cent of our sample were in partnership and 67.5 per cent were assistants. It therefore seemed unlikely that their responses would be influenced by a disproportionately advantaged or disadvantaged position within the profession.

In the case of the 1994 senior partners' survey, the principle area of under-representation was in the area of sole practitioners, where we failed to obtain a single response though they represent 32 per cent of the numbers of firms in the Legal Aid North Eastern Region (Annual Statistical Report 1994, p.25). This is not unexpected, as responses from smaller firms in both time series indicated that they felt the issue of equal opportunities was less applicable to the smaller firm (a view supported by statute of course) and they were therefore far less likely to respond. In contrast to the fears about the 1990 study, large firms were in fact over-represented in the 1994 study (15.8 per cent of sample over 11 partners as opposed to 4.4 per cent in the Region), but of course as major employers, an over-representation here was preferable.

Some consideration was given to weighting subsets at the data analysis stage, but given the difficulty of evaluating sampling error, this strategy was dropped in favour of leaving the raw data to be read in the context of identified sample bias.

Other data sources

In addition to the data gathered from the four questionnaire surveys, essential qualitative data were obtained from various other sources:

- Training Providers - written and verbal information from current and potential course providers was obtained through informal contacts, attendance at an AWS conference combined with a follow-up questionnaire. Feedback from AWS Returners Course delegates was also obtained by courtesy of the course organisers in both 1990 and 1994, who provided copies of their feedback questionnaires to supplement data in this area.

- Recruitment Agencies - information was also sought from the local recruitment agencies, in order to assess current local recruitment patterns and requirements of employers, with the aim of establishing how returners might fit into the current labour needs of local employers.

- The Association of Women Solicitors - liaison with local and national representatives from the AWS provided information on the role that the AWS plays in pursuing the interests of women returners and other female members of the profession, and the degree of support the Association obtains from the Law Society.

- Local Law Societies - apart from their provision of assistance with introductory publicity, representatives from the local law societies were also interviewed to establish their current and potential role in assisting returners, specifically in terms of maintaining contacts with women in their areas who have left private practice.

- 'Model Firms' and Other Employers - in order to view the policies and attitudes of our sample of employers in a wider context of changing staffing and personnel policy, data was gathered both from solicitors' firms known to have implemented 'model' returners and retainers schemes and also from the Crown Prosecution Service (CPS). Information was also gathered from employers in other sectors, notably manufacturing, commerce and retail chains, which have also implemented comprehensive retainer and returner policies.

Follow-up interviews

Interview subjects were purposively sampled in both 1990 and 1994 to represent key individuals from each survey sample. Interviews were based on a semi-structured technique, combining elements of ethnographic (Spradley, 1979) and hierarchically focused technique (Tomlinson, 1989). A key characteristic of ethnographic interviewing is its concentration on 'descriptive' questions (using event histories or definitions as a key), and its emphasis on respondents as 'informants', the real experts on their lives. Closed or 'opinion' questions were avoided as far as possible.

After the 1994 survey and interview series, there appeared to be strong prima facie evidence that some of the key changes in the profession, such as the increasing importance of 'practice development' in legal practices, were significant in their effects on women's careers in law, and a revised interview schedule was designed for use with a purposive sample of women in the area. It also became clear that some aspects of these changes were opaque to women, precisely because of the gendered and sexualised character of the practices involved, but that this data was important for our study. We therefore made the decision to interview a very small sample of male solicitors practising in the areas covered by our research, in order to simply get some bearings on the male world and ethos with which the women in our sample had to contend. This data was supplemented by the earlier interviews with Senior Partners. The following table lists the characteristics of interviewees:

Table A.2 Interview respondents by type of firm and age

Women	20-35	36-50	51+	Total
In-House Lawyers		2		2
Corporate Firms	5	7		12
General Practice	2	9	1	12
Academic/lecturers	4	2	2	8
Advice/Law Centre	1	1		2
Students	5	3		8
CPS	1			1
Sole Practitioner		1		1
Out of Practice	1			1
TOTALS	**19**	**25**	**3**	**47**

Six of the interviewees were of 'South Asian' origin, but there were no African-Caribbean British respondents. The table above does not include five respondents who were also interviewed in 1990 and 1994, so the total number of interviews undertaken is 57. The women are assigned in this table to the category occupied when last interviewed: their employment histories actually reflect the statistical picture we have recounted in the main text. So the lecturers were also able to recount their experiences in a range of firms, and the reasons they had turned from practice to teaching law (five of them had worked in the corporate commercial sector, three in medium-sized general practices). Of the two in-house lawyers, one had previously worked in commercial firms, the other in general practice. Seven of the respondents had either been equity partners, or still were at the time of the interview. Three of the respondents were salaried partners. This is a higher proportion than the national average reported in Chapter Four, and the sampling was intended to produce this ratio, as we were most concerned to explore the way in which comparatively successful women viewed the profession. We also interviewed two personnel officers.

Of the male sample, three were in the younger age band and worked for commercial corporate firms, 13 were between 36-50, of whom six worked in the corporate commercial sector, and eight were over 51, all of whom had worked in general practice. In addition in 1994 interviews were conducted with a management consultant, a representation firm, a legal recruitment agency and two personnel officers.

Interviews lasted between an hour and an hour and a half. In 1990 and 1994, most of the interviews were conducted on a face-to-face basis. In 1997, they were conducted by telephone, which we found improved both their fluency and the readiness of respondents to discuss 'difficult' topics.

Regional context of the research

In order to protect the confidentiality of our research, we will identify the sites of our research by name, and we will omit some of the details from this description. The research was based in adjacent rural and urban areas in the North of England although some of the 1997 interviewees were drawn from London. Although these regions can not be claimed to be 'typical' of law practice in the UK as a whole, particularly given the concentration of lawyers in the capital city, nevertheless, the region embraces a wide range of geographical and socio-economic features, from the small market town of S* to the revived urban centre of A*. Similarly, the practices in this area reflect the differentiation of the profession, and equally illustrate the extent of change over the past decade and a half in the structure, ethos and self-image of the profession.

A*

A* is the second largest metropolitan district in England and is one of the UK's principal manufacturing and commercial centres. It is a regional centre and forms part of a connurbation which has a population of over two million. There is a working population of around 340,000 people in A*. Enquiries in 1990 identified 95 solicitors' firms ranging from sole-practitioners to branches of large national commercial firms. In terms of recruitment, senior partners in A*'s firms complained of the difficulty in competing with London employers who usually attract over 50 per cent of trainee staff (Law Society Annual Statistical Reports, 1990 and 1994). On the other hand, recruiting agencies reported in 1990 that private practice had not been affected by the recession as severely as the South East and that redundancies had been minimal. By 1994, one recruitment agency reported that the market was saturated, although some employers were still seeking staff or planning to recruit. The number of women solicitors employed in practices in A* was estimated in 1990 to be around 150. It proved impossible to form an accurate estimate of numbers of women solicitors out of practice in the region. During the seven years of the research, the pattern of firms in A* followed the national trends, with a number of large mergers and takeovers, and some growth of the sector including smaller firms and sole practitioners.

The Hinterland

The * region covers a large part of the rural North and is commonly viewed as far more 'traditional' in outlook than A*. It includes three urban centres: B* (population of 46,700), S* (population of 2,455) and U* (population of 13,445). All three centres provide an interesting contrast to A* in terms of types of firms and work undertaken and also exhibit some interesting differences between each other.

B* is an old mill town which has traditionally attracted a high number of immigrants, in the past Irish and East Europeans and currently people from the Asian subcontinent. It may be described as a predominantly working class, low income town which has, during the last few years, suffered from industrial blight although it has diversified into light manufacturing. Legal aid work forms a substantial proportion of the practice of most solicitors' firms in the town and is considered to bring an adequate return because of the low business overheads. In 1990 employers complained of difficulties in attracting legal staff in general and some complained of particular problems of attracting women: even in 1994, four employers required staff.

U*, 10 miles away, is known as the 'gateway to the * National Park'. It is an attractive market town with some light manufacturing industry but a larger service sector. S*, 20 miles further into a National Park, is a small market and tourist centre. Solicitors in these latter two centres complained in both 1990 and 1994 of difficulties in general of attracting staff which they felt were largely due to the relatively remote character of the region.

They also indicated that shortage of staff was a particular problem given the extremely wide geographical area they had to cover, for instance one solicitor who undertook a lot of criminal litigation explained that in one week she might have to cover a very large number of courts spread over a wide geographical area. As with B*, we were advised that the commercial viability of many of the U* and S* firms depended on legal aid work. Just 19 women were identified as practising in these areas in 1990. Again it proved impossible to form an accurate estimate of all non-practising solicitors located in the area.

Data analysis procedures

The survey instruments used in 1990 and 1994 produced a substantial amount of quantitative data, but also gave respondents the opportunity to answer open questions of their future ambitions, their general views on the treatment of women in the profession, and the prospects for women in general. The quantitative results were analysed using SPSS release 3.0 in 1990 and 4.0 in 1994. Because of the sample size and the number of sub-sets of the sample, as well as our caution about sample bias, we did not undertake any substantial multivariate analysis. Some group differences were evaluated using chi-square contingency tables, but in some instances, the sub-sets these produced were rather small. Hagan and Kay have argued for the limitations of significance tests and the value of raw data properly contextualised, and we would agree with them (1995, p.210).

The responses to open questions were analysed manually in 1990, but in 1994 this analysis was supported by SPSS's text listing facility, which made the quantification of different responses easier. The interviews were analysed manually, using a card-based system of categorisation.

Bibliography

Abbott, Andrew (1988), *The System of Professions: an Essay on the Division of Expert Labour*, Chicago, University of Chicago Press.

Abdela, L. (1991), *Breaking through glass ceilings*, London, Metropolitan Authorities Recruitment Agency.

Abel, R. (1988), *The Legal Profession in England and Wales*, Oxford, Basil Blackwell.

Abel-Smith, B. and Stevens, R. (1967), *Lawyers and the Courts*, London, Heinemann.

ACLEC (1996), *First Report on Legal Education and Training*, London, Lord Chancellor's Advisory Committee on Legal Education and Conduct.

Adelman, S. and Foster, K. (1992), 'Critical Legal Theory: The Power of Law', in Grigg-Spall, I. and Ireland, P. (eds), *The Critical Lawyers Handbook*, London, Pluto Press, pp.39-43.

Adkins, L. (1995), *Gendered Work*, Milton Keynes, Open University Press.

Alfieri, A.V. (1991), 'Reconstructive Poverty Law Practice: learning lessons of client narrative', *The Yale Law Journal*, 100, pp.2107-47.

Allen, I. (1988), *Doctors and their careers*, London, Policy Studies Institute.

Allen, I. (1991), *Any Room at the Top?*, Policy Studies Institute.

American Bar Association (1990), *Lawyers and Balanced Lives: A Guide to Drafting and Implementing Workplace Policies for Lawyers*, New York: American Bar Association, Commission on Women in the Profession.

Anderson, C.D. and Tomaskovic-Devey, D. (1995), 'Patriarchal pressures: an exploration of organisational processes that exacerbate and erode gender earnings inequality', *Work and Occupations*, 22, 3, pp.328-56.

Arber, S. and Ginn, J. (1995), 'The mirage of gender equality: occupational success in the labour market and within marriage', *British Journal of Sociology*, 46, 1, pp.21-44.

Armytage, W.H.G. (1964), *Four hundred years of English education*, Cambridge, Cambridge University Press.

The Association of Personnel Managers (1990), *Maximising Female Resources*, Unpublished Report.

The Association of Women Solicitors (n.d.), *Guidelines for Part-time Working*, London, Association of Women Solicitors.

Atkinson, J. (1989), 'Four Stages of Adjustment to the Demographic Downturn', *Personnel Management*, 21, 3, pp.20-4.

Bacchi, C.L. (1996), *The Politics of Affirmative Action: 'Women', Equality and Category Politics*, London, Sage.

Baker, J.H. (1990), *An Introduction to Legal History*, London, Butterworths.

Bankowski, Z. and Mungham, G. (1976), *Images of Law*, London, Routledge.

Barrett, M. (1987), 'The Concept of Difference', *Feminist Review*, 26, pp.29-41.

Barrett, M. and McIntosh, M. (1982), *The Anti-Social Family*, London, Verso.

Bass, I. (1998), 'Politics of a good day at the office', *Guardian*, 7 March, pp.28-9.

Bawdon, F. (1994), 'The lore of legal fashion', *The Times*, 27 September, p.34.

Bawdon, F. (1996), 'The Time Out', *Law Society Gazette*, 17 April, p.24.

Baxter, J. (1992), 'Domestic Labour and Income Inequality', *Work Employment and Society*, 6, 2, pp.229-49.

Becker, G. (1985), 'Human capital, effort and the sexual division of labour', *Journal of Labor Economics* (Supp. 1) 3: S33-S58.

Becker (1991), *A treatise on the family*, Cambridge, Mass: Harvard University Press.

Beechey, V. and Perkins, T. (1987), *A matter of hours: women, part-time work and the labour market*, Cambridge, Polity.

Bell, J. and Johstone, J. (1998), 'General transferable skills in the Law curriculum': Report of a DfEE funded discipline Network Project, Leeds University, DfEE.

Berry-Lound, D. (1990), 'Towards the Family-friendly Firm?', *Employment Gazette*, February, pp.85-91.

Biklen, S.K. (1997), *School Work, Gender and the cultural construction of teaching*, New York, Teachers' College Press.

Birks, M. (1960), *Gentlemen of the Law*, London, Stevens.

Bottero, Wendy (1992), 'The Changing Face of the Professions? Gender and Explanations of Women's Entry to Pharmacy', *Work, Employment and Society*, 6, 3, pp.329-46.

Bottomley, A. (1992), 'Feminism: Paradoxes of the Double Bind', in I. Grigg-Spall and P. Ireland (eds), *The Critical Lawyers Handbook*, London, Pluto Press, pp.22-9.

Bottomley, A. (eds) (1996), *Feminist Perspectives on the Foundational Subjects of Law*, London, Cavendish Publishing.

Bourdieu, P. (1977), *Outline of a Theory of Practice*, Cambridge, Cambridge University Press.

Bourdieu, P. (1984), *Distinction: a social critique of the Judgement of Taste*, Cambridge, Mass: Harvard University Press.

Bourdieu, P. (1987), 'The Force of Law: Toward a Sociology of the Juridical Field', *Hastings Law Journal*, 38, pp.805-52.

Bourdieu, P. (1990), *The Logic of Practice*, Cambridge, Polity.
Bourdieu, P. (1990a), *In Other Words*, Cambridge, Polity.
Bourdieu, P. (1991), *Language and Symbolic Power*, Cambridge, Polity.
Bradley, H. (1989), *Men's Work, Women's Work: a sociological history of the sexual division of labour in employment*, London, Allen & Unwin.
Bradshaw, A. and Thomas, P. (1995), *Leaving the profession: a survey of solicitors not renewing practising certificates*, Cardiff Law School for the Association of Women Solicitors, unpublished mimeo.
Braidotti, R. (1993), *Nomadic Subjects: Embodiment and Sexual Difference in Contemporary Feminist Theory*, Columbia, Columbia University Press.
Brannen, J. (1989), 'Childbirth and occupational mobility', *Work, Employment and Society*, 3, 2, pp.179-201.
Brannen, J. and Moss, P. (1991), *Managing Mothers*, London, Unwin Hyman.
Braverman, H. (1974), *Labour and Monopoly Capital: the degradation of work in the twentieth century*, New York, Monthly Review Press.
Breugel, I. (1979), 'Women as a reserve army of labour: a note on recent British experience', *Feminist Review*, 3, pp.12-23.
Breugel, I. (1996), 'Whose myths are they anyway?: a comment', *British Journal of Sociology*, 47, 1, pp.175-77.
Bridgeman, J. and Millns, S. (1998), *Feminist Perspectives on Law: Law's engagement with the female body*, London, Sweet and Maxwell.
Bristol Law Society (1989), *Women and the Recruitment Crisis* - Report by a Special Committee of the Council, Unpublished.
Brockman, J. (1992), 'Resistance by the Club', *Canadian Journal of Law & Society*, 7, pp.47-92.
Brown, R., Curran, M. and Cousins, J. (1983), 'Changing Attitudes to Employment', *Dept. of Employment Research Paper*, No.40, London, HMSO.
Burrage, Michael (1996), 'From a gentlemen's to a public profession: status and politics in the history of English solicitors', *International Journal of the Legal Profession*, 3,1/2, pp.45-81.
Butler, J. (1990), *Gender Trouble: Feminism and the Subversion of Identity*, London, Routledge.
Cain, M. and Harrington, C. (1994), *Lawyers in a Postmodern World*, Milton Keynes, Open University Press.
Cain, P.A. (1990), 'Feminism and the Limits of Equality', *Georgia Law Review*, 24, pp.803-14.
Cameron, I. (1993), 'Formulating an Equal Opportunities Policy', *Equal Opportunities Review*, 47, Jan-Feb, pp.12-23.
Campbell, M. (1989), *Towards a local labour market strategy*, Policy Research Unit, Leeds Metropolitan University.

Caplow, S. and Scheindlin, S. (1990), 'Portrait of a Lady: the woman lawyer in the 1980s', *New York Law School Law Review*, 35, 2, pp.391-446.

Caplow, T. (1954), *The Sociology of Work*, New York, McGraw Hill.

Carlin, J.E. (1962), *Lawyers on their own: a study of individual practitioners in Chicago*, New Brunswick NJ, Rutgers University Press.

Carrier, S. (1995), 'Family Status and Career Situations for Professional Women', *Work Employment and Society*, 9, 2, pp.343-58.

Carter, M.J. and Carter, S.B. (1981), 'Women's recent progress in the professions or, women get a ticket to ride after the gravy train has left the station', *Feminist Studies*, 7, 3, pp.476-504.

Carty, A. (1991), 'English Constitutional Law from a Postmodernist perspective', in P. Fitzpatrick (ed), *Dangerous Supplements: resistance and renewal in jurisprudence*, London, Pluto Press, pp.182-206.

Chambers, D. (1989), 'Accommodation and Satisfaction: Women and Men Lawyers and the Balance of Work and Family', *Law and Social Inquiry* 14, pp.251-79.

Chambers, G. and Harwood, S. (1990), *Solicitors in England and Wales: Practice, Organisation and Perceptions*, London, The Law Society.

Chambers, M. (1990), *Chambers and Partners' Directory of The Legal Profession 1990*, London, Chambers and Partners Publishing Ltd.

Chambers, M. (1997), 'Part-time Partners: the Linklaters Initiative', *Commercial Lawyer*, 19, pp.21-4.

Chambliss, E. (1997), *Review of Dissonance and Distrust* by Margaret Thornton, *Journal of Law and Society*, 24, 4, pp.583-5.

Cockburn, C. (1983), *Brothers: Male Dominance and Technological Change*, London, Pluto Press.

Cockburn, C. (1985), *Machinery of Dominance: Women, Men and Technical Knowhow*, London, Pluto Press.

Cockburn, C. (1989), 'Equal Opportunities: the Short and the Long-term Agenda', *Industrial Relations Journal*, 20, 3, pp.213-25.

Cockburn, C. (1991), *In the Way of Women: men's resistance to sex equality in organisations*, Basingstoke, Macmillan.

Cockshutt, J. (1961), *The Services of a Solicitor. The Law Society's Guide*, London, Hodder and Stoughton.

Coe, T. (1992), *The Key to the Men's Club*, Corby, Northants, Institute of Management.

Cohn, S. (1985), *The Process of Occupational Sex-Typing: the Feminisation of Clerical Work in Great Britain*, Philadelphia, Temple University Press.

Cohn, S. (1994), Review of *Professions and Patriarchy* by Anne Witz, *Work and Occupations*, 21, 2, pp.218-21.

Cole, W. (1997), *Solicitors in Private Practice - Their Work and Expectations*, Research Study No.26, London, The Law Society.

Coleman, M. (1996), 'Barriers to career progress for women in education: the perceptions of female headteachers', *Educational Research*, 38, 3, pp.317-32.

Colgan, F. and Tomlinson, F. (1991), 'Women in Publishing - jobs or careers', *Personnel Review*, 20, 5, pp.16-26.

Collier, R. (1991), 'Masculinism, Law and Law Teaching', *International Journal of the Sociology of Law*, 19, pp.427-51.

Collier, R. (1998), '(Un)Sexy bodies: the making of professional legal masculinities' in C. McGlynn (ed), *Legal Feminisms: theory and practice*, Ashgate/Dartmouth, London, pp.21-45.

Collier, R. (1998a), ''Nutty Professors', 'Men in Suits' and 'New Entrepreneurs': Corporeality, Subjectivity and Change in the Law School and Legal Practice', *Social and Legal Studies*, 7, 1, pp.27-53.

Collinson, D. and Hearn, J. (1994), 'Naming Men as Men: Implications for Work, Organisation and Management', *Gender Work and Organisation*, 1, pp.2-32.

Collinson, D.L., Knights, D. and Collinson, M. (1990), *Managing to Discriminate*, London, Routledge.

Collinson, M. and Collinson, D. (1996), '"It's only Dick": the sexual harassment of women managers in insurance sales', *Work, Employment and Society*, 10, 1, pp.29-56.

Cooper Ramo, R. (1997), 'Gender bias is still a problem in the US legal profession', in J. Smerin, 'Different for Girls?', *Law Society Gazette*, 94, 12, 26 March, pp.17-18.

Coopers & Lybrand (1996), *Financial Management in law firms - 1996*, London, Coopers & Lybrand and The Lawyer.

Cope, N. (1993), Glass Ceiling Clouded with Hot Air, *Independent*, 2 November, p.31.

Cornell, D. (1991), *Beyond Accommodation: Ethical Feminism, Deconstruction and the Law*, New York and London, Routledge.

Corti, L., Laurie, H. and Dex, S. (1995), *Highly qualified women*, Employment Department Research Series, No.50, ESRC Research Centre on Micro-social change, HMSO.

Coser, L. (1974), *Greedy institutions: Patterns of undivided commitment*, New York, Free Press.

Cotterrell, R. (1989), *The Politics of Jurisprudence: a critical introduction to Legal Philosophy*, London, Butterworth.

Cox, L. (1997), 'Mentoring rarely works for women lawyers because of competitiveness and the "Queen Bee syndrome"', in J. Smerin, 'Different for Girls?', *Law Society Gazette*, 94, 12, 26 March, p.18.

Crompton, R. (1994), 'Women and the Service Class', in R. Crompton and M. Mann, *Gender and Stratification*, Cambridge Polity Press.

Crompton, R. (1997), 'Gender and Employment: current debates', *Social Science Teacher*, 26, 2, pp.2-7.

Crompton, R., Hantrais, L. and Walters, P. (1990), 'Gender Relations and Employment', *British Journal of Sociology*, 41, 3, pp.329-49.

Crompton, R. and Sanderson, K. (1990), *Gendered Jobs and Social Change*, London, Unwin Hyman.

Cunningham, J. (1995), 'Women: should a groper get his hands on the Law Society', *Guardian*, 10 July, p.4.

Curnow, B. (1989), 'Recruit, retrain, retain: Personnel Management and the 3R's', *Personnel Management*, November, pp.40-7.

Curran, B.A. (1986), 'American Lawyers in the 1980s: A Profession in Transition', *Law and Society Review*, 20, pp.19-52.

Curran, M. (1988), 'Gender and Recruitment: people and places in the labour market', *Work, Employment and Society*, 2,3, pp.335-51.

Daniel Bates Consultants (1995), *Sexual Discrimination in the Legal Profession*, London, Daniel Bates.

Davidson, M.J. and Cooper, C.L. (1992), *Shattering the Glass Ceiling: the woman manager*, London, Paul Chapman.

Davies, C. and Rosser, J. (1986), 'Gender in the labour process - the case of women and men lawyers', in D. Knights and H. Willmott (eds), *Gender and the Labour Process*, Aldershot, Gower, pp.94-116.

Davies, C. and Rosser, J. (1987), 'A male pathway unwilling to bend', *The Health Service Journal*, 5 February, pp.158-9.

Davies, M. (1997), Taking the inside out: sex and gender in the legal subject', in N. Naffine and R.J. Owens (eds), *Sexing the subject of law*, Sidney, Sweet & Maxwell, pp.25-46.

Derber, C. (1982), *Professionals as Workers*, Boston, G.K. Hall.

Dex, S. (1987), *Women's Occupational Mobility*, London, Macmillan.

Dezalay, Y. and Garth, B. (1997), 'Law, Lawyers and Social Capital: "Rule of Law" versus relational capitalism', *Social and Legal Studies*, 6, 1; pp.109-41.

Dicey, A.V. (1909), *Letters to a friend on votes for women*, London, John Murray.

Dickens, L. (1992), *Whose Flexibility? Discrimination and equality issues in a typical work*, London, Institute of Employment Rights.

Dixon, J. and Seron, C. (1991), 'Lawyers in Love: Labor Market Segmentation and the effects of family status on the earnings of male and female lawyers' (unpublished manuscript).

Dixon, J. and Seron, C. (1995), 'Stratification in the Legal Profession: sex, sector and salary', *Law and Society Review* 29, 3, pp.381-412.

Drachman, V. (1989), 'My "partner" in law and life: marriage in the lives of women lawyers in late 19th and early 20th-century America', *Law & Social Inquiry*, 14, pp.221-50.
Dyer, C. (1994), 'Sex is a law letter word', *Guardian*, 8 May, p.18.
Edgell, S. (1980), *Middle Class Couples*, London, Allen and Unwin.
Edwards, S. (1996), *Sex, Gender in the Legal Process*, London, Blackstone.
Elliot, L. (1997), 'How housework could clean up', *Guardian*, 7 October, p.1.
Elshtain, J. (1982), *Public Man, Private Woman: Women in Social and Political Thought*, Oxford, Martin Robertson.
Employment, Department of (1980), *Women and Employment, a Lifetime Perspective*, London, Office of Population Censuses and Surveys.
Employment, Department of (1988), *Employment for the 1990's*, London, HMSO.
Epstein, C.F. (1981), *Women in Law*, New York, Basic Books.
Epstein, C.F. (1991), 'Faulty Framework: consequences of the difference model for women in the law', *New York Law School Law Review*, 35, 2, pp.309-36.
Epstein, C.F., Saute, R., Oglensky, B. and Gever, M. (1995), 'Glass Ceilings and open doors: women's advancement in the legal profession', A Report to the Committee on Women in the Profession, The Association of the Bar of the City of New York, *Fordham Law Review*, 64, November, pp.306-449.
Equal Opportunities Commission (1995), *The Life Cycle of Inequality - Women and Men in Britain in 1995*, London, Equal Opportunities Commission.
Estes, S.B. and Glass, J.L. (1996), 'Job changes following childbirth: are women trading compensation for family-responsive work conditions?', *Work and Occupations*, 23, 4, pp.405-36.
Faulkner, N. (1997), *Summary of material from archives of Association of Women Solicitors*, Nicholas Faulkner Associates, mimeo.
Fegan, E. (1996), 'Ideology after Discourse: A reconceptualization for Feminist analyses of the law', *Journal of Law and Society*, 27, 2, pp.173-97.
Figes, K. (1994), *Because of her Sex*, London, Pan Books.
Filby, M.P. (1992), 'The figures, the personality and the bums: service work and sexuality', *Work, Employment and Society*, 6, 1, pp.23-42.
Fineman, M.A. (1990), 'Challenging law, establishing differences: the future of feminist legal scholarship', *Florida Law Review*, 42, pp.25-4.
Fineman, M.A. (1991), 'Societal factors affecting the creation of legal rules for distribution of property at divorce', in M.A. Fineman and N.S. Thomadsen (1991), *At the Boundaries of Law: Feminism and Legal Theory*, Routledge, New York, pp.265-279.
Fineman, M.A. (1992), 'The Neutered Mother', *Miami Law Review*, 46, pp.653-88.
Fineman, M.A. and Thomadsen, N.S. (eds) (1991), *At the Boundaries of Law*, New York, Routledge.

Fitzpatrick, P. (1991), 'The Abstracts and Brief Chronicles of the Time: Supplementing Jurisprudence', in P. Fitzpatrick (ed), *Dangerous Supplements, Resistance and Renewal in Jurisprudence*, London, Pluto Press, pp.1-33.

Flood, J. (1996), 'Megalawyering in the global order: the cultural, social and economic transformation of global legal practice', *International Journal of the Legal Profession*, 3, 2, pp.169-214.

Fogarty, M.P., Allen, I. and Walters, P. (1981), *Women in Top Jobs*, London, Heinemann Educational Press.

Foster, S.E. (1995), 'The Glass Ceiling in the Legal Profession: why do law firms still have so few female partners?', *UCLA Law Review*, 42, pp.1631-89.

Foucault, M. (1979), *Discipline and Punish*, Harmondsworth, Penguin.

Foucault, M. (1980), *Power/Knowledge*, Brighton, Harvester Press.

Fox, W.M. (1989), 'Being a Woman, Being a Lawyer and Being a Human Being - Women and Change', *Fordham Law Review*, 57, pp.955-83.

Fredman, S. (1992), 'European Community Discrimination Law: a critique', *Industrial Law Journal*, 21, 2, pp.119-34.

Fredman, S. (1997), *Women and the Law*, Oxford, Clarendon Press.

French, K. (1995), 'Men and Locations of Power - Why Move Over?', in C. Itzin and J. Newman, *Gender, Culture and Organisational Change*, London, Routledge, pp.54-67.

Frug, M.J. (1985), 'Rereading Contracts: a feminist analysis of a contracts casebook', *American University Law Review*, 34, pp.1065-140.

Frug, M.J. (1992), *Postmodern Legal Feminism*, New York, Routledge.

Galanter, M. (1983), 'Mega-Law and Mega-Lawyering in the Contemporary United States', in *The Sociology of the Professions*, R. Dingwall and P. Lewis (eds), London, MacMillan Press, pp.152-76.

Galanter, M. (1992), 'Law abounding: Legalisation around the North Atlantic', *Modern Law Review*, 10, pp.1-26.

Galanter, M. and Palay, T. (1990), 'Why the big get bigger: The Promotion - to Partner Tournament and the Growth of Large Law Firms', 76, *Virginia Law Review*, p.747.

Galanter, M. and Palay, T. (1991), *The Tournament of Lawyers: the Transformation of the Big Law Firm*, Chicago, University of Chicago Press.

Garlick, H. (1990), 'Mothers, lawyers and jugglers', *Independent*, 23 November, p.19.

Gaskell, J. (1995), 'Gender and the School-Work Transition in Canada and the USA', in L. Bash and A. Green (eds), *World Yearbook of Education 1995*, London, Kogan Page, pp.80-91.

Gebel, R. (1980), 'Reification in Legal Reasoning from Research in Law and Sociology', *Critical Legal Studies*, 3, pp.25-46.

Gillies (1991), 'Strategic Moves', *The Lawyer*, 29 January 1991, p.2.
Gilligan, C. (1982), *In a different voice: Psychological Theory and Women's Development*, Cambridge, Harvard University Press.
Gilson, R.J. and Mnookin, R. (1985), 'Sharing among the Human Capitalists: an economic inquiry into the corporate law firm and how partners share profits', *Stanford Law Review*, 41, pp.567-95.
Ginn, J. and Sandell, J. (1997), 'Balancing home and employment: stress reported by social services staff', *Work, Employment and Society*, 11, 3, pp.413-34.
Glaser, J. (1994), 'Women teachers and white collar workers: domestic circumstances and paid work', *Work Employment and Society*, 8, 140, pp.87-100.
Goldberg, S. (1993), *Why men rule: A theory of male dominance*, Chicago, Open Court.
Golden, B. (1997), 'Getting Equal', *AWS Newsletter*, March, p.5.
Goodrich, P. (1993), 'Gynaetopia: Feminine Genealogies of Common Law', *Journal of Law and Society*, 20, 3, pp.236-308.
Goodrich, P. and Hachamovitch, Y. (1991), 'Time out of mind: an introduction to the semiotics of the Common Law', in P. Fitzpatrick (ed), *Dangerous Supplements: resistance and renewal in jurisprudence*, London, Pluto Press, pp.159-81.
Gordon, R. (1988), 'Law and Theology', from *Tikkun*, 3, 1, pp.14-86.
Gordon, W.H. (1984), 'The Right of Women to Graduate in Medicine - Scottish Judicial Attitudes in the Nineteenth Century', *The Journal of Legal History*, 5, 2, pp.136-51.
Goriely, T. (1996), 'The Development of Criminal Legal Aid in England and Wales', in R. Young and D. Wall (eds), *Access to Criminal Justice*, London, Blackstone Press, pp.26-54.
Granfield, R.C. (1996), 'Lawyers and Power; reproduction and resistance in the Legal Profession', *Law and Society Review*, 30, 1, pp.205-23.
Granovetter, M. (1985), 'Economic Action and Social Structure - the Problem of Embeddedness', *American Journal of Sociology*, 91, 3, pp.481-510.
Graycar, R. and Morgan, J. (1990), *The Hidden Gender of Law*, Leichhardt NSW, The Federation Press.
Gregson, N. and Lowe, M. (1993), 'Renegotiating the domestic division of labour? A study of dual-career household in North East and South East England', *Sociology*, 28, 1, pp.55-78.
Greig, Grata Flos. (1909), 'The Law as a Profession for Women', *Commonwealth Law Review*, 6, pp.145-54.
Griffith, J.A.G. (1977), *The Politics of the Judiciary*, London, Fontana Press.

Grigg-Spall, I. and Ireland, P. (1992), 'Afterword: Law's (Un)spoken (Pre)sumptuous (Pre)suppositions', in I. Grigg-Spall and P. Ireland (eds), *The Critical Lawyers' Handbook*, Pluto Press, pp.126-40.

Grint, K. (1991), *The Sociology of Work*, Cambridge, Polity.

Gross, K. (1990), 'Foreword: She's my lawyer and she's a woman', *New York Law School Law Review*, 35, 2, pp.293-307.

Hagan, J. and Kay, F. (1995), *Gender in Practice: A study of lawyers' lives*, New York, Oxford University Press.

Hakim, C. (1979), *Occupational Segregation*, Research Paper No.9, Department of Employment, London, HMSO.

Hakim, C. (1992), 'Explaining trends in occupational segregation: the measurement, causes and consequences of the sexual division of labour', *European Sociological Review*, 8, pp.127-52.

Hakim, C. (1995), 'Five feminist myths about women's employment', *British Journal of Sociology*, 45, 3, pp.429-56.

Hakim, C. (1996), *Key issues in women's work: female heterogeneity and the polarisation of women's employment*, London, Athlone Press.

Hakim, C. (1996a), 'The sexual division of labour and women's heterogeneity', *British Journal of Sociology*, 47, 1, pp.178-87.

Halford, S. and Savage, M. (1995), 'Restructuring Organisations, Changing People: Gender and Restructuring in Banking and Local Government', *Work, Employment and Society*, 9, 1, pp.97-122.

Hall, E. (1993), 'Smiling, deferring and flirting. Doing gender by giving "good service"', *Work and Occupations*, 20, 4, pp.452-71.

Halpern, D. (1994), *Entry into the Legal Professions*, London, The Law Society.

Hammersley, M. (1992), *Social Research: Philosophy, Politics and Practice*, London, Sage and Open University.

Hanlon, G. (forthcoming), *Lawyers, the State and the Market - Professionalism Revisited*, London, Macmillan.

Hansard Society, The (1990), *The Report of the Hansard Society Commission on Women at the Top*, London, The Hansard Society.

Hantrais, L. and Letablier, M. (1996), *Families and Family Policy in Europe*, London, Longman.

Hantrais, L. and Walters, P. (1994), 'Making it in and Making out: women in professional occupations in Britain and France', *Gender, Work and Organisation*, 1, 1, pp.23-32.

Hardill, I., Green, A., Dudleston, A. and Owen, D. (1997), 'Who decides what? Decision making in dual career households', *Work, Employment and Society*, 11, 2, pp.313-26.

Harrington, M. (1992), *Women Lawyers: rewriting the rules*, New York, Alfred Knopf.

Harris, O. (1996), 'Introduction: inside and outside the law', in O. Harris (ed), *Inside and Outside the Law: Anthropological studies of authority and ambiguity*, London, New York, Routledge, pp.1-15.

Harrison, Brian (1978), *Separate Spheres: the opposition to women's suffrage in Britain*, London, Croom Helm.

Hartmann, H. (1979), 'Capitalism, Patriarchy and Job Segregation by Sex', in Z.R. Eisenstein (ed), *Capitalist Patriarchy and the case for Socialist Feminism*, New York, Monthly Review.

Hartmann, H. (1981), 'The unhappy marriage of Marxism and Feminism: towards a more progressive union', in L. Sargent (ed), *The unhappy marriage of Marxism and Feminism: a debate on Class and Patriarchy*, London, Pluto.

Harvard Law Review (1996), 'Why Law Firms cannot afford to maintain the mommy track', *Harvard Law Review*, 109, 6, pp.1375-92.

Heaney, M. (1992), 'Slow progress towards equality', *The Lawyer*, 28 April, p.16.

Hearn, J. and Parkin, W. (1995), *'Sex' at 'Work': the power and paradox of organisation sexuality*, London, Harvester Wheatsheaf, 2nd Edition.

Hearn, J., Sheppard, D., Tancred Sherritt, P. and Burrell, G. (eds) (1989), *The Sexuality of Organisation*, London, Sage.

Heinz, J.P. and Laumann, E.O. (1982), *Chicago Lawyers: the Social Structure of the Bar*, New York, Russell Sage Foundation.

Henwood, F. (1996), 'WISE Choices? Understanding occupational decision-making in a climate of equal opportunities for women in science and technology', *Gender and Education*, 8, 2, pp.199-214.

Heuston, R.F.V. (1964), *The Lives of the Lord Chancellors 1885-1940*, Oxford, Clarendon Press.

Hewson, B. (1995), 'A Recent Problem?', *New Law Journal*, 5 May, pp.626-7.

Hewson, B. (1997), 'Male and Gender Bias', *New Law Journal*, 11 April, p.537.

Hochschild, A. (1983), *The Managed Heart: Commercialisation of human feeling*, Berkeley, University of California Press.

Hochschild, A. (1989), *The second shift: working parents and the revolution at home*, New York, Viking Penguin.

Holdsworth, A. (1988), *Out of the Doll's House: the story of women in the twentieth century*, London, BBC Books.

Holland, L. and Spencer, L. (1992), *Without Prejudice? Sex equality at the bar and in the judiciary*, Bournemouth, TMS Consultants.

Horwitz, M.J. (1977), *The Transformation of American Law 1780-1860*, Cambridge, Mass, Harvard University Press.

Hughes, K.D. (1996), 'Transformed by Technology? The changing nature of women's "traditional" and "non-traditional" white collar work', *Work, Employment and Society*, 10, 2, pp.227-50.

Hughes, S. (1991), *The Circuit Bench - a woman's place?*, London, The Law Society.

Hunt, A. (1993), *Explorations in Law and Society: toward a constitutive theory of law*, New York, London, Routledge.

Hurstfield, J. (1992), 'Equal opportunities in the legal profession', *Equal Opportunities Review*, 45, pp.13-22.

Innes, S. (1995), *Making it Work - Women, Change and Challenge in the 90's*, London, Chatto & Windus.

Itzin, C. (1995), 'The Gender Culture in Organisations', in C. Itzin and J. Newman (eds), *Gender, Culture and Organisational Change*, London, Routledge, pp.30-54.

Itzin, C. (1995a), 'Crafting strategy to create women-friendly work', in C. Itzin and J. Newman (eds), *Gender, Culture and Organisational Change*, London, Routledge, pp.127-52.

Itzin, C. (1995b), 'Gender, culture, power and change: a materialist analysis', in C. Itzin and J. Newman (eds), *Gender, Culture and Organisational Change*, London, Routledge, pp.246-72.

Itzin, C. and Newman, J. (eds) (1995), *Gender, Culture and Organisational Change*, London, Routledge.

Itzin, C. and Phillipson, C. (1995), 'Gendered Ageism: a double jeopardy for women in organisations', in C. Itzin and J. Newman (eds), *Gender, Culture and Organisational Change*, London, Routledge, pp.81-90.

Jack, R. and Jack, D.C. (1989), 'Women Lawyers: Archetypes and Alternatives', *Fordham Law Review*, 57, pp.933-9.

Jackson, C. (1997), *Accountants with attitude: a career survey of women and men in the profession*, Institute for Employment Studies Report No.342, Brighton, Institute for Employment Studies.

Jackson, E. (1993), 'Contradictions and coherence in feminist responses to law', *Journal of Law and Society*, 20, 4, pp.398-411.

Jenkins, J. (1997), *Quality of Solicitors' Practice Management*, Law Society, London.

Johnson, T.J. (1972), *Professions and Power*, London, Macmillan.

Johnson, T.J. (1989), 'Review of A. Abbott; "The System of Professions"', in *Work, Employment and Society*, 2, 3, pp.413-7.

Kaldenberg, D.O., Becker, B.W. and Zvonkovic, A. (1995), 'Work and Commitment among Young Professionals: A study of male and female dentists', *Human Relations*, 48, 11, pp.1355-77.

Kanter, R.M. (1977), 'Some effects of proportions on group life: skewed sex ratios and responses to token women', *American Journal of Sociology*, Vol.82, pp.965-90.

Kanter, R.M. (1977a), *Men and women of the corporation*, New York, Basic Books.

Kaufman, D. (1984), 'Professional women: how real are the recent gains?', in Freeman, J. (ed), *Women: a Feminist Perspective*, Palo Alto Mayfield.

Kaufman, R.V. (1974), 'The patron-client concept and macro politics: prospects and problems', *Comparative Studies in Society and History*, 16, pp.284-308.

Kaye, J.S. (1988), 'Women Lawyers in Big Firms: A study in progress toward gender equality', *Fordham Law Review*, 57, pp.111-26.

Kennedy, D. (1992), 'Legal Education as Training for Hierarchy', in I. Grigg-Spall and P. Ireland (eds), *The Critical Lawyers' Handbook*, London, Pluto Press, pp.51-61.

Kennedy, D. (1993), *Sexy Dressing*, Cambridge, Mass: Harvard University Press.

Kennedy, H. (1992), *Eve was framed*, London, Chatto and Windus.

Kingson, J.A. (1988), 'Women in the Law say path is limited by mommy track', *New York Times*, 8 August, p.1.

Laband, D. and Lentz, B. (1992), 'Is there sex discrimination in the Legal profession? Further evidence on Tangible and Intangible margins', *The Journal of Human Resources*, XXVIII, 2, pp.230-58.

Lahey, K.A. (1991), 'Reasonable Women and the Law', in M.A. Fineman and N.S. Thomadsen (eds), *At the boundaries of law: Feminism and Legal Theory*, New York and London, Routledge, pp.3-21.

Larkin, G. (1983), *Occupational Monopoly and Modern Medicine*, London, Tavistock.

Larson, M.S. (1977), *The Rise of Professionalism*, Berkeley, University of California Press.

The Law Society (1919), *Annual Report of the Council*, London, The Law Society.

The Law Society (1988), *Equal in the Law: Report of the Working Party on Women's Careers*, London, The Law Society.

The Law Society (1989), *Equal Opportunities in Solicitors' Firms*, London, The Law Society.

The Law Society (1990), *Annual Statistical Report 1990*, London, The Law Society.

The Law Society (1994), *Annual Statistical Report 1994*, London, The Law Society.

The Law Society (1997), *News Release: New survey reveals continuing inequality between male and female solicitors*, 7 July, London, The Law Society.

Law Society Gazette (1995), 'Gender Gap', *Law Society Gazette* 92/08, Commemorative Issue, 22 February, no page numbers.

Law Society Gazette (1996), 'The Lot of the Woman Lawyer', *Law Society Gazette* 93/14, 17 April, pp.26-7.

Law Society Gazette (1997), 'Different for Girls', *Law Society Gazette* 94/12, 25 March, p.18.

Law Times (1913), 'Women as solicitors', *Law Times*, 5 July, 135, p.232.

Law Times (1914), 'Women and the Law', *Law Times*, 4 April, 136, p.578.

Law Times (1914), 'Women as solicitors', *Law Times*, 11 April, 136, pp.599-600.

Law Times (1917), 'Women as solicitors', *Law Times*, 10 March, 142, p.331.

The Lawyer (1991), 'Solicitor tops working-mum league', *The Lawyer*, 15 October, p.3.

The Lawyer (1992), 'Women find more bias in private firms', *The Lawyer*, 25 February, p.1.

The Lawyer (1992), 'An historic structure', *The Lawyer*, 5 May, p.17.

The Lawyer (1997), 'CC to take hard line on leavers after Wilkinson episode', *The Lawyer*, 28 October, p.1.

Legge, K. (1987), 'Women in personnel management: uphill climb or downhill slide', in Spencer, A. and Podmore, D. (eds), *In a Man's World*, London, Tavistock, pp.33-60.

Leigh-Kile, D. (1998), *Lawyers on the Spot*, London, Vision.

Lentz, B. and Laband, D. (1995), *Sex Discrimination in the Legal Profession*, Quorum Books, USA.

Levi-Strauss, C. (1969), *The elementary structures of kinship*, Boston, Beacon Press.

Lewis, S. and Lewis, J. (eds) (1996), *The Work-Family Challenge: Rethinking Employment*, London, Sage.

Lewis, V. (1996), *Trends in the Solicitors' Profession: Annual Statistical Report 1996*, Chancery Lane, London, The Law Society.

Lewis, V. (1997), *Annual Statistical Report 1997*, Chancery Lane, London, The Law Society.

Liff (1989), 'Assessing Equal Opportunities Policies', *Personnel Review*, 18, 1, pp.27-34.

Liff, Sonia (1997), 'Tell Me What You Want ...: Opportunities and Pitfalls on the Road to Gender Equality', *Work, Employment and Society*, 11, 3, pp.555-63.

Lissenburgh, S. (1994), *Value for money: the costs and benefits of giving part-time workers equal rights*, London, Trades Union Congress.

Littleton, C.A. (1987), 'Reconstructing Sexual Inequality', *California Law Review*, 75, pp.1274-90.

Longrigg, C. (1998), 'If you want to get ahead then get a suit, women lawyers told', *Guardian*, 21 March, p.3.

MacCorquodale, P. and Jensen, G. (1993), 'Women in the Law: Partners or Tokens?', *Gender and Society*, 7, 4, pp.582-93.

MacKinnon, C. (1987), *Feminism Unmodified: discourses on life and law*, London, Harvard University Press.

Macran, S., Joshi, H. and Dex, S. (1996), 'Employment after childbearing - a survival analysis', *Work, Employment and Society*, 10, 2, pp.273-96.

McCabe, M. (1995), 'A proactive approach to equal opportunities', *New Law Journal*, 7, 4, pp.482-3.

McConville, M., Hodgson, J., Bridges, L. and Pavlovic, A. (1994), *Standing Accused: The Organisation and Practices of Criminal Defence Lawyers in Britain*, Oxford, Clarendon Press.

McGivney, V. (1993), *Women, Education and Training*, Leicester, NIACE.

McGlynn, C. (1996), 'Pregnancy dismissals and the Webb Litigation', *Feminist Legal Studies*, IV, 2, pp.229-42.

McGlynn, C. (1996a), 'Sex Discrimination at the Margins', *New Law Journal*, 15 March, pp.379-81.

McGlynn, C. (1997), 'Young women do not want to have to be superwomen in order to achieve career success', in J. Smerin, 'Different for Girls?', *Law Society Gazette*, 94/12, 26 March, p.19.

McGlynn, C. (1998), 'The Business of Equality' in C. McGlynn (ed), *Legal Feminisms*, Aldershot, Ashgate/Dartmouth, pp.101-16.

McGlynn, C. and Graham, C. (1995), *Soliciting Equality: Equality and Opportunity in the Solicitors' Profession*, London, Young Women Lawyers.

Maine, H.S. (1885), *Popular Government*, London.

Maley, Y. (1994), 'The Language of the Law', in J. Gibbons (ed), *Language and the Law*, London, Longmans, pp.11-59.

Mansnerus, L. (1993), 'Why Women are Leaving the Law', *Working Women*, April, pp.64-7 and 93, New York.

Market Assessment Publications (1996), *Working Women*, London, Market Assessment Publications.

Marks, L. (1990), 'Alternative Work Schedules in Law; it's about time!', *New York Law School Law Review*, 35, 2, pp.361-7.

Marks, P. (1988), *Solicitors Career Structure Survey*, London, The Law Society.

Marks, S.R. (1977), 'Multiple roles and role strain: some notes on human energy, time and commitment', *American Sociological Review*, 42, pp.921-36.

Markus, M. (1987), 'Women, success and civil society: submission to, or subversion of, the achievement principle', in S. Benhabib and D. Cornell (eds),

Feminism as Critique: Essays in the Politics of Gender in Late Capitalist Societies, Cambridge, Polity, pp.96-109.

Marsden, P.V., Kalleberg, A.L. and Cook, C.R. (1993), 'Gender Differences in Organisational Commitment: Influences of Work Positions and Family Roles', *Work and Occupations*, 20, 3, pp.368-90.

Martin, R. (1994), 'A feminist view of the reasonable man: an alternative approach to liability in negligence for personal injury', *Anglo-American Law Review*, 23, 3, pp.334-74.

Maynard, M. and Purvis, J. (1994), 'Doing Feminist Research', in M. Maynard and J. Purvis (eds), *Researching Women's Lives from a Feminist Perspective*, London, Taylor and Francis, pp.1-9.

Menkel-Meadow, C. (1989), 'Exploring a research agenda of the feminisation of the legal profession: theories of gender and social change', *Law and Social Inquiry*, 14, pp.289-319.

Menkel-Meadow, C. (1989a), 'Feminisation of the Legal Profession: The Comparative Sociology of Women Lawyers', in R. Abel and P. Lewis (eds), *Lawyers in Society: Comparative Theories*, University of California Press, Berkeley, Vol.3, pp.196-255.

Merry, S.E. (1992), 'Anthropology, law and transnational processes', *Annual Review of Anthropology*, 21.

Mews, H. (1969), *Frail Vessels: Woman's role in Women's Novels from Fanny Burney to George Eliot*, University of London, London, The Athlone Press.

Mill, J.S. (1869), *The Subjection of Women*, London, Longman, 2nd ed.

Millerson, G. (1964), *The Qualifying Associations*, London, Routledge.

Mills, Dame Barbara (1997), 'What does a woman want?', Text of the Second Fawcett Library Annual Lecture, 12/11/96, London Guildhall University, The Fawcett Library.

Molyneux, P. (1986), 'Association of Women Solicitors - membership survey', *Law Society Gazette*, 83, pp.3082-4.

Moorhead, R. (1997), *Protecting whom? The impact of the minimum salary: a survey into salary and debt levels of trainees and LPC students*, London, Institute of Advanced Legal Studies.

Morgan, D. (1984), 'Gender', in R. Burgess (ed), *Key variables in social investigation*, London, Routledge, pp.31-53.

Morgan, G. and Knights, D. (1991), 'Gendering Jobs: corporate strategy, managerial control and the dynamics of job segregation', *Work, Employment and Society*, 5, 2, pp.181-200.

Morison, J. and Leith, P. (1992), *The Barristers' World: and the nature of law*, Open University Press, Milton Keynes.

Mossman, M.J. (1990), 'The Past as Prologue', in A. Asau and J. Penner (eds), *Lawyering and Legal Education into the 21st Century*, Winnipeg Legal Research Institute.

Mossman, M.J. (1990), 'Women lawyers in the 20th Century: rethinking the Image of Portia', in R. Graycar (ed), *Dissenting Opinions: Feminist Explorations in Law and Society*, Australia, Allen and Unwin.

Mossman, M.J. (1991), 'Feminism and legal method: the difference it makes', in M.A. Fineman and N.S. Thomadsen (eds), *At the Boundaries of Law*, New York, Routledge, pp.283-300.

Mossman, M.J. (1994), 'Lawyers and Family Life: New directions for the 1990's (Part One)', *Feminist Legal Studies*, 2, 1, pp.61-82.

Mossman, M.J. (1994), 'Lawyers and Family Life: New Directions for the 1990's: Part Two, the Search for Solutions, *Feminist Legal Studies*, 2, 2, pp.150-82.

Mucciante, T. (1991), 'Obstacles to equality', *The Lawyer*, 17 September, pp.15-6.

Murgatroyd, L. and Neuburger, H. (1997), 'A household satellite account for the UK', *Economic Trends*, 527, pp.63-71, London, Office for National Statistics.

Murphy, R. (1984), 'The structure of closure: a critique and development of Weber, Collins and Parkin', *British Journal of Sociology*, 35, 3, pp.547-67.

Murray, G. (1987), 'Women Lawyers in New Zealand: Some questions about the politics of equality', *International Journal of the Sociology of Law*, 15, 4, pp.439-57.

Murray, J. (1984), *Strongminded women*, Harmondsworth, Middlesex, Penguin.

Murray, M. (1995), *The Law of the Father? Patriarchy in the transition from feudalism to capitalism*, London, Routledge.

Naffine, N. and Owens, R.J. (1997), *Sexing the subject of law*, Sidney, Sweet & Maxwell.

Nelson, R. (1988), *Partners with Power: the Social Transformation of the Large Law Firm*, Berkeley, University of California Press.

New Ways to Work (1993), *Change at the Top; Working flexibly at senior and managerial levels in organisations*, London, National Westminster Bank.

New Ways to Work (1994), 'Job sharing solicitors', *New Ways to Work Newsletter*, July, pp.3-4.

Newell, S. (1993), 'The superwoman syndrome: gender differences in attitudes towards equal opportunities at work, and towards domestic responsibilities at home', *Work, Employment and* Society, 7, pp.275-89.

Newman, C. (1957), *The Evolution of Medical Education in the Nineteenth Century*, London, Oxford University Press.

Newman, J. (1995), 'Gender and cultural change', in C. Itzin and J. Newman (eds), *Gender, Culture and Organisational Change*, London, Routledge, pp.11-29.

Newman, J. (1995a), 'Making connections: frameworks for change', in C. Itzin and J. Newman (eds), *Gender, Culture and Organisational Change*, London, Routledge, pp.246-72.

Nicolson, P. (1995), 'When it comes to disaster, she's a natural', *Independent*, 1 March, p.30.

Nott, S. (1989), 'Women in the Law - Part I', *New Law Journal*, 2 June, pp.749-51.

O'Brien, M. (1981), *The politics of reproduction*, London, Routledge & Kegan Paul.

O'Donovan, K. (1981), 'Before and after: the impact of feminism on the academic discipline of law', in D. Spender (ed), *Men's Studies Modified*, Oxford, Pergamon, pp.175-87.

O'Donovan, K. (1985), *Sexual Divisons in the Law*, London, Weidenfeld, Nicholson.

Okin, S.M. (1979), *Women in Western Political Thought*, Princeton, Princeton University Press.

Okin, S.M. (1989), *Justice, Gender and the Family*, USA, Basic Books.

Olive, C. (1992), 'The Path to Partnership', *The Lawyer*, 5 May, p.17.

Olsen, F. (1990), 'Feminism and Critical Legal Theory: an American perspective', *International Journal of the Sociology of Law*, 18, pp.199-215.

Pankhurst, Sylvia (1931), *The Suffragette Movement*, London.

Parkin, Frank (1979), *Marxism and Class Theory: a bourgeois critique*, London, Tavistock.

Pateman, C. (1988), *The Sexual Contract*, Oxford, Polity Press.

Paterson, A. (1996), 'Professionalism and the legal services market', *International Journal of the Legal Profession*, 3,1/2, pp.139-68.

Payne, J. (1991), *Women, Training and the Skills Shortage*, London, Policy Studies Institute.

Pexton, M. (1990), 'Being a workaholic will not always help your firm', *Legal Business*, November, p.49.

Pierce, J. (1996), *Gender Trials: Emotional Lives in Contemporary Law Firms*, Berkeley, University of California Press.

Podmore, D. and Spencer, A. (1982), 'The Law as a sex-typed profession', *Journal of Law and Society*, 9, 1, pp.21-36.

Podmore, D. and Spencer, A. (1982a), 'Women Lawyers in England: the experience of inequality', *Work and Occupations*, 9, pp.21-36.

Podmore, D. and Spencer, A. (1986), 'Gender in the Labour Process - the Case of Women and Men Lawyers', in D. Knights and H. Willmott (eds), *Gender and the Labour Process*, Aldershot, Gower, pp.36-53.

Podmore, D. and Spencer, A. (1987), 'Equality in the Law', in G. Lee and R. Loveridge (eds), *The Manufacture of Disadvantage*, Milton Keynes, Open University Press, pp.20-32.

Polachek, S. (1981), 'Occupational self-selection: a human capital approach to sex differences in occupational structure', *Review of Economics and Statistics*, 63, pp.60-9.

Porter, H. (1997), 'Smashing the glass ceiling', *Guardian*, 26 May, pp.2-9.

Power, M. (1997), *The Audit Society*, Oxford, Oxford University Press.

Pringle, R. (1989), *Secretaries' Talk*, London, Verso.

Rajan, A. and Eupen, P. (1990), *Good Practices in the Employment of Women Returners*, Brighton Institute of Manpower Studies Report No.183.

Rees, T. (1992), *Women and the Labour Market*, London, Routledge.

Reynell Legal Recruitment Consultants (1997), *The Law at Work - the view from within the legal profession, Report on a survey of assistant solicitors*, Reynell Ltd., London.

Rhode, D.L. (1988), 'Perspectives on professional women', *Stanford Law Review*, 40, pp.1163-207.

Rhode, D.L. (1991), 'The "No-Problem" Problem: Feminist Challenges and Cultural Change', *The Yale Law Journal*, 100, pp.1731-93.

Rhode, D. (1994), 'Feminism and the State', *Harvard Law Review*, 107, pp.961-1213.

Richardson, K. (1991), 'Flexible working for women', *Law Society Gazette*, 83/3, pp.25-6.

Rifkin, J. (1980), 'Toward a theory of law and patriarchy', *Harvard Women's Law Journal*, 3, 1, pp.83-95.

Rights of Women (1994), 'Women and the Law': Conference Report, March, London, Rights of Women.

Roach Anleu, S. (1992), 'Women in Law: Theory, Research and Practice', *ANZJS*, 28, 3, pp.391-410.

Roach Anleu, S. (1992a), 'Recruitment Practice and Women Lawyers' Employment', *Sociology*, 26, 4, pp.651-72.

Roberts, H.E. (1973), 'Marriage, Redundancy or Sin: the Painter's View of Women in the First Twenty-five years of Victoria's Reign', in M. Vicinus (ed), *Suffer and Be Still: Women in the Victorian Age*, Indiana University Press, Bloomington and London, pp.45-76.

Rose, N. (1996), 'Winning over in-house counsel', *Law Society Gazette*, 93/30, 14 August 1996, p.8.

Rosen, A. (1974), *Rise up Women*, London, Routledge.

Rosenberg, J., Perlstadt, H. and Phillips, W.R. (1993), 'Now that we are here: discrimination, disparagement, and harrassment at work and the experience of women lawyers', *Gender and Society*, 7, 3, pp.415-33.

Ross, D. (1990), *Bridging the Gap - A Report on Women in the Law*, London, Quarry Dougall Consulting Group.

Rowe, R. and Snizek, W.E. (1995), 'Gender differences in work values: perpetuating the myth', *Work and Occupations*, 22, 2, pp.5-29.

Sachs, A. (1993), 'Women in the Law: Desperately Seeking Daycare', *American Bar Association Journal*, 79, 6, pp.58-62.

Sachs, A. and Wilson, J.H. (1978), *Sexism and the Law*, London, Martin Robertson.

Sage, A. (1993), 'Law firms hostile to anti-bias proposals', *Independent*, 19 April, p.3.

Sanders, A. (1996), 'Access to justice in the police station: an elusive dream?', in R. Young and D. Wall (eds), *Access to Criminal Justice: Legal Aid, Lawyers and the Defence of Liberty*, London, Blackstones, pp.254-75.

Saunders, N. (1996), 'From Cramming to Skills - the development of Solicitors' education and training since Ormrod', *Law Teacher*, 30, 2, p.168.

Scales, A. (1993), 'The emergence of feminist jurisprudence: an essay', in P. Smith (ed), *Feminist Jurisprudence*, Oxford, OUP.

Schwartz, F.N. (1989), 'Management Women and the New Facts of Life', *Harvard Business Review*, Jan-Feb, 1989, pp.65-76.

Seron, C. and Ferris, K. (1995), 'Negotiating Professionalism', *Work and Occupations*, 22, 1, pp.22-48.

Sheppard, D.L. (1989), 'Organisation, power and sexuality: the image and self-image of women managers', in J. Hearn, D.L. Sheppard, P. Tancred-Sheriff and G. Burrell (eds), *The Sexuality of Organisation*, London, Sage.

Shiner, M. (1997), *Entry into the Legal Professions: the Law Student Cohort Study Year 4*, RPPU Research Study No.25, London, Policy Studies Institute for the Law Society.

Sidaway, J. (1995), 'Gender and Status in the Private Practice Firm', in *Removing the Barriers: Legal Services and the Legal Profession*, Proceedings of the Annual Research Conference of the Law Society 1995, Law Society, London.

Sidaway, J. (1997), 'Male and Female Solicitors' Remuneration Study Summary', Information Sheet released by the Law Society, London.

Sidaway, J. (1997), 'Salary Lottery', *Law Society Gazette*, 94/27, 9 July, pp.16-7.

Sidaway, J. and Cole, B. (1996), *The Panel: a study of private practice*, Research Study No.20, Law Society, London.

Sidaway, J. and Lewis, V. (1996), *Law Society Annual Statistical Report*, London, Law Society.

Simmons, M. (1996), 'The great divide between the sexes is still evident in the legal profession', *Law Society Gazette*, 93/12, 17 April, p.27.

Skordaki, Eleni (1996), 'Glass slippers and glass ceilings: women in the legal profession', *International Journal of the Legal Profession*, 3, 2, pp.7-43.

Smart, C. (1989), *Feminism and the Power of Law*, London, Routledge.

Smart, C. (1991), 'Feminist Jurisprudence', in P. Fitzpatrick (ed), *Dangerous Supplements: Resistance and Renewal in Jurisprudence*, London, Pluto Press, pp.133-58.

Smart, C. (1992), 'The Woman of Legal Discourse', *Social and Legal Studies*, 1, 29.

Smerin, J. (1995), 'Groups find little sex pest evidence', *Law Society Gazette*, 92/18, 11 May, p.6.

Smerin, J. (1995), 'Mears in direct appeal to Council', *Law Society Gazette*, 92/38, 25 October, p.2.

Smith, P. (ed) (1993), *Feminist Jurisprudence*, Oxford, Oxford University Press.

Solicitors Journal, Comment (1989), 'The New Elite', *Solicitors Journal*, 133, 31, 4 August, p.983.

Sommerlad, H. (1994), 'The myth of feminisation: women and cultural change in the legal profession', *International Journal of the Legal Profession*, 1, 1, pp.31-53.

Sommerlad, H. (1994a), 'Issues in the retention of women solicitors: a regional study', Unpublished report prepared for the Law Society by Leeds Metropolitan University.

Sommerlad, H. (1995), 'Managerialism and the legal profession: a new professional paradigm', *International Journal of the Legal Profession*, 2, pp.159-86.

Sommerlad, H. (1996), 'Criminal legal aid reforms and the restructuring of legal professionalism', in R. Young and D. Wall (eds), *Access to Justice: Legal Aid, Lawyers and the Defence of Liberty*, London, Blackstones, pp.292-312.

Sommerlad, H. (1998), 'The gendering of the professional subject: commitment, choice and social closure in the legal profession', in C. McGlynn (ed), *Legal Feminisms*, Ashgate/Dartmouth, London, pp.3-20.

Sommerlad, H. and Allaker, J. (1991), 'Retrieve or retain: training for women returners to private practice', Unpublished report prepared for the Law Society by Leeds Metropolitan University.

Sommerlad, H. and Sanderson, P. (1997), 'The legal labour market and the training needs of women returners in the United Kingdom', *Journal of Vocational Education and Training*, 49, 1, pp.45-64.

Spelman, E. (1988), *Inessential woman*, Boston, Beacon Press.

Spradley, J.P. (1979), *The Ethnographic Interview*, New York, Holt Reinhart & Winston.

Spurr, S.J. (1990), 'Sex discrimination in the legal profession: a study of promotion', *Industrial and Labour Relations Review*, 43, 4, pp.406-17.

Stanko, E. (1988), 'Keeping women in and out of line: sexual harassment and occupational segregation', in S. Walby (ed), *Gender Segregation at Work*, Milton Keynes, Open University Press, pp.91-9.

Stanley, L. and Wise, S. (1983), '"Back into the personal" or: Our attempt to construct "feminist research"', in G. Bowles and R. Klein (eds), *Theories of Women's Studies*, London, Routledge and Kegan Paul, pp.192-209.

Stapeley, S. (1996), 'Social Climbing', *Law Society Gazette* 93/35, 25 September, p.38.

Stebbings, Anne-Marie (1994), 'Implementing a competence system in the professions: from theory to practice', *International Journal of the Legal Profession*, 1, 1, pp.97-108.

Steele, M. and Peach, J. (1993), 'The Best of Both Worlds? Recruitment and Retention of Women at Work', *Department of Human Resource Management*, University of Strathclyde, Occasional Paper No.4.

Steele, M., Snape, E. and Gilbert, K. (1990), *Women Returners to the Scottish Labour Market*, Commissioned Report for the Scottish Development Agency, June, Department of Human Resource Management, University of Strathclyde.

Stuart, L. (1998), 'Career women are providing a glass act', *Guardian*, 7 March, p.30.

Sugarman, D. (1996), 'The best organised and most intelligent trade union in the country? The private and public life of the Law Society, 1825-1914', *International Journal of the Legal Profession*, 3/1-2, pp.83-136.

Thomas, P. and Bradshaw, A. (1995), 'Survey of Solicitors not renewing practising certificates: November 1994-October 1995', in *Removing the Barriers: Legal Services and the Legal Profession*, Proceedings from the Law Society Annual Research Conference 1995, Chancery Lane, London, The Law Society.

Thompson, E.P. (1977), *Whigs and Hunters*, Harmondsworth, Penguin.

Thornton, M. (1986), 'Feminist Jurisprudence: illusion or reality?' *Australian Journal of Law & Society*, 3, pp.5-29.

Thornton, M. (1996), *Dissonance and Distrust: Women in the Legal Profession*, Melbourne, Oxford University Press.

Tolfree, P. (1990), *Employment in the 1990's*, London, Croner.

Tomlinson, P. (1989), 'Having it Both Ways: hierarchical focusing as research interview method', *British Educational Research Journal*, 15, 2, pp.155-76.

Trappe, H. (1996), 'Work and family in women's lives in the German Democratic Republic', *Work and Occupations*, 23, 4, pp.354-77.

Travis, A. (1998), 'How to be a Judge: The Usual Suspects', *Guardian*, 25 February, p.13.
UKIPG (United Kingdom Inter-professional Group) (1990), *Women in the Professions*, London, The Law Society.
Urry, J. (1990), *The Tourist Gaze: Leisure and travel in contemporary societies*, London, Sage.
Veares, C. (1998), 'Female students anticipate bias', *The Lawyer*, 17 February, p.2.
Vicinus, M. (1973), *Suffer and Be Still: Women in the Victorian Age*, Indiana University Press, Bloomington and London.
Wajcman, J. (1996), 'The domestic basis for the managerial career', The Sociological Review, 44, 4, pp.609-29.
Walby, S. (1986), *Patriarchy at Work: Patriarchal and capitalist relations in employment*, Cambridge, Polity Press.
Walby, S. (1990), *Theorising Patriarchy*, Oxford, Basil Blackwell.
Wall, D. and Johnstone, J. (1997), 'The Industrialization of Legal Practice and the Rise of the New Electric Lawyer: The impact of information technology upon Legal Practice in the UK (1)', *International Journal of the Sociology of Law*, 25, pp.95-116.
Wallach, S. (1992), 'Law; Up the Legal Ladder Slowly', *Independent*, 15 May, p.20.
Walters, P. (1994), 'Women professionals in Britain and France', paper delivered at Law Society's Annual Research Conference, June.
Ward, S. (1995), 'Law Society chief strikes new blow in battle of sexes', *Guardian*, 21 October, p.5.
Ward, S. (1996), 'Perks of the Job', *Law Society Gazette*, 14 August, p.24.
Weale, S. (1997), 'To Britain's most dangerous feminist: a daughter', *Guardian*, 2 September, p.7.
Weber, L. (1990), 'Professionalism and Gender: a practical guide', *Michigan Bar Journal*, 69, pp.898-902.
Weber, M. (1968), *Economy and Society*, Glencoe, Free Press.
West, R.L. (1991), 'The difference in women's hedonic lives: a phenomenological critique of feminist legal theory', in M.A. Fineman and N.S. Thomadsen (1991), *At the Boundaries of Law: Feminism and Legal Theory*, Routledge, New York, pp.115-34.
Wharam, A. (1986), 'Probable Demand for Lawyers and Law Degree Courses for the Next Ten Years', *The Law Teacher*, 20, 3, pp.180-86.
White, D. and Jenkins, P. (1995), *The Official Lawyers' Handbook*, Petersfield, Harriman House Ltd.
Wilkinson, H. (1994), *No Turning Back: Generations and the Genderquake*, Demos, London.

Willetts, J. (1997), 'Getting in the business is not that difficult if women persevere and borrow a few strategies from the boys', in J. Smerin, 'Different for girls?', *Law Society Gazette*, 94/12, 26 March, pp.18-9.

Williams, J.C. (1990), 'Sameness Feminism and the Work/Family Conflict', *New York Law School Law Review*, 35, pp.347-60.

Willis, J. (1996), 'Women Solicitors: Equality in Practice', Paper delivered at 'Women in the Law' Conference, University of Durham, August.

Witz, A. (1992), *Professions and Patriarchy*, London, Routledge.

Young, I.M. (1987), 'Impartiality and the Civic Public: some implications of feminist critiques of moral and political theory', in S. Benhabib and D. Cornell (eds), *Feminism as Critique: Essays on the Politics of Gender in Late-capitalist Societies*, Cambridge, Polity, pp.56-76.

Young, I.M. (1990), *Justice and the Politics of Difference*, Princeton New Jersey, Princeton University Press.

Index

References from Notes indicated by ‘n’ after page preference

For Product Safety Concerns and Information please contact our EU representative GPSR@taylorandfrancis.com Taylor & Francis Verlag GmbH, Kaufingerstraße 24, 80331 München, Germany

Batch number: 10725921

Printed by Printforce, the Netherlands